Modern ITALIAN Grammar

Modern Italian Grammar: A practical guide is an innovative reference guide to Italian, combining traditional and function-based grammar in a single volume.

The *Grammar* is divided into two parts. The shorter section covers traditional grammatical categories such as nouns, verbs and adjectives. The larger section is carefully organized around language functions and notions such as:

- giving and seeking information
- putting actions into context
- expressing likes, dislikes and preferences
- comparing objects and actions

All grammar points and functions are richly illustrated and information is provided on register and relevant cultural background. Written by experienced teachers and academics, the *Grammar* has a strong emphasis on contemporary usage. Particular attention is paid to indexing and cross-referencing across the two sections.

This is the ideal reference grammar for learners of Italian at all levels, from elementary to advanced. It will prove invaluable to those with little experience of formal grammar, as no prior knowledge of grammatical terminology is assumed and a glossary of terms is provided. The book will also be useful to teachers seeking back-up to functional syllabuses, and to designers of Italian courses.

Anna Proudfoot is Head of Italian at Oxford Brookes University and **Francesco Cardo** is currently teaching at the Liceo Classico/Scientifico E. Majorana in Pozzuoli, Naples.

Routledge Modern Grammars

Series concept and development – Sarah Butler

Other books in the series:

Modern Italian Grammar Workbook

Modern French Grammar
Modern German Grammar
Modern Spanish Grammar

Modern
ITALIAN
Grammar

A practical guide

Anna Proudfoot and Francesco Cardo

London and New York

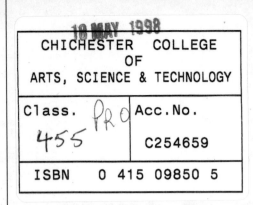
First published 1997
by Routledge
11 New Fetter Lane, London EC4P 4EE

Simultaneously published in the USA and Canada
by Routledge
29 West 35th Street, New York, NY 10001

Typeset in Utopia by Solidus (Bristol) Limited
Printed and bound in Great Britain by TJ Press Ltd, Padstow, Cornwall

The authors have asserted their moral rights in accordance with Section 77 of the Copyright,
Designs and Patents Act 1988

British Library Cataloguing in Publication Data
A catalogue record for this book is available from the British Library

Library of Congress Cataloguing in Publication Data
Proudfoot, Anna.
Modern Italian grammar: a practical guide/Anna Proudfoot and Francesco Cardo.
p. cm.
Includes index.
 1. Italian language – Textbooks for foreign speakers – English.   2. Italian language –
 Grammar.   I. Cardo, Francesco, 1951– .   II. Title.
 PC1129.E5P76   1996
 858.2 '421–dc20   96-1193

   ISBN 0-415-09849-1 (hbk)
   ISBN 0-415-09850-5 (pbk)

Contents

Part B Functions

I Giving and seeking factual information

Contents

Contents

Introduction

Modern Italian Grammar follows an entirely new approach to learning Italian. It embraces a new way of looking at grammar not as an ultimate goal, but as the tool with which we construct a dialogue or a piece of writing.

Modern Italian Grammar is specifically designed to be accessible to the English reader not brought up in the Italian tradition of grammar and language analysis. It is unique both in its combination of formal grammar reference section and its guide to usage organized along functional lines, and because it has been compiled by an English mother-tongue teacher of Italian and an Italian native speaker, working closely together.

It is the ideal reference text to use with newer language courses, for both beginner and advanced learner.

The course books and textbooks published over the last two decades are based on the principles of the *communicative* approach to language learning, which recognizes that the objective of any language learner is to communicate, to get one's message across, and that there can be many different ways of doing this, rather than a 'right' way and a 'wrong' way.

The communicative approach emphasizes language *functions* rather than structures. Traditional reference grammars present language by structure, making them inaccessible to learners who have no knowledge of grammatical terminology. *Modern Italian Grammar* presents language by *function*, with examples of usage and full explanations of how to express specific functions in Part B. At the same time it retains the traditional presentation of language by *structure* in Part A, which illustrates language forms and grammatical systems in a schematic way: word formation and morphology, verb conjugations, tenses, use of conjunctions and verb constructions.

The *language functions* included have been based on the communicative functions listed in Nora Galli de Paratesi's *Livello Soglia* (1981), itself based on J.A. van Ek's *The Threshold Level* (1975), the statement of key language functions supported by the Council of Europe. We have expanded them to provide a richer variety of examples more suited to our target readership. The division into functional areas also takes account of general linguistic *notions*, which can occur in more than one function; these include notions such as presence or absence, time and space, cause and effect. Notions and functions are integrated throughout Part B, while the structures illustrated in Part A are accessed through extensive cross-referencing.

In our choice of examples, we have included as many different contexts as possible. Some examples are typical of everyday dialogue or writing; some have been taken from the press or television, others from contemporary texts.

Our guides and inspiration in putting together this grammar have been some of the recognized authorities in the area of Italian grammar in the last decade or so: to them go our thanks and our recognition of the great debt we owe them. Anna-Laura and Giulio Lepschy (*The Italian Language Today*, Routledge, 1991); Marcello Sensini (*Grammatica della lingua italiana*, Mondadori, 1990): Maurizio Dardano and Pietro Trifone (*Grammatica Italiana*, Zanichelli, 3rd edn, 1995); Luca Serianni (*Grammatica italiana. Italiano comune e lingua letteraria*, UTET, 2nd edn, 1991); Giampaolo Salvi and Laura Vanelli (*Grammatica essenziale di riferimento della lingua italiana*, De Agostini/Le Monnier, 1992).

The latter three texts, in particular, have to some extent departed from traditional Italian grammar terminology. In *Modern Italian Grammar* we have also made innovations both in terminology and in presentation. In many cases, we have had to make choices, and there may be areas where our choice differs from that of our colleagues. One such area is terminology.

We have deliberately departed from the practice of translating **passato remoto** as 'past definite' or 'past historic', since this only reinforces in the learner's mind the idea that the **passato remoto** should be used to describe events far-off in time, while the **passato prossimo** is used for more recent events, a concept which misleads. We have followed Salvi-Vanelli in defining the former as 'simple perfect' (**perfetto semplice**) and the latter as 'compound perfect' (**perfetto composto**) which better illustrates the difference in these verb forms, and at the same time brings the focus back to the important distinction between *perfect* and *imperfect* aspect.

In conclusion, we are conscious of the fact that our grammar represents the beginning of a journey rather than an end. We have had to find our own way, and make our own judgements, in an area as yet uncharted. We may have erred on our way, but hope we have not foundered totally! We trust that our colleagues will be sympathetic with our dilemma and forgiving of any shortcomings. We look to them and to the users of the grammar for advice and suggestions as to how the text might be improved in future years, and we wish our readers '**Buono studio**'.

How to use this book

Part A of the book is a reference guide to the grammatical structures or 'building blocks' of Italian: noun group, verbs, pronouns, conjunctions, prepositions, adverbs. Where possible, tables are used to illustrate forms and patterns.

Part B shows how grammar structures are used to express communicative 'functions' such as giving personal information, asking someone to do something, describing something, etc. These structures are divided into four broad Sections: I Giving and seeking factual information; II Actions affecting ourselves and others; III Expressing emotions, feelings, attitudes and opinions; IV Putting in context. A final Section, Section V, looks at special types of language, for example the formal register, bureaucratic language, and the language of telephone and letter.

The *table of contents* at the front of the book shows the content of each Section and chapter, for Part A and Part B. It is not in alphabetical order but set out according to the layout of the book.

At the end of the book, there is a full *index* for the whole book. Grammar structures, communicative functions and key words are all listed in alphabetical order, using both Italian and English terms.

If you want to know how to express a particular *function*, for example 'Asking if something is available' or 'Introducing yourself', simply look it up in the index or in the table of contents. In Part B, you will find all the different ways in which you can say what you want, with an indication of where you can find further information on the grammar structures used, and references to related functions found in other parts of the book.

If, on the other hand, you know the grammatical name for the *structure* you want to use, for example personal pronouns or impersonal **si**, you can look that up in the index instead. You will find each grammar structure explained in Part A. Part A is also useful as an easy-to-use quick reference section, where you can remind yourself of the correct form, or check on a verb ending, for example. A *glossary*, which immediately follows this short guide, gives definitions of the grammatical terms used in this book, with examples.

Note that throughout the book an asterisk is used to denote a form or wording that does not exist or is incorrect, shown for purposes of demonstration.

Lastly, *keywords* are also indexed to make it easier for the reader to look up a particular point. Both Italian and English keywords are included here, grammar terminology as well as Italian examples; you will find both **lei** and 'personal pronouns', for example, listed in the index.

We hope you enjoy learning Italian using this book as a guide. Remember that some spoken skills such as pronunciation, intonation and stress cannot simply be learnt from a book. But grammar structures are the foundation of any language, and this book will teach you how to use these structures to express what you want to say.

Glossary

abstract noun a noun which refers to a concept or quality rather than a person or object. Examples are **la felicità** 'happiness', **la miseria** 'poverty'.

active construction an active construction occurs in a sentence in which the subject of the sentence is the person carrying out the action, or the event taking place (as opposed to a *passive* construction where the subject is the person *affected* by the action): **mio marito** *fuma* **troppo** 'my husband smokes too much', **gli ospiti** *rimangono* **fino a sabato** 'the guests are staying until Saturday'. A verb can therefore have an *active* form: *chiudiamo* **la porta a mezzanotte** 'we shut the door at midnight' or a *passive* form: **la porta** *viene chiusa* **a mezzanotte** 'the door is shut at midnight'.

adjective describes or gives information about a noun. Adjectives can be descriptive (such as **grande** 'big', **bianco** 'white', **vecchio** 'old', **italiano** 'Italian'), demonstrative (**questo** 'this', **quel** 'that'), indefinite (**qualche** 'some', **alcuni** 'some, a few', **certo** 'certain'), interrogative (**quale** 'which', **quanto** 'how much, how many') or possessive (**mio** 'my', **tuo** 'your' etc): *alcuni nostri* **amici** 'Some friends of ours', **la** *vecchia* **casa in campagna** 'the old house in the country'.

adverb gives information about a verb, saying how, for example, something is done: **bene** 'well', **male** 'badly', **subito** 'immediately', **cortesemente** 'politely'. Adverbs can also add further information about an adjective or another adverb: *tanto* **stanco** 'so tired', *poco* **bene** 'not very well', *molto* **male** 'very badly'.

agreement in Italian, adjectives, articles and, in some cases, past participles have to 'agree with' the noun or pronoun they accompany or refer to. This means that their form varies according to whether the noun/pronoun is masculine or feminine (gender), singular or plural (number): *la* **casa bianca** 'the white house', *i miei* **sandali sono rott***i* 'my sandals are broken', **loro sono andat***i* 'they went'.

article Italian has three types of article: the definite article **il**, **lo** (etc.) 'the', the indefinite article **un**, **una** (etc.) 'a' and the partitive **dei**, **delle**, **degli** (etc.) 'some, any': *il* **ragazzo** 'the boy', *una* **lezione** 'a lesson', *dei* **bambini** 'some children'.

auxiliary verb auxiliary verbs such as **avere**, **essere** are used in combination with the past participle to form compound tenses, both active *ho* **mangiato** 'I have eaten', *siamo* **andati** 'we have gone' and passive *è stato* **licenziato** 'he was sacked'. See also **modal verb**.

clause is a section or part of a sentence which contains a subject and a verb. Complex sentences are made up of a series of clauses. The main clause (or clauses) is the part of a sentence which makes sense on its own and does not depend on any other element in the sentence. A subordinate clause always depends on another clause, and is often introduced by a conjunction such as **che**. There are different types of subordinate clause, e.g. relative clauses: **ho visto il ragazzo** *che piace a mia sorella* 'I saw the boy that my sister likes'; purpose clauses: **ho portato la macchina dal meccanico** *perché controllasse i freni* 'I took the car to the mechanic so that he could check the brakes'.

comparative when one person, object or activity is compared with another, a comparative form is used: **mia figlia nuota** *meglio* **della sua** 'my daughter swims better than hers', **la pasta napoletana è** *migliore* **di quella siciliana** 'Neapolitan pasta is better than Sicilian pasta'.

compound noun a noun formed by joining together one or more words, either nouns or other parts of speech: **asciugamano** 'a towel' (verb **asciugare** 'to dry' + noun **mano** 'hand'), **capotreno** 'chief guard on train' (noun **capo** 'chief' + noun **treno** 'train').

compound tenses are tenses consisting of more than one element. In Italian, the compound tenses are formed by the auxiliary **avere** or **essere**, and the past participle: *ho mangiato* **troppo** 'I have eaten too much', *siamo andati* **a casa** 'we went home'. See also **simple tenses**.

conditional this is not strictly a tense, but a verb mood. It can be used on its own, particularly as a polite way of expressing a request: **Le** *dispiacerebbe* **aprire la finestra?** 'Would you mind opening the window?' It can also be used in conditional sentences, where the meaning of the main sentence is dependent on some condition being fulfilled: *andrei* **in vacanza anch'io, se avessi tempo** 'I would go on holiday too if I had the time'.

conjugation the way in which verb forms change according to the person, tense or mood: (**io**) *vado* 'I go', (**noi**) *andremo* 'we will go', **le ragazze** *sono andate* 'the girls went', **voleva che io** *andassi* **a casa sua** 'he wanted me to go to his house', etc. The word conjugation is also used to mean the regular patterns of verbs ending in -**are**, -**ere**, -**ire** to which verbs belong.

conjunction a linking or joining word, usually linking two words, phrases or clauses within a sentence: **Marco** *e* **Davide** 'Marco and Davide', **con amore** *ma* **con disciplina** 'with love but with discipline', **sono andata a letto** *perché* **ero stanca** 'I went to bed because I was tired', **i giudici dicono** *che* **bisogna cambiare la legge** 'the judges say that the law should be changed'. Conjunctions can either be coordinating, linking two phrases or clauses of equal weight, or subordinating, linking main clause and subordinate clause.

countable a noun is countable if it can normally be used in both singular and plural, and take the indefinite article **un, una** (etc.): **un bicchiere** 'a glass', **una pizza** 'a pizza', whereas an uncountable noun is one which is not normally found in the plural e.g. **zucchero** 'sugar' or an abstract noun such as **tristezza** 'sadness'.

declension this means the way in which nouns and adjectives decline, in other words, change their endings according to whether they are singular or plural, masculine or feminine: **un ragazzo** 'a boy', **una ragazza** 'a girl', **due ragazzi** 'two boys', **due ragazze** 'two girls'. This pattern of endings is known as the declension.

definite article see **article**

demonstrative a demonstrative adjective or pronoun is one which demonstrates or indicates the person or object we are talking about: *questo* **carrello** 'this trolley', *quel* **professore** 'that teacher', *quelle* **tagliatelle** 'those tagliatelle'.

direct object a direct object, whether noun or pronoun, is one which is directly affected by the action or event. A direct object can be living or inanimate. It is always used with a **transitive** verb: **i miei figli hanno mangiato** *tutti i cioccolatini* 'my sons ate all the chocolates'. When a direct object pronoun is used with a compound tense, the past participle changes its ending to agree with it: *Li* **ho** vist*i* **in città ieri sera** 'I saw them in town yesterday evening'.

feminine see **gender**

finite verb a verb that has a subject and is complete in itself, as opposed to **infinitives** or **participles**, which have to depend on another verb: **ieri** *siamo andati* **in piscina** 'yesterday we went to the swimming pool', **domani i ragazzi** *torneranno* **a scuola** 'tomorrow the kids will go back to school'.

gender all nouns in Italian have a gender: they are either masculine or feminine, even if they are inanimate objects. Even where living beings are concerned, grammatical gender is not always the same as natural gender: *una* **tigre** 'a tiger' (either sex unless specified), *un* **ippopotamo** 'a hippopotamus'. Gender is important since it determines the form of noun, article and adjective.

gerund the Italian **gerundio** is a verb form ending in **-ando** or **-endo**: **parlando** 'speaking', **sorridendo** 'smiling', **finendo** 'finishing'. The Italian gerund is often used with the verb **stare** to express a continuous action or event: **sto** *finendo* 'I'm just finishing', **stavano ancora** *mangiando* 'they were still eating'. The English gerund – the '-ing' form – is not used in exactly the same way. For example, it is often used with the value of a noun: 'Studying is boring' while in Italian this sentence would be expressed by an infinitive: **Studiare è noioso.**

idiomatic an idiomatic expression is one which cannot normally be translated literally, for example **ubriaco fradicio** literally 'soaking drunk' but more idiomatically 'dead drunk'. Frequently a common verb such as **fare** 'to do' can have a range of idiomatic meanings, often adding a pronoun, for example: **farcela** 'to be able to, to manage to', **non** *ce la faccio* **a finire questo gelato** 'I can't manage to finish this ice cream'.

imperative the imperative mood is the verb mood used to express orders, commands or instructions: *state* **fermi** 'keep still', *si accomodi* 'sit down', *andiamo* 'let's go'. See also **subjunctive**.

impersonal (verbs, verb forms) impersonal verbs or verb forms do not refer to any one particular person. They can generally be translated by the English 'it' form and use the third person form: *occorre* **pulire prima la casa** 'it is necessary to clean the house first', **non** *serve* **protestare** 'it's no good protesting'. These verbs can be personalised by the addition of a personal pronoun, usually the indirect object: **non mi** *occorre* **questo maglione** 'I don't need this thick sweater'.

indefinite an adjective or pronoun used to refer to a person or thing in a general way, rather than a **definite** person or thing. Examples are: **alcuni** 'some', **certi** 'certain, some', **qualche** 'some'.

indefinite article see **article**

indicative the verb mood we use most in speaking and writing is the indicative mood. Within this mood are a full range of tenses: present **mangio** 'I eat', past **ho mangiato** 'I have eaten', future **mangerò** 'I will eat', etc. The verb mood used to express uncertainty is the subjunctive, which also has a full range of tenses. See **subjunctive**.

indirect object an indirect object, whether noun or pronoun, is one which is indirectly affected by the action or event. An indirect object can be found with a **transitive** verb which already has one direct object: **ho mandato delle cartoline** *ai miei amici* 'I sent some postcards to my friends' or it can be used with an intransitive verb which does not take a direct object, in which case it may be found together with a preposition such as **a**, **da**: **Marco telefonava** *a sua madre* **ogni sera** 'Marco used to phone his mother every evening'.

infinitive the infinitive of a verb is the form always given in a dictionary and is recognized by its endings **-are**, **-ere**, **-ire**: for example **chiacchierare** 'to chat', **sorridere** 'to smile' and **partire** 'to leave'. It cannot be used on its own but depends on a finite verb form, often a modal verb: **vorrei** *ringraziare* **i telespettatori** 'I would like to thank the TV audience' or else is found linked with a preposition: **abbiamo fatto un salto in centro per** *comprare* **dei regali** 'we took a quick trip into town to buy some presents'.

interrogative words are used to ask direct or indirect questions. They include **chi** 'who', **come** 'how', **cosa** 'what', **dove** 'where', **quale** 'which', **quando** 'when', **perché** 'why'.

intransitive verbs see also **transitive verbs**. Intransitive verbs are verbs which *cannot* be used with a direct object. Some intransitive verbs can be used with an indirect object: *ho telefonato a* **Maria Teresa** 'I telephoned [to] Maria Teresa'. Some are always used without any object: *siamo arrivati* **alla stazione con un'ora di ritardo** 'we arrived at the station an hour late'. Many of these verbs take the auxiliary **essere**, but some take **avere**: *abbiamo camminato* **molto** 'we walked a lot'. Sometimes a verb which can be used transitively in English ('to walk the dog') cannot be used transitively in Italian (**camminare**). Some verbs can be used both transitively and intransitively.

invariable nouns are nouns that have the same form for both singular and plural: **un** *film*, **dei** *film* 'a film, some films' or for both masculine and feminine: **un** *artista*, **un'***artista* 'an artist'. An invariable adjective is one which does not change form to agree with the noun, whether masculine or feminine, singular or plural: **un vestito** *rosa*, **una giacca** *rosa* 'a pink jacket', **dei pantaloni** *rosa* 'some pink trousers', **delle calze** *rosa* 'some pink stockings'.

irregular (noun or verb) one which does not follow one of the standard patterns of forms or endings: **un uov***o* 'one egg', **due uov***a* 'two eggs'; **andare** 'to go': **vado** 'I go', **vai** 'you go', **va** 'he/she goes', **andiamo** 'we go', **andate** 'you (plural) go', **vanno** 'they go'.

masculine see **gender**

modal verb a verb which is used with a verb infinitive to *modify* what is being said: in Italian the modal verbs are **potere** 'to be able to', **dovere** 'to have to', **volere** 'to want to': *posso* **lavorare domani** 'I can work tomorrow', *devo* **lavorare domani** 'I have to work tomorrow', *voglio* **lavorare domani** 'I want to work tomorrow'.

moods the seven main ways in which verbs can express actions or events are known as moods. The four finite moods – all of which, except the imperative, have a full range of tenses – are the *indicative* (e.g. **vado** 'I go'), *subjunctive* (e.g. **che io vada** 'that I may go'), *conditional* (e.g. **andrei** 'I would go') and *imperative* (**vada!** 'go!'). The three 'indefinite' moods are: infinitive, gerund, participle.

negative a statement is negative when it specifies an action or event which has not taken place or will not take place. Negative words or phrases turn a positive statement or question into a negative one. Examples of negative words in Italian include: **nessun** 'no', **nessuno** 'nobody', **niente** 'nothing', **non . . . mai** 'not . . . ever, never', **non . . . ancora** 'not yet', **non . . . più** 'no longer, no more'.

noun a noun indicates a person, place, thing, or event, for example: **l'Italia** 'Italy', **l'assistente** 'the language assistant', **la festa** 'the party'. Nouns are inextricably linked to the articles (**il**, **un**, etc.) and to any adjectives that accompany them. All nouns have a gender and this determines the form of the adjectives and articles that go with them.

number is the distinction between *singular* and *plural*. Verb forms alter according to the number of the subject: **il ragazzo** *nuota* 'the boy swims', **i ragazzi** *nuotano* 'the boys swim'.

object in grammatical terms, an object is the person or thing affected by the action or event, as opposed to the subject, which is the person or thing responsible for it. See **direct object**, **indirect object**.

participle (present, past) verbs normally have a present participle and a past participle. Unlike other (finite) verb forms, it cannot be used on its own but is found together with other verb forms. The *past participle* is used with the verb **avere** or **essere** to form the **passato prossimo** tense: **non abbiamo *mangiato* gli hamburgers** 'we didn't eat hamburgers'. When used with **essere**, it agrees with the subject: **nel 1994 siamo *andati* a Los Angeles** 'in 1994 we went to Los Angeles'. The *present participle*, ending in -**ante**, -**ente** is less frequently used and changes form when used as an adjective or noun, for example: **i cantanti**.

partitive article see **article**

passato composto is the term used for the *compound past*, a past tense formed by auxiliary and participle: **ho mangiato** 'I ate', **sono andato** 'I went'. Some books call it the **passato prossimo** 'perfect tense'.

passato remoto see **passato semplice**

passato semplice we have used the term **passato semplice** 'simple past' to denote the past tense which is simple, not compound, e.g. **andai** 'I went' (as opposed to **sono andato** 'I went'). Some books call this tense **passato remoto**, English 'past definite', 'past historic' or 'past absolute'.

passive construction a passive construction occurs in a sentence in which the subject of the sentence is the person or thing *affected by* the action or event taking place (as opposed to an *active construction* where the subject is the person *carrying out* the action): **tutti gli studenti sono stati promossi** 'all the students were moved up a class', **il concerto è stato anticipato** 'the concert was put forward'.

person the verb subject can be a first person (**io** 'I'), second person (**tu** 'you') third person (**lui**, **lei** 'he, she') and so on. Most verbs have three singular persons (English 'I, you, he/she'), and three plural (English 'we, you, they').

personal pronouns can be subject pronouns **io, tu, lui** 'I, you, he', etc; direct object pronouns **mi, ti, lo, la** 'me, you, him, her', etc; indirect object pronouns **mi, ti, gli, le** 'to me, to you, to him, to her', etc; disjunctive pronouns, used as stressed direct object or after a preposition (**con**) **me, te, lui, lei** '(with) me, you, him, her', etc. See also **pronouns**.

plural see **number**

possessive adjectives and/or pronouns denote ownership: **il *mio* orologio** 'my watch', **la *nostra* macchina** 'our car'.

preposition a word which gives further information about a person, action or event, for example, on time or place, value or purpose: **ci siamo sposati *nel* 1975** 'we got married in 1975', **sono nata *a* Milano** 'I was born in Milan', **una macchina *da* caffè** 'a coffee machine', **un francobollo *da* L.900** 'a nine hundred lire stamp', **siamo venuti *per* imparare l'italiano** 'we came to learn Italian'.

pronoun a word which stands in for and/or refers to a noun. There are various categories of pronoun: demonstrative, such as **hai visto *quello*?** 'have you seen that man?'; indefinite, such as **alcuni** 'a few people'; interrogative, such as **chi?** 'who?'; personal, such as **io** 'I', **noi** 'we, us', **lo** 'it'; possessive, such as **il mio** 'my, mine', **i suoi** 'his, hers' (masculine plural form); reflexive, such as **mi, ti, si** 'myself, yourself, himself/herself'; relative, such as **quello che** 'the one who'.

question direct questions sometimes begin with a question word: **dove vai stasera?** 'where are you going this evening?' and sometimes not: **hai tempo di parlarmi?** 'do you have time to speak to me?' Indirect questions are introduced by words such as **chiedere** 'to ask': **mi ha chiesto se avevo tempo di parlargli** 'he asked me if I had time to speak to him'.

reflexive verb a verb that can be used with a reflexive pronoun, equivalent of English 'myself, himself', indicating that the subject and the object are one and the same: *mi lavo* 'I wash', *si è fatto* **male** 'he hurt himself'. Sometimes the verb can only be used reflexively, and no object is actually present: **molte volte i drogati** *si vergognano* **di quello che fanno** 'often drug addicts are ashamed of what they do'.

regular a regular noun or verb is one which follows one of the main noun or verb patterns, in **-are**, **-ere**, **-ire**, and whose forms and endings can therefore be predicted, for example **parlare** 'to speak', **sorridere** 'to smile', **partire** 'to leave'.

relative a relative pronoun introduces a relative clause, in which it gives more information about a person or thing mentioned specifically, or even an event referred to: **ho visto la studentessa** *che* **veniva sempre nel mio ufficio** 'I saw the student who was always coming to my office', **è andato alla discoteca senza chiedere il permesso, ciò** *che* **mi ha fatto arrabbiare** 'he went to the disco without asking permission, which made me angry'.

reported speech, also known as indirect speech, is a way of relating words spoken or written by someone else. Reported speech is usually introduced by verbs such as **dire** 'to say, to tell', **scrivere** 'to write', **annunciare** 'to announce' and the conjunction **che**: **i giornali** *annunciano che* **i soldati hanno massacrato migliaia di bambini** 'the newspapers say that the soldiers have massacred thousands of children'.

sentence a sentence must have a verb and a subject. It can be either a simple sentence (one subject, one verb): **gli ospiti dormivano** 'the guests were asleep', or a complex sentence (main clause and one or more subordinate clauses): **mentre i turisti dormivano, i ladri hanno portato via tutto** 'while the tourists were asleep, the thieves took everything'.

simple tenses those which are formed of one word only. See also **compound tenses**.

singular see **number**

stem see **verb stem**

subject the subject is usually a noun, pronoun or proper name denoting the person or object performing the action or the event taking place: *mia madre* ha comprato un tailleur 'my mother bought a suit', *la festa* si svolge a maggio 'the festival takes place in May'. In the case of a passive construction, the subject is the person or thing affected by the action: *gli studenti* sono stati criticati dagli insegnanti 'the students were criticized by their teachers'. With Italian verbs, it is not always essential to have a subject mentioned since it is understood from the verb form: *abbiamo mangiato* a mezzogiorno 'we ate at midday'.

subjunctive the subjunctive mood is used to express doubt or uncertainty. It is almost always used in complex sentences where one clause depends on another: abbiamo comprato un cagnolino in modo che i bambini *imparino* a prendere cura degli animali 'we bought a puppy so that the children can learn how to look after animals', or where the subordinate clause depends on a main verb expressing uncertainty: dubito che lui *possa* farcela 'I doubt if he can manage it'. However it can be found standing on its own, when used as an imperative form: *Vada* via! 'Go away!'

subordinate (clauses) a subordinate clause is one which depends on another clause, usually the main clause in a sentence. It can be introduced by a conjunction such as **che** 'what', **perché** 'because' or a relative pronoun such as **che** 'who, which'. See **clause, conjunction**.

superlative when one or more persons, objects or activities are compared with others, or a comparison is implied, to express the one which is superior to all the rest: la casa della mia amica Matilde era *la più grande* del paese 'my friend Matilde's house was the biggest in the village', abbiamo fatto *il meglio* possibile 'we did as well as we could'. See also **comparative**.

tense a finite verb form which normally provides a clue as to the time setting (present, past, future) for an action or event: andremo a New York 'we will go to New York', i miei amici ci sono stati 'my friends have been there'. Occasionally the grammatical verb tense does not correspond to the time setting; for example the future can be used for a present time setting: Sono le 4.00. Mio marito sarà già a Palermo 'It's 4 o'clock. My husband will be at Palermo by now', and the imperfect can be used to express a polite request: volevo un francobollo da L.750 'I wanted a L.750 stamp'.

transitive verbs are verbs which *can* always be used transitively, in other words with a direct object: *ho fumato* una sigaretta 'I smoked a cigarette'. Sometimes no object is used: *ho fumato* 'I smoked', but the verb is still a transitive verb since it can – and often does – take an object. Some verbs can be used both transitively and intransitively, e.g. **aumentare** 'to increase', **diminuire** 'to decrease', **cambiare** 'to change': *abbiamo aumentato* il prezzo del biglietto 'we have increased the price of the ticket', il prezzo del biglietto *è aumentato* 'the price of the ticket has increased'.

verb a verb describes an action, event or state. It always has a subject and can also have an object. Its form varies according to mood and tense, and the person, gender and number of its subject.

verb stem the stem of a verb is its 'base', the part of the verb which is left when you take away **-are**, **-ere-**, **-ire** from the infinitive form. In a regular verb the ending changes but the stem does not normally change. In an irregular verb, the stem may change too.

voice verbs normally have two voices: *active* and *passive*.

PART A

Structures

1 *The noun group*

1.1 *What is a noun?*

The main function of *nouns* in any language is to denote an entity (person, object, etc.) or concept (situation, abstract idea, etc.). Nouns are generally used together with *articles* (the, a) and/or *adjectives* (describing physical or other characteristics) which provide information about the entity or concept. Together they form a group of words called the *noun group*; two examples are shown below:

una *(article)* **grande** *(adjective)* **casa** *(noun)*   a big house
la *(article)* **ragazza** *(noun)* **inglese** *(adjective)*   the English girl

Although the noun group may contain other elements (for example adverbs, prepositional phrases, etc.), in this chapter we will deal only with the three basic elements of noun/article/adjective, analysing them one by one. Since in Italian the three components of the noun group cannot only be considered separately, but as a whole in which the various components have to 'agree', we will also look at how they are used together.

1.2 *The noun*

The noun is the focus of the noun group, and in fact the article and adjectives always agree with the noun in *gender* (masculine or feminine) and *number* (singular or plural). The two grammatical features of gender and number determine the form of noun, article and adjective.

Gender

All Italian nouns have either a masculine or a feminine gender. Gender is a purely *grammatical* term. Nouns referring to human beings or animals sometimes have the same *grammatical* gender as their *natural* gender, but not always (see below). Italian native speakers rarely find this a problem. However speakers of other languages often find it difficult to remember the gender of nouns and this creates a problem when it comes to making the other components of the noun group 'agree' with the noun.

With non-animate objects, there is not always an obvious explanation for their gender. Why, for example, should **sera** 'evening' be feminine, while **giorno** 'day' is masculine? Non-Italian speakers either have to learn and memorize the genders of words or consult a dictionary. Italian dictionaries usually indicate the gender of nouns with abbreviations such as **s.m.** (**sostantivo maschile**) and **s.f.** (**sostantivo femminile**).

Grammatically speaking, Italian does not always have a male and a female of each animal species, for example:

>**una tigre** 'tiger' is always feminine
>**un ippopotamo** 'hippopotamus' is always masculine

In order to provide the missing half, we have to say:

>**una tigre maschio**   a male tiger
>**un ippopotamo femmina**   a female hippopotamus

Some animals – as in English – have two distinct names for the male and the female of the species:

>**un cane** 'dog'   **una cagna** 'bitch'
>**un gallo** 'cock'   **una gallina** 'hen'

Some professional and other titles sometimes have a distinct form for the feminine. Nouns whose masculine form ends in **-e** either have a feminine form in **-a** or add the ending **-essa**:

-a

signore	Mr	**signora**	Mrs
cameriere	waiter	**cameriera**	waitress
padrone	landlord	**padrona**	landlady
infermiere	nurse	**infermiera**	nurse

-essa

dottore	**dottoressa**	doctor
professore	**professoressa**	teacher
studente	**studentessa**	student
presidente	**presidentessa**	president
principe	**principessa**	prince/princess
conte	**contessa**	count/countess
duca	**duchessa**	duke/duchess
barone	**baronessa**	baron/baroness

Nouns whose masculine form ends in **-tore** normally have feminine endings in **-trice**.

-trice

imperatore	**imperatrice**	emperor/empress
ambasciatore	**ambasciatrice**	ambassador
senatore	**senatrice**	senator

direttore	**direttrice**	director
attore	**attrice**	actor/actress
pittore	**pittrice**	painter
scultore	**scultrice**	sculptor
scrittore	**scrittrice**	writer
autore	**autrice**	author

The use of the masculine/feminine forms of professional titles such as
professore/professoressa, **direttore/direttrice** is fully illustrated in Chapter 20
Social contacts.

Number

Unlike gender, the grammatical concept of *singular* or *plural* (number) causes
no problem for speakers of English. Occasionally (as in English) a singular noun
is used to refer to a collective entity that one might expect to be grammatically
plural, for example **la gente** 'people'.

Common noun patterns

The gender and number determine the ending of the noun. These patterns of
endings are called *inflexions*. Italian nouns can be divided into several different
groups, according to their patterns of inflexion. The three most common
patterns (also followed by most adjectives, see below) are:

		Singular	Plural
1	Masculine	**-o**	**-i**
2	Feminine	**-a**	**-e**
3	Masculine or feminine	**-e**	**-i**

Note: Nouns in the third group (**-e**) have the same ending whatever the gender.

Examples

		Singular		Plural	
1	Masculine	**tavolo**	table	**tavoli**	tables
		albero	tree	**alberi**	trees
		sbaglio	mistake	**sbagli**	mistakes
		ragazzo	boy	**ragazzi**	boys
2	Feminine	**donna**	woman	**donne**	women
		parola	word	**parole**	words
		scuola	school	**scuole**	schools
		ragazza	girl	**ragazze**	girls
3	Masculine	**padre**	father	**padri**	fathers
		studente	student	**studenti**	students

	Singular		Plural	
	bicchier*e*	glass	**bicchier***i*	glasses
Feminine	**madr***e*	mother	**madr***i*	mothers
	occasion*e*	occasion	**occasion***i*	occasions
	chiav*e*	key	**chiav***i*	keys

In the plural, nouns ending in **-co**, **-go**; **-ca**, **-ga**; **-cia**, **-gia** present variations in their ending, as shown below:

Nouns ending in -co, -go
Masculine nouns ending in **-co** or **-go** in the singular normally form the plural as follows:

in **-chi**, **-ghi**, keeping the hard **c**, **g** sound, if the stress falls on the penultimate syllable:

     fuo*co* fuo*chi* 'fire'   a*go* a*ghi* 'needle'
     bu*co* bu*chi* 'hole'   albèr*go* albèr*ghi* 'hotel'
     sac*co* sac*chi* 'sack'   su*go* su*ghi* 'sauce'

and also in **catà**lo*go* **catà**lo*ghi* 'catalogue', **dià**lo*go* **dià**lo*ghi* 'dialogue' and a few more nouns

in **-ci**, **-gi**, with soft **c**, **g** sound, if the stress – indicated here by an accent for the purpose of clarity – falls on the third last syllable:

     mèdi*co* mèdi*ci* 'doctor'   aspàra*go* aspàra*gi* 'asparagus'
     mòna*co* mòna*ci* 'monk'   biòlo*go* biòlo*gi* 'biologist'

and also in **amì***co* **amì***ci* 'friend', **nemì***co* **nemì***ci* 'enemy', **gre***co* **gre***ci* 'Greek', **por***co* **por***ci* 'pig'.

Nouns ending in -ca, -ga
Feminine nouns ending in **-ca**, **-ga** in the singular form their plural in **-che**, **-ghe**, spelt with an '**h**' to represent the 'hard' **c**, **g** sound:

     ami*ca* ami*che* 'friend'
     le*ga* le*ghe* 'league'

Nouns ending in -cia, -gia
Feminine nouns ending in **-cia**, **-gia** in the singular form their plural as follows:

in **-cie**, **-gie** when the stress falls on the '**i**' (as indicated in the examples below), and when the last syllable is preceded by a vowel:

     farma*cìa* farma*cìe* 'pharmacy'   bu*gìa* bu*gìe* 'lie'
     ca*mìcia* ca*mìcie* 'shirt'   ciliè*gia* ciliè*gie* 'cherry'
     a*càcia* a*càcie* 'acacia'   va*lìgia* va*lìgie* 'suitcase'

in **-ce**, **-ge** when the ending is preceded by a consonant:

     aràn*cia* aràn*ce* 'orange'   spià*ggia* spià*gge* 'beach'
     provìn*cia* provìn*ce* 'province'   fran*gia* fran*ge* 'fringe'
     fac*cia* fac*ce* 'face'   pio*ggia* pio*gge* 'rain'

Notice that the pronunciation of -**cia** is similar to the 'ch' in English 'charm', that of -**gia** is like the 'j' in 'jacket', -**cie** as in 'chest', -**gie** as in 'jet'. There is no difference in pronunciation between the -**cie** of **camicie** and the -**ce** of **arance**. The **i** is pronounced and given its full value as a syllable only when stressed as in **farmacìe** and **bugìe**.

Note: In the plural, nouns ending in -**io** sometimes double the final **i**, sometimes not, according to whether it is stressed or unstressed:

> stud*io* stud*i*
> z*io* z*ii*

1.2.4 Other noun patterns

A large number of Italian nouns do not follow the patterns shown above. Here are some other noun patterns:

Masculine or feminine nouns with singular ending in -a

Singular -**a** (Masculine/Feminine)	Plural -**i** (Masculine)/-**e** (Feminine)

atlet*a*	athlete	atlet*i*	atlet*e*
autist*a*	driver	**autist***i*	**autist***e*
artist*a*	artist	**artist***i*	**artist***e*
colleg*a*	colleague	**collegh***i*	**collegh***e*
giornalist*a*	journalist	**giornalist***i*	**giornalist***e*

The nouns in the above group refer to categories of people. The singular ending -**a** is used whether they are male or female, but the plural form is different according to the 'natural' gender. A large number of these nouns end in -**ista** (English '-ist') indicating an ideology (**socialista**, **marxista**), profession (**chitarrista**, **dentista**) or sport (**ciclista**, **tennista**).

Masculine nouns with singular ending in -a

Singular -**a** (Masculine)	Plural -**i** (Masculine)

problem*a*	problem	**problem***i*
programm*a*	programme	**programm***i*
sistem*a*	system	**sistem***i*
Pap*a*	Pope	**Pap***i*
poet*a*	poet	**poet***i*
monarc*a*	monarch	**monarch***i*

This pattern is similar to masculine and feminine nouns with singular ending in -**a**, but has only masculine forms.

Masculine nouns ending in -ca, -ga (**monarca, collega**) normally add the -h- in a similar way to the feminine nouns ending in -ca, -ga shown on p.6, but note **il belga, i belgi.**

Feminine nouns with singular ending in -o, *plural in* -i

The two nouns shown below are both feminine in the singular but differ in the plural: **mani** is feminine, while **echi** is masculine.

Singular		Plural
man*o* (Feminine)	hand	**man***i* (Feminine)
ec*o* (Feminine)	echo	**ech***i* (Masculine)

See 1.2.5 Invariable nouns, below, for other examples of feminine nouns ending in -o.

Masculine nouns with singular in -o, *feminine plural in* -a
A number of masculine nouns become feminine in the plural, with an irregular ending in -a:

Singular Masculine		Plural Feminine
uov*o*	egg	**uov***a*
migli*o*	mile	**migli***a*
pai*o*	pair	**pai***a*

Masculine nouns with singular in -o, *masculine plural in* -i, *feminine plural in* -a
Some masculine nouns have the regular masculine plural in -i as well as a feminine plural in -a.

Singular Masculine		Plural in -i Masculine	Plural in -a Feminine
dit*o*	finger	**dit***i*	**dit***a*
bracci*o*	arm	**bracc***i*	**bracci***a*
ginocchi*o*	knee	**ginocch***i*	**ginocchi***a*
labbr*o*	lip	**labbr***i*	**labbr***a*
oss*o*	bone	**oss***i*	**oss***a*
gest*o*	gesture	**gest***i*	**gest***a*
lenzuol*o*	sheet	**lenzuol***i*	**lenzuol***a*
mur*o*	wall	**mur***i*	**mur***a*
url*o*	shout	**url***i*	**url***a*

There are however differences in the meaning of the two different plurals; the -a plural generally emphasizes the collective nature of the plural as a group or set, while the -i ending tends to denote either a more figurative sense or the plural as a collection of separate/individual elements.

For example, **le dita** are the fingers of your hand, when talked about 'collectively' (**Ho** *le dita* **gelate** 'My fingers are frozen') while **i diti** are the fingers considered 'individually or separately' (**Ho *due diti* rotti** 'I have two broken fingers').

Le mura are the collective walls of a city (**Lucca è una città circondata da mura romane** 'Lucca is a city surrounded by Roman walls'), while **i muri** refers to all other kinds of walls. **Le ossa** is the plural form normally used when talking about the skeletal system (**Mi fanno male le ossa** 'My bones ache') while the masculine plural **gli ossi** is used when talking about separate bones, e.g. broken bones or dog bones (**Ho dato due ossi al cane** 'I gave the dog two bones').

1.2.5

Invariable nouns

Invariable nouns have the same form in the plural as in the singular. These include:

Nouns with stress falling on last syllable
These are mainly feminine in gender, coming from an older form, of Latin origin, ending in **-tate** (**civitate**, **qualitate**) now abbreviated and ending in **-à**.

	Singular		Plural
Feminine	**città**	town	**città**
	università	university	**università**
	libertà	freedom	**libertà**
Masculine	**caffè**	coffee	**caffè**

Feminine nouns ending in -i

Singular		Plural
crisi	crisis	**crisi**
ipotesi	hypothesis	**ipotesi**
analisi	analysis	**analisi**

Feminine nouns ending in -ie

serie	series	**serie**
specie	species/kind	**specie**

Feminine nouns with abbreviated singular
These end mainly in **-o** and are usually abbreviations, often derived from compound words (**automobile** > **auto**, **fotografia** > **foto**):

Singular		Plural
auto	car	**auto**
moto	motorbike	**moto**
radio	radio	**radio**
foto	photo	**foto**
bici	bike	**bici**

Nouns of one syllable

	Singular		Plural	
Masculine	**re**	king	**re**	
	sci	ski	**sci**	
Feminine	**gru**	crane	**gru**	

Words borrowed from another language

	Singular		Plural	
Masculine	**bar**	bar, café	**bar**	
	sport	sport	**sport**	
	film	film	**film**	
	computer	computer	**computer**	
Feminine	**reclame**	advert	**reclame**	
	gaffe	gaffe	**gaffe**	
	brioche	brioche	**brioche**	

Note: Remember not to add '-s' in the plural, however tempting (**il film** – **i film**).

— 1.2.6 —
Nouns with extremely irregular plurals
Here are a few nouns whose plural form is extremely irregular:

	Singular		Plural	
Masculine	**uomo**	man	**uomini**	men
	dio	god	**dei**	gods
	bue	ox	**buoi**	oxen
Feminine	**ala**	wing	**ali**	wings
	arma	arm	**armi**	arms

1.3   *The article*

— 1.3.1 —
What is an article?
There are two types of article in Italian, as there are in English: the *definite article* (**articolo determinativo**) and the *indefinite article* (**articolo indeterminativo**). They distinguish the generic from the specific, the known from the unknown:

> **In giardino c'è *un* cane.**
> There is a dog in the garden. (unknown dog)

> **In giardino c'è *il* cane.**
> There is the dog in the garden. (our dog or a dog we know about)

In Italian the form of the article has to agree with the *gender* and *number* of the noun it is attached to, but also varies according to the *initial letter* of the word immediately following it, whether noun or adjective.

1.3.2

Indefinite article *un, uno, una, un'*

```
Masculine un   + vowel or consonant
          uno + s+consonant
                z, gn, ps, pn, x, semi-vowel i (j, y)
Feminine  un'  + vowel
          una + consonant
```

The form of the indefinite article for a masculine singular noun is **un**, becoming **uno** before a word starting with **s** + another consonant, **z, gn, ps, pn, x**, the semi-vowel **i (j, y)**:

> **un telefono** 'a telephone'
> **un espresso** 'an espresso'
> **un nuovo studente** 'a new student'
> **uno studente nuovo** 'a new student'
> **uno spuntino** 'a snack'
> **uno gnomo** 'a gnome'
> **uno psichiatra** 'a psychiatrist'
> **uno zoo** 'a zoo'
> **uno xenofobo** 'a xenophobe' (someone who hates foreigners)
> **uno yogurt** 'a yogurt'
> **uno iugoslavo** 'a Yugoslav'
> **uno pneumatico** 'a tyre'

With a feminine singular noun the indefinite article is **una**, but this changes to **un'** before a word starting with a vowel (a, e, i, o, u):

> **una bottiglia** 'a bottle'
> **una spremuta** 'a fresh fruit juice'
> **un'aranciata** 'an orangeade'
> **un'ampia distesa di neve** 'a wide expanse of snow'

Partitive article dei, delle, degli

```
Masculine dei   + consonant
          degli + vowel
                  s+consonant
                  z, gn, ps, pn, x, semi-vowel i (j, y)
Feminine  delle + any letter
```

With plural nouns the function of the indefinite article is taken by the *partitive article*, translated by English 'some':

Masculine
> *dei* **libri** 'some books'
> *degli* **studenti** 'some students'
> *degli* **amici** 'some (male) friends'

Feminine   *delle* **amiche** 'some (female) friends'
                  delle **camere** 'some rooms'

The *partitive* article indicates some *part* (an unspecified number) of a group or category of things/persons; it is formed by the preposition **di** combined with the *definite article*, and follows a similar pattern, changing according to gender, number and the word that follows (see 1.3.3).

A partitive article can also be used in the singular, indicating a quantity of 'uncountable' things, persons or abstract concepts:

Vorrei *del* pane.   I'd like some bread.
Ho visto *della* gente che   I saw some people running.
correva.
C'è ancora *della* speranza.   There is still some hope.

Note: See Chapter 11 for more details on using **del**, **della**.

1.3.3 Definite article

	Singular	Plural
Masculine	**il** + consonant	**i** + consonant
	l' + vowel	**gli** + vowel, **s**+consonant, **z, gn, ps, pn, x,** semi-vowel **i (j, y)**
	lo + **s**+consonant, **z, gn, ps, pn, x,** semi-vowel **i (j, y)**	
Feminine	**la** + consonant	**le** + any letter
	l' + vowel	

Masculine nouns
In the singular, masculine nouns normally take the article **il** but this changes to **lo** before a word starting with **s** + another consonant, **z, gn, ps, pn, x** (semi-vowel), **i (j, y)** and to **l'** before words starting with a vowel.

In the plural, masculine nouns take the article **i** but this changes to **gli** before a word beginning with a vowel or with **s** + another consonant, **z, gn, ps, pn, x**, and semi-vowel **i (j, y)**.

il **famoso cantante** 'the famous singer'
lo **strano inglese** 'the strange Englishman'
lo **Ionio** 'the Ionian'
lo **Yuppie** 'the Yuppie'
*l'***inglese pazzo** 'the mad Englishman'
i **ragazzi italiani** 'the Italian boys'

> *gli* **studenti italiani** 'the Italian students'
> *gli* **stranieri** 'the foreigners'
> *gli* **zii americani** 'the American uncles'
> *gli* **Iugoslavi** 'the Yugoslavs'
> *gli* **yacht** 'the yachts'
> *gli* **alberghi** 'the hotels'

Feminine nouns
In the singular feminine nouns take the article **la**, which becomes **l'** before a word beginning with a vowel. Feminine plural nouns take the article **le**, which is *not* abbreviated in the plural.

> *la* **bottiglia grande** 'the large bottle'
> *la* **spremuta** 'the fresh fruit juice'
> *l'***aranciata** 'the orangeade'
> *l'***ampia distesa di neve** 'the wide expanse of snow'
> *le* **automobili bianche** 'the white cars'
> *le* **spagnole** 'the Spanish women'

1.3.4 — **Use of definite or indefinite articles**
The use of definite or indefinite article depends on whether the person or object is known or unknown, individual or class/species, as in the examples below:

A particular, clearly identified thing or things, known or visible to the speaker and to the person(s) addressed:

> **Dammi** *gli* **stuzzicadenti.**
> Give me *the* tooth-picks.

Referring to *any* tooth-picks, without reference to a particular or known set:

> **Dammi** *degli* **stuzzicadenti.**
> Give me *some* tooth-picks.

Known or unknown, specified or unspecified

(a)   The *definite* article is used to specify *known* persons or things

> **Flavia vuole portare** *l'amico* **alla festa.**
> Flavia wants to take her friend to the party. (particular friend or boyfriend)

> **Vorrei** *la camera* **che abbiamo avuto l'anno scorso.**
> I would like the room we had last year. (specific room)

(b)   The *indefinite* article is used, as in English, for an *unknown or unspecified* individual or thing:

> **Flavia vuole portare** *un amico* **alla festa.**
> Flavia wants to take *a* friend to the party. (an unspecified friend)

> **Vorrei *una camera* per stasera, per favore.**
> I would like a room for tonight. (any old room, unspecified)

Individual or class/species
(a)   The *definite* article is used when we want to identify a whole *class or species* of things or creatures, distinct from other species or categories, (e.g. an animal species, a category of films):

> ***Il* delfino è un mammifero.**
> The dolphin is a mammal. (Dolphins are mammals.)

> **Mi piacciono *i* film americani.**
> I like American films.

Note how English only uses the definite article 'the' in the singular ('the dolphin').

(b)   The *indefinite* article is used to talk about an individual dolphin or film (unless it is a particular dolphin or film known to us):

> **Guarda! C'è *un* delfino!**
> Look! There is *a* dolphin!

> **Ho visto *un* bel film americano alla televisione.**
> I saw *a* nice American film on TV.

These are only general guidelines. In many cases the use or omission of the articles is a matter of different linguistic habits.

Some particular uses of the definite article
In Italian we *always* use the definite article with the proper names of geographical features such as mountains, rivers, etc.:

> ***le* Alpi, *gli* Alburni**
> *the* Alps, *the* Alburni

> ***il* Tamigi, *la* Senna**
> *the* Thames, *the* Seine

but not with the names of cities:

> **Firenze**   **Londra**
> Florence   London

Except when qualified in some way:

> ***la* Firenze del Settecento**
> eighteenth-century Florence

We use it with the names of countries or nations:

Amo *l'*Italia.
I love Italy.

Il Brasile è campione del mondo.
Brazil is world champion.

We don't use it with the preposition in:

Vivo *in* Italia.
I live in Italy.

Andiamo *in* Spagna.
We go to Spain.

Unless the country is qualified in some way:

Si vive meglio *nell'*Italia meridionale.
One lives better in southern Italy.

Note: For the use of the article with prepositions **in**, **a**, etc., see Chapter 4 Prepositions.

When speaking of somebody's profession we use the article with **fare**,

Faccio *l'*ingegnere.
I am *an* engineer.

but omit it with **essere** (note how English usage differs):

Sono ingegnere.
I am *an* engineer.

We can summarize these patterns in the following way:

Noun	Article	Examples
Class/group/species	Definite	**Il cavallo è un animale docile.** The horse is a docile animal.
Individual member	Indefinite	**Ho comprato *un* cavallo.** I've bought a horse.
Known	Definite	**Il mio cavallo si chiama Dolly.** My horse's name is Dolly.
Unknown	Indefinite	**C'è *un* cavallo nel campo.** There is a horse in the field.

1.4 The adjective

What is an adjective?

An adjective is a word that qualifies the meaning of a noun by adding some specification or description to it.

There are many different categories of adjective including demonstrative (**questo, quello**), interrogative (**quale**), possessive (**mio, tuo . . .**), indefinite (**alcuni, qualche**) and negative (**nessun**). But in this chapter we only cover the use of **aggettivi qualificativi**: *descriptive adjectives*, which describe qualities (physical or otherwise) of a person or thing, and *classifying adjectives*, such as nationality, which describe the category or classification that the person or thing belongs to. The other types of adjectives will be shown in Chapter 3, together with the corresponding pronouns.

Common adjective patterns

Almost all descriptive adjectives follow the same basic patterns as the nouns (see 1.2.3 above), with their ending depending on gender and number. There are two 'classes' or groups of adjectives:

	1			2	
	Singular	Plural		Singular	Plural
Masculine	-o	-i	Masculine/		
Feminine	-a	-e	Feminine	-e	-i

In the first group, there are four different endings for feminine/masculine/singular/plural. In the second group, the ending is the same for both masculine and feminine:

	1			2	
	Singular	Plural		Singular	Plural
Masculine	**piccolo**	**piccoli**	Masculine/		
Feminine	**piccola**	**piccole**	Feminine	**grande**	**grandi**

The gender and number of the adjective must agree with the noun to which it refers (see 1.2.3):

	Singular	Plural	Singular	Plural
Masculine	**libro piccolo**	**libri piccoli**	**libro grande**	**libri grandi**
	balcone piccolo	**balconi piccoli**	**balcone grande**	**balconi grandi**
Feminine	**penna piccola**	**penne piccole**	**penna grande**	**penne grandi**
	stazione piccola	**stazioni piccole**	**stazione grande**	**stazioni grandi**

1.4.3
Exceptions to this pattern
Only a few descriptive adjectives have a different pattern from those shown above:

Adjectives with singular **-a** (for both masculine and feminine), have masculine plural in **-i** and feminine plural in **-e**. Many of these have endings such as **-ista**, **-asta, -ita, -ida, -ota** (for nouns with similar endings, see 1.2.4 above):

Singular	Plural	
Masculine/Feminine	Masculine	Feminine
social*ista*	socialist*i*	socialist*e*
entusia*sta*	entusiast*i*	entusiast*e*
ipocr*ita*	ipocrit*i*	ipocrit*e*
suic*ida*	suicid*i*	suicid*e*
idi*ota*	idiot*i*	idiot*e*
Il Partito Socialista	**i paesi socialisti**	**le idee socialiste**
La bandiera socialista		

1.4.4
Invariable adjectives
Invariable adjectives have the same ending, whatever their gender and number, and retain the same form whatever noun they are referring to. The most common invariable adjectives are:

Some colours: **blu, rosa, viola, lilla, beige ...**

> **un libro blu, una penna blu, i giornali blu, le chiavi blu**

Colours indicated by two words: **verde bottiglia, giallo canarino, bianco latte ...**

> **camicia verde bottiglia** 'bottle green shirt'
> **pantaloni giallo canarino** 'canary yellow trousers'
> **lampadine bianco latte** 'milk-white light bulbs'

pari 'even', 'equal', **dispari** 'odd' and **impari** 'uneven', 'unequal':

> **numero pari** 'even number'
> **carte dispari** 'odd-numbered playing cards'
> **pari condizioni** 'equal conditions'
> **una lotta impari** 'an unequal struggle'

arrosto 'roast':

> **pollo arrosto** 'roast chicken'
> **patate arrosto** 'roast potatoes'
> **carne arrosto** 'roast meat'

1.4.5
Position of adjectives
Unlike English, and many other languages, the most common position for the adjective in the Italian noun group is after the noun. This is the usual

non-emphatic position occupied by the adjective, when it expresses a basic, intrinsic characteristic of the noun:

> **Ho visto un film *interessante.***
> I saw an interesting film.

> **Abbiamo visitato una città *storica.***
> We visited an historic city.

Adjectives of shape, colour, nationality almost *always* come *after* the noun. Note that they never have a capital letter in Italian:

> **una tavola *rotonda*** 'a round table'
> **una maglia *bianca*** 'a white sweater'
> **uno studente *francese*** 'a French student'

Adjectives qualified, for example, by an adverb or a prepositional phrase also come after the noun:

> **una persona *enormemente simpatica*** 'a really nice person'
> **un viaggio *pieno di problemi*** 'a journey full of problems'

As well as participles used as adjectives:

> **le mele *cotte*** 'cooked apples'

However, in Italian, unlike in English where adjectives almost always come before the noun ('an interesting film'), the order of the noun group is flexible, and the position of the adjectives can change the emphasis of the sentence.

Although Italian descriptive adjectives, particularly the most common (e.g. **nuovo**, **vecchio**, **giovane**, **piccolo**, **bello**, **brutto**) are placed after the noun when used to specify it or distinguish it from similar objects, they can be placed before when there is a need to describe the noun with some emphasis or imagination:

> **Dammi il cacciavite *piccolo.***
> Give me the *small* screwdriver. (not the big one)

> **Sul tavolo c'era un *piccolo* cacciavite.**
> There was a *small* screwdriver on the table. (description of screwdriver)

> **Sandra è una ragazza *bella.***
> Sandra is a *beautiful* girl. (not merely nice)

> **Sandra è una *bella* ragazza.**
> Sandra is a *really beautiful* girl.

> **Ho comprato una macchina *nuova.***
> I bought a *new* car. (rather than a second-hand one)

> **Paola si è messa un *nuovo* vestito.**
> Paola put on a *new* dress. (another, a different one)

Some adjectives have a completely different meaning from their common one when their position is changed, expressing their *literal* meaning when used *after*, but a quite different, often *figurative*, meaning when used *before*:

> **un film *bello*** 'a *nice* film'
> **un *bel* problema** 'a *pretty difficult* problem'

> **Preferisco avere regole *certe*.**
> I prefer to have *reliable* rules.

> **Non capisco *certe* regole.**
> I don't understand *certain* (some) rules.

> **un ufficiale *alto*** 'a *tall* officer'
> **un *alto* ufficiale** 'a *high-ranking* officer'

> **un uomo *grande*** 'a *big* man' (e.g. Pavarotti)
> **un *grande* uomo** 'a *great* man' (e.g. Napoleon)

> **Ci sono molti studenti *poveri*.**
> There are many *poor* students.

> ***Poveri* studenti! L'esame sarà duro!**
> *Poor* students! The exam will be hard!

Note that **bello**, when placed *before* the noun (as in **un *bel* problema**), follows the same pattern of change as the definite article (see 1.3.3) and the adjective **quello** (see 3.8.1). Also the adjective **buono** takes the form of the indefinite article (see 1.3.2): ***buon* esempio, *buono* studio, *buona* fortuna**, etc.

Comparative adjectives

One way of making a comparison between two different people, objects or other elements, is to use a *comparative adjective*.

> **La mia macchina è *veloce come* la tua.**
> My car is as fast as yours.

> **La mia macchina è *più veloce* della tua.**
> My car is faster than yours.

> **La mia macchina è *meno veloce* della tua.**
> My car is less fast than yours.

'as . . . as'

This is formed by using the words **come** or **quanto** to introduce the second element of the comparison. As a reinforcement we can also use the words **tanto**, **altrettanto** or **così** before the first element:

> **Il mio nuovo ufficio è comodo *quanto* quello di prima.**
> My new office is *as* comfortable *as* the one I had before.

La mia collega è *tanto* carina *quanto* efficiente.
My colleague is *as* pretty *as* she is efficient.

Qui le melanzane non sono *care come* in Inghilterra.
Here aubergines are not *as* dear *as* in England.

'more/less than'

The words **più** and **meno** are used to make a descriptive adjective into a comparative, while **di** or **che** introduce the second element of the comparison:

Sandro è *più bravo di* Angelo a bridge.
Sandro is better than Angelo at bridge.

È stato *meno facile di* quanto pensassi.
It was less easy than I expected.

È *più facile* criticare *che* risolvere i problemi.
It's easier to criticize than to solve problems.

Sara è *più carina che* intelligente.
Sara is prettier than she is intelligent.

The choice of **di** or **che** depends on what part of speech the second element of the comparison is, and on its position in the sentence:

più/meno ... di + noun, pronoun, adverb, numeral
più/meno ... che + adjective, verb, noun/pronoun preceded by preposition

Note: further examples of usage are shown in Chapter 17 Comparatives.

Special forms of comparative

A few very common adjectives have a special form of comparative:

buono	'good'	*migliore* (**più buono**)
cattivo	'bad'	*peggiore* (**più cattivo**)
grande	'big'	*maggiore* (**più grande**)
piccolo	'small'	*minore* (**più piccolo**)

The regular form of comparative (shown in brackets) is also possible. While there is little difference between **più buono/migliore** and **più cattivo/peggiore**, there is a difference of meaning between **maggiore** and **più grande**.

Maggiore can mean 'bigger, older/elder' in a physical sense, but can also mean 'greater' in an abstract sense. Similarly, **minore** can mean 'the smaller' or 'younger', but can also mean 'less, the lesser' when referring to an abstract quality:

Ho due sorelle. *La maggiore* si chiama Diana.
I have two sisters. The elder is called Diana.

Noi abbiamo *una maggiore* responsabilità di voi.
We have a greater responsibility than you.

> **Il mio fratello *minore* frequenta la scuola elementare.**
> My little (younger) brother goes to elementary school.

> **Lui lavora con *minore* impegno da quando si è sposato.**
> He works with less commitment since he got married.

Relative superlatives

To refer to something or somebody as having *the most* of a certain quality, in relation to other individuals, we use **il più** together with the relevant adjective. This is called the *relative* superlative:

> **Silvia è *la più brava* studentessa della nostra classe.**
> Silvia is the best student in our class.

> **Pavarotti è *il* tenore italiano *più famoso* del mondo.**
> Pavarotti is the most famous Italian tenor in the world.

> **Il Po è *il più lungo* fiume italiano.**
> The Po is the longest Italian river.

Again, a few common adjectives have a special form of relative superlative, as well as the regular one:

> **buono** 'good'   ***il migliore*** (**il più buono**) 'the best'
> **cattivo** 'bad'   ***il peggiore*** (**il più cattivo**) 'the worst'
> **grande** 'big'   ***il maggiore*** (**il più grande**) 'the biggest', 'oldest'
> **piccolo** 'small'   ***il minore*** (**il più piccolo**) 'the smallest', 'youngest'

As with the comparative, there can be a difference of meaning between the two forms **il maggiore/il più grande** and **il minore/il più piccolo**:

> **Secondo me, il problema *maggiore* dei giorni nostri è la droga.**
> In my opinion, the greatest problem in our time is that of drugs.

Absolute superlatives

Absolute superlatives indicate the greatest possible degree of a quality, but without any comparison being made. Superlative adjectives are formed in Italian by adding the suffix **-issimo** to the end of the adjective:

> **un uomo bell*issimo*** 'a very handsome man'
> **un'organizzazione efficient*issima*** 'a very efficient organization'
> **degli important*issimi* clienti** 'some very important clients'

However, it is also possible in Italian to use the adverb **molto** to modify the adjective, in a similar way to the English 'very':

> **un uomo *molto bello*** 'a very handsome man'
> **un'organizzazione *molto efficiente*** 'a very efficient organization'
> **dei clienti *molto importanti*** 'some very important clients'

As seen above, when modified by any adverb (**molto, poco, troppo, abbastanza, piuttosto**) the adjective generally follows the noun:

dei clienti *piuttosto importanti* 'some rather important clients'

Notice that, when modified by the superlative suffix **-issimo**, the endings of the adjectives have the same pattern as adjectives in the first group (ending in **-o/-a/-i/-e**) (see 1.4.2 above), even if they belong to the second group (**-e, -i**). So we have:

Adjective in the first group	**bello/a/i/e**	**bellissimo/a/i/e**
Adjective in the second group	**importante/i**	**importantissimo/a/i/e**

The common adjectives **buono, cattivo, grande, piccolo**, mentioned above, also have two forms of absolute superlative:

buono 'good'	**ottimo/buonissimo** 'best'
cattivo 'bad'	**pessimo/cattivissimo** 'worst'
grande 'big'	**massimo/grandissimo** 'biggest', 'greatest'
piccolo 'small'	**minimo/piccolissimo** 'smallest', 'least'

For the comparative and superlative of adverbs, see Chapter 6.

1.5 *Agreement of noun, article and adjective*

The great majority of Italian descriptive adjectives have the same pattern of endings as the nouns (the two patterns are shown above); only a few are invariable (see 1.2.3). Nouns, adjectives and articles used together in a noun group must agree in number and gender.

For example, if we use a feminine singular noun such as **borsa** 'bag', we have to use the feminine singular *article* **la** and *adjective* **rossa**:

la borsa rossa 'the red bag'

If we use a masculine plural noun such as **sandali** 'sandals', we have to use the masculine plural *article* **i** and *adjective* **rossi**:

i sandali rossi 'the red sandals'

The English articles and adjectives are identical in both examples 'the red . . .' while in Italian they have very different forms (**la . . . rossa/i . . . rossi**) depending on the gender and number of the noun to which they are attached.

1.5.1 Noun and adjective of same pattern

When noun and adjective belong to the same pattern of endings, the agreement will be obvious:

> **Sul tavolo c'è un piatt*o* rotond*o*.**
> On the table there is a round dish.

> **Ho conosciuto due ragaz*ze* italian*e*.**
> I met two Italian girls.

Noun and adjective of different patterns

It is more difficult to remember how to make the agreement when the noun and adjective belong to different patterns and therefore have different endings:

> **Sul tavolo c'è un piatt*o* grand*e*.**
> There is a large dish on the table.

> **Ho conosciuto due ragaz*ze* ingles*i*.**
> I met two English girls.

> **Il programm*a* era noios*o*.**
> The programme was boring.

> **La radi*o* era rott*a*.**
> The radio was broken.

More than one noun (same gender)

If an adjective refers to more than one noun of the same gender, it will be plural and have the same gender as the nouns:

> **Ho comprato un libro e un vocabolario tedesch*i*.**
> I bought a German book and German dictionary.

> **Ho comprato una grammatica e un'agenda tedesch*e*.**
> I bought a German grammar and a German diary.

More than one noun (different genders)

If the two nouns are of different genders then the adjective is generally masculine plural:

> **Ho comprato un vocabolario e una grammatica tedesch*i*.**
> I bought a German dictionary and a German grammar.

However, if the second of the two nouns – the one nearest to the adjective – is feminine plural, the adjective may sometimes agree with it:

> **Ho comprato un vocabolario e due grammatiche tedesch*e*.**
> I bought a German dictionary and two German grammars.

2 Verbs

2.1 General features of verbs

2.1.1
Introduction

Actions, events and situations are expressed by the use of *verbs*. Italian has a complex system of different verb forms. In the first section of this chapter we shall introduce the general features of Italian verbs, both regular and irregular, with a brief explanation of basic grammatical terminology which will help you to understand these features. In the second section, the different verb forms are illustrated in table form for regular and the most common irregular verbs, and also for the passive forms of the four regular verb types. Finally, in the third section, we shall look at the different verb moods and tenses individually with brief explanations of their use. Part B of the book illustrates usage more fully.

2.1.2
Grammatical subject

Usually the subject of a verb is the 'author' or *doer* of an action, the 'protagonist' of an event:

> **Noi part*iamo* per l'America.**
> We leave for America.

> **Franco e Teresa part*ono* per l'America.**
> Franco and Teresa leave for America.

Sometimes we talk of *facts* rather than *actions*. Here the 'subject' of the verb is not doing anything, but is the *theme*, or main topic, expressed by the verb:

> **Giulia *è* bionda.**
> Giulia is blonde.

> **Questo film *dura* due ore.**
> This film lasts two hours.

However, the *grammatical subject* of the verb is not always the '*real*' subject or 'doer' of the action. This is the case with *passive* verbs (see Chapter 19).

2.1.3
Persons of the verb

The different forms of the verb, determined by its grammatical subject, are called the *persons* (this is a purely grammatical term, not necessarily referring to human beings):

1	Singular first person (the speaker)	I
2	Singular second person (the person addressed)	you
3	Singular third person (the 'third party')	he, she, it
4	Plural first person (the speaker + other people)	we
5	Plural second person (the people addressed)	you
6	Plural third person (the 'third parties')	they

In each tense, Italian verbs have six different endings, depending on who or what is carrying out the action. The different endings immediately identify the 'person' – the subject of the action – unlike in English where only the third person singular has a distinctive ending ('I eat', 'you eat', 'he eats'). The first and second persons are usually evident in the context of communication (speaker/writer and receiver):

> **Quanti anni hai? Ho trent'anni.**
> How old are you? I am thirty.

Using a subject pronoun to refer to the third person is also often unnecessary where the person (or thing) has already been mentioned:

> **Quanti anni ha Maria? Ha venticinque anni.**
> How old is Maria? She is twenty-five.

Consequently, it is not necessary to use subject pronouns (English 'I', 'you', 'he/she' . . .) in Italian, unless we need to give particular emphasis to the subject. (See also Chapter 8.)

2.1.4

Verb conjugations

The fact that Italian verbs have a pattern of six distinct verb endings in each of the tenses creates a large number of different forms of the same verb (almost 100!), also called *inflexions*. Fortunately, most verbs follow common patterns of change (or inflexion) known as conjugations. Each verb has a part (the *stem*), which carries its meaning, and an *inflected* part (the ending) which identifies the *person*, the *tense*, the *mood* and other features.

The regular conjugation patterns are shown in the verb tables below (2.2) for easy reference. Traditionally we distinguish three conjugations defined by the form that the verb takes in the *infinitive* (the infinitive is the form used in dictionary entries):

> *1st conjugation* ending in **-are** as **parl-*are*** 'to speak'
> *2nd conjugation* ending in **-ere** as **cred-*ere*** 'to believe'
> *3rd conjugation* ending in **-ire** as **dorm-*ire*** 'to sleep'

The verbs of the 3rd conjugation (ending in **-ire**) follow two distinct patterns, the second of which, with ending in **-isco**, as in **fin-*ire*/fin-*isco*** 'to finish', is the most frequent. Both patterns however are considered as belonging to the same conjugation, because of the **-ire** ending of the infinitive.

2.1.5 **Moods and tenses**

Moods
The different forms and uses of Italian verbs are traditionally grouped in seven *moods*. These convey the different characteristics of the actions or facts that the speaker or writer wants to communicate: certainty or doubt, straightforwardness or politeness, command, etc. . . .

The seven moods are:

Indicative	Infinitive
Conditional	Participle
Subjunctive	Gerund
Imperative	

The different verb *forms* for each verb mood will be listed below in the tables of regular and irregular conjugations and then described in separate paragraphs. The ways in which moods are used to express distinct *communicative functions* and meanings are illustrated in Part B.

Tenses
The word *tense* denotes the different verb forms which indicate the relationship between the action or event referred to and the time of speaking or writing (or another reference point in time). There are different tenses for each mood of verbs (except the imperative).

Sometimes in Italian different tenses are used to distinguish features of verbs other than time relationships. For example, perfect and imperfect tenses can express the *aspect* of the action (see Chapter 13), while different subjunctive and conditional tenses can express different degrees of doubt, possibility, politeness . . . (see Sections III and IV).

Simple and compound tenses
Many tenses of Italian verbs are formed using the past participle of the main verb along with either **avere** or **essere** as *auxiliary verb*. These are called compound tenses. One major area of difficulty for students of Italian is knowing which verbs use **avere** in compound tenses, and which use **essere**. In order to do this, it is useful to understand the difference between *transitive* and *intransitive* verbs (see 2.1.6 below).

All *passive* forms of verbs (see 2.1.7 below) are compound forms, commonly formed with the auxiliary **essere**.

2.1.6 **Transitive/intransitive verbs: use of *avere* or *essere* in compound tenses**
The actions that we express by using verbs can be 'completed' with an *object*. There may be a *direct object* as in:

Lucia scrive *una lettera.*	Lucia writes a letter.
Cerchiamo *una casa.*	We look for a house.

Here the action of the verb can be completed by answering the question **che cosa?** 'what?'. The direct object of the verb is the noun that can answer this question without the use of a preposition (in this case **una lettera** and **una casa**):

Che cosa scrive Lucia?	What is Lucia writing?
Lucia scrive *una lettera.*	Lucia is writing a letter.
Che cosa cerchiamo?	What are we looking for?
Cerchiamo *una casa.*	We're looking for a house.

If we can ask and answer the question **che cosa?**, the verb is *transitive*, and it will use the auxiliary **avere** in compound tenses:

Lucia *ha scritto* una lettera.	Lucia wrote a letter.
***Abbiamo cercato* una casa.**	We looked for a house.

But some Italian verbs cannot be completed by a direct object and the question **che cosa?** would not make sense; these are *intransitive verbs* and they normally use **essere** as auxiliary:

> ***Andiamo* in ufficio alle 9.**
> We go to the office at 9 o'clock.

> **Il treno per Napoli *parte* alle 6.**
> The train to Naples leaves at 6 o'clock.

> ***Siamo andate* in ufficio alle 9.**
> We went to the office at 9 o'clock.

> **Il treno per Napoli *è partito* alle 6.**
> The train to Naples left at 6 o'clock.

Because it determines their different uses, especially in the compound tenses, knowing whether verbs are transitive or intransitive is very important. Check by either looking in a dictionary or seeing whether you can ask and answer the question **che cosa?** 'what?'. In dictionaries all verb entries carry the following indications:

v.t. or **v.tr.**	**verbo transitivo**
v.i. or **v.intr.**	**verbo intransitivo**

Speakers of English find it difficult to distinguish transitive from intransitive verbs, because English compound tenses only use the auxiliary 'to have' in the active forms and the auxiliary 'to be' in passive forms ('I have criticized my colleagues'; 'I am criticized by my colleagues').

Problems arise also from the fact that many English verbs used transitively and intransitively have an Italian counterpart which can only be used intransitively. Below we show some examples of English phrases which cannot be translated directly into Italian, since the verbs **camminare**, **volare**, **guidare**, **viaggiare** are not generally used transitively:

To walk the dog . . .   I'm Sharon. Fly me!
Drive me home . . .   Travel the world with
                                          Airmiles!

Verbs that can be used both transitively and intransitively
Some verbs can be used both transitively (with direct object) and intransitively
(without direct object), for example **cominciare, finire, aumentare, diminuire,
cambiare, crescere, passare**:

> **Il professore *comincia* la lezione alle 11.00.**
> The teacher begins the lesson at 11 o'clock.

> ***Finiamo* le vacanze in agosto.**
> We finish our holidays in August.

Here the subjects of these actions – beginning and finishing – are persons and
the verbs have direct objects (the lesson, the holidays). But sometimes the same
verbs have a non-personal subject, and cannot logically have a direct object:

> **La lezione *comincia* alle 11.00.**
> The lesson begins at 11 o'clock.

> **Le vacanze *finiscono* in agosto.**
> The holidays finish in August.

In simple tenses, the forms of the verbs are identical, whether transitive or
intransitive. But the compound forms in the past and future tenses vary
according to whether they are used transitively or intransitively:

> **Il professore *ha cominciato* la lezione.**
> The teacher began the lesson.

> **La lezione *è cominciata* alle 11.**
> **The lesson began at 11.00 o'clock.**

> ***Abbiamo finito* le vacanze in agosto.**
> We finished the holidays in August.

> **Le vacanze *sono finite* in agosto.**
> The holidays finished in August.

Verbs such as **correre, vivere, saltare** *must* take **avere** when used transitively:

> ***Ho vissuto* una vita d'inferno.**
> I have lived a life of hell.

> ***Hanno corso* un grosso rischio.**
> They ran a great risk.

> **Oggi *ho saltato* il pranzo.**
> Today I skipped lunch.

When used *intransitively,* the choice of **avere**/**essere** is more a matter of personal choice and linguistic habit:

> *Ho vissuto/Sono vissuto* **in Inghilterra per 25 anni.**
> I lived in England for 25 years.

> **Giuliana** *ha corso/è corsa* **a casa.**
> Giuliana ran home.

> **I bambini** *sono saltati/hanno saltato* **giù dal letto.**
> The kids jumped down from the bed.

Verbs like these are marked in dictionaries as **v.tr. e intr.** (verb transitive and intransitive).

Verbs using the auxiliary avere *even when used intransitively*
Generally Italian transitive verbs use the auxiliary **avere**, while intransitive verbs use the auxiliary **essere** in the compound tenses. However, there are quite a few verbs which use the auxiliary **avere** even when used intransitively. Here are the most common:

camminare 'to walk'   **passeggiare** 'to walk'   **viaggiare** 'to travel'
dormire 'to sleep'   **piangere** 'to cry'
giocare 'to play'   **riposare** 'to rest'

> *Ho camminato* **per due ore.**
> I walked for two hours.

> **Come** *hai dormito?*
> How did you sleep?

> *Avete giocato* **a carte?**
> Did you play cards?

2.1.7   **Voice: active, passive, reflexive**

Introduction
'*Voice*' describes the relationship of the verb action with its subject and object, shown in italics in the examples below. The different voices or relationships are:

(a) Active voice
Normally (see 2.1.2) the grammatical subject of the verb is the doer of the action or the main theme of the event, in which case the verb is active:

> *Gianni* **guarda** *Luisa.*
> Gianni watches Luisa.

> *Il meccanico* **ripara** *la macchina.*
> The mechanic repairs the car.

(b) Passive voice
Sometimes the person or object on the receiving end of the action is the
grammatical subject, and in this case the verb is passive:

> **Luisa è guardata *da Gianni.***
> Luisa is watched by Gianni.

> **La macchina è riparata *dal meccanico.***
> The car is repaired by the mechanic.

In the second example, the real subject of the action is clearly the mechanic (the
one who repairs the car), but the grammatical subject of the passive verb is the
car.

(c) Reflexive and pronominal voice
A verb form is reflexive when its subject and object are the same:

> **Gianni *si* guarda allo specchio.**
> Gianni looks at himself in the mirror.

There are other verb forms which are not strictly speaking reflexive but are
similar in form.

The following paragraphs look at the *passive* and *reflexive/pronominal* forms in
detail.

The passive form
The *passive* of Italian verbs is formed by the use of the auxiliary **essere** and the
past participle, using the same tense as the corresponding active form. The
passive conjugation of verbs is shown in the verb tables in 2.2. The passive can
also be formed using **venire** or **andare** as auxiliary instead of **essere** (see 19.2) or
by using the pronoun **si** and the third person of the verb (see 19.4). Only
transitive verbs can have a passive form (see 2.1.6).

Passive sentences (sentences based on a passive verb) are used when we want
to focus on the action itself or the object of an action, rather than on the doer or
author of an action. For more examples on the use of the passive, see Chapter
19.

Reflexive and pronominal forms
Reflexive verb forms:
Reflexive verbs are active verb forms accompanied by a reflexive pronoun (see
Chapter 3 Pronouns). Look at these two examples:

> **Il sig. Franchi *sta lavando* la macchina.**
> Mr Franchi *is washing* the car.

> **Il sig. Franchi *si sta lavando.***
> Mr Franchi *is washing himself.*

In the first example above, the direct object of the action of washing is the car. It is something separate from the person who is doing it (the subject of the action).

In the second example, both the subject and the object of the action are the same person (**Il sig. Franchi**). This is the reflexive form, in which the reflexive pronoun refers to the person carrying out the action, but at the same time is also the object of it.

The position of the reflexive pronoun is the same as that of all other unstressed pronouns (see Chapter 3): usually before the verb, but sometimes attached to the end of it, as with infinitives, gerunds and **voi**, **tu** imperatives:

> **Prego, *si* accomodi.**
> Please, have a seat (make *yourself* comfortable).

> **In genere i giovani italiani *si* vestono alla moda.**
> In general young people in Italy dress fashionably.

> **Sono le 9. Dovete preparar*vi* a uscire.**
> It's 9 o'clock. You must get *yourselves* ready to go out.

> **Prepara*ti* ad uscire!**
> Get yourself ready to go out!

In the compound tenses, reflexive verbs are conjugated with the verb **essere**, even though the verbs are *transitive* (cf. **lavare**, **alzare**) and normally take **avere** in the compound tenses. The past participle has to agree with the subject:

> **Stamattina i bambini si sono alzat*i* alle 6.**
> This morning the children got (themselves) up at 6 o'clock.

> **Mi sono vestit*a* con calma.**
> I got dressed unhurriedly.

Pronominal verb forms:
Pronominal verb forms are verb forms which use the reflexive pronoun. In Italian they are used much more frequently than in English because we can use them not only in a true reflexive pattern, but also in many other ways. In true reflexives (see above), the subject and object of the verb are one and the same. Although this is not the case with pronominal verb forms, they still embody the concept of 'reciprocal' or 'reflexive' action (an action relating or reflecting back to the subject).

The different uses of the *pronominal verb form* will become clear from the examples below:

(a) Indirect reflexive
The reflexive always indicates an action that is related to the person carrying out the action (the subject). Note the use of the auxiliary **essere** in the compound tenses:

Giulio *si* lava le mani.
Giulio washes *his* hands.

***Mi* metto la giacca.**
I put on *my* jacket.

Stamattina non *mi* sono fatto la barba.
This morning I didn't shave (*myself*).

In the examples above, the actions are clearly not truly reflexive, since the subjects and the objects of the actions are not exactly identical: **Giulio . . . le mani**, **io . . . la giacca**, **io . . . la barba**. However we use the reflexive pronoun to stress the fact that the object of the action is *closely related* to the person who does it, and indeed is either part of his/her body (**le mani**, **la barba**) or a personal belonging (**la giacca**). In the last example, the participle can also agree with the *object*:

Stamattina non *mi* sono fatt*a* la barba.

The reflexive pronoun can also be omitted in which case the construction no longer takes **essere** in the compound tenses:

Giulio lava le mani.
Metto la giacca.
Non ho fatto la barba.

(b) Reciprocal reflexive (each other)
A reciprocal action is when two persons do something to each other:

Arrivederci. *Ci vediamo* domani.
Bye. See you tomorrow.

Mario e Nicoletta *si sposano* domani.
Mario and Nicoletta are getting married tomorrow.

Dove *vi siete conosciuti* tu e Maria?
Where did you and Maria meet (each other)?

***Ci siamo incontrati* in Spagna.**
We met (each other) in Spain.

Note how in the examples above the reflexive pronoun marks an event or action taking place *within* the subject; the two persons are at the same time the subject and the object of a reciprocal action.

The same actions can be expressed by the active form, in which case one person is the subject and the other is the object:

Domani Mario *sposa* Nicoletta.
Tomorrow Mario will marry Nicoletta.

> **Dove (tu)** *hai conosciuto* **Maria?**
> Where did you meet Maria?

> *Ho incontrato* **il dott. Rossi in Spagna.**
> I met Dr Rossi in Spain.

(c) Emotions or involvement expressed with reflexive pronouns

In Italian we can use the reflexive pronoun simply to stress the subjective side of an event, the importance of this event to the person (the self) who is involved in it and who is its (grammatical) subject:

> **Stasera** *ci* **vediamo un bel film.**
> Tonight we'll watch a nice film.

> **Ho fame! Voglio mangiar***mi* **una pizza!**
> I'm hungry! I really want a pizza!

> **Mannaggia!** *Mi* **sono dimenticata le chiavi!**
> Damn! I've forgotten the keys!

In the examples above, the objects of the verbs are totally separate from, and not part of, the subjects. However the use of the reflexive pronoun shows the *intensity* felt by the persons carrying out these actions.

The same sentences can be expressed without using the reflexive pronouns, but then the statements will sound much less emotional, more objective:

> **Stasera vediamo un bel film.**
> **Voglio mangiare una pizza.**
> **Ho dimenticato le chiavi.**

There are a few Italian verbs that are always (or almost always) used with a reflexive pronoun, because of the 'psychological' and subjective meaning they convey, for example:

vergognarsi 'to be ashamed'	**innamorarsi** 'to fall in love'
pentirsi 'to regret, repent'	**arrabbiarsi** 'to get angry'
accorgersi 'to realize, to be aware'	**divertirsi** 'to have fun'

> **Non vergognar***ti* **di questo errore, non è colpa tua.**
> Don't be ashamed of this mistake. It's not your fault.

> **Giulia** *si* **è pentita di aver accettato quel lavoro.**
> Giulia regretted having accepted that job.

> **Sbrigati! Non** *ti* **accorgi che è tardi?**
> Hurry up! Don't you realize that it's late?

> **Non arrabbiar***ti***!**
> Don't be angry!

> *Vi* **siete divertiti a Roma?**
> Did you have a good time in Rome?

(d) 'Si passivante'

In some cases the reflexive pronoun **si** is used to give a passive meaning to the active form of the verb:

> *Si* **parla italiano.**
> Italian is spoken.
>
> **Nella mia famiglia** *si* **parlano tre lingue.**
> In my family three languages are spoken.
>
> **Dal terrazzo** *si* **vedono i tetti della città.**
> From the terrace the roofs of the city can be seen (one can see the roofs).

In the first example, the pronominal form is identical to the impersonal form ('one' speaks Italian) mentioned in 2.1.8. However, when there is a plural subject, as in the second two examples, the verb is plural, so it becomes clear that the construction is passive ('three languages are spoken, the roofs can be seen').

Impersonal *si*

The pronoun **si** is also used to express the *impersonal* form of verbs, i.e. in cases when no subject of the verb is mentioned, or rather when the subject cannot be identified with a particular person or thing (English would use the indeterminate subject 'one'):

> *Si* **lavora meglio con il fresco.**
> One works better in cool weather.
>
> **Stasera** *si* **va a ballare.**
> Tonight everybody is going to dance.
>
> **A tavola non** *si* **invecchia.**
> One doesn't get old at the dinner table.
> (Popular saying, meant to discourage people from hurrying when eating.)

Notice that the impersonal form is always formed with **si** and the third person singular of the verb.

2.2 Verb tables

All the examples shown in the tables in 2.2.1 use the auxiliary **avere** in the compound tenses. Certain verbs use **essere** instead (see 2.2.4 **essere**, for example). The simplified tables in 2.2.2 show how **essere** is used to form the passive verb forms.

Regular verbs: active conjugation

Here are the complete conjugations of four very common Italian verbs. We call these patterns *regular* because the *stems* of these verbs normally remain the same (or *invariable*) throughout the whole system of moods and tenses. Learning the changes of the *ending* (the *variable* part of the verb) will allow us to know all the possible forms of most Italian verbs. Notice the two patterns of the 3rd conjugation, and remember that the pattern in **-isco** is the more frequent.

1st Conjugation   2nd Conjugation   3rd Conjugation

Infinitive (**Infinito**)

Present (**Presente**)

parl-*are*	**cred-*ere***	**dorm-*ire***	**fin-*ire***

Past (**Passato**)

avere parlato	**avere creduto**	**avere dormito**	**avere finito**

Indicative (**Indicativo**)

Present (**Presente**)

parl-*o*	**cred-*o***	**dorm-*o***	**fin-*isco***	1st pers. sing.
parl-*i*	**cred-*i***	**dorm-*i***	**fin-*isci***	2nd pers. sing.
parl-*a*	**cred-*e***	**dorm-*e***	**fin-*isce***	3rd pers. sing.
parl-*iamo*	**cred-*iamo***	**dorm-*iamo***	**fin-*iamo***	1st pers. plur.
parl-*ate*	**cred-*ete***	**dorm-*ite***	**fin-*ite***	2nd pers. plur.
parl-*ano*	**cred-*ono***	**dorm-*ono***	**fin-*iscono***	3rd pers. plur.

Imperfect (**Imperfetto**)

parl-*avo*	**cred-*evo***	**dorm-*ivo***	**fin-*ivo***
parl-*avi*	**cred-*evi***	**dorm-*ivi***	**fin-*ivi***
parl-*ava*	**cred-*eva***	**dorm-*iva***	**fin-*iva***
parl-*avamo*	**cred-*evamo***	**dorm-*ivamo***	**fin-*ivamo***
parl-*avate*	**cred-*evate***	**dorm-*ivate***	**fin-*ivate***
parl-*avano*	**cred-*evano***	**dorm-*ivano***	**fin-*ivano***

Compound Perfect (**Passato prossimo**)

ho parlato	**ho creduto**	**ho dormito**	**ho finito**
hai parlato	**hai creduto**	**hai dormito**	**hai finito**
ha parlato	**ha creduto**	**ha dormito**	**ha finito**
abbiamo parlato	**abbiamo creduto**	**abbiamo dormito**	**abbiamo finito**
avete parlato	**avete creduto**	**avete dormito**	**avete finito**
hanno parlato	**hanno creduto**	**hanno dormito**	**hanno finito**

Simple Perfect (**Passato remoto**)

parl-*ai*	**cred-*etti*** (**cred-*ei***)	**dorm-*ii***	**fin-*ii***
parl-*asti*	**cred-*esti***	**dorm-*isti***	**fin-*isti***
parl-*ò*	**cred-*ette*** (**cred-*é***)	**dorm-*ì***	**fin-*ì***
parl-*ammo*	**cred-*emmo***	**dorm-*immo***	**fin-*immo***
parl-*aste*	**cred-*este***	**dorm-*iste***	**fin-*iste***
parl-*arono*	**cred-*ettero***	**dorm-*irono***	**fin-*irono***
	(**cred-*erono***)		

parlare	credere	dormire	finire

Pluperfect (**Trapassato prossimo**)

avevo parlato	avevo creduto	avevo dormito	avevo finito
avevi parlato	avevi creduto	avevi dormito	avevi finito
aveva parlato	aveva creduto	aveva dormito	aveva finito
avevamo parlato	avevamo creduto	avevamo dormito	avevamo finito
avevate parlato	avevate creduto	avevate dormito	avevate finito
avevano parlato	avevano creduto	avevano dormito	avevano finito

Past Anterior (**Trapassato remoto**)

ebbi parlato	ebbi creduto	ebbi dormito	ebbi finito
avesti parlato	avesti creduto	avesti dormito	avesti finito
ebbe parlato	ebbe creduto	ebbe dormito	ebbe finito
avemmo parlato	avemmo creduto	avemmo dormito	avemmo finito
aveste parlato	aveste creduto	aveste dormito	aveste finito
ebbero parlato	ebbero creduto	ebbero dormito	ebbero finito

Simple Future (**Futuro semplice**)

parl-*erò*	cred-*erò*	dorm-*irò*	fin-*irò*
parl-*erai*	cred-*erai*	dorm-*irai*	fin-*irai*
parl-*erà*	cred-*erà*	dorm-*irà*	fin-*irà*
parl-*eremo*	cred-*eremo*	dorm-*iremo*	fin-*iremo*
parl-*erete*	cred-*erete*	dorm-*irete*	fin-*irete*
parl-*eranno*	cred-*eranno*	dorm-*iranno*	fin-*iranno*

Future perfect (**Futuro anteriore**)

avrò parlato	avrò creduto	avrò dormito	avrò finito
avrai parlato	avrai creduto	avrai dormito	avrai finito
avrà parlato	avrà creduto	avrà dormito	avrà finito
avremo parlato	avremo creduto	avremo dormito	avremo finito
avrete parlato	avrete creduto	avrete dormito	avrete finito
avranno parlato	avranno creduto	avranno dormito	avranno finito

Subjunctive (**Congiuntivo**)

Present (**Presente**)

parl-*i*	cred-*a*	dorm-*a*	fin-isc-*a*
parl-*i*	cred-*a*	dorm-*a*	fin-isc-*a*
parl-*i*	cred-*a*	dorm-*a*	fin-isc-*a*
parl-*iamo*	cred-*iamo*	dorm-*iamo*	fin-*iamo*
parl-*iate*	cred-*iate*	dorm-*iate*	fin-*iate*
parl-*ino*	cred-*ano*	dorm-*ano*	fin-isc-*ano*

Imperfect (**Imperfetto**)

parl-*assi*	cred-*essi*	dorm-*issi*	fin-*issi*
parl-*assi*	cred-*essi*	dorm-*issi*	fin-*issi*
parl-*asse*	cred-*esse*	dorm-*isse*	fin-*isse*
parl-*assimo*	cred-*essimo*	dorm-*issimo*	fin-*issimo*

parlare	credere	dormire	finire
parl-*aste*	cred-*este*	dorm-*iste*	fin-*iste*
parl-*assero*	cred-*essero*	dorm-*issero*	fin-*issero*

Perfect (**Passato**)

abbia parlato	abbia creduto	abbia dormito	abbia finito
abbia parlato	abbia creduto	abbia dormito	abbia finito
abbia parlato	abbia creduto	abbia dormito	abbia finito
abbiamo parlato	abbiamo creduto	abbiamo dormito	abbiamo finito
abbiate parlato	abbiate creduto	abbiate dormito	abbiate finito
abbiano parlato	abbiano creduto	abbiano dormito	abbiano finito

Pluperfect (**Trapassato**)

avessi parlato	avessi creduto	avessi dormito	avessi finito
avessi parlato	avessi creduto	avessi dormito	avessi finito
avesse parlato	avesse creduto	avesse dormito	avesse finito
avessimo parlato	avessimo creduto	avessimo dormito	avessimo finito
aveste parlato	aveste creduto	aveste dormito	aveste finito
avessero parlato	avessero creduto	avessero dormito	avessero finito

Conditional (**Condizionale**)

Present (**Presente**)

parl-*erei*	cred-*erei*	dorm-*irei*	fin-*irei*
parl-*eresti*	cred-*eresti*	dorm-*iresti*	fin-*iresti*
parl-*erebbe*	cred-*erebbe*	dorm-*irebbe*	fin-*irebbe*
parl-*eremmo*	cred-*eremmo*	dorm-*iremmo*	fin-*iremmo*
parl-*ereste*	cred-*ereste*	dorm-*ireste*	fin-*ireste*
parl-*erebbero*	cred-*erebbero*	dorm-*irebbero*	fin-*irebbero*

Past (**Passato**)

avrei parlato	avrei creduto	avrei dormito	avrei finito
avresti parlato	avresti creduto	avresti dormito	avresti finito
avrebbe parlato	avrebbe creduto	avrebbe dormito	avrebbe finito
avremmo parlato	avremmo creduto	avremmo dormito	avremmo finito
avreste parlato	avreste creduto	avreste dormito	avreste finito
avrebbero parlato	avrebbero creduto	avrebbero dormito	avrebbero finito

Imperative (**Imperativo**)

tu parl-*a*	cred-*i*	dorm-*i*	fin-isc-*i*
lui parl-*i*	cred-*a*	dorm-*a*	fin-isc-*a*
noi parl-*iamo*	cred-*iamo*	dorm-*iamo*	fin-*iamo*
voi parl-*ate*	cred-*ete*	dorm-*ite*	fin-*ite*
loro parl-*ino*	cred-*ano*	dorm-*ano*	fin-isc-*ano*

Participle (**Participio**)

Present (**Presente**)

parl-*ante*	cred-*ente*	dorm-*ente*	(fin-*ente*)

Past (**Passato**)

parl-*ato*	cred-*uto*	dorm-*ito*	fin-*ito*

Gerund (**Gerundio**)

Present (**Presente**)

parl-*ando*	cred-*endo*	dorm-*endo*	fin-*endo*

Past (**Passato**)

avendo parlato	avendo creduto	avendo dormito	avendo finito

2.2.2

Regular verbs: passive conjugation

Here is a simplified table (showing only the third person singular of each tense) of the passive forms of four regular verbs.

Notice how each passive tense is formed by the corresponding tense of the auxiliary **essere** (see below 2.2.4, for the full conjugation of **essere**) and the past participle. In this table the participle is masculine singular, but in actual use it agrees with the gender and number of the subject (see below), as do all compound forms of verbs using **essere**.

Remember that only *transitive* verbs (see above 2.1.6) can have a passive form.

	guardare	credere	sentire
Infinitive			
Present	*essere* guardato/a/i/e	*essere* creduto/a/i/e	*essere* sentito/a/i/e
Past	*essere stato* guardato	*essere stato* creduto	*essere stato* sentito
Indicative			
Present	*è* guardato	*è* creduto	*è* sentito
Imperfect	*era* guardato	*era* creduto	*era* sentito
Compound Perfect	*è stato* guardato	*è stato* creduto	*è stato* sentito
Simple Perfect	*fu* guardato	*fu* creduto	*fu* sentito
Pluperfect	*era stato* guardato	*era stato* creduto	*era stato* sentito
Past Anterior	*fu stato* guardato	*fu stato* creduto	*fu stato* sentito
Simple Future	*sarà* guardato	*sarà* creduto	*sarà* sentito
Future Perfect	*sarà stato* guardato	*sarà stato* creduto	*sarà stato* sentito
Subjunctive			
Present	*sia* guardato	*sia* creduto	*sia* sentito
Imperfect	*fosse* guardato	*fosse* creduto	*fosse* sentito
Past	*sia stato* guardato	*sia stato* creduto	*sia stato* sentito
Pluperfect	*fosse stato* guardato	*fosse stato* creduto	*fosse stato* sentito

Conditional

Present	*sarebbe* guardato	*sarebbe* creduto	*sarebbe* sentito
Past	*sarebbe stato* guardato	*sarebbe stato* creduto	*sarebbe stato* sentito

Imperative

Present	*sia* guardato	*sia* creduto	*sia* sentito

Gerund

Present	*essendo* guardato	*essendo* creduto	*essendo* sentito
Past	*essendo stato* guardato	*essendo stato* creduto	*essendo stato* sentito

2.2.3

Irregular verb conjugation: introduction

Irregular verbs are those that not only change the endings, but also change the stem in some of the tenses.

Italian has a large number of irregular verbs, most of them in the 2nd conjugation, including many verbs frequently used in everyday language.

Sometimes the irregular changes of the stem are unique to one verb (as in the case of **avere** and **essere**). Sometimes several verbs may be grouped under a common pattern of irregularity, and this can help us to memorize the many (but not always unpredictable!) deviations from the norm.

The complete conjugations of five irregular verbs are shown below (2.2.4) in table form. These verbs have been chosen not only because of their frequency of use, but also because in some cases their patterns are followed by several other irregular verbs.

A complete list of irregular verbs in alphabetical order is in Appendix II.

2.2.4

Irregular verbs *avere, essere, dovere, potere, volere*

These five verbs are among the most frequently used in Italian, and also among the most irregular. They share a common characteristic: they are often used in combination with another verb. The verbs **avere** and **essere** are used as *auxiliary* verbs, combining with the *past participles* of other verbs to form all compound tenses, while **dovere** 'must', **potere** 'can', **volere** 'will' are very often used in combination with another verb in the *infinitive* form, to complement its meaning. When used in this way, they are called **verbi servili** verbs 'modal'.

> Ieri *ho dovuto chiudere* io l'ufficio.
> *I* had to close the office yesterday.

> Quando *potremo incontrare* il dott. Salvi?
> When can we meet Dr Salvi?

> *Voglio tornare* a casa presto stasera.
> I want to go home early tonight.

The verb **essere** is highly irregular, with varied stems in almost all tenses. **Avere,**

dovere, **potere**, **volere** also have varying stems in their present indicative tenses, but a common pattern of contraction in their future and present conditional tense with the vowel **-e-** dropping to give **av-rei**, **dov-rei**, **pot-rei**, **vor-rei** (instead of *av-erei, *dov-erei, *pot-erei, *vol-erei); and **av-rò**, **dov-rò**, etc. (instead of *av-erò, *dov-erò, etc.). NB: Use of the asterisk is explained on p. xv.

In the tables below, note how the compound tenses of **essere** take **essere** as their auxiliary, and the participle has to agree in number and gender.

Infinitive (**Infinito**)

Present (**Presente**)

av-*ere*	ess-*ere*	dov-*ere*	pot-*ere*	vol-*ere*

Past (**Passato**)

avere avuto	essere stato	avere dovuto	avere potuto	avere voluto

---

Indicative (**Indicativo**)

Present (**Presente**)

ho	son-o	dev-o (debbo)	poss-o	vogli-o
hai	se-i	dev-i	puo-i	vuo-i
ha	è	dev-e	può	vuol-e
abb-iamo	s-iamo	dobb-iamo	poss-iamo	vogl-iamo
av-ete	si-ete	dov-ete	pot-ete	vol-ete
hanno	s-ono	dev-ono (debbono)	poss-ono	vogli-ono

Imperfect (**Imperfetto**)

av-evo	ero	dov-evo	pot-evo	vol-evo
av-evi	eri	dov-evi	pot-evi	vol-evi
av-eva	era	dov-eva	pot-eva	vol-eva
av-evamo	eravamo	dov-evamo	pot-evamo	vol-evamo
av-evate	eravate	dov-evate	pot-evate	vol-evate
av-evano	erano	dov-evano	pot-evano	vol-evano

Compound Perfect (**Passato prossimo**)

ho avuto	sono stato	ho dovuto	ho potuto	ho voluto
hai avuto	sei stato	hai dovuto	hai potuto	hai voluto
ha avuto	è stato	ha dovuto	ha potuto	ha voluto
abbiamo avuto	siamo stati	abbiamo dovuto	abbiamo potuto	abbiamo voluto
avete avuto	siete stati	avete dovuto	avete potuto	avete voluto
hanno avuto	sono stati	hanno dovuto	hanno potuto	hanno voluto

Simple Perfect (**Passato remoto**)

ebbi	fui	dov-ei (dovetti)	pot-ei	volli
av-esti	fo-sti	dov-esti	pot-esti	vol-esti
ebbe	fu	dov-é (dovette)	pot-é	voll-e
av-emmo	fummo	dov-emmo	pot-emmo	vol-emmo
av-este	fo-ste	dov-este	pot-este	vol-este
ebbero	furono	dov-erono (dovettero)	pot-erono (potettero)	vollero

avere	essere	dovere	potere	volere

Pluperfect (**Trapassato prossimo**)

avere	essere	dovere	potere	volere
avevo avuto	ero stato	avevo dovuto	avevo potuto	avevo voluto
avevi avuto	eri stato	avevi dovuto	avevi potuto	avevi voluto
aveva avuto	era stato	aveva dovuto	aveva potuto	aveva voluto
avevamo avuto	eravamo stati	avevamo dovuto	avevamo potuto	avevamo voluto
avevate avuto	eravate stati	avevate dovuto	avevate potuto	avevate voluto
avevano avuto	erano stati	avevano dovuto	avevano potuto	avevano voluto

Past Anterior (**Trapassato remoto**)

avere	essere	dovere	potere	volere
ebbi avuto	fui stato	ebbi dovuto	ebbi potuto	ebbi voluto
avesti avuto	fosti stato	avesti dovuto	avesti potuto	avesti voluto
ebbe avuto	fu stato	ebbe dovuto	ebbe potuto	ebbe voluto
avemmo avuto	fummo stati	avemmo dovuto	avemmo potuto	avemmo voluto
aveste avuto	foste stati	aveste dovuto	aveste potuto	aveste voluto
ebbero avuto	furono stati	ebbero dovuto	ebbero potuto	ebbero voluto

Simple Future (**Futuro semplice**)

avere	essere	dovere	potere	volere
av-rò	sa-rò	dov-rò	pot-rò	vor-rò
av-rai	sa-rai	dov-rai	pot-rai	vor-rai
av-rà	sa-rà	dov-rà	pot-rà	vor-rà
av-remo	sa-remo	dov-remo	pot-remo	vor-remo
av-rete	sa-rete	dov-rete	pot-rete	vor-rete
av-ranno	sa-ranno	dov-ranno	pot-ranno	vor-ranno

Future Perfect (**Futuro anteriore**)

avere	essere	dovere	potere	volere
avrò avuto	sarò stato	avrò dovuto	avrò potuto	avrò voluto
avrai avuto	sarai stato	avrai dovuto	avrai potuto	avrai voluto
avrà avuto	sarà stato	avrà dovuto	avrà potuto	avrà voluto
avremo avuto	saremo stati	avremo dovuto	avremo potuto	avremo voluto
avrete avuto	sarete stati	avrete dovuto	avrete potuto	avrete voluto
avranno avuto	saranno stati	avranno dovuto	avranno potuto	avranno voluto

Subjunctive (**Congiuntivo**)

Present (**Presente**)

avere	essere	dovere	potere	volere
abbia	sia	debba	possa	voglia
abbia	sia	debba	possa	voglia
abbia	sia	debba	possa	voglia
abbiamo	siamo	dobbiamo	possiamo	vogliamo
abbiate	siate	dobbiate	possiate	vogliate
abbiano	siano	debbano	possano	vogliano

Imperfect (**Imperfetto**)

avere	essere	dovere	potere	volere
av-essi	fo-ssi	dov-essi	pot-essi	vol-essi
av-essi	fo-ssi	dov-essi	pot-essi	vol-essi
av-esse	fo-sse	dov-esse	pot-esse	vol-esse
av-essimo	fo-ssimo	dov-essimo	pot-essimo	vol-essimo
av-este	fo-ste	dov-este	pot-este	vol-este
av-essero	fo-ssero	dov-essero	pot-essero	vol-essero

avere	essere	dovere	potere	volere

Perfect (**Passato**)

abbia avuto	sia stato	abbia dovuto	abbia potuto	abbia voluto
abbia avuto	sia stato	abbia dovuto	abbia potuto	abbia voluto
abbia avuto	sia stato	abbia dovuto	abbia potuto	abbia voluto
abbiamo avuto	siamo stati	abbiamo dovuto	abbiamo potuto	abbiamo voluto
abbiate avuto	siate stati	abbiate dovuto	abbiate potuto	abbiate voluto
abbiano avuto	siano stati	abbiano dovuto	abbiano potuto	abbiano voluto

Pluperfect (**Trapassato**)

avessi avuto	fossi stato	avessi dovuto	avessi potuto	avessi voluto
avessi avuto	fossi stato	avessi dovuto	avessi potuto	avessi voluto
avesse avuto	fosse stato	avesse dovuto	avesse potuto	avesse voluto
avessimo avuto	fossimo stati	avessimo dovuto	avessimo potuto	avessimo voluto
aveste avuto	foste stati	aveste dovuto	aveste potuto	aveste voluto
avessero avuto	fossero stati	avessero dovuto	avessero potuto	avessero voluto

Conditional (**Condizionale**)

Present (**Presente**)

av-rei	sa-rei	dov-rei	pot-rei	vor-rei
av-resti	sa-resti	dov-resti	pot-resti	vor-resti
av-rebbe	sa-rebbe	dov-rebbe	pot-rebbe	vor-rebbe
av-remmo	sa-remmo	dov-remmo	pot-remmo	vor-remmo
av-reste	sa-reste	dov-reste	pot-reste	vor-reste
av-rebbero	sa-rebbero	dov-rebbero	pot-rebbero	vor-rebbero

Past (**Passato**)

avrei avuto	sarei stato	avrei dovuto	avrei potuto	avrei voluto
avresti avuto	saresti stato	avresti dovuto	avresto potuto	avresti voluto
avrebbe avuto	sarebbe stato	avrebbe dovuto	avrebbe potuto	avrebbe voluto
avremmo avuto	saremmo stati	avremmo dovuto	avremmo potuto	avremmo voluto
avreste avuto	sareste stati	avreste dovuto	avreste potuto	avreste voluto
avrebbero avuto	sarebbero stati	avrebbero dovuto	avrebbero potuto	avrebbero voluto

Imperative (**Imperativo**)

–	–	–	–	–
abbi	sii	–	–	vogli
abbia	sia	–	–	voglia
abbiamo	siamo	–	–	vogliamo
abbiate	siate	–	–	vogliate
abbiano	siano	–	–	vogliano

Participle (**Participio**)

Present (**Presente**)

avente	(ente)	–	(potente)	volente

avere	essere	dovere	potere	volere
Past (**Passato**)				
avuto	stato	dovuto	potuto	voluto
Gerund (**Gerundio**)				
Present (**Presente**)				
avendo	essendo	dovendo	potendo	volendo
Past (**Passato**)				
avendo avuto	essendo stato	avendo dovuto	avendo potuto	avendo voluto

2.3 *Moods and tenses of verbs*

In this section, we look at each *mood* and *tense* of verbs individually, with a brief illustration of their use.

2.3.1 Infinitive mood (*Infinito*)

The infinitive is the basic form of verbs, and the one used as dictionary entry (in other words, the name of the verb). It is the infinitive form (-**are**, -**ere**, -**ire** or -**rre**) that tells us which conjugation a verb belongs to.

The infinitive has a present and a past tense. The past is formed by the past participle and the infinitive **avere** or **essere**. When formed with **essere**, the past infinitive changes form to agree with the verb subject (see examples below).

Present		Past	
and*are*	to go	essere *andato/a/i/e*	to be gone
viv*ere*	to live	essere *vissuto/a/i/e*	to have lived
sent*ire*	to hear	avere *sentito*	to have heard

Irregular infinitives
There are two groups of 2nd conjugation verbs with an irregular infinitive (i.e. not ending in the usual -**ere** form):

(a) Verbs with infinitive in -**urre**
Several verbs have an infinitive in -**urre**, which is a contracted form of the original infinitive *-**ucere** (***producere**, etc.). In fact several of the tenses are based on the original stem in *-**duc**- (see 2.3.3 below for the present indicative forms).

> **produrre** 'to produce' **introdurre** 'to introduce, insert'
> **condurre** 'to conduct, lead' **tradurre** 'to translate'

and a few more. . .

(b) Verbs with infinitive in **-orre**

Several verbs have an infinitive in **-orre**. In their present indicative, these verbs follow the **-go** pattern shown below (2.3.3). Their infinitive is a contracted form of the original ***ponere**:

porre 'to place, put'   **proporre** 'to propose'   **supporre** 'to suppose'

Some uses of the infinitive

Verbs used in the infinitive generally *depend* on another verb:

> **Dobbiamo *partire* alle 7.**
> We must leave at 7 o'clock.

> **Sai *usare* il computer?**
> Can you use the computer?

> **Penso di *avere capito*.**
> I think I have understood.

> **Non riesco a *sentire* la tua voce.**
> I can't hear your voice.

In most cases the infinitive is linked to preceding verbs by a preposition such as **di** or **a** (see the last two examples above and Chapter 4 Prepositions). However with the verbs **potere, dovere, volere, sapere, preferire, desiderare, amare, osare**, no preposition is needed.

In Italian the subject of the infinitive must be the same as that of the verb on which it depends. Otherwise two separate finite verbs must be used, usually linked by **che**. So English sentences such as 'I want you to come soon' cannot be translated directly as ***voglio tu venire presto**, but have to be translated as **voglio che tu venga presto**, in order to make clear that the two different verbs have different subjects.

An exception to this is when the main verb of the clause is **fare** or **lasciare**:

> ***Fammi passare.***
> Let me pass.

> ***Lasciali parlare.***
> Let them speak.

> ***Ho fatto entrare* i signori.**
> I allowed the gentlemen to come in.

Infinitive as imperative: The infinitive can be used by itself, without depending on another verb, when it is used to tell somebody *not to do* something, i.e. as a *negative* imperative, in the second person singular (see 21.2):

> **Zitto,** *non parlare.*
> Be quiet, don't speak.

> *Non sporgersi* **dal finestrino.**
> Don't lean out of the window.

Here something that was originally the imperative of a verb used reflexively **non ti scordare . . .** 'do not forget . . .!' has now become the name of a flower:

> *Nontiscordardimé* 'Forget-me-not'

Infinitive as a noun: Infinitive verbs are often used instead of nouns, sometimes preceded by the definite article, in the masculine singular form:

> *Lavorare* **stanca.**
> Work is tiring.

> *Mangiare* **è necessario per vivere.**
> Eating is necessary for life.

> *Il sapere* **degli antichi si trasmette di generazione in generazione.**
> The wisdom of the ancients is handed down from generation to generation.

2.3.2   Indicative mood: introduction

The indicative mood is used to express straightforward statements of facts, objective descriptions, real and definite situations, etc.

We shall look here at the eight tenses of the indicative mood, both regular and irregular forms, with a brief reference to their use, covered in detail in Part B.

2.3.3   Present indicative (*Indicativo presente*)

The forms of the present indicative of the three regular conjugations are shown in the verb tables above (2.2).

In addition to **avere, essere, dovere, potere, volere** shown in the verb tables, some common verbs with an irregular present indicative are illustrated below.

Irregular present indicatives: 1st conjugation
Some verbs in the *1st conjugation* present potential difficulties of spelling. These are the regular verbs ending in **-care, -gare**, such as **cercare, pagare**:

In order to maintain the hard **-g-** sound, the letter **-h-** is added before endings which include the vowel **-i-** (2nd person singular **-i** and 1st person plural **-iamo**):

cer*care* 'to look for'	pa*gare* 'to pay'
cerco	pago
cer*chi*	pa*ghi*
cerca	paga
cer*chiamo*	pa*ghiamo*
cercate	pagate
cercano	pagano

In verbs ending in **-ciare** and **-giare**, where the **-i-** is present to make the **-c-** or **-g-** soft before **o**, **a**, and *is not pronounced as a separate vowel*, there is no doubling of the **-i-** in the 2nd person singular and 1st person plural forms:

comin*ciare* 'to begin'	man*giare* 'to eat'
comincio	mangio
cominc*i*	mang*i*
comincia	mangia
cominc*iamo*	man*giamo*
cominciate	mangiate
cominciano	mangiano

The only verbs of the *1st conjugation* with a truly irregular present indicative are:

andare 'to go'	**dare** 'to give'	**fare** 'to do'	**stare** 'to stay'
vado	do	faccio	sto
vai	dai	fai	stai
va	dà	fa	sta
andiamo	diamo	facciamo	stiamo
andate	date	fate	state
vanno	danno	fanno	stanno

Stare is used very often in combination with the gerund in the progressive tenses, for example **sto scrivendo** 'I am writing'; see also Chapter 12.

Irregular present indicatives: 2nd conjugation
Verbs ending in **-cere**, **-gere**, **-scere** have hard **-c-**, **-g-**, **-sc-** sounds before endings with the vowel **-o** but soft **-c-**, **-g-**, **-sc-** sound before the vowels **-e**, **-i**:

vincere 'to win'	**piangere** 'to cry'	**conoscere** 'to know'
vin*co*	pian*go*	cono*sco*
vin*ci*	pian*gi*	cono*sci*
vin*ce*	pian*ge*	cono*sce*
vin*ciamo*	pian*giamo*	cono*sciamo*
vin*cete*	pian*gete*	cono*scete*
vin*cono*	pian*gono*	cono*scono*

Many verbs in the *2nd conjugation* are irregular in the present indicative tense as well as in other tenses (see also verb tables above, 2.2). Although some verbs appear irregular, their forms are in fact regular but based on an older form of the infinitive (see 2.3.1), for example:

tradurre 'to translate'	**bere** to drink'
traduc-o	bev-o
traduc-i	bev-i
traduc-e	bev-e
traduc-iamo	bev-iamo
traduc-ete	bev-ete
traduc-ono	bev-ono

Here are a few more irregular 2nd conjugation verbs:

The verb **sapere** is irregular both in the ending and in its stem changes:

sapere 'to know'

---

so
sai
sa
sappiamo
sapete
sanno

The verb **scegliere** has a pattern in which the stem alternates between **-lg-** and **-gl-**:

scegliere 'to choose'

---

scelgo
scegli
sceglie
scegliamo
scegliete
scelgono

Verbs following a similar pattern to **scegliere** are: **accogliere** 'to welcome', **accolgo/accogliamo**; **cogliere** 'to pick', **colgo/cogliamo**; **raccogliere** 'to collect', **raccolgo/raccogliamo**; **sciogliere** 'to melt', **sciolgo/sciogliamo**; and **togliere** 'to take away', **tolgo/togliamo**.

The following verbs have in common a pattern in which some persons are formed with **-g-** and some without (see Appendix II for a complete list). The verb **tenere** changes not only its endings but the stem **ten/tien**:

rimanere 'to remain'	**tenere** 'to keep'	**porre** 'to put'
rimango	tengo	pongo
rimani	tieni	poni
rimane	tiene	pone
rimaniamo	teniamo	poniamo
rimanete	tenete	ponete
rimangono	tengono	pongono

Verbs following the pattern of **tenere** are: **mantenere** 'to maintain', **ottenere** 'to obtain', **ritenere** 'to retain', **sostenere** 'to sustain' and other similar compounds.

Verbs following the pattern of **porre** are: **imporre** 'to impose', **proporre** 'to propose', **supporre** 'to suppose', etc.

Irregular present indicatives: 3rd conjugation
The most important irregular verbs of the *3rd conjugation* are the following:

dire 'to say'	salire 'to go up'	uscire 'to go out'	venire 'to come'
dico	salgo	esco	vengo
dici	sali	esci	vieni
dice	sale	esce	viene
diciamo	saliamo	usciamo	veniamo
dite	salite	uscite	venite
dicono	salgono	escono	vengono

The verb **uscire** has the stem change **esc-/usc-**. Another verb with the same pattern is **riuscire** 'to succeed', **riesco/riusciamo**.

The verb **venire** has the stem change **ven-/vien-**. Other verbs following its pattern are: **avvenire** 'to happen', **divenire** 'to become', **rinvenire** 'to find', **svenire** 'to faint', etc.

Uses of the present indicative
Verbs in the present indicative express actions, facts and situations that happen or are going on *at the moment when we speak or write*. This applies to:

(a) Actions and facts happening at the precise *moment of speech*:

> **Mara, il telefono *suona*. Rispondi, per favore.**
> Mara, the phone is ringing. Please answer it!

(b) Something that happens *regularly*, with continuity or which is *always* true (in the present as well as in the past and future):

> **Nel mio ufficio il telefono *suona* continuamente di mattina.**
> In my office the phone rings continuously in the mornings.

> **La domenica le campane della chiesa *suonano* alle 8 meno 10.**
> On Sundays the church bells ring at ten to eight.

> **Gli italiani *fumano* più degli inglesi.**
> Italians smoke more than English people.

> **Le balene *sono* mammiferi.**
> Whales are mammals.

There are two situations in which the present indicative is used to refer to facts that are *not* in the present time:

(c) Referring to the *future*, as happens frequently in conversational situations (see Chapter 14).

> **Domani *arrivano* gli ospiti spagnoli.**
> Tomorrow the Spanish guests are coming.

> **L'anno prossimo *compriamo* una macchina nuova.**
> Next year we'll buy a new car.

(d) As an *historical present* in order to render the description of past events more vivid (see Chapter 13 on the past). This is done when the events are described in a narrative way and is very common in history books and news reports:

> **Nel 1870 Roma *diventa* capitale d'Italia.**
> Rome became the capital of Italy in 1870.

> **Al quinto rigore Baggio *sbaglia* e l'Italia *perde* il Campionato del Mondo.**
> At the fifth penalty Baggio missed the penalty kick and Italy lost the World Cup.

2.3.4 **Future indicative (*Indicativo futuro*)**

Forms
The forms of the future indicative of the three regular conjugations are shown in the verb tables. Several verbs have an irregular future indicative. In most cases, the irregularity consists in the *contraction* of the stem (***anderò** to **andrò**, etc.) and in some cases the subsequent assimilation of the consonant groups **nr**, **lr**, etc. to **rr** as in the irregular infinitives (**trarre**, **porre**, **bere**) already seen above:

andare	*andrò*	avere	*avrò*
dovere	*dovrò*	potere	*potrò*
rimanere	*rimarrò*	sapere	*saprò*
venire	*verrò*	volere	*vorrò*

and also in:

vedere	*vedrò*	cadere	*cadrò*
bere	*berrò*		

See Appendix II for further examples and translations.

A similar *contracted* pattern can be seen in the present tense of the conditional of the same verbs **andare** (*andrei*), **bere** (*berrei*), **potere** (*potrei*).

The future of **essere** is very irregular: *sarò, sarai, sarà,* etc.

Uses of the future
The future indicative tense is naturally mainly used to refer to facts that *will* happen in a time subsequent to that when we speak. However Italians use this tense of verbs only very sparingly, often preferring to use the present tense instead (see Chapter 14).

The future tense is also used in Italian to express probability, as in English 'it will probably be', with no relation to future time (see 26.4.2):

> **Che ore sono? *Saranno* le tre meno dieci.**
> What time is it? It must be (about) ten to three.

> **Suona il telefono. Chi *sarà*? Sarà Davide.**
> The phone is ringing. Who could it possibly be? It will be Davide.

2.3.5

Future perfect (*futuro anteriore*)

Forms
The future perfect is a *compound* tense formed of the future tense of the auxiliary **avere** or **essere** together with the past participle of the verb. The forms of the future perfect are shown in the verb tables (2.2).

Uses of the future perfect
The future perfect is used to indicate facts or actions that will take place in the future (in relation to the moment when we are speaking or writing), but *before* facts or actions that will happen even later; it is a sort of 'past in the future':

> **Non** *so* se *avrò finito* **il lavoro quando** *arriverà* **il cliente.**
> I don't know whether I will have finished the job by the time the customer comes.

> *Stiamo aspettando* **la fattura. Quando** *avremo ricevuto* **la fattura, Le** *invieremo* **i soldi.**
> We are waiting for the invoice. When we've received the invoice, we'll send you the money.

Each of the three verbs in these sentences could be illustrated by a time sequence:

Now	Future Perfect	Future
→	→	→
non so	**avrò finito**	**arriverà**
stiamo aspettando	**avremo ricevuto**	**invieremo**

The examples show the position in time of the actions expressed by the future perfect (**avrò finito**/**avremo ricevuto**): they are in the *future* with reference to the moment of speaking, but are in the *past* in relation to a second reference point placed in the future (**arriverà, invieremo**). More examples of the use of the future perfect can be found in 14.7.

2.3.6

Imperfect indicative (*Indicativo imperfetto*)

Forms
The forms of the imperfect of the three regular conjugations are shown in the verb tables. The imperfect indicative is formed by adding the endings **-avo**, **-evo**, **-ivo** (for the 1st, 2nd and 3rd conjugations respectively) to the stem of the verb. It is the most regular of all the tenses of Italian verbs.

The imperfect of the 2nd conjugation verbs with a contracted infinitive in **-urre** is regular, but follows the pattern of the stem in **duc-**, giving **produrre**: **produc-evo, produc-evi . . .**, tradurre: **traduc-evo, traduc-evi . . .**, etc.

Similarly, the verbs with a contracted infinitive in **-orre** have a regular imperfect based on the stem in **pon-**; **disporre, dispon-evo; imporre, impon-evo . . .**

The contracted infinitive **bere** has a regular imperfect **bev-evo**.

The only true irregular imperfect is that of **essere: ero, eri . . .** (see verb tables).

Uses of the imperfect

The imperfect indicative is mainly used to refer to the past as will be shown in Chapter 13. The use of this tense should always be considered in the context of *aspect*. The choice of aspect (*imperfect* or *perfect*) is very important when referring to the past in Italian, particularly in situations where the two forms are used in the same sentence.

Here is a summary of the most common cases when the imperfect indicative is used:

(a) To describe a past action/fact in its duration (as going on and not completed):

> *Guardavo* **la televisione quando c'è stato il terremoto.**
> I was watching TV when the earthquake struck.

(b) To describe situations, compose a 'picture' with facts or events happening at the same time in the past:

> *Era* **mezzanotte,** *pioveva* **e la macchina** *correva* **silenziosa.**
> It was midnight, it was raining and the car ran silently.

(c) For past actions repeated regularly as a habit:

> *Prendevamo* **sempre il caffè alle 11.**
> We used to have a coffee at 11 o'clock.

(d) To relate the background, cause or situation in which an event happened:

> **Non ho mangiato perché non** *avevo* **fame.**
> I didn't eat because I wasn't hungry.

> *Erano* **già le 5 quando hai telefonato.**
> It was already 5 o'clock when you phoned.

(e) To refer to the 'future in the past', instead of using the compound conditional (see Chapter 14 and 30.5.2):

> **La settimana scorsa mi hanno detto che tu** *venivi* **(saresti venuto) ieri.**
> Last week I was told that you'd come yesterday.

In a few cases the imperfect indicative is *not* used to refer to past time, but as a substitute for a different verb 'mood' (such as conditional or subjunctive):

(f) To express a polite request or statement (instead of using the present conditional – see Chapter 38) or to express embarrassment:

> *Volevo* **(or vorrei) delle rose.**
> I'd like some roses.

> **Buongiorno,** *cercavo* **un libro di Umberto Eco.**
> Good morning, I'm looking for a book by Umberto Eco.

> **Mi scusi, non** *volevo* **disturbare.**
> Excuse me, I don't want to disturb you.

(g) In hypothetical clauses ('if' clauses) where the 'if' condition is unlikely to happen, or can no longer happen, as a replacement for the compound conditional and subjunctive (see Chapter 38). (This is more common in *spoken* than in written Italian.)

> **Se** *andavi* **più piano non** *facevi* **l'incidente.**
> If you had gone more slowly, you wouldn't have had the accident.

2.3.7

Compound perfect (*passato prossimo*)

Forms
The compound perfect is formed by the present indicative of the auxiliary **avere** or **essere** and the past participle (see verb tables in 2.2).

Of the two forms of the perfect (compound and simple) the compound is by far the more frequently used, especially in spoken language. The uses of the compound perfect and other past tenses are illustrated in Part B.

Uses of the compound perfect
The compound perfect refers to facts that are seen as completed, but have some relation to the present, generally in one of the following two contexts:

(a) The past events are very near to the present time:

> *Ho* **appena** *preso* **un caffè.**
> I've just had a coffee.

> *Avete capito* **quello che** *ho detto***?**
> Did you understand what I said?

(b) The facts or events, even if they are in the distant past, still have some relationship with the present time or with the person who is speaking:

> *Siamo venuti* **in Inghilterra vent'anni fa.**
> We came to England 20 years ago (and we are still here).

> **La Basilica di S.Pietro** *è stata costruita* **nel '500.**
> St Peter's Basilica was built in the 16th century (and you can still see it now).

Because of these characteristics the compound perfect is very frequently used in conversational Italian, allowing the speaker to relate the facts of the past to the present.

Simple perfect (*passato remoto*)

Forms

The forms of the simple perfect (**passato remoto**) of the three regular conjugations are shown in the verb tables (2.2).

Note in particular that the simple perfect of certain 2nd conjugation verbs has alternative forms for the first person singular and third person singular and plural:

> **credei/credetti** 'I believed'
> **credé/credette** 'he/she believed'
> **crederono/credettero** 'they believed'

The simple perfect is often irregular. The most common irregularity is the short -**si** ending alternating with the longer form based on the stem of the infinitive, e.g. **chiesi/chiedesti, posi/ponesti**:

chiedere 'to ask'	**dire** 'to say'	**prendere** 'to take'	**vivere** 'to live'
chie-*si*	dis-*si*	pre-*si*	vis-*si*
chied-*esti*	dic-*esti*	prend-*esti*	viv-*esti*
chie-*se*	dis-*se*	pre-*se*	vis-*se*
chied-*emmo*	dic-*emmo*	prend-*emmo*	viv-*emmo*
chied-*este*	dic-*este*	prend-*este*	viv-*este*
chie-*sero*	dis-*sero*	pre-*sero*	vis-*sero*

Most verbs with this irregular pattern are 2nd conjugation verbs, and in some cases (e.g. **mettere, muovere, sapere, vedere**) the stem has a vowel change as well:

mettere	misi/mettesti
muovere	mossi/muovesti
sapere	seppi/sapesti
vedere	vidi/vedesti

A complete list of all these irregular verbs is in Appendix II.

There are a few verbs in the 1st and 3rd conjugations which show a similar pattern:

fare 'to do, make'	**venire** 'to come'	**dare** 'to give'
feci	venni	diedi
facesti	venisti	desti
fece	venne	diede
facemmo	venimmo	demmo
faceste	veniste	deste
fecero	vennero	diedero

Note the extremely irregular forms of:

avere	ebbi/avesti
essere	fui/fosti
piacere	piacqui/piacesti

Use of simple perfect

We use the simple perfect (**passato remoto**) whenever we want to express the distance of past events, not just in terms of time, but mainly in terms of their 'separateness' (remoteness) from the present situation (see Chapter 13):

> **Vissi male a Milano. Perciò sono tornato a Napoli.**
> I had a bad time living in Milan. That's why I came back to Naples (and I am still here).

> **I dinosauri *scomparvero* 65 milioni d'anni fa.**
> Dinosaurs disappeared 65 million years ago.

Although it tends to be used very seldom in conversational Italian, except perhaps in parts of the south, the simple perfect is very common in written language, especially narrative and historical language, because of the precise way in which it defines the past. Typically it is the tense of fairy tales, when events are placed in a far and abstract past, in a different dimension separate from the reality of the present:

> *Come* andò *che maestro Ciliegia, falegname,* trovò *un pezzo di legna che piangeva e rideva come un bambino.*

> **Appena maestro Ciliegia ebbe visto quel pezzo di legno, *si rallegrò* tutto e, dandosi una fregatina di mani per la contentezza, *borbottò* a mezza voce:**
> **– Questo legno è capitato a tempo: voglio servirmene per fare una gamba di tavolino.**
> **Detto fatto, *prese* subito l'ascia arrotata per cominciare a levargli la scorza e a digrossarlo; ma quando *fu* lì per lasciare andare la prima asciata, *rimase* col braccio sospeso in aria, perché *sentì* una vocina sottile che *disse* raccomandandosi:**
> **– Non mi picchiar tanto forte!**
> (*Pinocchio*, by Collodi, I Libri di Gulliver, 1983)

2.3.9

Pluperfect (*trapassato prossimo*)

The pluperfect can be thought of as the 'past of the past'. It is formed by the past participle and the imperfect of **avere** or **essere**. The forms of the pluperfect of the three regular conjugations are shown in the verb tables.

It is used to refer to an event previous to an event placed in the past (see Chapters 13, 30 and 36).

> **Ricordo che tu *eri arrivato* da poco quando Maria ha telefonato.**
> I remember that you had just arrived when Maria called.

> **Penso che alle 7 Franco *aveva* già *chiuso* il negozio.**
> I think Franco had already closed the shop at 7 o'clock.

If we place the two examples on a 'time line' it is easier to see where the pluperfect stands in the sequence of events:

Pluperfect	Past	Present
→	→	→
eri arrivato	**quando Maria ha telefonato**	**ricordo**
aveva chiuso	**alle 7**	**penso**

2.3.10

Past anterior (*trapassato remoto*)

The **trapassato remoto** is formed by the simple perfect of the auxiliary **avere** or **essere** and the past participle. The forms of the **trapassato remoto** of the three regular conjugations are shown in the verb tables.

The **trapassato remoto** is the form of pluperfect used when the main event or action is expressed by a verb in the simple perfect. Its use is rare and generally limited to the literary and more formal registers of the written language, and it is always introduced by a conjunction such as **dopo**, **appena**:

> **Dopo che *ebbe salutato*, uscì in fretta.**
> After he had said goodbye, he went out in a hurry.

> **Appena *fu uscita*, tutti si misero a ridere.**
> As soon as she had gone out, everybody started laughing.

2.3.11

Conditional mood: introduction

The conditional mood is used to express a fact, action or event which can/will only take place subject to some *condition*.

There are two tenses of the conditional mood: the *present* and the *past*.

2.3.12

Present conditional (*Condizionale presente*)

Forms

For the regular verbs, the present conditional is formed by adding the specific endings -**rei**, -**resti**, etc. to the stem of the verb: the forms of the conditional of the three regular conjugations are shown in the verb tables.

The verbs with an irregular present conditional show the same pattern already seen for the future indicative (see 2.3.4 above), with the contracted forms:

avere	*avrei*	dovere	*dovrei*
potere	*potrei*	volere	*vorrei*
andare	*andrei*	venire	*verrei*
bere	*berrei*	sapere	*saprei*
vedere	*vedrei*		

The only truly irregular conditional is that of **essere**: *sarei, saresti*, etc. (see 2.2.4).

Uses of the present conditional

(a) The condition may be explicitly mentioned, usually by using a clause beginning with **se** 'if'. In Italian this is called **periodo ipotetico**. This type of sentence is made up of two parts: the condition and the consequence. The *condition* is introduced by **se** 'if such and such were to happen' and expressed by a verb in the indicative or, more often, the subjunctive mood. The *consequence*, if the condition were to be met, is expressed by a verb in the indicative or, more often, *conditional* mood 'this would be the result'.

> **Se fossi ricco, non** *lavorerei.*
> If I were rich, I wouldn't work.

> **Se Lei mi stimasse davvero, mi** *darebbe* **più responsabilità.**
> If you really valued me, you would give me more responsibility.

You will find more details on the **periodo ipotetico** in Chapter 38.

(b) The conditional is often used *without* a **se** clause, or any explicit mention of a condition. This is true both in Italian and English ('could', 'would', 'should' forms).

An example of this is when it is used to express politeness, for example in making a request:

> *Vorrei* **un caffè.**
> I would like a coffee.

> *Potrebbe* **aprire la finestra?**
> Could you open the window?

The politeness of these requests lies in their being subject to some implicit condition: 'I'd like a coffee (if it is available)', 'Could you open the window (if it isn't too much trouble)'.

(c) Again with the function of 'softening' a statement, the conditional is used in many other contexts, for example to show uncertainty, or to express an opinion less forcefully:

> **Secondo me** *dovresti* **riposarti.**
> I think you should rest.

> **Io** *sarei* **per la soluzione più facile.**
> I would be for the easier option.

2.3.13

Past conditional (*Condizionale passato*)

Forms
The past conditional is formed by the present conditional of **avere** or **essere** and the past participle of the verb (see verb tables above, 2.2). The past conditional of the three regular conjugations is:

parlare	*avrei parlato*
credere	*avrei creduto*
partire	*sarei partito*

Uses of the past conditional
The past conditional is used in a similar way to the present conditional shown above, but mainly referring to past time:

(a) Expressing a condition:

> **Ieri non *sarei arrivato* in ritardo se avessi preso il treno.**
> I wouldn't have been late yesterday if I had taken the train.

(b) Expressing politeness:

> **Avrei preferito un caffè.**
> I would have preferred a coffee.

(c) Softening a statement:

> **Penso che la sig.ra Prati *avrebbe dovuto* pagare in contanti.**
> I think Mrs Prati should have paid in cash.

Note: This tense is also used to express an action which took place or was to take place after a point referred to in the past (the so-called 'future in the past', see Chapters 30 and 36):

> **La mia segretaria mi ha detto che *avrebbe prenotato* l'albergo subito.**
> My secretary told me that she would reserve the hotel immediately.

> **Dieci anni fa non immaginavo che tu *avresti fatto* una carriera così brillante.**
> Ten years ago I didn't imagine that you would have such a brilliant career.

2.3.14 **Subjunctive mood: introduction**

The subjunctive mood is mainly used to express something which is subjective rather than objective, uncertain rather than definite, a concept rather than a reality. Its most common use is in expressions of doubt, hope, supposition:

> **Non sono certo che mi *abbiano capito*.**
> I'm not certain they understood me.

> **Speriamo che lui *venga* in tempo.**
> Let's hope he'll arrive in time.

> **Penso che *siano* le 3 e 20.**
> I think it must be twenty past three.

Verbs in the subjunctive mood always *depend* directly or indirectly on another verb, linked by **che**, as in the examples above, or by a conjunction, thereby forming a complex sentence of at least two verbs. Only in a few cases is the subjunctive used by itself, without being connected to another verb.

The 'indefinite' or 'subjective' nature of the verb phrase may be found in the *main* verb on which the subjunctive depends, as in the examples above; in the *conjunction* that links the two verbs (**nonostante** 'although', **affinché** 'in order to', etc.); or in the *pronoun* or *adjective* (**qualsiasi** 'whatever', etc.):

> **Ti scrivo affinché tu *sappia* la verità.**
> I write to let you know the truth.

> **Nonostante le *abbia scritto* un mese fa, Paola non mi ha ancora risposto.**
> Although I wrote to her a month ago, Paola hasn't yet replied (to me).

> **Qualsiasi canzone lei *canti* è sempre un piacere ascoltarla.**
> Whatever song she sings, it is always a pleasure to listen to her.

But often it is the subjunctive itself that provides a 'subjective' emphasis to what we say. The choice of indicative or subjunctive to convey the same facts, can shift the meaning of a sentence from the objective to the subjective, from the reality to the idea. Let's see two examples:

(a)   **Ho bisogno dell'assistente che *parla* italiano.**
        I need the assistant who speaks Italian.
        (just that particular one who is known to speak Italian)

        Ho bisogno di un assistente che *parli* italiano.
        I need an assistant who can speak Italian.
        (someone who might be able to speak Italian)

The first of these two statements refers to a known, and actually existing, person (as shown also by the use of the definite article '*l'*assistente') and the statement sounds like a definite request that I expect to be met. In the second, the person I need may or may not be available, and therefore my need is presented as a 'subjective' desire, an ideal, that cannot necessarily be met.

(b)   **Sembra che l'Olivetti *sta* per lanciare un nuovo computer.**
        It seems that Olivetti is about to launch a new computer.

        Sembra che l'Olivetti *stia* per lanciare un nuovo computer.
        It seems that Olivetti might be about to launch a new computer.

In the first sentence, the news is presented as almost certain, while the second sentence, by using the subjunctive, implies a higher degree of doubt or uncertainty about the reliability of the news. These and other uses of the subjunctive in different contexts are illustrated fully in Part B, Sections III and IV.

It is often said that the subjunctive mood is used ever less frequently in modern Italian. It is true that Italians tend to associate the frequent use of subjunctive with the more formal, sophisticated and, in particular, written registers of the language, to express nuances of meaning. However, using the indicative instead of the subjunctive not only conveys a more informal style, but also a different meaning, and may well change substantially the message that we want to convey.

2.3.15

Uses of the subjunctive

In some cases, it is almost compulsory to use the subjunctive, even in the most familiar context of communication. This is particularly true when there is an explicit reference to the subjective value of a statement:

(a) With *verbs* expressing hope, doubt, expectation, desire, fear, emotion such as:

sperare 'to hope'	**desiderare** 'to wish'
illudersi 'to illude oneself'	**dubitare** 'to doubt'
temere 'to fear'	**sospettare** 'to suspect'

Spero che *abbiate capito*.
I hope you understood.

Temo che *sia* troppo tardi.
I'm afraid it is too late.

Non illuderti che il Napoli *possa* vincere il campionato.
Don't delude yourself that 'Napoli' can win the championship.

Non avrei mai sospettato che tu *fossi* capace di mentire.
I would never have suspected you of being able to lie.

(b) With the following *conjunctions* (this is not a complete list but will help you understand the contexts when the subjunctive is required; see also Part B, Sections III and IV):

prima che 'before'	**come se** 'as if'
tranne che, a meno che 'unless'	**se** 'if'
malgrado, benché, sebbene 'although'	
nonostante 'despite'	

Prima che *sia* troppo tardi, dobbiamo pagare il telefono.
We must pay the phone bill, before it is too late.

Parlava come se *avesse* il raffreddore.
He was speaking as if he had a cold.

Dovete sbrigarvi, a meno che non *vogliate* fare tardi.
You must hurry up, unless you want to be late.

Malgrado *fossero* in tre, non sono riusciti a sollevare l'armadio.
Although there were three of them, they couldn't lift the cupboard.

> **Sebbene** *siano* **stanchi, i ragazzi vogliono uscire stasera.**
> The kids want to go out tonight, although they're tired.

> **Se** *fossi* **in te non le parlerei.**
> If I were you I wouldn't speak to her.

The most common conjunction used to introduce the subjunctive is **se** 'if' in the so-called '**periodo ipotetico**'. However, whether to use the subjunctive after **se** is also a matter of choice (see Chapter 38).

(c) When the verb is introduced by an *indefinite pronoun* or *adjective* (see Chapter 3) such as **chiunque, qualunque, qualsiasi**:

> **Chiunque** *bussi* **alla porta, non aprire.**
> Whoever knocks on the door, don't open.

> **Sono pronta a fare qualsiasi cosa tu mi** *chieda.*
> I'm ready to do whatever you ask me to do.

Even in the examples shown in this paragraph, many Italians might use the indicative instead of the subjunctive. However it is useful to get into the habit of using the subjunctive in the 'essential' cases and is especially important for those who need to communicate formally in Italian.

2.3.16

Tenses of the subjunctive

Verbs in the subjunctive mood always, except in a few cases, *depend* on another verb (i.e. the main verb of a complex sentence). This means that we also need to look at how each *tense* of the subjunctive expresses a different *time relationship* with the main verb.

There are four tenses of the subjunctive: *present, perfect, imperfect, pluperfect.* The regular conjugations of these tenses are shown in the verb tables above (2.2).

2.3.17

Present subjunctive (*Congiuntivo presente*)

The regular conjugation of the present subjunctive has the same ending in the three singular persons: **-i/-i/-i** for the 1st conjugation and **-a/-a/-a** for the 2nd and 3rd conjugations:

guardare	guard-*i*
credere	cred-*a*
dormire	dorm-*a*
finire	finisc-*a*

Note the following irregular verb forms:

avere *abbia*	essere *sia*
andare *vada*	dare *dia*
fare *faccia*	stare *stia*
dire *dica*	

And see Appendix II.

The present subjunctive is used when we want to mention something that is contemporary or future (there is no future tense in the subjunctive). It is almost always linked to a main verb in the *present* tense:

> **Spero che tu** *capisca.*
> I hope you understand.

> **Mi sembra che il telefono non** *funzioni.*
> I think the telephone must be out of order.

> **Credo che l'agenzia di viaggio ci** *prenoti* **l'aereo oggi stesso.**
> I think the travel agency is booking our flight today.

A more detailed study of the time relationship of the subjunctive and the verb it depends on is found in Part B.

2.3.18

Perfect subjunctive (*Congiuntivo passato*)

The perfect subjunctive is formed by the present subjunctive of the auxiliary **avere** or **essere** and the past participle. The forms of the perfect subjunctive for the three regular conjugations are found in the verb tables above (2.2).

The perfect subjunctive is used to refer to a past fact linked to a main verb, usually in the present tense:

> **Mi sembra che ieri il telefono non** *abbia funzionato.*
> I think the phone must have been out of order yesterday.

> **Credo che l'agenzia di viaggio ci** *abbia prenotato* **l'aereo ieri.**
> The travel agency should have reserved our flight yesterday, I think.

> **Marco penserà che tu** *sia uscito.*
> Marco will think you have gone out.

2.3.19

Imperfect subjunctive (*Congiuntivo imperfetto*)

The ending of the imperfect subjunctive is the same for both 1st and 2nd persons singular: **-assi, -essi, -issi** in the **-are, -ere, -ire** conjugations respectively (**io/tu guard-***assi*, **cred-***essi*, **dorm-***issi*, **fin-***issi*). The forms of the imperfect subjunctive for the three regular conjugations are found in the verb tables.

Irregular forms to be noted are

> essere *fossi*   dare *dessi*
> fare *facessi*   stare *stessi*
> bere *bevessi*   dire *dicessi*

And see Appendix II.

The imperfect subjunctive is used for events or actions taking place at the same time as the action of the main verb in the past:

> **Speravo che tu *capissi.***
> I hoped you understood.

> **Ieri mi sembrava che il telefono non *funzionasse.***
> Yesterday I thought the phone was out of order.

> **Credevo che l'agenzia di viaggio *prenotasse* l'aereo il giorno stesso.**
> I assumed that the travel agency was reserving our flight that same day.

The imperfect subjunctive is also used for a present or future action, which depends on a main verb in the present conditional:

> **Vorrei che voi *parlaste* con il capo.**
> I'd like you to speak to the boss.

> **Sarebbe bene che domani *arrivasse* in orario.**
> It would be good if he arrived on time tomorrow.

> **Compreresti una Rolls Royce, se *avessi* i soldi?**
> Would you buy a Rolls Royce, if you had the money?

2.3.20
Pluperfect subjunctive (*Congiuntivo trapassato*)
The pluperfect subjunctive is formed by the imperfect subjunctive of **avere** or **essere** and the past participle. The forms of the pluperfect subjunctive for the regular conjugations are shown in the verb tables (2.2).

It is used to refer to a past event referred to by a main verb in the past tense:

> **Speravo che *avessi capito.***
> I hoped you had understood.

> **Mi sembrava che il telefono non *avesse funzionato.***
> I thought the phone had been out of order.

> **Credevo che l'agenzia ci *avesse prenotato* l'aereo già da un mese.**
> I assumed the travel agency had already reserved our flight a month before.

2.3.21
Other uses of the subjunctive
In a few cases the subjunctive is used by itself without depending on another verb.

(a) To give an order or invite somebody to do something, when using the polite **Lei/Loro** form. In this function the present subjunctive serves as the 3rd person form of the imperative, both singular and plural:

Prego, *dica*!
Can I help you? (*literally*: Please, tell me.)

Prego, si *accomodi*.
Please, have a seat.

***Esca* immediatamente!**
Get out immediately!

Prego signori, *vengano* di qua.
Please come over here, gentlemen.

(b) In exclamations, to express a wish or a threat:

Dio *salvi* la Regina.
God save the Queen.

***Viva* l'Italia!**
Long live Italy!

Dio ti *benedica*.
God bless you.

Ti *venga* un accidente.
Drop dead.

The verb can be introduced by the words **magari** 'if only' or **se** 'if':

Magari *potessi* andare in vacanza. . . .
If only I could go on holiday. . . .

Se *avessi* vent'anni!
If I were 20 years old!

Here, the subjunctive, although used alone, still depends on a main verb, although it is implicit rather than actually stated:

(Spero che) ti *venga* un accidente.
(I hope that) something horrible happens to you.

(Mi auguro che) Dio ti *benedica*.
(I wish that) God would bless you.

Se *avessi* vent'anni (farei tante cose).
If I were young (I would do lots of things).

2.3.22 — **Imperative mood: introduction**

The forms of the imperative for the three regular conjugations are shown in the verb tables (2.2). The imperative only has one tense: the present (see tenses). The imperative is the mood we use when we want to give orders or to ask somebody to do something, so it has no 1st person singular form.

Ama **il prossimo tuo come te stesso.**
Love your neighbour like yourself.

Credetemi, **sono sincero.**
Believe me, I am sincere.

Prendimi **l'ombrello, per favore.**
Please, get my umbrella for me.

Aiuto, *datemi* **una mano.**
Help, give me a hand.

The polite 'you' form, the 3rd person **Lei/Loro**, uses the present subjunctive as a polite 'imperative' form of giving an order, inviting or advising someone to do something (see subjunctive above, 2.3.21).

Signora, *guardi* **che belle scarpe.**
Look what beautiful shoes, madam.

Dott. Bianchi, *finisca* **quella lettera e poi** *venga* **da me.**
Dr Bianchi, could you please finish that letter and then come to see me.

Mi *dia* **il telefono, per favore.**
Give me the telephone, please.

Note how in the examples above the imperative **tu** or **voi** form is combined with any pronoun used – whether direct or indirect object – while with the **Lei** form, the pronoun comes before (see also Chapter 3).

For more illustrations of the use of the imperative, see Chapter 21.

2.3.23

Some irregular imperatives

A few verbs have an irregular imperative, in the **tu** form:

avere	*abbi*
essere	*sii*
sapere	*sappi*

With the five verbs **andare, dare, dire, fare, stare**, the shortened imperative forms are normally marked nowadays with an apostrophe, to distinguish them from the prepositions **di, da** or the third person singular of the present indicative **da, fa, sta**. These shortened imperative forms are very often replaced by the second person indicative forms **vai, fai**, etc.:

Infinitive	Imperative	Indicative
andare	*va'*	*vai*
dire	*di'*	*dici*
dare	*da'*	*dai*
fare	*fa'*	*fai*
stare	*sta'*	*stai*

Abbi **pazienza!**	Be patient!
Sii **prudente!**	Be prudent (drive carefully)!
Dammi **la penna, per favore!**	Please give me the pen!
Fammi **un piacere.**	Do me a favour.
Vallo **a trovare.**	Go to see him.

The last example is very colloquial use; normally the direct object pronoun would be attached to the end of the infinitive, rather than the first verb (**Vai a trovarlo**).

Negative imperative

To ask somebody *not* to do something we use *non* + **infinitive** if speaking in the 2nd person singular (**tu**). For all other forms of the imperative, simply add *non*.

> **Teresa,** *non giocare* **in casa con la palla.**
> Teresa, don't play indoors with the ball.

> **Bambini,** *non andate* **lontano.**
> Children, don't go far away.

> **Franco,** *non preoccuparti.*
> Don't worry, Franco.

> **Non si** *preoccupi,* **avvocato.**
> Don't worry, (lawyer).

The gerund (*Gerundio*)

The present gerund is formed by adding the endings **-ando** for the 1st conjugation and **-endo** for the 2nd and 3rd conjugations, to the verb stem:

> am-*ando*   ved-*endo*   part-*endo*   fin-*endo*

The past gerund is formed by the gerund of the auxiliary **avere** or **essere** and the past participle:

amare	**avendo amato**
vedere	**avendo visto**
partire	**essendo partito/a/i/e**
finire	**avendo finito**

The present gerund indicates an action happening at the same time as that of the main verb, be it past, present or future:

> **Il prof. Neri parla** *leggendo* **gli appunti.**
> Prof. Neri speaks reading from notes.

> **Il prof. Neri ha parlato** *leggendo* **gli appunti.**
> Prof. Neri spoke reading from notes.

> **Il prof. Neri parlerà** *leggendo* **gli appunti.**
> Prof. Neri will speak reading from notes.

2.3.27
The past gerund indicates an action that took place before that of the main verb:

> *Avendo distribuito* **gli appunti in inglese, il prof. Neri parla in italiano.**
> Having distributed notes in English, Prof. Neri speaks in Italian.

> *Avendo distribuito* **gli appunti in inglese, il prof. Neri ha parlato in italiano.**
> Having distributed notes in English, Prof. Neri spoke in Italian.

> *Avendo distribuito* **gli appunti in inglese, il prof. Neri parlerà in italiano.**
> Having distributed notes in English, Prof. Neri will speak in Italian.

2.3.28
Uses of the gerund
The gerund is always used in connection with another verb on which it is closely dependent. The subject of the gerund must be the same as that of the main verb (unless explicitly stated).

English '-ing'
The English verb form '-ing' cannot be translated by the Italian gerund when used as an adjective or a participle modifying a noun. In Italian we use a *relative* clause with **che**:

> **C'è un uomo** *che bussa* **alla porta.**
> There is a man knocking at the door.

> **Ho visto uno studente** *che leggeva* **'Panorama'.**
> I saw a student reading *Panorama*.

Using the gerund with pronouns
When the gerund has an unstressed pronoun as direct or indirect object, the pronoun is attached to the end of the verb (see Chapter 3):

> **Guardando***li* **bene ho capito che quei francobolli erano falsi.**
> Looking at them carefully I realized that those stamps were false.

> **Dando***le* **più fiducia otterrai migliori risultati da lei.**
> By putting more trust in her, you will get better results from her.

Progressive (stare + gerund)
One of the most common uses of the gerund is with **stare** (see also Chapter 12) to describe an action *in progress*:

> *Sto preparando* **il caffè.**
> I'm making coffee.

> **Non ho risposto al telefono perché** *stavo facendo* **la doccia.**
> I didn't answer the phone because I was having a shower.

In the *past*, the progressive form is *always* formed with the *imperfect* of **stare**. The progressive form, expressing an action in its duration, rather than when completed, is the most typical example of the *imperfect* aspect of verbs (see Chapter 13).

2.3.29

Present participle (*Participio presente*)

The present participle is formed by the endings **-ante/i** in the 1st conjugation and **-ente/i** in the 2nd and 3rd conjugations. In modern Italian this form is very rarely used as a verb, and has taken on the function of adjective or noun.

Adjectives:	**affascinante** 'fascinating'
	bollente 'boiling hot'
	ignorante 'ignorant'
	imbarazzante 'embarrassing'
	importante 'important'
	potente 'powerful'
	rilevante 'relevant'
	soddisfacente 'satisfactory'
	splendente 'splendid'
	urgente 'urgent'
Nouns:	**amante** 'lover'
	agente 'agent'
	cantante 'singer'
	comandante 'commander, commandant'
	dipendente 'dependant, employee'
	dirigente 'manager, director'
	insegnante 'teacher'
	stampante 'printer'
	studente 'student'

and many more . . .

As a verb it is sometimes used in very formal and bureaucratic language:

> Gli impiegati *perdenti il posto* riceveranno una pensione.
> The employees losing their jobs will receive a pension.

> *Vivente il padre*, i figli non ricevono l'eredità.
> The father being alive, the children shall not receive the inheritance.

But in general it is preferable to use a gerund, a relative clause (**che . . .**) or time clause (**quando . . .** or **mentre . . .**):

> Gli impiegati *che perdono* il posto riceveranno una pensione.
> *Mentre* il padre *è in vita*, i figli non ricevono l'eredità.

2.3.30

Past participle (*Participio passato*)

Unlike the present, the past participle is one of the most frequently used forms of Italian verbs. It is found in all *compound tenses* of verbs, together with the auxiliary **avere** or **essere**. The regular past participle is formed by the endings -**ato** for the 1st, -**uto** for the 2nd, and -**ito** for the 3rd conjugation.

> **guard*ato***   **cred*uto***   **dorm*ito***   **fin*ito***

Its endings have to agree with the subject (in the case of verbs taking the auxiliary **essere**) or sometimes the object of the verb (see below), following the pattern of adjectives in -**o/a/i/e** (see 1.5).

Irregular past participles

There are many verbs with an irregular past participle. All verbs with irregular past participles are listed with translations in Appendix II. But some basic groups can be identified:

(a) Verbs, mainly of the 2nd conjugation, with past participle in -**so** such as:

accendere	*acceso*	chiudere	*chiuso*	correre	*corso*
decidere	*deciso*	mettere	*messo*	perdere	*perso*
prendere	*preso*	scendere	*sceso*	apparire	*apparso*

(b) Verbs of the 2nd and 3rd conjugations with past participle in -**to** such as:

chiedere	*chiesto*	leggere	*letto*	rispondere	*risposto*
rompere	*rotto*	scegliere	*scelto*	scrivere	*scritto*
vedere	*visto*	porre	*posto*		
			(and **composto, esposto**, etc.)		
tradurre	*tradotto*	produrre	*prodotto*		
aprire	*aperto*	dire	*detto*	morire	*morto*
nascere	*nato*	offrire	*offerto*	venire	*venuto*
vivere	*vissuto*				

Note: **essere** *stato*.

These verbs are more fully illustrated in Appendix II.

Uses of the past participle

The past participle is used in two ways:

(a) In compound tenses when it is used with auxiliary **avere** or **essere**:
When the auxiliary is **avere**, the participle ends in -**o** (masculine singular), and does not change to agree with the subject of the verb:

> **L'avv. Serpe non aveva capit*o* il suo problema e la sig.ra Brandi gli ha scritt*o* un pro-memoria.**
> Dr Serpe didn't understand her problem so Mrs Brandi wrote a memorandum for him.

> **Sandro e Lucia hanno lavorat*o* bene.**
> Sandro and Lucia did a good job.

But if the verb is preceded by a *direct object pronoun* the participle agrees with its gender and number (see also Chapter 3):

> **Avete vist*o* quelle pratiche? Sì, *le* abbiamo vist*e*.**
> Did you see those files? Yes, we've seen them.

> **Hai vist*o* Elisa? Sì, *l*'ho vist*a*.**
> Did you see Elisa? Yes, I saw her.

When the auxiliary is **essere** the past participle always agrees with the gender and number of the *subject*:

> **È arrivat*o* il mio stipendio?**
> Has my salary arrived?

> **È arrivat*a* la posta?**
> Has the mail arrived?

> **Ci siamo accort*i* troppo tardi del nostro errore.**
> We realized our mistake too late.

> **Le fatture non sono stat*e* ancora ricevut*e* dal cliente.**
> The invoices haven't yet been received by the customer.

(b) As a verb form on its own

If used as a verb form by itself the past participle can have the same function as an adjective (i.e. qualifying a noun). Its ending is in agreement with the gender and number of the noun it qualifies:

> **Oggi non c'era posta indirizzat*a* a Lei, sig. Sini.**
> There was no mail addressed to you today, Mr Sini.

> **Oggi non c'erano lettere indirizzat*e* a Lei, sig. Sini.**
> There were no letters addressed to you today, Mr Sini.

> **Dove sono i pacchi arrivat*i* oggi?**
> Where are the parcels that arrived today?

It can also have the function of a verb in its own right, expressing an action *completed* before the action expressed in the main clause; the subject can be the same as that of the main verb or a different one:

> **Appena *arrivati*, abbiamo preso un caffè.**
> As soon as we arrived, we had a coffee.

> **Appena *arrivato* Franco, prendiamo un caffè.**
> As soon as Franco has arrived, we'll have a coffee.

> ***Sconfitto* l'esercito borbonico a Calatafimi, Garibaldi avanzò verso Palermo.**
> After defeating the Bourbon army at Calatafimi, Garibaldi advanced towards Palermo.

Past participle + pronouns

The past participle can also take an unstressed pronoun as its object (direct or indirect), in which case the pronoun is attached to the end of the participle (see also Chapter 3):

> **Vista*la* arrivare, ho chiamato Sara dal balcone.**
> As I saw her arriving, I called Sara from the balcony.

> **Consegnati*gli* i documenti, sono tornato in ufficio.**
> After delivering the documents to him, I came back to the office.

3 Pronouns

3.1 What is a pronoun?

A pronoun (pro + noun) is literally a word that takes the place of, or fulfils the function of, a noun in certain specific circumstances.

There are several types of *pronouns* in Italian (as there are in English): *personal, relative, demonstrative, possessive, indefinite*. Each type of pronoun is covered separately in this chapter.

3.2 Personal pronouns

Personal pronouns are the main thread of any spoken or written discourse. Their function is to refer to somebody or something known to both speaker and listener, either because they are actually present or because they have already been mentioned in the conversation or in the text. In Italian, personal pronouns have the same gender and number as the noun to which they refer.

3.3 Stressed personal pronouns

Stressed pronouns are *only* used when we want to identify clearly the person to whom we refer, usually to distinguish them from somebody else (see Chapters 8–10). They almost always refer to people, rather than to things or animals.

Stressed pronouns are normally quite separate from other words, and in particular from the verb. For this reason they are sometimes called *disjunctive* (*unjoined*) pronouns. This gives them a more emphatic position in the sentence. They are distinguished from the more common unstressed pronouns by three main characteristics: (a) their *form* (b) their *position* and (c) the *stress* that falls on them.

3.3.1 Subject pronouns

Subject pronouns are used to emphasize the person or thing responsible for the action (see Chapters 8 and 9). The forms of the subject pronouns are as follows:

io 'I'	**noi** 'we'
tu 'you'	**voi** 'you' (plural)
lui 'he'	**loro** 'they'
lei 'she'	**Loro** 'you' (formal, plural)
Lei 'you' (formal)	

Other, much less used, subject pronouns are:

egli, esso 'he'	**essi** 'them' (masculine)
ella, essa 'she'	**esse** 'them' (feminine)

These pronouns are limited to formal spoken and written language. In modern Italian they are used infrequently.

In Italian use of subject pronouns with verbs is not essential, unlike in English (see Chapter 2), since the endings of Italian verbs always show who the subject (or 'person') is, without the need for a pronoun. So the use of pronouns is limited to cases when we need to give special emphasis to the subject:

Chi te l'ha detto?	**Me l'ha detto *lui.***
Who told you that?	*He* told me.

Io sono scozzese, *lei* è gallese.
I am Scottish, *she* is Welsh.

Object pronouns

3.3.2

Object pronouns are used to refer to the person or thing that is the target of an action, and *stressed* object pronouns place particular emphasis on it. For this reason they are generally much less used than the corresponding *unstressed* forms (see 3.4). For the uses of stressed pronouns, see Chapters 8, 9 and 18.

The forms of the stressed object pronouns are as follows:

me 'me'	**noi** 'us'
te 'you'	**voi** 'you' (plural)
lui 'him'	**loro** 'them'
lei 'her'	**Loro** 'you (formal, plural)
Lei 'you' (formal)	

These pronouns can be used as the direct object of a verb, such as:

Vorrei vedere *te* al posto mio!
I'd like to see *you* in my place!

or, preceded by a preposition, as the indirect object or other complement of a verb:

> **Dai *a me* quei soldi!**
> Give that money *to me*!

> **Devi parlare più forte *con lui*, perché è duro d'orecchi.**
> You should speak louder *to him*, because he's hard of hearing.

Indirect object pronouns (indicating the person or thing *at which* the action of the verb is directed) also have an unstressed form, used without the preposition **a** (see 3.4.2).

When any preposition is present, only stressed pronouns can be used.

3.3.3

Reflexive pronouns (stressed)

Reflexive pronouns refer to the object or other complement of a verb, when it is the same person as the subject. This is expressed in English by the use of '-self' ('himself', 'ourselves' etc.).

Here are the stressed (emphatic) forms (for the unstressed forms, see 3.4.2):

me (**stesso/a**) 'myself'	**noi** (**stessi/e**) 'ourselves'
te (**stesso/a**) 'yourself'	**voi** (**stessi/e**) 'yourselves'
sé (**stesso/a**) 'him/herself'	**sé** (**stessi/e**) 'themselves'

The use of **stesso**, to increase the emphasis given to the pronoun, is optional. (It is not necessary to omit the accent on **sé** when it is followed by **stesso**, although many writers do.)

> **Dovrebbe criticare *sé stesso* invece di dare la colpa agli altri.**
> He ought to be more critical of himself instead of putting the blame on others.

> **Ama il prossimo tuo come *te stesso*.**
> Love thy neighbour as thyself.

3.4   *Unstressed personal pronouns*

The most common way to refer to somebody or something, without mentioning them explicitly, is to use *unstressed pronouns* (see Chapter 18). Because they are always used in conjunction with a verb, they are also called *conjunctive* pronouns. The unstressed pronouns can be *direct* or *indirect object*, *reflexive*, or *partitive*, depending on their relationship with the verb.

The unstressed pronouns are always used *without a preposition*. (With a preposition e.g. **a**, **da**, **di**, **con**, **per**, the stressed forms should always be used.) Their normal position is *before* the verb. When the verb is in the infinitive, imperative, gerund or participle, however, the pronouns are attached *to the end* of the verb:

Pronto! *Mi* **senti?**	**Sì,** *ti* **sento bene!**
Hello! Can you hear me?	Yes, I can hear you well!
Da*mmi* **lo zucchero.**	**Il caffè** *mi* **piace dolce.**
Give me the sugar.	I like my coffee sweet.

Non dir*glielo. Glielo* **dirò io.**
Don't tell her (it). I'll tell her (it).

Although, in writing, these pronouns are separate words, when we speak they combine with the verb, which usually comes immediately after, so they sound like a single utterance (**misènti, tisènto**). When they follow the verb, they are actually attached to it, in writing as well as in speech (**dammi, dirglielo**). This shows how closely pronoun and verb are linked.

Direct object pronouns

Direct object pronouns are those used with transitive verbs (see Chapter 2). They indicate the thing, person or entity which the action of the verb directly affects, in other words, its 'object', and are much more frequently used than the stressed pronouns seen above.

mi 'me'	**ci** 'us'
ti 'you'	**vi** 'you' (plural)
lo 'him, it'	**li** 'them'
la 'her, it'	**le** 'them'
La 'you' (formal)	

Indirect object pronouns

We use the indirect object pronouns to indicate that the action of a verb is aimed *at* or *to* something or somebody (see Chapter 18).

The forms are as follows:

mi 'to me'	**ci** 'to us'
ti 'to you'	**vi** 'to you' (plural)
gli 'to him'	**gli** (**loro**†) 'to them'
le 'to her'	
Le 'to you' (formal)	

†In written Italian, and occasionally in formal spoken Italian, the pronoun **loro** (coming after the verb) can be used instead of **gli**.

Reflexive pronouns

The unstressed reflexive pronouns are the following:

> **mi** 'myself'   **ci** 'ourselves'
> **ti** 'yourself'   **vi** 'yourselves'
>
> **si** 'himself/herself'   **si** 'themselves'

Notice how in the first and second person, the unstressed pronouns (**mi**, **ti**, **ci**, **vi**) are identical in form. Only in the third person, are the indirect object, direct object and reflexive pronouns different from each other: **lo/gli/si**, **la/le/si**, **li/gli/si**, **le/gli/si**.

The reflexive pronouns have the same function as the direct object pronouns seen above, but are used when the *object* and the *subject* of the verb are the *same person*.

> **Io *mi* lavo (Io lavo me stesso) tutte le mattine alle 7.**
> I wash (myself) every morning at 7 a.m.

> **Guarda*ti* allo specchio!**
> Look at yourself in the mirror!

> **I miei figli *si* stanno preparando per gli esami.**
> My children are getting (themselves) ready for the exams.

In addition to this genuinely *reflexive* use, these pronouns are also used with the various *pronominal* forms of verbs (see 2.1.7).

3.4.4   *Ne*

Ne *used as partitive*
In the examples below, the pronoun **ne** is called *partitive* because it refers to a part or quantity of something or somebody:

> **Desidera del pane?**
> Would you like some bread?

> **Si, *ne* vorrei un chilo.**
> Yes, I would like one kilo (of it).

> **È squisito questo gelato. Vuoi assaggiar*ne* un po'?**
> This ice-cream is delicious. Would you like to taste a little bit (of it)?

> **Oggi sono arrivate molte telefonate. Solo io *ne* ho ricevut*e* dieci.**
> Today we have had a lot of telephone calls. I alone have had ten (of them).

> **Oggi sono arrivati molti clienti. Solo io *ne* ho ricevut*i* cinque.**
> Today a lot of customers have come. I myself have seen five (of them).

Ne is therefore used almost always with an indication of *quantity.* It may be a number, a specification of weight or length, or a pronoun, for example **molto, poco, troppo, abbastanza, un po'** ... (for more examples see Chapter 11).

Ne is invariable (does not change form). It may refer to any noun (masculine, feminine, singular or plural). Notice however that, although invariable in form, **ne** 'reflects' the noun to which it refers. In fact, in the compound tenses, the past participle generally agrees with the noun that **ne** represents, as in the last two examples above (see 3.4.7).

Notice also how **ne** occupies the same position in the sentence as the other unstressed pronouns: *before* the verb (or *after* an infinitive, certain imperative forms, the gerund and participle: see 3.4).

Other uses of **ne**
There are a few cases in which **ne** is used without a 'partitive' meaning.

(a) Meaning **di questo ... di quello**, but without any reference to quantity:

> **Non ho comprato quella macchina e** *me ne* **pento.**
> I didn't buy that car and I regret it.

> **Franco lavora troppo, ma non se** *ne* **lamenta.**
> Franco works too much, but he doesn't complain about it.

(b) Meaning **da questo ... da quello** 'from':

> **I miei affari vanno bene.** *Ne* **ricavo un buon profitto.**
> My business is going well. I'm making a good profit (out of it).

> **Questo ufficio è male organizzato e** *ne* **deriva molta confusione.**
> This office is badly organized and a great deal of confusion arises from this (fact).

(c) With **andare** or other verbs in idiomatic expressions as:

> **Vatte***ne***! Andateve***ne***!**
> Go away! Get out of here!

> **Non ce la faccio più. Me** *ne* **vado!**
> I can't stand it any more. I'm going away!

> **Chi se** *ne* **frega!**
> Who cares!? (rather coarse)

> **Non me** *ne* **importa niente!**
> I don't care at all! (colloquial but not vulgar)

> **Non** *ne* **posso più!**
> I can't bear it any more!

> **Non** *ne* **vale la pena!**
> It is not worth the effort!

Oggi ho la febbre. È meglio che me *ne* stia a casa.
Today I am ill. I'd better stay at home.

For more examples of the use of **ne** as an adverb of place, see Chapter 6.

Particle *ci*

Like **ne**, **ci** can be used as a pronoun, as an adverb of place, or idiomatically in several expressions. Like the other conjunctive pronouns, it is positioned before the verb normally, but after an infinitive, certain imperatives, the gerund or participle.

(a) As an adverb of place, either static or implying movement, with verbs such as **abitare, mettere, venire, andare**:

> **C'è ...**   **Ci sono ...**
> There is ...   There are ...

> **C'era una volta (una principessa) ...**
> Once upon a time there was (a princess) ...

> **Ci vado quest'estate.**
> I'm going there this summer.

> **Napoli mi piace molto. Ci abito da dieci anni.**
> I like Naples a lot. I've lived here ten years now.

When found with an unstressed direct object pronoun or **ne**, **ci** used as an adverb of place occupies a different position according to what the pronoun is: **mi ci, ti ci, ce lo, ce la, vi ci, ce li, ce le, ce ne**. The combination **ci ci** is best avoided.

> **Chi mi porta all'aeroporto? *Ti ci* porto io.**
> Who's taking me to the airport? I'll take you there.

For further examples of its use as an adverb of place, see Chapter 6.

(b) As a pronoun, used with a verb taking **a**, to replace either **a** + noun or **a** + a verb phrase:

> **Tu fumi ancora? Perché non *ci* rinunci veramente? (ci = a fumare)**
> Are you still smoking? Why don't you really give *it* up?

> **L'Italia mi manca molto. *Ci* penso spesso. (ci = all'Italia)**
> I miss Italy a lot. I often think *about it*.

(c) Used idiomatically with certain verbs:

> **Non *ci* vedo.**
> I can't see anything.

> **Ce l'hai?**
> Have you got it?

(d) With a reflexive verb, to replace impersonal **si**:

If the impersonal **si** were used with the third person of a reflexive verb **si alza**, this would produce *In Italia si si alza presto. To avoid repetition and confusion, the first **si** changes into **ci**: **In Italia** *ci* **si alza presto** ('In Italy one gets up early').

3.4.6

Compound pronouns (indirect + direct)

Unstressed pronouns are often used in combination with each other and with the particles **ci** and **ne**. When indirect and direct object (3rd person only) pronouns are combined, the indirect object pronoun (and reflexive **si**) comes first. In the case of **mi, ti, ci, vi, si**, the **-i** ending changes to **-e. Gli** combines with a direct object pronoun to form a single word. The table below shows the combinations of direct (3rd person only), indirect pronouns and **ne**. Remember that **ci** acts in the same way both when it is a pronoun and when it is an adverb (see 3.4.5).

	lo	*la*	*li*	*le*	*ne*
mi	me lo	me la	me li	me le	me ne
ti	te lo	te la	te li	te le	te ne
gli, le	glielo	gliela	glieli	gliele	gliene
si	se lo	se la	se li	se le	se ne
ci	ce lo	ce la	ce li	ce le	ce ne
vi	ve lo	ve la	ve li	ve le	ve ne
gli, loro	glielo	gliela	glieli	gliele	gliene

These compound pronouns, like all the other unstressed pronouns, are normally placed before the verb, but after the infinitive, imperative, participle or gerund (see 3.4). They also form a single utterance with the verb: **te l'ho detto** (**teloddètto**) 'I told you'.

> **Che bella rosa!** *Me la* **dai?**
> What a beautiful rose! Will you give it to me?
>
> **No non voglio dar*tela*!**
> No, I don't want to give it to you!
>
> *Gliel'***ho detto io.**
> I told her it.
>
> **Per favore, di*glielo* tu.**
> Please tell her it.

3.4.7

Agreement with participle

When using compound tenses of the verbs, such as the **passato prossimo**, the *participle* must agree with the gender and number of the direct object pronouns, including **ne**, which in turn agree with the gender and number of the noun they are replacing (apart from **ne** which is invariable in form):

Hai visto la mia macchina nuova? Sì, l(a)'ho vist*a*.
Did you see my new car? Yes, I saw it.

Hai visto l'ultimo film di Fellini? No, non l(o)'ho vist*o*.
Did you see the last Fellini film? No, I didn't see it.

Hai visto i bambini? Sì, *li* ho vist*i*.
Did you see the children? Yes, I saw them.

Hai visto le Olimpiadi? No, non *le* ho vist*e*.
Did you see the Olympics? No, I didn't see them.

Hai comprato le bibite? Sì, *ne* ho comprat*e* due.
Have you bought the drinks? Yes, I bought two.

Hai comprato le pesche? Sì, *ne* ho comprat*e* un chilo.
Have you bought peaches? Yes, I bought a kilo of them.

3.5   *Relative pronouns*

Relative pronouns have a double function: (a) like the personal pronouns, they
refer to a previously mentioned person or thing; (b) they also act as a link
between two sentences or clauses. The sentence introduced by a relative
pronoun is called the relative clause.

Puoi restituirmi la penna *che* ti ho prestato?
Can you return me the pen that I lent you?

3.5.1   *Che*

Che is by far the most common of all Italian relative pronouns, and indeed one
of the most frequently used words in the Italian language. It is used to refer to
persons, animals or things, and it is *invariable* (does not change form). In the
relative clause it can be either the subject or the direct object of the verb.

Subject:

L'albero *che* cresce davanti alla mia finestra è una quercia.
The tree that grows in front of my window is a oak.

Ricordi lo scrittore *che* ha vinto il Premio Strega?
Do you remember the writer who won the Strega Prize?

Object:

L'albero *che* ho tagliato stamattina era una quercia.
The tree that I cut down this morning was an oak.

**Ricordi lo scrittore *che* l'Università ha invitato a fare una
conferenza?**
Do you remember the writer whom the University invited to give
a talk?

When used as a relative pronoun **che** can never be preceded by a preposition.

3.5.2

Cui

Cui is the relative pronoun used with the function of indirect object or other complement of the verb. It is usually preceded by a preposition (**a, da, con, per** ...). Like **che**, **cui** is invariable and can refer to any noun (masculine, feminine, singular or plural) without change of form.

> **Questo è l'ufficio *in cui* dobbiamo trasferirci l'anno prossimo.**
> This is the office which we have to move into next year.

> **Sto lavorando sulla pratica *di cui* ti ho parlato ieri.**
> I am working on the file which I spoke to you about yesterday.

> **Oggi quella signora *a cui* abbiamo mandato la fattura è venuta a pagare.**
> Today the lady to whom we sent the invoice came to pay.

When **cui** is used as an *indirect object* as in the last example above, indicating the person or thing *at whom/ which* the action of the verb is directed, the preposition **a** can be omitted:

> **Vorrei gli indirizzi di tutte le ditte *cui* abbiamo inviato il nostro catalogo.**
> I would like to have the addresses of all the companies to whom we sent our catalogue.

> **Il problema *cui* ti riferisci è stato già affrontato.**
> The problem to which you are referring has already been dealt with.

Cui is also used as a *possessive adjective* (English 'whose'). It is then placed between the definite article and the noun, without a preposition:

> **Bisogna trovare la persona *le cui* chiavi sono rimaste sul mio tavolo.**
> We have to find the person whose keys have been left on my table.

> **Verrà assunto il candidato *il cui* curriculum risulterà più adatto.**
> The candidate whose CV turns out to be the most suitable will be employed.

3.5.3

Il quale, la quale, i quali, le quali

These are used instead of **che** and **cui**, when we need to specify more clearly which noun the relative pronoun is referring to. Unlike **che** and **cui**, these pronouns vary in gender and number, as too does the definite article used with them, so it is clearer which noun they are referring to.

Il quale however is used only rarely as a replacement for **che**, and then only in a formal context, for example in legal or bureaucratic language (see the first example below). It is more commonly found with a preposition (note the combined forms) replacing **cui**, but again only when there is a need for precision in the reference. Compare the examples below with those above:

> **Tutta la corrispondenza deve essere firmata dal Direttore, *il quale* ne assume la responsabilità legale.**
> All correspondence must be signed by the Director, who assumes legal responsibility for it.

> **Sto lavorando sulla pratica *della quale* ti ho parlato ieri.**
> I am working on the file which I spoke to you about yesterday.

> **Vorrei gli indirizzi di tutte le ditte *alle quali* abbiamo inviato il catalogo.**
> I would like to have the addresses of all the companies to which we sent the catalogue.

> **Verrà assunto il candidato, il curriculum *del quale* risulterà più adatto.**
> The candidate whose CV turns out to be most suitable will be employed.

── 3.5.4 ── ## *Chi*

Chi is more commonly found as an interrogative in questions or indirect questions:

> **Mi ha chiesto *chi* ha telefonato.**
> He asked me who phoned.

As a relative, **chi** is used only to refer to people, never to things. It has the function of a 'double' pronoun: **quello che, uno che** 'those who', 'the people who . . .':

> **Le Pagine Gialle sono utili soprattutto a *chi* lavora nel commercio.**
> The Yellow Pages are especially useful to those who are in business.

> **I nostri prodotti sono disegnati per *chi* apprezza la funzionalità.**
> Our products are designed for people who appreciate the functional approach.

Notice that **chi** is always used with a singular verb (even when it refers to more than one person). Note also that, unlike the other relative pronouns, it does not refer explicitly to a noun but is complete in itself.

Here are five sayings of popular wisdom, in which **chi** is used (we leave their interpretation and translation to you):

> *Chi* cerca trova.
> *Chi* va piano va sano e va lontano.
> *Chi* di spada ferisce di spada perisce.
> *Chi* tace acconsente.
> *Chi* troppo vuole nulla stringe.

3.6 *Interrogative pronouns and adjectives*

Interrogatives are used to ask questions, mainly about three different aspects:
(a) quantity (b) quality (c) identity (see also Chapter 15).

Quantity:	**Quanto, quanta, quanti, quante?**		
	How much, how many?		
Quality:	**Quale, quali? Che?**		
	Which, which one(s)? What?		
Identity:	Persons	**Chi?**	**Quale?**
		Who? Whom?	Which?
	Things	**Che, che cosa, cosa?**	**Quale?**
		What?	Which?

Quanto, quale and **che** are used both as pronouns (by themselves) and as
adjectives (accompanying a noun). **Chi, che cosa** and **cosa** are used only as
pronouns. Here are a few examples distinguishing the two different functions
(for more examples see Chapter 15):

Pronoun	Adjective
Quant'è?	**Quanti libri hai comprato?**
How much is it?	How many books did you buy?
Quante ne vedi?	**Quante cassette vedi?**
How many do you see?	How many cassettes do you see?
Qual è?	**Quale libro hai comprato?**
Which one is it?	Which book did you buy?
Quali preferisci?	**Quali canzoni preferisci?**
Which ones do you prefer?	Which songs do you prefer?
	Quali amici hai invitato?
	Which friends did you invite?
Chi hai invitato?	
Whom did you invite?	
Che vuoi?	**Che dolce vuoi?**
What do you want?	Which cake do you want?
Che cosa beve?	**Che vino beve?**
What would you like to drink?	Which wine would you like?

3.7   *Possessive pronouns and adjectives*

Possessives indicate the person to whom something or somebody belongs. Like personal pronouns they have six grammatical 'persons' ('my', 'your', 'his', etc.). In Italian each of the six persons has *four* different endings which agree with the noun which they specify (except **loro** which is invariable); for example *il mio* **ragazzo**, *la mia* **macchina**, *i miei* **amici**, *le mie* **scarpe**.

Possessive *pronouns* and *adjectives* are identical in form (whereas English has the variation 'my'/'mine', 'your'/ 'yours', etc.). The pronouns are used on their own to refer to something that has already been mentioned or that is actually present. The adjectives are always attached to a noun.

Adjective:	**Questa è *la mia* scrivania.** This is my desk.
Pronoun:	**E questa è *la tua.*** And this is yours.

The following table shows all the forms of the possessive:

	Singular		Plural	
	Masculine	Feminine	Masculine	Feminine
1	**mio**	**mia**	**miei**	**mie**
2	**tuo**	**tua**	**tuoi**	**tue**
3	**suo**	**sua**	**suoi**	**sue**
4	**nostro**	**nostra**	**nostri**	**nostre**
5	**vostro**	**vostra**	**vostri**	**vostre**
6	**loro**	**loro**	**loro**	**loro**

3.7.1

Use of article with possessives

While in English possessives are *never* accompanied by articles, in Italian the contrary happens: possessives are *always* preceded by an article, except in a few cases. Both article and possessive must agree in gender and number with the noun to which they are attached:

il suo **computer**	'his/her computer'
la sua **macchina**	'his/her car'
i suoi **soldi**	'his/her money'
le sue **colleghe**	'his/her colleagues' (female)

The only exception to this rule is with relatives, but only when they are used in the *singular*:

mia madre	*mio* padre	*mia* sorella	*mio* fratello	*mia* cugina
'my mother'	'my father'	'my sister'	'my brother'	'my cousin' (female)

Note the use of the article with more than one relative:

i miei genitori	*le mie* cugine
'my parents'	'my cousins' (female)

With **loro** 'their', the article is *always* used:

la loro **madre**	*il loro* **zio**
'their mother'	'their uncle'

Again, the article is always used when the noun is qualified in some way by a suffix (e.g. as a term of affection) or an adjective:

la sua **sorellina**	*il mio* **amato zio**
'his/her little sister'	'my beloved uncle'

It is also used – although this is not a firm rule – with **nonno**, **nonna** 'grandfather', 'grandmother' and with the affectionate terms **babbo**, **papà**, **mamma**:

(il) mio nonno	**(la) mia nonna Giuseppina**
'my grandfather'	'my grandmother Giuseppina'
(la) mia mamma	**(il) mio babbo/(il) mio papà**
'my mummy'	'my daddy'

Finally, when used as possessive *pronouns* (i.e. not attached to a noun) the article is often omitted:

> **Di chi sono questi occhiali? Sono** *miei*!
> Whose spectacles are these? They are mine!

3.7.2

Position and omission of the possessive

The possessive adjective is usually placed before the noun. When it follows the noun, it carries a strongly emphatic or emotional meaning:

> **Mamma** *mia*!   **Dio** *mio*!   **Signora** *mia*!   **Figlio** *mio*!

> **Qui siamo in casa** *nostra*!
> Here we are in our own place!

> **Questo dev'essere opera** *tua*!
> This must be your work! (ironical)

In English the possessive is commonly used to indicate personal belongings, or relationships, and parts of the body. In Italian, however, when the relationship or ownership is obvious, as in the examples shown, the possessive is not used; this is particularly true when referring to parts of the body:

> **Porterò** *la* **macchina.**
> I'll bring *my* car.

> **Aveva una giacca sul** *le* **spalle.**
> She had a jacket over *her* shoulders.

> **Lavati** *le* **mani!**
> Wash *your* hands!

> **Mettiti *il* cappotto!**
> Put on *your* coat!

— 3.7.3 —
Possessives as nouns

In a few cases possessives are used on their own, as nouns rather than as pronouns:

> **i miei/i tuoi** 'My/your' (parents)
> **la sua/la vostra del 20.6.95** 'Your (letter) of 20.6.95' (in business correspondence)
> **Alla tua!/Alla nostra!** 'To your/our (health)!' (when making a toast)

— 3.7.4 —
Proprio

Proprio is used as a possessive adjective in three particular contexts:

(a) It can reinforce a normal possessive (like English 'own'):

> **L'ho visto con *i miei propri* occhi!**
> I saw it with my own eyes!

(b) In the third person it can replace **suo**, **loro**, to avoid ambiguity (but only when it refers to the subject of the sentence):

> **Anna disse a Clara che aveva bisogno dei *propri* soldi.**
> Anna told Clara that she needed her (Anna's) money.

> **Quando scrive per il direttore, Luciana preferisce usare il *proprio* computer.**
> When she writes for the manager, Luciana prefers to use her own computer.

(c) It is always used when the subject is an *indefinite* pronoun such as **tutti**, **ognuno**, **nessuno** or impersonal **si** 'one' (see Chapter 19):

> **Tutti fanno i *propri* interessi.**
> Everybody looks after their own interests.

> **Nessuno ammette facilmente i *propri* errori.**
> Nobody easily admits to their mistakes.

> **In tempo di guerra si faceva il *proprio* dovere senza esitazione.**
> In times of war, one did one's duty, without hesitation.

3.8   *Demonstrative pronouns and adjectives*

Demonstratives are used to *indicate* something or somebody actually present when we speak, for example:

> **Dammi *questo* libro.**
> Give me this book.

> **Metti** *quella* **bottiglia in frigorifero.**
> Put that bottle in the fridge.

They can also refer to something or somebody not physically present, but previously mentioned in the discourse. In this function they are useful in connecting two different statements:

> **Ho comprato una macchina familiare, perché** *questa* **mi sembrava più adatta per la nostra famiglia.**
> I bought an estate car, because I thought this was more suitable for our family's needs.

3.8.1

Questo, quello

These demonstratives can be used as adjectives (qualifying a noun as in the first two examples above), or on their own as pronouns (in the last example).

Questo and **quello** correspond exactly to the English 'this' and 'that', indicating respectively something or somebody near to or far away from the speaker/writer (in terms of space, time or position in the discourse).

Note: There is a third demonstrative in Italian: **codesto** used to refer to something far away from the speaker, but near to the person addressed (it is relatively uncommon except in Tuscany).

> **Dammi** *codesto* **libro.**
> Give me that book (the one you have).

In today's language the use of **codesto** is restricted to bureaucratic language, when we want to refer to an office, company or firm (as we do in English by saying 'your company'):

> **Informiamo** *codesta* **spettabile ditta che i nostri prezzi subiranno una variazione dal 30/6 p.v.**
> We would like to inform your company that our prices will change as from 30/6 next.

Questo has four different endings that agree with the gender and number of the noun to which it refers:

> *questo* **vestito** 'this dress'
> *questa* **cravatta** 'this tie'
> *questi* **pantaloni** 'these trousers'
> *queste* **scarpe** 'these shoes'

> **Volevo un paio di scarpe e ho comprato** *queste.*
> I wanted a pair of shoes and I bought these.

> **Cambiati i pantaloni.** *Questi* **sono più comodi.**
> Change your trousers. These are more comfortable.

Quello behaves differently according to whether it is a pronoun or an adjective:

(a) as a pronoun it has four possible endings **-o/-a/-i/-e**, according to the noun to which it refers:

> **Questo vestito è mio.** *Quello* **è tuo.**
> This dress is mine. That one is yours.
>
> **Questa cravatta è mia.** *Quella* **è tua.**
> This tie is mine. That one is yours.
>
> **Questi pantaloni sono miei.** *Quelli* **sono tuoi.**
> These trousers are mine. Those are yours.
>
> **Queste scarpe sono mie.** *Quelle* **sono tue.**
> These shoes are mine. Those are yours.

(b) as an *adjective* it changes its ending, with the same pattern as the definite article (see 1.3.3), and depending on the word that follows:

Il vestito 'dress'	*Quel* vestito	*La* scarpa 'shoe'	*Quella* scarpa
*L'*ombrello 'umbrella'	*Quell'*ombrello	*L'*amica 'friend'	*Quell'*amica
Lo scialle 'shawl'	*Quello* scialle		
I vestiti	*Quei* vestiti	*Le* scarpe 'shoes'	*Quelle* scarpe
Gli ombrelli	*Quegli* ombrelli	*Le* amiche	*Quelle* amiche
Gli scialli	*Quegli* scialli		

Note: The pattern of the demonstrative **quello**, and of the definite article, is followed by another very common adjective: **bello** (see 1.4.5).

3.8.2 **Other demonstrative pronouns: *ciò; costui, costei, costoro; colui, colei, coloro***

These demonstratives are used *only* as pronouns. They are used instead of **questo/quello** but mainly in written language.

(a) **Ciò** refers only to events or ideas, in particular to something that has just been mentioned, usually in the form of a whole phrase, clause or sentence such as:

> **Il treno è arrivato con un'ora di ritardo, e** *ciò* **ci ha fatto perdere l'appuntamento.**
> The train arrived one hour late, and this caused us to miss the appointment.
>
> **Non posso spiegarvi perché abbiamo deciso di partire. Di** *ciò* **abbiamo già parlato nella riunione di ieri.**
> I can't explain why we decided to leave. We already talked about it at yesterday's meeting.

ciò che/... cui is used when referring to something explained subsequently in a *relative* clause:

> **Non ho capito *ciò che* hai detto.**
> I didn't understand what you said.

> **Vorrei spiegarvi *ciò di cui* ha parlato ieri il direttore.**
> I'd like to explain to you what the manager talked about yesterday.

(b) A more formal way to refer to people, is to use **costui/costei/costoro** instead of **questo/questi** and **colui, colei, coloro** instead of **quello/quelli**:

> **Chi è *costui*?**
> Who is this gentleman?

> **Abbiamo inviato una lettera a tutti *coloro che* parteciperanno al congresso.**
> We sent a letter to all those who will take part in the congress.

3.9   *Indefinite pronouns and adjectives*

Indefinite pronouns and *indefinite adjectives* designate somebody or something without a definite specification. In Italian they take various forms.

Indefinites can be divided into three different groups, according to their different grammatical function: (a) as pronouns only; (b) as adjectives only; (c) as pronouns and adjectives. This list shows only the indefinites most commonly used.

3.9.1

Pronouns: *uno, qualcuno, ognuno, chiunque, qualcosa, niente, nulla*
The following are used *only* as pronouns, on their own and not attached to a noun. They are all used only in the singular.

Uno/a 'one', 'somebody', refers to a single person or thing:

> **C'è *uno* che ti cerca.**
> There is a man looking for you.

> **Non ho mai conosciuto *una* come te.**
> I've never met anybody like you.

> **Che belle prugne. Me ne dai *una*?**
> What nice plums! Would you give me one?

Ognuno/a 'each one' (see also **ciascuno** and **ogni** below):

> **Ho comprato un regalo ad *ognuno*.**
> I bought a present for each one.

Ci sono 15 linee telefoniche, *ognuna* con un numero diverso.
There are 15 telephone lines, each with a different number.

Qualcuno/a 'someone', 'some(thing)', refers to an undefined, but small number of people or things:

C'è *qualcuno* alla porta.
There is somebody at the door.

Ho fatto molte fotografie. Vuoi vederne *qualcuna*?
I took a lot of photographs. Do you want to see some?

Chiunque 'anyone', 'whoever', is invariable and refers only to persons. When introducing a relative sentence it is often followed by a verb in the subjunctive (see 2.3.15).

Chiunque può rivolgersi al direttore.
Anyone can go to the manager.

Chiunque sia, non voglio rispondergli.
Whoever it may be, I don't want to answer.

Non aprire mai la porta a *chiunque* chieda di entrare.
Never open the door to anyone who asks to come in.

Qualcosa 'something' is invariable and refers only to things. Note that its gender is usually considered masculine (although **cosa** is feminine) and note the use of **di** (**qualcosa di buono**) when an adjective is used:

C'è sempre *qualcosa* da fare.
There is always something to be done.

Vorrei *qualcosa di buono* da mangiare.
I'd like something good to eat.

Qualcosa è stato fatto, nonostante le difficoltà.
Something has been done, in spite of all the difficulties.

Niente, nulla 'nothing' are also invariable. When placed after a verb, they require a second negative (**non**) before the verb.

Non c'è *niente* da fare.
There is nothing to do.

Non fa *niente*!
It's all right! (Don't worry!)

Non è successo *niente*.
Nothing happened. (Everything is all right.)

Nulla è più bello di una giornata di sole.
Nothing is more beautiful than a sunny day.

3.9.2

Adjectives: *ogni, qualche, qualunque, qualsiasi*

The following are used *only* as adjectives, modifying a noun. They are all *invariable* and used only in the *singular*.

Ogni 'every, each'

> **Faccio la doccia *ogni* giorno.**
> I have a shower every day.

> ***Ogni* volta che entro in ufficio c'è sempre una telefonata per me.**
> Each time I come into my office, there is always a telephone call for me.

> **Dobbiamo controllare i registri *ogni* tre settimane.**
> We must check the registers once every three weeks.

Qualche 'some' is unique in always taking a singular noun, with a plural meaning:

> ***Qualche* volta anche tu sbagli.**
> Sometimes even you make mistakes.

> **Dammi *qualche* francobollo.**
> Give me a few stamps.

> **I soldi arriveranno fra *qualche* giorno.**
> The money will arrive in a few days.

Qualunque, qualsiasi 'any'. Notice that the corresponding pronoun (for referring to persons, see 3.9.1) is **chiunque**:

> **Può venire a trovarmi in *qualunque* momento.**
> You may come to see me at any time.

> **Chiamami pure a *qualunque* ora.**
> Call me at any time.

> **Bisogna essere preparati a *qualsiasi* eventualità.**
> One should be ready for any eventuality.

> **Dobbiamo essere capaci di risolvere *qualsiasi* problema si presenti.**
> We should be able to solve any problem that might arise.

Note the different meaning of **qualunque** when used after the noun:

> **Oggi non è un giorno *qualunque*. È il mio compleanno.**
> Today is not just any old day. It's my birthday.

3.9.3

Pronouns and adjectives: *alcuno, ciascuno, nessuno, tale, altro*

The following are used both as pronouns and as adjectives:

Alcuno/a/i/e 'some', 'a few', is sometimes used as an adjective, with *plural* nouns, instead of the more common **qualche**, which is always singular (see above 3.9.2). In the singular it is only used in *negative* sentences, as an alternative to the more common **nessuno** (see below).

> **Sul mio tavolo ci sono *alcune* pratiche importanti.**
> There are a few important files on my desk.

> **Non ho *alcuna* paura.**
> I have no fear at all.

> **Non c'è *alcun* dubbio.**
> There is no doubt at all.

Ciascuno/a 'each (one)' is only used in the *singular*. It can be used instead of the more common **ogni** (adjective) and **ognuno** (pronoun), see above 3.9.1 and 3.9.2.

> **Nel mio giardino *ciascuna* pianta ha un'etichetta.**
> In my garden each plant has got a label.

> **Ho tre figli e devo sempre comprare un regalo a *ciascuno*.**
> I have three children and I must always buy a present for each (one).

Nessuno/a 'no(one)', 'nobody', is only *singular*. Like **niente, nulla** (see above 3.9.1), when it comes after the verb, it takes a second negative **non**, before the verb.

> **Non c'è *nessuno*.**
> There is nobody.

> **Non c'è *nessun* dubbio.**
> There is no doubt.

> **Non ho visto *nessuna* macchina per strada.**
> I didn't see any cars on the road.

> ***Nessuno* conosce il futuro.**
> Nobody knows the future.

Tale/i 'such', 'a certain', can be singular or plural. When used as a pronoun it refers to an unidentified person (English 'chap', 'bloke', 'fellow'), and is usually preceded by **un** or **quel**:

> **Di là c'è *un tale* che ti cerca.**
> There is a bloke asking for you, next door.

> **Dica a *quel tale* di aspettarmi.**
> Tell that chap to wait for me.

Ho avuto una *tale* paura, che sono rimasto paralizzato.
I was so scared that I froze.

Altro/a/i/e 'other', 'another', can be singular or plural. Used as a pronoun, **altro** can refer to people or things, or can be used in idiomatic expressions, as in the last two examples.

Desidera un *altro* caffè?
Would you like another coffee?

Sì, grazie, ne vorrei un *altro*.
Yes, please, I'd like another one.

Non mi interessa quello che dicono gli *altri*.
I am not interested in what others say.

Desidera qualcos'*altro*?
Would you like anything else?

Ci sono degli *altri*?
Is there anybody else?

Senz'*altro*!
Certainly!

***Altro* ché!**
No wonder!

4 Prepositions

4.1 *What is a preposition?*

In Italian there are eight prepositions which are used more than any others:

di, a, da, in, con, su, per, tra (or **fra**)

The basic function of a *preposition* is to introduce some additional information to a verb or a noun, in the form of a '*complement*' (something which *completes* the verb):

Abbiamo parlato *di* Anna.
We talked about Anna.

Qual è il numero *di* Teresa?
What is Teresa's phone number?

The complement can be either a noun:

Vado *a* Roma.
I go to Rome.

Or a verb:

Vado *a* lavorare.
I go to work.

When prepositions introduce a verb, as in the last example above, their function is very similar to that of *conjunctions* (see Chapter 5) except for the differences shown below:

Prepositions (for example **di**) always introduce verbs in the *infinitive* (**parlare**):

Spero *di* parlare con Carlo domani.
I hope I'll talk to Carlo tomorrow.

Conjunctions (such as **che**) introduce verbs in the indicative, conditional or subjunctive moods (here, **parli**):

Spero *che* tu parli con Carlo domani.
I hope you'll talk to Carlo tomorrow.

4.2   *Combined prepositions and articles*

Six of the eight important prepositions listed above combine with the *definite article* to give the forms shown below:

	lo	*l'*	*i*	*gli*	*la*	*le*
a	allo	all'	ai	agli	alla	alle
da	dallo	dall'	dai	dagli	dalla	dalle
di	dello	dell'	dei	degli	della	delle
in	nello	nell'	nei	negli	nella	nelle
su	sullo	sull'	sui	sugli	sulla	sulle
con	collo	coll'	coi	cogli	colla	colle

Note particularly how **in** + the definite article changes to **nel**, **nella**, etc.

In the case of **con** the combination with the article is optional, and rarely used in writing. In the other five cases the use of the compound form is essential.

4.3   *Use of prepositions with nouns*

We now give a few detailed examples showing the basic uses of the most common prepositions. Some examples have been chosen to stress the difference between Italian and English usage. Note especially those cases in which *no* preposition is needed in English, and particularly where we use **di** and **a** in Italian. A good dictionary can provide even more examples.

4.3.1

Di

Di is the most frequently used of all Italian prepositions. Although it is often translated by the English 'of', its meaning is rather undefined, and in fact it has many different functions, some of which are shown below:

Specification:	la **difficoltà** *del* **lavoro** 'the difficulty of the job'
	frutta *di* **stagione** 'fresh fruit'
Belonging:	la **macchina** *di* **Giulia** 'Giulia's car'
	la **casa** *di* **mio padre** 'my father's house'
	di **chi è la giacca?** 'whose jacket is this?'
Origin:	sono *di* **Napoli** 'I am from Naples'
	Anna è *di* **Ayr** 'Anna is from Ayr'
Comparison:	sono **più alto** *di* **te** 'I'm taller than you'
Material:	**tavolo** *di* **legno** 'wooden table'
	cavo *d'***acciaio** 'steel cable'
Author:	la '**Commedia**' *di* **Dante** 'the "Comedy" by Dante'
	'**Amarcord**' *di* **F. Fellini** ' "Amarcord" by F. Fellini'
Topic:	**parliamo** *di* **affari** 'let's talk about business'
	una lezione *di* **storia** 'a lecture on history'
Time:	*di* **giorno**, *di* **notte** 'by day, by night'

	*d'***inverno fa freddo** 'it's cold in winter'
Place/ Movement:	*di* **qui**, *di* **là** 'over here, over there'
	di **sopra**, *di* **sotto** 'upstairs, downstairs'

Note how, before a word beginning with a vowel, **di** is elided to **d'**.

See 4.4 below for the use of **di** with verbs.

For the use of **di** + article (**del**, **dello . . .**) as a partitive or indefinite article see 1.3.2 and 11.6.1.

--- 4.3.2 ---

A

The basic relationship (or 'complement') expressed by the preposition **a** is that of direction towards some person, place or time (i.e. the *indirect object* of the action expressed by a verb). However, as in the case of **di**, this preposition has many and varied uses, beyond its basic meaning of 'to', 'at':

Indirect object:	**dire qualcosa** *a* **qualcuno** 'to say something to somebody'
	ho scritto *a* **mia sorella** 'I wrote to my sister'
'To' (place):	**andiamo** *a* **Parigi** 'we're going to Paris'
	vado *a* **casa** 'I'm going home'
'In'/'at' (place):	**vivo** *a* **Parma** 'I live in Parma'
	lavoro *all'***Università** 'I work at the University'
Time:	*alle* **tre** 'at three o'clock'
	a **mezzanotte** 'at midnight'
Means:	**andiamo** *a* **piedi** 'let's walk'
	lavorato *a* **mano** 'hand-made'
Manner:	**spaghetti** *alle* **vongole** 'spaghetti with clams'
	ragù *alla* **bolognese** 'Bolognese meat sauce'
Quality:	**televisione** *a* **colori** 'colour TV'
	pentola *a* **pressione** 'pressure cooker'

Note that movement *to* a place can be expressed by other prepositions such as **in** and **da**:

> **vado** *a* **scuola** 'I'm going to school'
> **vado** *in* **ufficio** 'I'm going to the office'
> **vado** *da* **Roberta** 'I'm going to Roberta's'

Also note that we always need to use **a** to express the *indirect object* even when the preposition can be omitted in English (except with *unstressed* pronouns, see last example below):

> **ho dato il libro** *a* **Paolo** 'I gave Paolo the book'
> **ho dato il libro** *a* **lui** 'I gave *him* the book'
> *gli* **ho dato il libro** 'I gave him the book'

When followed by a word beginning with a vowel, **a** can change to **ad** to help pronunciation:

> **ho dato il libro** *ad* **Anna** 'I gave the book to Anna'

For the use of **a** with verbs, see 4.4 below.

4.3.3

Da

The basic meaning of **da** is direction *from* some point in space or in time, and in fact it is often used with **venire**. However **da** is used to represent many other relationships; it can even indicate movement *to* somewhere, when used with **andare** (but only when the objective is an individual, indicated by name or by trade, as in the second set of examples):

From a place:	**veniamo *da* Genova** 'we come from Genoa'
	veniamo *dall'*Inghilterra 'we come from England'
To a place:	**andiamo *da* Giorgio** 'we go to Giorgio's' (home)
	andiamo *dal* dentista 'we go to the dentist's' (surgery)
At a place:	**stasera dormi *da* me** 'tonight you're staying at my place'
	Lucia è *dal* direttore 'Lucia is in the manager's office'
Through a place:	**il treno passa *da* Pisa** 'the train passes through Pisa'
	è uscito *dalla* finestra 'he went out through the window'
Agent:	**fu colpito *da* una palla** 'he was hit by a ball'
	amato *da* tutti 'loved by everyone'
Since:[†]	**lavoro *da* tre anni** 'I've been working for three years'
	viaggiamo *dalle* sette 'we have been travelling since seven o'clock'
Function:	**spazzolino *da* denti** 'toothbrush'
	crema *da* barba 'shaving-cream'
Cause:	**morte *da* infarto** 'death from heart attack'
	stress *da* lavoro 'work-related stress'
Manner:	**vita *da* cani** 'dog's life'
	giochi *da* bambini 'child's play'
Value:	**moneta da L200** 'L200 coin'

[†]For this use of **da** with verbs, see Chapter 12.

4.3.4

In

The basic meaning of **in** is not different from that of the corresponding preposition in English, but it indicates both position in space and time, as well as movement *into* somewhere:

'In' (place):	**i bicchieri sono *in* cucina** 'the glasses are in the kitchen'
	abito *in* Francia 'I live in France'
'To' (place):	**vado *in* Francia** 'I'm going to France'
	domani vengo *in* ufficio 'I'll come to the office tomorrow'
'In' (time):	**mi sono laureato *nel* '76** 'I graduated in 1976'
	mi preparo *in* 5 minuti 'I'll get ready in five minutes'
Means:	**devo andare *in* macchina** 'I must go by car'
	pagheremo *in* dollari 'we'll pay in dollars'
Matter:	**rifiniture *in* pelle** 'trimmings in leather'
	camicia *in* seta grezza 'raw silk shirt'
Mood/ style:	***in* buona fede** 'in good faith'
	voglio vivere *in* pace 'I wish to live in peace'

Con

Basically **con** corresponds to the English 'with':

Together:	**stasera ceno *con* Gigi** 'I'll have dinner with Gigi tonight'
	***con* chi stai parlando?** 'who are you talking to?' (*literally*: 'with whom are you talking?')
Means:	**lavoro molto *col* telefono** 'I work on the telephone a lot'
	si accende *con* il telecomando 'it's switched on by remote control'

Su

su indicates a position, for example English 'on' 'upon' 'above' or a topic:

On:	**i piatti sono *sul* tavolo** 'the dishes are on the table'
	andiamo a sciare *sulle* Dolomiti 'we go skiing in the Dolomites'
Topic:	**notizie *sul* mercato** 'market report'
	un articolo *su* Pirandello 'an article on Pirandello'
Approximation:	**un uomo *sui* trent'anni** 'a man of around thirty'
	costa *sui* due milioni 'it costs about two million'

When indicating a position ('upon some place'), the preposition **sopra** is also commonly used (see 4.5):

i piatti sono *sopra* il tavolo 'the dishes are on the table'

Per

In addition to its basic meanings of English 'for', **per** is also used in several other contexts. Here are a few cases:

Through/along:	**siamo passati *per* Londra** 'we passed through London'
	andiamo *per* l'autostrada 'let's go by the motorway'
	parliamo *per* telefono 'we talk on the phone'
Destination:	**parto *per* il Giappone** 'I'm leaving for Japan'
	c'è posta *per* me? 'is there any mail for me?'
Limitation:	***per* me è sbagliato** 'as far as I am concerned, it is wrong'
	***per* ora aspettiamo** 'we'll wait, for the moment'
Distribution:	**catalogo *per* autore** 'catalogue by author'
	divisi *per* età 'divided by age group'
	5 *per* 5 fa 25 '5 times 5 makes 25'

For the use of **per** with verbs see below, 4.4.

Tra, fra

These two prepositions have exactly the same meaning. Their basic meaning is the English 'between' or 'among':

Between/among:	***fra* me e te** 'between you and me'
	***tra* la gente** 'among the people'
Distance:	***tra* un anno** 'in a year's time'
	***fra* tre chilometri** 'in three kilometres'

4.4   *Use of prepositions with verbs*

Prepositions often introduce a dependent clause in the infinitive such as:

Cerca *di* capire.	Try to understand.
Vieni *a* vedere.	Come to see.
Lavoro *per* guadagnare.	I work in order to earn money.

In this function the role of the preposition is similar to that of a conjunction, although with some special differences (see below).

Di, **a**, **da** and **per** are the prepositions most commonly used in this function. It is impossible to give precise rules on the use of these prepositions, which mainly depend on the verb they accompany. Use a dictionary to find out about the different constructions possible with each verb. Here are a few guidelines and examples.

Di is used when the dependent verb expresses the *object* (the *end*), or the *subject* of the action of the main verb. It is also frequently used with a verb of completion, or ending:

> **Penso *di* partire presto.**
> I'm thinking of leaving early.

> **Ho finito *di* scrivere.**
> I've finished writing.

> **Mi pare *di* impazzire.**
> I feel as if I am going mad. (*literally*: It seems to me to be going mad.)

> **Sforzati *di* mangiare.**
> Make an effort to eat.

A is mainly used to indicate the *aim, end* or *intention* of the main verb. It is also often used with a verb expressing 'beginning' or 'starting out':

> **Vado *a* sciare.**
> I'm going to ski.

> **Pensa *a* studiare.**
> You'd better think about studying.

> **Cominciate *a* lavorare.**
> Start working.

Da indicates that 'something must be done' – a *passive* sense – rather than that 'someone has to do something':

> **Ho molto *da* fare.**
> I've got a lot to do. (*literally*: a lot to be done)

> **Ci sono due lettere *da* scrivere.**
> There are two letters to write (to be written).

> **Cosa prende *da* bere?**
> What would you like to drink?

Per is used to state explicitly the *aim* of an action (as in English 'in order to'):

> **Sono venuto *per* parlarti.**
> I came in order to speak to you.

> **Ho bisogno di tempo *per* finire il lavoro.**
> I need time in order to complete the job.

Note how in Italian the verb introduced by a preposition must always have the same subject as the main verb. If the subject is different a *conjunction* (**che**, etc.) must be used, and the dependent verb cannot be in the infinitive, but has to be a *finite* verb in the indicative or subjunctive:

> **Credo *di* avere ragione.**
> I think I am right.

> **Credo *che* tu abbia ragione.**
> I think you are right.

Some very frequently used verbs introduce dependent verbs in the infinitive without the use of a preposition. The most important are: **dovere, potere, volere** (see Chapter 2), **sapere, fare, preferire, amare, osare**:

> **Vorrei dormire.**
> I'd like to sleep.

> **Non so nuotare.**
> I don't know how to swim.

> **Preferisco vivere da solo.**
> I prefer to live alone.

4.5   *Other prepositions*

In addition to the eight most common prepositions shown above, there are many other prepositions. Here are the most common, expressing:

(a) Position in space:

dentro 'inside'	**fuori** 'outside'	**davanti a** 'before'
dietro 'behind'	**vicino** 'near'	**lontano da** 'far from'
sotto 'under'	**sopra** 'on', 'above'	**lungo** 'along'
oltre 'beyond'	**verso** 'towards'	**presso** 'near', 'at'

(b) Position in time:

prima di 'before'   **dopo** 'after'   **durante** 'during'

(c) Other features:

mediante 'by means of'   **secondo** 'according to'   **senza** 'without'
insieme a 'together with'   **come** 'as'   **contro** 'against'

All these prepositions can be distinguished from the eight common prepositions illustrated previously because:

(a) They are all words of more than one syllable, and are often found together with another preposition, for example **prima di**, **davanti a**, **insieme a** . . .

(b) Some prepositions are also used as adverbs (see Chapter 6). As such, they can be used on their own to modify a verb, for example:

> **Arriverò** *dopo* **le cinque.**
> I shall arrive after five o'clock.

> **Arriverò** *dopo.*
> I shall arrive afterwards.

> **Si sieda** *davanti al* **banco.**
> Please, have a seat at the counter.

> **Si sieda** *davanti.*
> Please, have a seat in front.

(c) Some of these prepositions introduce either a noun or a verb complement:

> **Partirò** *prima di* **cena.**
> I'll leave before dinner.

> **Partirò** *prima di* **cenare.**
> I'll leave before having dinner.

5 Conjunctions

5.1   *What is a conjunction?*

The role of conjunctions ('joining words') is to link two sentences or parts of a sentence, either clauses, phrases or simply groups of words. The conjunctions, together with other elements such as pronouns and prepositions, help to connect the thread of logic that runs through any discourse or text. The links formed by conjunctions can be of two different types: coordination or subordination.

5.2   *Coordinating conjunctions*

Two clauses, or groups of words are called *coordinated* when they have the *same syntactical status*, for example:

When they are both subjects of the same verb:

> **Luciano *e* Gianni sono italiani.**
> Luciano and Gianni are Italian.

or they are clauses of equal weight/value:

> **Il cane dorme *e* il gatto mangia.**
> The dog is sleeping and the cat is eating.

The different types of coordinating conjunctions fulfil different functions, depending on the relationship between the two clauses or parts of the sentence.

5.2.1
Simple coordinating conjunctions
E 'and' is the most common of the coordinating conjunctions. When followed by a word beginning with a vowel it may change into **ed** to help pronunciation (**tu *ed* io . . .**).

Other simple coordinating conjunctions are:

anche, pure 'also'	**neanche, neppure** 'neither', 'nor'
o, oppure 'or'	

> **Flavia parla italiano ed *anche* spagnolo.**
> Flavia speaks Italian and also Spanish.

Marina si iscriverà all'Università di Siena *oppure* al Politecnico di Torino.
Marina will enrol at Siena University or else at the Politecnico in Turin.

Double conjunctions

Sometimes two or more conjunctions are used to create a relationship between several corresponding elements of a clause or sentence:

e ... e 'both ... and'	**o ... o** 'either ... or'
sia ... sia 'both ... and'	**né ... né** 'neither ... nor'
non solo ... ma anche 'not only ... but also'	

***Né* io *né* mio marito abbiamo il tempo di pulire la casa.**
Neither I nor my husband have time to clean the house.

Vediamo le stesse persone *sia* in città *sia* al mare.
We see the same people both in town and at the seaside.
(The pair **sia ... sia** is often substituted by the pair **sia ... che**.)

Napoli è una città interessante *non solo* dal punto di vista archeologico, *ma anche* dal punto di vista culturale.
Naples is an interesting city, not only from an archaeological point of view, but also from a cultural one.

Explanatory conjunctions

These connect one clause, phrase or sentence with a second one which *explains* the meaning of the first more fully:

cioè, infatti 'indeed', 'really'

Arriveremo domani, *cioè* sabato.
We will arrive tomorrow, in other words Saturday.

Non è andata bene l'ispezione. *Infatti* è andata malissimo.
The inspection didn't go well. In fact it went very badly.

Cioè can also be used to *correct* a previous statement:

Vado io a prendere il pane, *cioè* no, vai tu, perché sai dove andare.
I'll go and get the bread, no, *you* go, because you know where to go.

Contrasting conjunctions

These connect a clause or sentence, whose content is in *contrast* with the preceding one:

ma, però 'but'
tuttavia 'yet'
anzi, piuttosto 'on the contrary', 'rather'

Diana non è stupida, *anzi* è molto intelligente.
Diana is not stupid, on the contrary she's very intelligent.

Se c'è traffico, non fate l'autostrada, *piuttosto* prendete le strade di campagna.
If there's traffic, don't go on the motorway, rather take the country roads.

5.2.5 ### Conjunctions of sequence or consequence

These introduce a clause or sentence whose content is a direct follow-on or a *consequence* of the preceding one:

dunque, quindi, perciò, allora 'therefore', 'so', 'then'

Laura ha capelli biondi, *quindi* si capisce subito che è straniera.
Laura has blond hair, so people realize immediately that she's a foreigner.

Il bambino è nato prematuro, *perciò* è a rischio.
The baby was born premature so he's at risk.

Il treno è arrivato in ritardo e *allora* Marco ha preso il tassì per arrivare prima.
The train arrived late, so Marco took a taxi to get there quicker.

Each of these conjunctions produces a sequence of sentences or clauses that are connected, but still independent of each other, and which could just as well stand alone. These are called *coordinated* sentences.

5.3   *Subordinating conjunctions*

We say that a sentence is subordinate to another one when it has the function of completing it. There is a relationship of dependence, in which there is a *main* sentence and a *dependent* one. Certain specific conjunctions are used to indicate this relationship; their role is similar to that of prepositions in introducing a 'complement' (as seen in 4.1 and 4.4 above). Dependent sentences cannot stand alone, but exist only in relation to the main sentence.

Relationships of subordination are frequently found in Italian, certainly more so than in English, so it is important to understand the role of the various conjunctions. In Italian a dependent verb introduced by a *preposition* must be in the infinitive and its subject must be the *same* as that of the main verb (see 4.4 above):

Spero *di* vincere.
I hope to win.

A *subordinating conjunction*, instead, introduces a verb that can be in the indicative, conditional or subjunctive mood, and whose subject may be a *different* one from that of the main verb:

Indicative:	**So *che* loro hanno vinto.**
	I know they have won.
Conditional:	**Capisco *che* voi vorreste vincere.**
	I understand that you would like to win.
Subjunctive:	**Spero *che* la nostra squadra vinca.**
	I hope our team wins.

The mood and tense of the dependent verbs, introduced by the conjunction **che**, depends on the nature of the main verb (**so, capisco, spero**) and on the time relationship between the two verbs.

Some of the most common of these conjunctions, with a few examples, follow.

5.3.1

Che

Che is the most frequently used of all subordinating conjunctions. This function of **che** has to be distinguished from its function as a relative pronoun (see Chapter 3).

The different kinds of sentences introduced by **che** can be identified on the basis of their relationship with the main verb, on which they depend. (See Section IV throughout.) Here are some examples:

Object:	**Ho detto *che* sono stanco.**
	I said that I am tired.
Subject:	**È meglio *che* tu vada a letto.**
	It's better that you go to bed.
Consequence:	**Sono così stanco *che* andrei a letto subito.**
	I'm so tired that I'd go to bed immediately.
Comparison:	**È più facile dirlo *che* farlo.**
	It's easier to say it than to do it.

5.3.2

Perché

Cause:	**Mio figlio piange *perché* ha fame.**
	My son is crying because he is hungry.
Purpose:	**Ti parlo *perché* tu possa capirmi.**
	I am speaking to you so that you can understand.
Indirect question:	**Dimmi *perché* vuoi andare via.**
	Tell me why you want to go away.

For more information on purpose and reason, see Chapters 33 and 34; for indirect questions, see Chapter 31.

Se

Condition:	**Se piove non esco.**
	If it rains I won't go out.
	Se avessi i soldi farei un viaggio negli USA.
	If I had the money I'd go on a trip to the USA.
Indirect question:	**Dimmi se capisci.**
	Tell me whether you understand (or not).

For more details on the use of **se** in 'if' clauses, as in the first two examples, see 38.2 and 38.3.

Quando, mentre, appena

Time:	**Scrivimi *appena* arrivi.**
	Write to me as soon as you arrive.
	***Quando* l'ho visto l'ho salutato.**
	When I saw him I said hello.
	Sono arrivato *mentre* telefonavi.
	I arrived while you were on the phone.

For further information on time, see Chapter 36.

| *Indirect question*: | **Non so *quando* mi pagheranno.** |
| | I don't know when they'll pay me. |

Affinché, benché, sebbene, purché, prima che, senza che

Some conjunctions require the use of the *subjunctive* mood. This is because of the meaning of the conjunction, and the nature of the relationship between the main verb and the dependent verb (see 2.3.15):

Concessive:	**neanche se** 'not even if', **anche se** 'even if', **nonostante** 'despite', **benché** 'although', **sebbene** 'even though'
	Sono venuto in uffico, *nonostante* avessi la febbre.
	I came to the office, although I had a fever.
	Non vorrei una motocicletta *neanche se* me la regalassero.
	I wouldn't like to have a motorbike not even if I was given one for free.
Purpose:	**perché, affinché** 'so that', 'in order to'
	Il direttore ha dato un computer alla segretaria *perché* lavorasse meglio.

The manager bought the secretary a computer so that she could work better.

Restrictive: **a meno che** 'unless', **senza che** 'without', 'unless', **tranne che** 'except that', **salvo che** 'unless', 'except for', **nel caso (che)** 'just in case'

Possiamo andare, *a meno che* tu non abbia ancora da fare.
We can go now, unless you still have something to do.

Ti lascio le chiavi della macchina *nel caso* tu ne avessi bisogno.
I'll leave you my car keys, just in case you might need them.

For information on these types of sentences, see Chapters 33 and 39.

6 Adverbs

6.1

6.1   *What is an adverb?*

Adverbs are invariable words whose main function is to modify the meaning of a verb. This function can be compared to that of adjectives qualifying a noun.

Adjective:	**Viviamo una vita *tranquilla*.**
	We live a quiet life.
Adverb:	**Viviamo *tranquillamente*.**
	We live quietly.

However certain adverbs such as **molto**, **poco** (see 6.2.2) can also be used to modify other words, in particular adjectives or other adverbs:

La mia vita è *molto* tranquilla.
My life is very quiet.

Viviamo *molto* tranquillamente.
We live very quietly.

6.2   *Types of adverbs*

6.2.1   Adverbs formed with *-mente*

The most typical form of Italian adverbs is that derived from an adjective, with the addition of the suffix **-mente**. This is similar to the English pattern of adverbs formed with the suffix '-ly' (quiet/quiet*ly*, slow/slow*ly*).

(a) For adjectives in the first group (**-o**/**-a**/**-i**/**-e** type, see 1.4.2) **-mente** is added to the feminine singular form (ending in **-a**):

tranquillo	*tranquillamente*	**lento**	*lentamente*
attento	*attentamente*	**serio**	*seriamente*

(b) For adjectives in the second group (the **-e**/**-i** type), the suffix **-mente** is simply added to their singular form; with adjectives ending in **-le** and **-re**, the **e** is dropped first:

semplice	*semplicemente*	**veloce**	*velocemente*
faci*le*	*facilmente*	**particolare**	*particolarmente*

6.2.2

Adjectives used as adverbs

Some of the most commonly used adverbs in Italian are in fact also used as adjectives: **molto, poco, troppo, tanto, quanto.** When used as adjectives these words must agree in gender and number with the noun that they qualify, following the pattern **-o/-a/-i/-e.** They are, however, invariable (keeping the masculine singular form) when they are used as adverbs:

Used as an adjective:

Ho molt*i* amic*i*.	I have many (boy)friends.
Ho molt*e* amic*he*.	I have many (girl)friends.

Used as an adverb:

Lavoro molt*o*.	I work a lot.
Lavoriamo molt*o*.	We work a lot.
Carla è molt*o* stanca.	Carla is very tired.
Gianni è molt*o* stanco.	Gianni is very tired.

Many other adjectives are used as adverbs without any change in form:

Non ti capisco quando parli *veloce* (= velocemente).
I don't understand you when you speak fast.

Capisco bene quando parli *chiaro* (= chiaramente).
I understand well when you speak clearly.

6.2.3

Prepositional phrases used as adverbs

Another alternative to an adverb, is a phrase consisting of *noun and preposition*, for example:

Ha guidato *con molta attenzione.*
He drove with great care.

Gli studenti devono imparare a lavorare *in modo autonomo.*
The students have to learn to work independently.

For more information on the use of adverbial phrases, etc., see Chapter 37.

6.2.4

Simple adverbs

Some adverbs are not derived from, or connected to, any adjective. They are words used exclusively as adverbs. Here is a list of the most common of these, divided into categories by meaning.

Time:

ora, adesso 'now'	**allora** 'then'
ancora 'still'	**già** 'already'
tardi 'late'	**presto** 'soon', 'early'
oggi 'today'	**ieri** 'yesterday'
domani 'tomorrow'	**l'altro ieri** 'the day before yesterday'
dopo, poi 'after'	**prima** 'before'

	subito 'immediately'	**spesso** 'often'
	sempre 'always'	**mai** 'never'
Place:	**qui, qua** 'here'	**lì, là** 'there'
	quaggiù 'down here'	**quassù** 'up here'
	laggiù 'down there'	**lassù** 'up there'
	sopra 'above'	**sotto** 'beneath'
	altrove 'elsewhere'	**oltre** 'further'
	dentro 'inside'	**fuori** 'outside'
	dietro 'behind'	**davanti** 'in front'
	dappertutto 'everywhere'	
Question:	**come?** 'how?'	**dove?** 'where?'
	perché? 'why?'	**quando?** 'when?'
Quality:	**bene** 'well'	**male** 'badly'
	volentieri 'willingly'	
Doubt:	**forse** 'perhaps'	**quasi** 'almost'
Assertion:	**appunto** 'just', 'indeed', 'precisely', 'exactly'	

Some adverbs of time and place can be combined with a preposition (see Chapter 4), and attached to a noun or pronoun, for example, and used as *a preposition*:

> **dopo di, prima di, sopra a, sotto a, davanti a, dietro a, dentro a, fuori a/da, oltre a ...**

> **Siamo arrivati *dopo di* voi.**
> We arrived after you.

> **Mi piace sedermi *davanti al* caminetto.**
> I like to sit in front of the fireplace.

> **Mettetevi la giacca *prima di* uscire.**
> Put your jacket on before you go out.

A few of the most common adverbs can have a suffix added to them, which can convey a more limited intensity of meaning, or a particular tone, such as affection. This usage is mainly limited to spoken Italian:

> **Ha solo 1 anno, ma parla *benino*.**
> She's only one year old, but she speaks quite well.

> **Come ti senti adesso? *Maluccio*.**
> How do you feel now? Not too bad.

6.2.5

Unstressed adverbs of place: *ci, vi, ne*

One very common adverb of place is the unstressed particle **ci** (less commonly the form **vi**) used with the meaning of 'here/there' in expressions such as:

> **c'è, *ci* sono** 'there is', 'there are'
> ***ci* vado, *ci* vengo** 'I go there', 'I come here'

Ne as an adverb of place has the meaning of 'from here'/'from there' (see also 3.4.4):

> **Me *ne* vado** 'I'm going away'
> **Andatev*ene*** 'Go away'

These adverbs are similar to the corresponding unstressed personal pronouns (see 3.4), in form and behaviour; for example, they can also be combined with other pronouns, as in the examples above (see 3.4.4). However in these examples, their meaning and function is clearly that of an adverb.

6.3   *Comparative and superlative adverbs*

We can make comparisons with adverbs, as we do with adjectives, using comparative and superlative forms.

Adverb	Comparative	Superlative (absolute)
molto	*più*	*moltissimo*
poco	*meno*	*pochissimo*
sicuramente	più/meno sicuramente	sicurissimamente (molto sicuramente)
velocemente	più/meno velocemente	velocissimamente (molto velocemente)
presto	più/meno presto	prestissimo (molto presto)
tardi	più/meno tardi	tardissimo (molto tardi)

Two adverbs with 'special' forms are:

bene	*meglio*	benissimo (molto bene)
male	*peggio*	malissimo (molto male)

Some examples of usage:

> **Si scrive *più velocemente* col computer che a mano.**
> One can write faster with a computer than by hand.

> **Ieri sera siamo andati a letto *tardissimo*.**
> Yesterday evening we went to bed very late.

> **È *meglio* lavorare in gruppo che lavorare da soli.**
> To work in a team is better than to work alone.

> **Oggi mi sento *benissimo*.**
> Today I feel very well.

> **Teresa suona il piano *peggio* di Giovanni.**
> Teresa plays the piano worse than Giovanni.

> **Per favore guida *un po' più* piano.**
> Please drive a bit slower (a bit more slowly).

The superlatives shown above are *absolute* superlatives, i.e. they do *not* suggest a comparison; but it is also possible to form a *relative* superlative, by using **il più ... possibile** or, with the particular forms shown above, **il meglio/peggio possibile**:

> **Partiamo** *il più presto possibile.*
> Let us leave as early as possible.

> **Controlli il contratto** *il più attentamente possibile.*
> Check the contract as carefully as possible.

The superlative adverbs **il meglio** 'best', **il peggio** 'worst' can also have the function of nouns, as in the expressions below:

> **Do** *il meglio* **di me stesso quando posso lavorare in modo autonomo.**
> I give the best of myself when I can work independently.

> *Il peggio* **deve ancora venire.**
> The worst is still to come.

7 Numbers

7.1 ## What is a number?

Grammatically, numbers can be considered as belonging to several categories, depending on their different functions.

A number can be used as a *noun*:

> **Il *cinque* è un numero dispari.**
> Five is an odd number.

> **Ci vediamo alle *nove*.**
> See you at nine o'clock.

as an *adjective* (with a noun):

> **Mi servono *tre* fogli di carta.**
> I need three sheets of paper.

or as a *pronoun* (on its own):

> **Quanti fogli di carta ti servono? Me ne servono *tre*.**
> How many sheets do you need? I need three.

7.2 ## Cardinal numbers

Cardinals are the basic numbers. A list of cardinal numbers is shown at the end of this chapter. Note in particular the elision of the vowel in **ventuno**, **trentotto** and the acute accent in **trentatré**.

All cardinal numbers are invariable except **uno/una**, which is used also as an indefinite article, whose forms vary according to the word that follows (see 1.3.2 for all the possible variations). With numbers ending in **-uno**, the final vowel is often dropped:

> **trent*un* giorni** 'thirty-one days'

> **Ha compiuto vent*un* anni.**
> She's turned twenty-one.

Numbers with more than one element are joined together, for example:

4.944	4,944
quattromilanovecentoquarantaquattro	

When the first element is **cento** or **mille**, these can remain separate, but joined by **e**:

1.002	1,002
mille *e* due	

milione 'million' can also remain separate and *not* joined by **e**:

2.350.000	2,350,000
due milioni trecentocinquantamila	

Note the singular **mille** 'one thousand' but plural **-mila** in compounds: **duemila**, **tremila**, **centomila** 'two thousand', 'three thousand', 'one hundred thousand'.

Decimal point:

In Italian, contrary to English usage, a **virgola** 'comma' is used to denote the decimal point, while for figures above a thousand, a **punto** 'full stop' is used:

2,5	2.5
due *virgola* cinque	two point five
1.500	1,500
millecinquecento	

When describing how people or objects are arranged or distributed, we use the prepositions **a** (**a due a due**) or **per**:

Ragazzi, mettetevi in fila *due per due*.
Kids, get in line (line up) two by two.

Signori, entrate *uno per volta*, per favore.
Ladies and gentlemen, come in one at a time, please.

7.3   *Ordinal numbers*

Ordinal numbers (except the first ten, whose special forms can be seen in 7.9) are all formed by adding the suffix **-esimo**. The final vowel of the cardinal number drops before the suffix: **undic-esimo**, **dodic-esimo**, **quarant-esimo**, **cent-esimo**.

These numbers are basically used as adjectives and can be masculine, feminine, singular and plural, changing their ending (with the pattern **-o/-a/-i/-e**) in agreement with the noun to which they are attached:

Sto scrivendo il *sesto* capitolo.
I am writing the sixth chapter.

la *dodicesima* **notte** 'the twelfth night'

They come *after* the noun when used with the names of rulers, always written as a Roman number:

Enrico *VIII* 'Henry the eighth'

However in some cases they are used on their own, referring to something which is understood from the context, for example:

The gears of a car:

la prima, la quarta (marcia) 'first', 'fourth gear'

For schools, referring to classes, grades or years:

Mio figlio frequenta la prima (classe) media, e mia figlia la terza.
My son is in the first year of middle school, and my daughter is in the third.

Referring to units of time:

(minuti) primi, secondi 'minutes', 'seconds'

Ci vogliono due ore, quattro primi e trenta secondi.
It takes two hours, four minutes and thirty seconds.

decimi, centesimi (di secondo) 'tenths', 'hundredths of a second'

Ordinal numbers are also used in *fractions* as:

1/10 un decimo 'a tenth'
2/3 due terzi 'two-thirds'
5/12 cinque dodicesimi 'five-twelfths'

Note also:

la metà, il mezzo 'half'
mezza porzione di spaghetti al burro 'a half portion of spaghetti with butter'
mezzo litro di vino rosso 'half a litre of red wine'

7.4   *Calculations*

Here are some examples of basic arithmetical calculations in Italian:

+ **più** 'plus'	$5 + 6 = 11$ **cinque più sei uguale undici**
– **meno** 'less'	$9 - 3 = 6$ **nove meno tre uguale sei**
: **diviso** 'divided by'	$8 : 2 = 4$ **otto diviso due uguale quattro**
× **per** 'multiplied by'	$3 \times 8 = 24$ **tre per otto uguale ventiquattro**
= **uguale** 'equals'	

In informal speech, **fa** 'makes' is also used:

$2 + 2 = 4$ **due più due *fa* quattro**

<table>
<tr><td>**7.5**</td><td></td></tr>
</table>

7.5   *Percentages*

Percentages are always preceded by an article:

> *Il* 15% **del nostro fatturato consiste in prodotti alimentari.**
> 15% of our turnover is in foodstuffs.

> **La lira si è svalutata** *del* 20% **(venti percento).**
> The lira has been devalued by 20%.

> **Il mio reddito si è ridotto** *del* 50%.
> My income has been reduced by 50%.

Note the article **l'** used with an initial vowel sound:

> *l'* **ottanta percento** '80 per cent'

7.6   *Collective and approximate numbers*

Note the use of suffixes in the following:

> **una dec***ina* 'about ten'
> **una doz***zina* 'a dozen'
> **un'or***etta* 'a short hour' (just for an hour)

The suffix **-ina** is used with numbers to express approximation:

> **C'era** *una ventina di* **spettatori.**
> There were about twenty spectators.

> **Passo** *una quindicina di* **giorni in montagna.**
> I'm spending a fortnight in the mountains.

As is the suffix **-aio** in **centin***aio***, migli***aio**:

> *un centinaio* **di persone** 'about a hundred people'
> *un migliaio* 'about a thousand'

These have an irregular feminine plural form:

> *varie migliaia* **di clienti** 'several thousands of customers'

An approximation of someone's age is expressed by:

> **Era una donna** *sui* **quaranta.**
> She was a woman of around 40.

> **Aveva** *una quarantina* **di anni.**
> She was around 40.

Other collective numbers are:

un **paio** 'a pair' (irregular feminine plural *le* **paia**)
una **coppia** 'a couple'

7.7   *Dates*

The days of the month are referred to with cardinal numbers, except the first:

il *primo* gennaio 'the first of January'
il *due* aprile 'the second of April'

Partiamo il *dieci* marzo.
We'll leave on the tenth of March.

Note how the article **l'** is used with an initial vowel sound:

l'uno settembre 'the first of September'
l'otto giugno 'the eighth of June'
l'undici agosto 'the eleventh of August'

Years are usually written in figures and spoken in full (the century, however, can be omitted):

Sono nato *nel 1951* (*millenovecentocinquantuno*).
I was born in 1951.

Mia figlia è nata *il 29 luglio 1987* (*millenovecentottantasette*).
My daughter was born on the 29 July 1987.

Viviamo in Gran Bretagna *dall'89* (*ottantanove*).
We have lived in Britain since '89.

All dates expressed in numbers are *always* preceded by the *article*, as in the examples above.

Note the two different ways in which to describe centuries:

il ventesimo secolo/il Novecento 'the twentieth century' (the 1900s)
il quindicesimo secolo/il Quattrocento 'the fifteenth century' (the 1400s)
il quinto secolo 'the fifth century' (the 400s)

And note the following phrases:

i primi anni trenta 'the early thirties'
agli inizi degli anni '80 'at the beginning of the 80s'

7.8   *Weights and measures*

Units of weight include:

> **un etto** '100 grams'
> **un chilo** 'a kilo'
> **un quintale** '100 kilos'
> **una tonnellata** 'a metric ton'

Units of distance, length include:

> **un centimetro** 'a centimetre'
> **un decimetro** '10 cms'
> **un metro** 'a metre'
> **un chilometro** 'a kilometre'

Note:

> **Le pere costano 4.000 lire** *al* **chilo.**
> Pears cost L.4,000 per kilo.
>
> **Le cassette costano L.10.000** *l'una.*
> Cassettes cost L.10,000 each.
>
> **Il limite di velocità su autostrada è di 130 chilometri** *all'ora.*
> The speed limit on motorways is 130 kms per hour.

7.9   *Table of numbers*

Number	Cardinal	Ordinal
1	uno/una	primo/a/i/e
2	due	secondo/a/i/e
3	tre	terzo/a/i/e
4	quattro	quarto/a/i/e
5	cinque	quinto/a/i/e
6	sei	sesto
7	sette	settimo
8	otto	ottavo
9	nove	nono
10	dieci	decimo
11	undici	undicesimo
12	dodici	dodicesimo
13	tredici	tredicesimo
14	quattordici	quattordicesimo
15	quindici	quindicesimo
16	sedici	sedicesimo
17	diciassette	diciassettesimo

Structures

Number	Cardinal	Ordinal
18	diciotto	diciottesimo
19	diciannove	diciannovesimo
20	venti	ventesimo
21	ventuno	ventunesimo
22	ventidue	ventiduesimo
23	ventitré	ventitreesimo
...	...	...
30	trenta	trentesimo
31	trentuno	trentunesimo
32	trentadue	trentaduesimo
33	trentatré	trentatreesimo
...	...	...
40	quaranta	quarantesimo
41	quarantuno	quarantunesimo
42	quarantadue	quarantaduesimo
...	...	...
50	cinquanta	cinquantesimo
60	sessanta	sessantesimo
70	settanta	settantesimo
80	ottanta	ottantesimo
90	novanta	novantesimo
100	cento	centesimo
200	duecento	duecentesimo
300	trecento	trecentesimo
1.000	mille	millesimo
2.000	duemila	duemillesimo
10.000	diecimila	diecimillesimo
100.000	centomila	centomillesimo
1.000.000	un milione	milionesimo
1.000.000.000	un miliardo	miliardesimo

Time

Numbers are also used to express time of day. Since **l'ora** is feminine, the articles **l'**, **le** are used, sometimes combined with preposition **a**:

> **Sono *le 11.00***
> It's 11 o'clock.

> **Ci vediamo *alle 5.00* davanti alla libreria?**
> Shall we meet at 5 o'clock outside the bookshop?

> **E' già *l'una*.**
> It's already 1 o'clock.

PART B

Functions

I Giving and seeking factual information

8 Identification: giving personal information

Giving and eliciting personal information: introduction

In Italian, as in other languages, one of the simplest ways of giving information about yourself or others, is by using the verb **essere** 'to be' (see Chapter 2) as shown in this simple dialogue:

A: **Buongiorno, io** *sono* **Monica.** *Sono* **la nuova assistente di marketing. E voi?**
B: **Io** *sono* **Carlo,** *sono* **il direttore tecnico. E questo** *è* **il mio collega, Gerardo. *Siamo* colleghi da più di dieci anni!**
C: **Piacere, Monica.**
A: **Piacere, Gerardo. Di dove** *sei***?**
C: *Sono* **napoletano. E tu?**
A: **Io** *sono* **di Milano.**

A: Good morning. I'm Monica. I'm the new marketing assistant. What about you?
B: I'm Carlo, I'm the technical director. And this is my colleague, Gerardo. We've been colleagues for more than ten years!
C: Pleased to meet you, Monica.
A: Pleased to meet you, Gerardo. Where are you from?
C: I'm from Naples. And you?
A: I'm from Milan.

Tu *or* Lei?

There are two ways of addressing someone in Italian: **Lei** (formal) or **tu** (informal). **Lei** should be used when addressing someone you don't know well, or don't know at all, although young people meeting each other often use **tu** straightaway, as in the conversation above. You may at some point be invited to use the **tu** form with the words: **Diamoci del tu**.

When using **Lei** to address someone, the third person verb form is used (for example **Lei parla inglese?**), rather than the second person verb form (**Tu parli inglese?**) normally used when addressing someone directly. In our examples, we have shown both 'you' forms.

8.3   *Giving different kinds of personal information*

The verb **essere** 'to be' is used in most of the functions illustrated below, to supply the kind of personal information we exchange, for example, when meeting someone for the first time. (For 'Introductions', see also 20.2.)

In Italian the verb endings tell us which person is referred to (see Chapter 2). This means it is not necessary to use the *subject pronouns* **io, tu, lui,** etc. to indicate the person, so they are shown in our examples in brackets:

Giving one's name

(Io) *sono* **Anna.**	I am Anna.
(Lui) *è* **Franco.**	He is Franco.
(Loro) *sono* **Monica e Gerardo.**	They're Monica and Gerardo.

The verb **essere** can be replaced by the verb **chiamarsi** (see Chapter 2) 'to be called':

(Io) *mi chiamo* **Anna.**	My name is Anna.
(Lui) *si chiama* **Franco.**	His name is Franco.
Come *si chiama?*	What's his name?
Si chiama **Marco.**	His name's Marco.

8.3.2   Indicating relationship to speaker

Friends or colleagues

È una collega.
She is a (my) colleague.

È un amico.
He is a friend.

Note the use of the articles in *un* **mio,** *i* **miei:**

È un mio amico.
He's a friend of mine/my friend.

Sono i miei colleghi.
They are colleagues of mine/my colleagues.

Family relations

When we talk about family relations, we naturally often use the possessives **mio, tuo,** etc. (see Chapter 3). With relations, the definite article **il, la,** etc. is omitted, unless talking about relatives in the plural:

È mio fratello.
He is my brother.

È suo marito.
It's her husband.

Sono i suoi figli.
They're her children.

Here is a list of close relations, with English translation:

il padre 'father'	**la madre** 'mother'
il fratello 'brother'	**la sorella** 'sister'
il cugino 'cousin'	**la cugina** 'cousin' (feminine)
il marito 'husband'	**la moglie** 'wife'
il figlio 'son'	**la figlia** 'daughter'
lo zio 'uncle'	**la zia** 'aunt'
il suocero 'father-in-law'	**la suocera** 'mother-in-law'
il genero 'son-in-law'	**la nuora** 'daughter-in-law'
il cognato 'brother-in-law'	**la cognata** 'sister-in-law'
il nonno 'grandfather'	**la nonna** 'grandmother'
il nipote 'grandson', 'nephew'	**la nipote** 'granddaughter', 'niece'

Note that the words **la famiglia** and **i parenti** *do* need the definite article:

la mia **famiglia** 'my family'
il mio/ la mia **parente** 'my relative' (masculine/feminine)

Avoid confusing:

i miei *parenti*   'my relatives'
i miei *genitori*   'my parents'

8.3.3
Indicating profession

In Italian, when talking about one's profession, using **essere**, the indefinite article **un**, **una** (English 'a', 'an') is not used:

(Io) *sono insegnante.*	I am a teacher.
(Lui) *è ingegnere.*	He is an engineer.
(Loro) *sono medici.*	They're doctors.

When, on the other hand, we use the verb **fare**, the definite article is used:

Faccio *l'*insegnante.   I'm a teacher.

We have indicated some of the trades and professions you are more likely to come into contact with in Italy:

Professionals:

> **il medico** 'doctor'
> **il/la dentista** 'dentist'
> **il/la pediatra** 'paediatrician'
> **il ragioniere** 'accountant'
> **l'ingegnere** 'engineer'
> **l'architetto** 'architect'
> **l'insegnante** 'teacher' (masculine/feminine)
> **il professore/la professoressa** 'lecturer', 'secondary school teacher'
> **il maestro/la maestra** 'teacher' (in elementary school)

Builders and workmen:

> **il muratore** 'builder'
> **l'operaio** 'workman'
> **l'idraulico** 'plumber'
> **l'elettricista** 'electrician'

Shops, trade:

> **il pescatore** 'fisherman'
> **il fruttivendolo** 'greengrocer'
> **il droghiere** 'grocer'
> **il salumiere** 'salame seller' (grocer)
> **il fotografo** 'photographer'
> **il bagnino/la bagnina** 'beach attendant'

General:

> **l'impiegato/a** 'office employee'
> **lo/la statale** 'state employee'
> **il/la giornalista** 'journalist'
> **il commesso/la commessa** 'shop assistant'

For more on the masculine/feminine forms of professions, see 1.2.1 and 20.9.

Indicating role or position

Where one particular post or office is referred to, the definite article **il, la** is normally used, but see last example:

> **Sono *il direttore commerciale* dell'agenzia di viaggio.**
> I'm the commercial director of the travel agency.

> **È *la nuova insegnante* d'italiano.**
> She's the new Italian teacher.

> **Sono *capo* della sezione di Risorse Umane.**
> I'm head of Human Resources.

Indicating nationality

Generally, nationality is indicated by using **essere** with the appropriate adjective of nationality:

(Io) sono scozzese.	I am Scottish.
(Lei) è italiana.	She is Italian.
(Loro) sono francesi.	They're French.

Here is a selection of adjectives denoting the more common nationalities:

africano 'African'	**libanese** 'Lebanese'
americano 'American'	**libico** 'Libyan'
australiano 'Australian'	**lussemburghese**
austriaco 'Austrian'	'Luxembourgeois'
belga 'Belgian'	**neozelandese** 'New Zealand'
bosniaco 'Bosnian'	**norvegese** 'Norwegian'
britannico 'British'	**olandese** 'Dutch'
cinese 'Chinese'	**portoghese** 'Portuguese'
croato 'Croatian'	**scozzese** 'Scottish'
danese 'Danish'	**serbo** 'Serbian'
francese 'French'	**sloveno** 'Slovenian'
gallese 'Welsh'	**spagnolo** 'Spanish'
giapponese 'Japanese'	**sudafricano** 'South African'
greco 'Greek'	**svedese** 'Swedish'
indiano 'Indian'	**svizzero** 'Swiss'
inglese 'English'	**tedesco** 'German'
irlandese 'Irish'	**turco** 'Turkish'
italiano 'Italian'	

Note:

(a) In Italian, no capital letter is used for adjectives of nationality:

> **un collega *italiano*** 'an Italian colleague'

(b) The singular form of the adjective **belga** 'Belgian' is the same for masculine and feminine, but the plural form has two possible endings:

> **degli amici *belgi*** 'Belgian friends' (masculine)
> **delle amiche *belghe*** 'Belgian friends' (feminine)

(c) **inglese** is often used by Italians to denote 'British'.

Indicating marital status

Again **essere** is used:

> **(Io) sono sposato.**
> I am married.

> **(Lui) è divorziato.**
> He's divorced.

> **(Noi) siamo sposati da venti anni.**
> We've been married for twenty years.

Single is best expressed as **non sposato**:

> **Giorgio** *non è sposato.*
> Giorgio is single/not married.

Indicating religion

Here are some religions you might want to express in Italian:

cattolico 'Catholic'	**protestante** 'Protestant'
buddista 'Buddhist'	**musulmano** 'Muslim'
anglicano 'Anglican'	**ortodosso** 'Orthodox'
ebreo 'Jewish'	

> **La mia amica Fatiha è musulmana.**
> My friend Fatiha is Muslim.

On a form:

> **Religione: cattolica**
> Religion: Catholic

Details of other adjectives, for example, those that describe physical appearance (age, shape, size, etc.), are found in 10.2.

Indicating place of origin

Note that while English uses 'from' to express origin, Italian uses **di**:

> **(Io)** *sono di* **Napoli.**
> I'm from Naples.

> **(Lui)** *è di* **Firenze.**
> He's from Florence.

> **I miei colleghi** *sono di* **Londra.**
> My colleagues are from London.

However, when using the verb **venire**, to express the place where you come from, not necessarily where you were born, use **da** instead:

> *Vengo da* **Londra.**
> I come from London.

8.4   *Emphasizing the person referred to*

With stressed subject pronouns

In Italian, as this chapter's initial dialogue shows, the verb endings change or inflect; this means it is not necessary to use the *subject pronouns* **io**, **tu**, **lui**, etc.

(see Chapter 3) to indicate *who* we are referring to, so they have been shown in brackets. But the pronouns are sometimes used to *contrast* or *emphasise* the person or persons spoken about:

> *Io* sono inglese.
> I, myself, am English.

> *Lui* è italiano.
> He, in fact, is Italian.

They are also used – particularly when using the polite **Lei** form of address (see 8.2) – to make a question sound less abrupt:

> *Lei* è inglese?
> Are you English?

> *Lei* è di Londra?
> Are you from London?

8.4.2

With *questo*

We can also add the demonstrative pronoun **questo** 'this' in our introductions, although when introducing someone by name, it is preferable to use the subject pronouns:

Questa è una mia collega.	This is a colleague of mine.
Questi sono i miei studenti.	These are my students.
Queste sono le mie amiche.	These are my friends.
Lui è Franco.	He (This) is Franco.

8.5 Eliciting personal information

Essere can also be used to elicit information, sometimes with a question word (see 3.6 and 15.3):

Chi è lui?	Who is he?
Di dove sei/è?	Who are you?
*Di dov'*è Franco?	Where is Franco from?
Di dove sono gli studenti?	Where are the students from?

Often the form of the sentence and the word order are exactly the same, whether statement or question. To turn a statement into a question, we need only alter the intonation of the sentence, usually by raising the voice towards the end of the sentence:

Lei è sposata?	Are you married?
Tu sei insegnante?	Are you a teacher?
È un collega?	Is he a colleague?

In the following examples, note the use of **quale** (**qual**) where English would use the question word 'what'. **Quale** can be abbreviated to **qual** but must never be followed by an apostrophe.

Qual è il Suo cognome?	What is your surname?
Qual è il Suo indirizzo?	What is your address?

8.6 Dialoghi

Un incontro con amici

A: **Ciao, Mariella!**
B: **Ciao, Gianna. Che sorpresa!**
A: **Questo è mio cugino, Aurelio. È siciliano. Aurelio, questa è la mia amica, Mariella.**
B: **Ciao, Aurelio. Benvenuto a Pisa. Di dove sei?**
C: **Sono di Catania, ma mia madre è di Pisa.**
B: **Ah, anche il mio fidanzato è di Catania. Si chiama Carmelo. È ragioniere. I suoi sono di Messina, ma sono a Catania da molto tempo.**

Meeting friends

A: Hi Mariella!
B: Hi, Gianna. What a surprise!
A: This is my cousin, Aurelio. He's Sicilian. Aurelio, this is my friend Mariella.
B: Hi, Aurelio. Welcome to Pisa. Where are you from?
C: I'm from Catania, but my mother is from Pisa.
B: Ah, my boyfriend's from Catania too. He's called Carmelo. He's an accountant. His parents are from Messina, but they've been in Catania for some time.

There are several legal/bureaucratic terms used in the following dialogue: **residenza** 'residence' or 'home address', **domicilio** 'the place where you are presently living', **stato civile** 'married status': Italian ID documents attest to one's **Stato di Famiglia** which notes whether married, number of children, etc. Note too how the polite form **Suo** 'yours' is generally written with a capital letter.

All'ufficio di polizia

A: **Prego si accomodi. Dobbiamo compilare questo modulo con le Sue generalità. Le farò alcune domande:**
   Il Suo cognome?
B: **Smith.**
A: **Mi scusi. Come si scrive?**
B: **Esse-emme-i-ti-acca (*S*avona, *M*antova, *I*mola, *T*aranto, *H*otel).**
A: **E il nome?**
B: **Richard.**
A: **La nazionalità?**

B: **Australiana.**

A: **Residenza?**

B: **56 Ramsay Street, Sydney, Australia.**

A: **Qual è il Suo domicilio in Italia?**

B: **Hotel Miramare, Napoli.**

A: **Numero di telefono?**

B: **081-271638.**

A: **E il Suo stato civile?**

B: **Coniugato.**

A: **Qual è il numero del Suo passaporto?**

B: **0044998245.**

A: **Che professione fa?**

B: **Commerciante.**

A: **Va bene, grazie. Per ora basta. Le telefoneremo non appena avremo notizie della Sua pratica di permesso di soggiorno.**

At the police station

A: Please, sit down. We have to fill in this form with your particulars. I have to ask you some questions.
      Your surname?

B: Smith.

A: Sorry, how is that written?

B: S for sugar, M for mother, I for India, T for Tommy, H for Harry.

A: And your name?

B: Richard.

A: Nationality?

B: Australian.

A: Home address?

B: 56 Ramsay Street, Sydney, Australia.

A: What is your address in Italy?

B: Hotel Miramare, Naples.

A: And the telephone number?

B: 081-271638.

A: And your marital status?

B: Married.

A: What's the number of your passport?

B: 0044998245.

A: What is your profession?

B: Businessman/salesman.

A: That's fine, thanks. That's enough for now. We'll call you as soon as we have some news of your application for a residence permit.

9 Specifying people or objects

9.1 Introduction

The following dialogue shows how even at the simplest level, we can *indicate* our specific needs:

Al bar

A: **Buongiorno.**
B: **Buongiorno, un caffè per favore.**
A: **Va bene. E ... per la Signora?**
C: **Una birra piccola e un whisky.**
A: **Certamente. Una birra italiana, va bene?**
C: **Sì, va bene. Ma ... un whisky scozzese.**
A: **Naturalmente, Signora.**

At the café

A: Good morning.
B: Good morning. A coffee, please.
A: All right. And ... for Madam?
C: A small beer and a whisky.
A: Certainly. An Italian beer, is that all right?
C: Yes, OK. But ... a Scotch whisky.
A: Of course, Madam.

In the dialogue above, we identify what we want by using a simple noun (**una birra**) or noun and adjective combination (**una birra piccola**). We can also use a verb such as **volere**, **cercare**, **aver bisogno di** (see Chapter 23).

9.2 Specifying a known or particular person or object

9.2.1 Using a definite article *il, la*

When we have *one particular person or thing* in mind, we can express this by using the definite article **il**, **la**, etc. (see Chapter 1). As the examples show, we are generally referring to a known person or thing, for example, 'the speciality we've had before', 'the English girl someone told us about':

> **Vorrei assaggiare *la* specialità della casa.**
> I'd like to try *the* speciality of the house.

> **Mi presenti *la* ragazza inglese?**
> Will you introduce me to *the* English girl?

Alternatively, we may be referring to someone or something that is the only one, or the only one possible, in this set of circumstances ('the manager', 'the bill'):

> **Il direttore, per favore.**
> The manager, please.

> **Il conto, per piacere.**
> The bill, please.

9.2.2 **Using *questo, quello***

We use **questo** 'this' or **quello** 'that' (see Chapter 3) to refer to *this* or *that* person or object, either the one near us (**questo**), the one near the person addressed (**quello**), the one which we can see in front of us (**questo, quello**) or perhaps even the one that has just been talked about:

> **Vorrei assaggiare *quel* caffè speciale.**
> I'd like to try that special coffee.

> **Conosci *quelle* ragazze inglesi?**
> Do you know those English girls?

> ***Questo* scontrino non è per la valigia che è andata smarrita.**
> This baggage tag is not for the case that's gone missing.

The verb **essere** can be used with **questo, quello**:

> ***Questi sono* i miei appunti. Sono abbastanza completi, se vuoi copiarli.**
> These are my notes. They're quite complete, if you want to copy them.

> ***Quello è* il computer portatile che abbiamo comprato negli Stati Uniti.**
> That is the portable computer that we bought in the USA.

The question words **cosa** or **che cosa** 'what?' can be used to elicit specific information:

> ***Cosa sono* (questi)? Sono funghi secchi.**
> What are they/these? They're dried mushrooms.

> ***Che cosa sono* quelle foglie secche? Sono foglie di basilico.**
> What are those dry leaves? They're basil leaves.

9.3   Specifying the category or type

Sometimes we want to indicate a specific *type or category of person or thing*. We can do this using an *adjective* or combination of adjectives:

> **Cerco *un interprete italiano*.**
> I'm looking for an Italian interpreter.

> **Gli studenti hanno bisogno di *un libro semplice e chiaro*.**
> The students need a clear simple book.

9.4   Specifying ownership

One of the most important aspects of identification is *belonging*. We can indicate the person to whom things belong. Note how Italian uses **di** and the person involved; there is no equivalent of the English's ('Franco's', 'Anna's'):

> **Metti il maglione verde *di Alessandro*.**
> Put Alessandro's green sweater on.

> **Prendiamo la macchina *di mio cugino*.**
> Let's take my cousin's car.

> **Le ciabatte di plastica sono *dei bambini*.**
> The plastic flip-flops are the children's.

We can also use possessives such as **mio, tuo, suo** (see 3.7). Note that in Italian, the definite article **il, la** etc. is normally used:

> **Questo è *il mio* lavoro.**
> This is my work.

> **Questa è *la tua* cassetta?**
> Is this your cassette?

To *ask* who something belongs to, we use:

> **Di chi è...?**
> Whose is it? (*literally*: Of who is it?)

When used as a pronoun ('mine', 'yours'), the definite article **il, la** etc. is optional:

> ***Di chi è* questa maglia? È *mia*.**
> Whose is this sweater? It's mine.

> ***Di chi è* questo biglietto? È *il suo*.**
> Whose is this ticket? It's his.

> **Quel libro è *mio*.**

That book is mine.

Le carte da gioco erano *sue.*
The playing cards were hers.

9.5   *Specifying a person or object using a* che *clause*

Another way of being more specific is to use a **che** clause (see 3.5.1, 5.3.1 and 30.5, for more about *relative* clauses) to give more details.

The **che** clause can refer to a definite or actual object or category that we know about, in which case the *indicative* verb form is used:

> **In genere gli inglesi preferiscono bere le birre *che conoscono.***
> On the whole the English prefer to drink the beers that they know.

> **Questa è la bicicletta *che ho comprato l'anno scorso.***
> This is the bike I bought last year.

> **Il regista ha assunto l'attrice *che aveva girato dei film* con Pasolini.**
> The director employed the actress who had been in some of Pasolini's films.

If the **che** clause refers to something which may or may not exist, or be available, the *subjunctive* is sometimes used, particularly in more formal language; the examples here use the indicative, with the subjunctive shown in brackets:

> **Vorrei una birra *che non è (sia)* troppo forte.**
> I would like a beer that is not too strong.

> **Cerco un interprete *che sa (sappia)* parlare inglese.**
> I'm looking for an interpreter who can speak English.

10 Describing people or things

Introduction

The most common way of describing the characteristics of someone or something is to use an adjective or adjectives (see Chapter 1). In this chapter are some of the most frequently used categories of adjectives. We give a few examples in each category, but obviously there are many more to choose from in each group.

10.2 Adjectives used to describe people

This sort of adjective is best divided into *permanent* characteristics and *temporary* ones.

10.2.1. Permanent characteristics

Physical appearance
Common adjectives expressing *size* include:

grande 'large'	**piccolo** 'small'
alto 'tall'	**basso** 'small in stature'
grasso 'fat'	**magro** 'thin'

See Chapter 1 for the forms of adjectives, including those that are invariable.

> **La sua futura suocera era *alta e grassa.***
> His future mother-in-law was tall and fat.

> **È *bionda, sui quaranta anni.***
> She's blonde, around forty.

> **I ragazzi sono *alti, con capelli lunghi e castani.***
> The boys are tall, with long brown hair.

Common adjectives describing appearance:

> **bello** 'pretty', 'nice', 'handsome'
> **brutto** 'ugly', 'horrible'
> **handicappato** 'handicapped'

Character or temperament
Adjectives describing someone's character or temperament include:

aggressivo 'aggressive'	**cooperativo** 'cooperative'
prepotente 'domineering'	
intelligente 'intelligent'	**stupido** 'stupid'
furbo 'crafty'	**fesso** 'gullible', 'foolish'
gentile 'kind'	**crudele** 'cruel'
estroverso 'extrovert'	**introverso** 'introvert'
vivace 'lively'	**tranquillo** 'calm'
allegro 'happy', 'cheerful'	
disponibile 'available', 'helpful'	

Marco è *simpatico*.
Marco is nice.

Simona è *antipatica*.
Simona is unpleasant.

Quella ragazza è *simpatica*, bella e *intelligente*.
That girl is nice, pretty and intelligent.

Talents and skills
At opposite ends of the spectrum are:

portato 'naturally talented'
negato 'with no talent'

Insisteva che la bambina facesse lezioni di pianoforte, però Sara era proprio *negata*.
She insisted on the child doing piano lessons, but Sara was hopeless.

Per parlare bene una lingua, forse bisogna essere proprio *portati*.
To speak a language well, maybe you need to have a leaning for it.

The word **dotato** 'gifted' can be used without any specific talent being mentioned:

Il figlio della mia amica era un bambino molto *dotato*.
My friend's son was a very gifted child.

And when you are getting everything wrong, or dropping things:

Oggi sono proprio *imbranata*.
Today I'm all fingers and thumbs.

Nationality
Adjectives of nationality are illustrated earlier in 8.3.5.

> **Teresa parla bene il francese, perché ha uno zio *francese*.**
> Teresa speaks French well, because she has a French uncle.

Marital status
See also 8.3.6.

> **Teresa è *separata*.**
> Teresa is separated.

> **Walter e Gloria sono *sposati*.**
> Walter and Gloria are married.

Age
Here are some common adjectives denoting age:

> **vecchio** 'old'   **giovane** 'young'
> **anziano** 'old'
> **grande** 'big', 'old'   **piccolo** 'small', 'young'

Religion
Adjectives of religion are illustrated in 8.3.7.

10.2.2 Temporary characteristics

Physical state
Adjectives describing a temporary physical condition include:

> **bagnato** 'wet'
> **malato** 'ill'
> **stanco** 'tired'

> **I bambini erano *bagnati*.**
> The children were soaking wet.

> **La professoressa era *stanca*.**
> The teacher was tired.

Emotional state
Adjectives describing a temporary emotional state include:

> **felice** 'happy'
> **triste** 'sad'
> **contento** 'happy'
> **arrabbiato** 'angry'
> **calmo** 'calm'
> **nervoso** 'edgy'
> **stressato** 'stressed'
> **rilassato** 'relaxed'

Mio marito sarà *arrabbiato*.
My husband will be angry.

Il capo era proprio *seccato*.
The boss was really fed-up.

10.3 *Adjectives used to describe things*

Physical characteristics (generally permanent)

Size
Common adjectives include:

grande 'large'	**piccolo** 'small'
lungo 'long'	**corto** 'short'
alto 'tall'	**basso** 'low'
largo 'wide'	**stretto** 'narrow'
breve 'short'	

un viaggio breve 'a short journey'
una gonna corta 'a short skirt'

Mia zia abitava in un vicolo lungo e stretto.
My aunt lived in a long narrow alley.

Shape
Common adjectives include:

quadrato 'square'	**rotondo** 'round'
ovale 'oval'	**rettangolare** 'rectangular'

Colour
The commonest adjectives include:

bianco 'white'	**nero** 'black'
grigio 'grey'	**marrone** 'brown'
blu 'navy'	**azzurro** 'sky blue'
verde 'green'	**rosso** 'red'
giallo 'yellow'	**rosa** 'pink'
chiaro 'light'	**scuro** 'dark'
verde chiaro 'light green'	**rosso scuro** 'dark red'

Note that many adjectives of colour are invariable: they do not change form (see
Chapter 1 for the forms of adjectives). Examples are **blu**, **rosa**, **beige**.

Le case sulle Isole Eolie sono *piccole* e *bianche*.
The houses on the Aeolian islands are small and white.

> **Il giardino era** *quadrato.*
> The garden was square.

Composition and materials

Rather than use an adjective (English 'metallic', 'wooden'), Italian often uses a prepositional phrase, the preposition **di** 'of' or **in** 'in' with a noun such as **legno**, **cotone**, to describe what an object is made of (see 4.3.1).

Textiles:

di cotone 'cotton'	**di seta** 'silk'
di poliestere 'polyester'	**di viscosio** 'viscose'
di lana 'wool'	**di pelle** 'leather'
di cuoio 'leather'	
di materiale sintetico 'synthetic material'	

Metals:

di alluminio 'aluminium'	**di metallo** 'metal'
di ferro 'iron'	**di acciaio** 'steel'
di oro 'gold'	**di argento** 'silver'
di bronzo 'bronze'	**di ottone** 'brass'

Household materials:

di gomma 'rubber'	**di plastica** 'plastic'
di legno 'wood'	**di ceramica** 'china'

You can use either **fatto di** 'made of' or another participle of similar meaning, such as:

> **foderato di** 'lined with'
> **ricoperto di** 'covered with'
> **ripieno di** 'filled with'
> **rivestito di** 'covered with'

> **L'ascensore aveva le porte** *fatte di metallo.*
> The lift had metal doors.

> **La cucina è tutta** *in legno.*
> The kitchen is all in wood.

> **Per la stagione estiva la moda sarà tutta** *di cotone.*
> For the summer season, the fashion will be all cotton.

> **In montagna bisogna mettere una maglia** *di lana.*
> In the mountains you must put on a woollen sweater.

The *authenticity* of the material is expressed by:

vero 'real'
finto 'fake'
puro 'pure'
genuino 'genuine'
autentico 'authentic'
cento per cento 'hundred per cent'

Questa giacca è vera pelle.
This jacket is real leather.

Characteristics of the material include:

morbido 'soft'
duro 'hard'
forte 'strong'
debole 'weak'
resistente 'tough', 'long-lasting'
soffice 'soft'
liscio 'smooth'
ruvido 'rough'
elastico 'elastic', 'stretchy'

Nationality

La Buick è una macchina *americana*.
The Buick is an American car.

Le scarpe che ho comprato al mercato sono *italiane*.
The shoes I bought at the market are Italian.

Taste and smell
Adjectives describing something you can taste include:

buono 'good'
cattivo 'bad'
dolce 'sweet'
amaro 'bitter'
salato 'salty'
saporito 'tasty'
insipido 'tasteless'

10.3.2

State or condition
A few common adjectives expressing a temporary or permanent condition include:

sporco 'dirty'	**ordinato** 'tidy'
squallido 'squalid'	**disordinato** 'untidy'
pulito 'clean'	

> **La città è *sporca* e *squallida.***
> The town is dirty and squalid.

> **bagnato** 'wet'
> **asciutto** 'dry'
> **gonfio** 'swollen'

> **Avevamo lasciato la finestra aperta, e il divano era tutto *bagnato*.**
> We had left the window open, and the sofa was all wet.

> **Dopo la lunga passeggiata, avevo i piedi *gonfi*.**
> After the long walk, I had swollen feet.

10.3.3

Subjective qualities

Certain qualities depend on individual, and subjective, judgement:

> **bello** 'pretty', 'nice'
> **brutto** 'ugly', 'horrible'
> **gradevole** 'pleasant'
> **sgradevole** 'unpleasant'

> **Che brutta credenza!**
> What an ugly sideboard!

10.4 *Intensifying the meaning of the adjective*

There are various ways in which the meaning of the adjective can be intensified or strengthened.

10.4.1

By means of an adverb

The adverbs most commonly used for this purpose in Italian are:

> **molto** 'much'
> **tanto** 'much', 'so much'

These are used before the adjective in the same way as 'very', 'greatly', 'extremely' in English. You can also use:

> **parecchio** 'greatly', 'much'
> **veramente** 'really'
> **estremamente** 'extremely'
> **ben(e)** 'well', 'quite', 'much', 'pretty'
> **assai** 'very'
> **abbastanza** 'enough', 'a bit', 'quite'
> **piuttosto** 'rather'

> **Alcuni leghisti erano *molto* preoccupati dal patto con Berlusconi.**
> Some members of the Lega were very worried by the agreement with Berlusconi.

È una situazione *estremamente* instabile.
It's an extremely unstable situation.

Il cane era *ben* contento di vederci.
The dog was pretty happy to see us.

10.4.2
By means of the suffix *-issimo*
The suffix -issimo (see Chapter 1) can only be used for the shorter more common adjectives:

I ragazzi sono content*issimi* di andare in vacanza anche senza la mamma.
The kids are really happy to be going on holiday, even without their mother.

Il mio medico è simpatic*issimo*.
My doctor is really nice.

10.4.3
By means of a prefix
There are several prefixes which can be added to the beginning of an adjective, and although these are not very common, they are found more and more in journalism and in the spoken language. Always check with a dictionary before using one of these. The form you want may not exist, or else it may mean something different. The 'hyper' forms in particular (**arci-**, **ultra-**) are used for effect, e.g. in journalistic writing:

una stanza *surr*iscaldata 'an overheated room'
Lava *super*bianco! 'Washes whiter than white!'
Marco è *arci*contento 'Marco is over-the-moon'
*ultra*sinistra 'far left'
una madre *iper*protettiva 'an over-protective mother'
un whisky *stra*vecchio 'an "aged" whisky'

10.4.4
By means of a second adjective
There are several fixed phrases in which a second adjective is used to intensify the meaning of the first adjective, some of which are shown here:

Sono *stanca morta*.
I'm dead tired.

Gli studenti erano *ubriachi fradici*.
The students were extremely drunk (*literally*: soaking drunk).

Other pairs include:

bianco pallido 'white as a sheet'
freddo gelato 'icy cold'
caldo bollente 'boiling hot'
ricco sfondato 'filthy rich' (*literally*: bottomless rich)

10.4.5 **With a phrase indicating the extent or effect**

> bello *da impazzire* 'beautiful "to drive you mad"'
> brutto *da morire* 'ugly "to death"'

10.5 *Diminishing the strength of the adjective*

10.5.1 **With an adverb**

In the same way that certain adverbs can be used to intensify or strengthen the meaning of the adjective, a few adverbs can be used to produce the opposite effect. The adverb most commonly used for this purpose is **poco**:

> **Gli studenti sono *poco* motivati.**
> The students are not very motivated.

Other adverbs which can be used include:

> **scarsamente** 'barely'
> **appena** 'barely', 'hardly'
> **leggermente** 'slightly'

10.5.2 **By means of a suffix**

Suffixes which can be used with this meaning include **-ino**, **-etto**:

> **bellino** 'pretty' (rather than beautiful)
> **magrolino** 'skinny' (rather than thin)
> **piccolino** 'little', 'small'
> **poveretto** 'poor little ...'

They can only be used for the shorter more common adjectives, and, as for the suffixes used to intensify, caution is advised.

10.5.3 **With a prefix**

A prefix which can be used to imply the opposite is **in-** 'not', for example:

> **inutile** 'useless'
> **incapace** 'incapable'

10.6 *Describing a physical state using stare*

To describe how someone is (state of health) – not what he/she looks like – we use **stare**:

> **Come *sta*, signora? *Sto* bene, grazie.**
> How are you, signora? I'm well, thanks.

> **Mio padre *stava* molto male.**
> My father was very ill.

The difference in meaning between the two verbs is clear when they are used in a question starting with **Come ...?** 'How ...?':

Using **essere** to ask about physical appearance:

> **Com'è la tua amica?**
> What is your friend like?

> **È bionda, con capelli lunghi.**
> She's blonde, with long hair.

Using **stare** to ask about state of health:

> **Come *sta* la tua amica?**
> How's your friend?

> ***Sta* molto meglio adesso.**
> She's a lot better now.

Come stai?/Come sta? is one of the most common ways of greeting someone (see 20.1).

10.7 Dialogo

Incontro con gli amici

A: **Ciao Sergio, come stai?**
B: **Bene grazie e tu?**
A: **E Lucia come sta?**
B: **Non sta bene, è stanca e nervosa. Il suo lavoro è faticoso, ma per fortuna Lucia è una ragazza forte e sana e non sono preoccupato per lei.**
A: **Senti, oggi è una bella giornata. Usciamo insieme?**
B: **È una buona idea, Lucia sarà contenta.**
A: **Allora va bene. La mia macchina è comoda e grande. Guido io. Tu e Lucia potete stare rilassati e riposare.**

Meeting with friends

A: Hi, Sergio, how are you?
B: I'm fine and you?
A: How is Lucia doing?
B: She's not well, she's tired and edgy, Her job is hard, but luckily Lucia is a strong and healthy girl and I'm not worried about her.
A: Listen, it's a beautiful day today. Shall we go out together?
B: It's a good idea. Lucia'll be happy.
A: That's fine then. My car is big and comfortable. I'll drive. You and Lucia can relax and have a rest.

11 Talking about existence, presence and availability

Talking about existence and availability: introduction

There are various ways of talking about whether something or someone exists, is present and/or is available, in Italian. One of the simplest ways is to use **ci** 'there' and **essere** 'to be', while another way, often used in shops or restaurants, is to use the verb **avere** 'to have'; both are shown in this simple dialogue:

All'ufficio turistico

> **T = Turista** 'tourist', **I = Impiegato** 'employee'

T: **Buongiorno, *avete* una piantina della città?**

I: **Sì, *c'è* questa, che costa 5.000 lire; è compreso anche l'elenco dei monumenti. Oppure questa qua, che è gratuita.**

T: **Prendo questa, grazie. Dunque, noi vorremmo vedere l'*Aida* all'Arena. *Ci sono* dei biglietti per stasera?**

I: **Per stasera, no, purtroppo ... *non ce ne sono*. Ma se per voi va bene, *ce ne sono* due nella platea per domani sera.**

T: **Sì, per noi va bene. Quanto costano?**

I: **50.000 lire ciascuno.**

T: **Va bene, li prendo. Senta, *c'è* una trattoria vicino al teatro?**

I: **Sì, *ce n'è* una molto buona proprio a due passi dal teatro. Si chiama 'Da Alfredo'. Se vuole, posso chiamare e prenotare un tavolo.**

T: **No, grazie, non fa niente.**

I: **Prego, signore. Arrivederci.**

At the tourist information office

> T = Tourist, E = Employee

T: Hello, do you have a map of the town?

E: Yes, there's this one, which is 5,000 lire; the list of monuments is included too. Or else this one, which is free.

T: I'll take this one, thanks. Now, we'd like to see 'Aida' at the Arena. Are there any tickets for this evening?

E: Not for this evening, no, unfortunately. But if it's all right for you, there are two tickets in the stalls for tomorrow evening.

T: Yes, that's fine for us. How much are they?

E: 50,000 lire each.

T: OK, I'll take them. Listen, is there a restaurant near the theatre?

E: Yes, there's a very good one very near the theatre. It's called 'Da Alfredo'. If you want, I can call and book a table.

T: No, thank you, it's not important.

E: All right, sir. Goodbye.

11.2   *Talking about existence and/or presence*

Depending on the circumstances, you can use one or other of the following verbs or verb phrases:

> **essere + ci** 'to be there'
> **esistere** 'to exist'
> **essere presenti** 'to be present'
> **trovarsi** 'to be there' (position)

11.2.1 *essere + ci*

Present tense: **c'è** 'there is', **ci sono** 'there are'.

In the singular form, the combination of **ci** and **è** is shortened to **c'è**:

> **c'è** 'there is'
> **c'è?** 'is there?'

The plural form is:

> **ci sono** 'there are'
> **ci sono . . .?** 'are there?'

You can ask about a specific person or thing, or one known to you, using **il/la**:

> *C'è* **il medico oggi? Sì,** *c'è.*
> Is the doctor here today? Yes, he's here.

> *Ci sono* **i nostri amici? Sì,** *ci sono.* **Sono arrivati mezz'ora fa.**
> Are our friends here? Yes, they're here. They arrived half an hour ago.

You can ask about an unknown or unspecified person or thing using **un/una**, and with/without **dei/delle** in the plural:

> **Scusi,** *c'è* **un gabinetto? Sì,** *c'è* **un gabinetto lì in fondo.**
> Excuse me, is there a toilet? Yes, there's a toilet over there.

> *Ci sono* **ospiti? Sì,** *ci sono* **degli ospiti appena arrivati.**
> Are there any guests? Yes, there are some guests just arrived.

Of course, **ci** can be used with other tenses of **essere**, for example:

Future:

> **Ci sarà qualcuno in ufficio?**
> Will there be anyone in the office?

Imperfect:

> **Il pomeriggio, non c'era mai nessuno in ufficio.**
> In the afternoon, there was never anyone in the office.

 ### Esistere

> **Per quanto riguarda l'alloggio, *esistono* varie sistemazioni.**
> As for accommodation, there are various arrangements.

Note that **esistere** forms the **passato prossimo** with **essere**:

> **Ma *sono esistiti* i dinosauri o no?**
> But did the dinosaurs exist or not?

11.2.3 — Essere presente/i
This phrase is often used for resources found naturally, as well as for other contexts:

> **I giacimenti di metano *sono presenti* in grandi quantità nella valle padana.**
> Deposits of methane are present in large quantity in the Po Valley.

> **Mio marito non era *presente* quel giorno.**
> My husband was not present that day.

11.2.4 — Trovarsi
We use **trovarsi** mainly when referring to geographical position:

> **La mia casa *si trova* vicino al mare.**
> My house is near the sea.

> **Oggi *ci troviamo* in un piccolo paese della Basilicata.**
> Today we are in a small village in Basilicata.

11.3 Expressing occurrence

Here are some expressions indicating occurrence of events:

> **succedere** 'to happen'
> **accadere** 'to happen'
> **può darsi** 'to come about'
> **svolgersi** 'to take place'

> **tenersi** 'to take place', 'to be held'
> **fare** 'to hold'
> **capitare** 'to happen'
> **aver luogo** 'to take place'
> **verificarsi** 'to take place'
> **ricorrere** 'to recur', 'take place'

11.3.1 *Succedere/accadere*

These verbs, particularly **succedere**, are by far the most common of all the verbs meaning 'to happen'. Both these verbs and **capitare** (see 11.3.5) can be used impersonally, meaning 'it happens' in which case they are followed by **di** and verb infinitive, or **che** and a clause:

> **Anche nel Parco Nazionale, non** *succede* **quasi mai di vedere gli orsi.**
> Even in the National Park, it hardly ever happens that you see the bears.

> **Molti incidenti stradali** *accadono* **nel momento del rientro dalle vacanze.**
> Many road accidents take place when people come back from their holidays.

> **Può** *succedere* **che si dimentica di spegnere il gas.**
> It can happen that one forgets to turn off the gas.

11.3.2 *Può darsi*

Sometimes the phrase **può darsi** 'it may be', 'it may happen' is used, followed by a **che** clause, usually with the verb in the *subjunctive*:

> **Può darsi che la segretaria l'abbia già mandata.**
> It may be that the secretary has already sent it.

11.3.3 *Svolgersi/tenersi*

When talking about an event taking place, you can use the verbs **svolgersi** or **tenersi** 'to take place':

> **Il Palio di Siena** *si svolge* **due volte all'anno nella Piazza del Campo.**
> The Palio of Siena takes place twice a year in the Piazza del Campo.

> **La Fiera di Milano** *si tiene* **nel quartiere di San Siro.**
> The Milan Trade Fair takes place in the San Siro district.

11.3.4 *Fare*

You can also use the verb **fare**, with **si** to make it passive (literally 'to be made'):

> **Le gare** *si facevano* **ogni anno nello stesso periodo.**
> The competitions were held every year at the same time.

11.3.5 *Capitare, aver luogo*

Both these verbs can be used to express 'to happen'. **Capitare** can be followed by **di** and verb infinitive (see 11.3.1).

> **È mai *capitato* un incidente del genere?**
> Has anything like that ever taken place?

> **Ti *è* mai *capitato* di vedere un fantasma?**
> Has it ever happened to you to see a ghost?

> **I funerali *avranno luogo* giovedì alle 17.00.**
> The funeral will take place on Thursday at 5 p.m.

11.3.6 *Verificarsi/ ricorrere*

The verb **ricorrere** is used when an event recurs regularly:

> **La festa dell'Assunzione *ricorre* il 15 agosto.**
> The holy day of the Assumption is on 15 August every year.

When talking about one single occurrence or regular event, you can use **verificarsi**:

> **Il miracolo di San Gennaro si è verificato anche quest'anno davanti a migliaia di fedeli.**
> The miracle of San Gennaro happened this year too, in front of thousands of faithful.

11.4 Talking about presence, attendance and participation at an event

In addition to using **essere** (**ci**), or **trovarsi** (see 11.2), the following verbs can be used:

> **partecipare** 'to be at', 'to take part in'
> **assistere** 'to be at', 'to take part in'
> **frequentare** 'to attend', 'to go'

11.4.1 *Assistere*

> **Al concerto di Pavarotti, *hanno assistito* 30.000 spettatori.**
> 30,000 spectators were at Pavarotti's concert.

11.4.2 *Partecipare*

This verb implies a more active role:

> **Il Capo di Stato *ha partecipato* al Vertice del G7 a Napoli.**
> The Head of State took part in the G7 Summit in Naples.

Frequentare

Attendance at a place (e.g. school, bar) can be expressed by **frequentare**:

> **I miei figli *frequentano* una scuola privata.**
> My children go to a private school.

> **Il direttore *frequentava* il bar di fronte.**
> The manager went to the café opposite.

11.5 Expressing availability

When talking about availability, most of the verbs and verb phrases listed below, with the exception of **avere**, can be used to refer either to a person or a thing:

> **avere** 'to have' (e.g in a shop or restaurant)
> **rimanere** 'to be left' (over)
> **essere disponibile** 'to be available'
> **essere libero/occupato** 'to be free'/'engaged'

Avere

In shops, offices, restaurants, hotels or similar situations, **c'è**, **ci sono** can be replaced by the verb **avere** 'to have' to express or enquire about availability:

> ***Avete* una mappa della città?**
> Do you have a map of the town?

> ***Abbiamo* questa qui, che costa cinquemila lire.**
> We have this one, which costs five thousand lire.

When **avere** is used with a direct pronoun such as **lo, li, ci** is often added (see 3.4.5). **Ci** changes into **ce** when used before these pronouns:

> ***Avete* la Repubblica? No, non *ce l'abbiamo* oggi.**
> Do you have the 'Repubblica'? No, we haven't got it today.

> ***Ha* il passaporto, signora? Sì, *ce l'ho*.**
> Do you have your passport, madam? Yes, I do have it.

Rimanere

The concept of 'quantity remaining', 'left' is expressed by **rimanere**:

> ***È rimasto* un po' di dolce?**
> Is there any cake left?

> **Del vecchio paese di prima, non *è rimasto* più niente.**
> There's nothing left now, of the old village that was.

> ***Sono rimaste* ancora due o tre persone nella sala.**
> There are still two or three people left in the hall.

11.5.3

Essere disponibile/i

Also often used in shops or business situations, is the adjective **disponibile** 'available'. It has to agree with the noun referred to:

> **Le buste** *sono disponibili* **in vari formati.**
> The envelopes are available in various formats.

> **Il direttore sarà** *disponibile* **dopo la riunione.**
> The manager will be available after the meeting.

11.5.4

Essere libero, occupato, impegnato

The adjectives **libero**, **occupato** can be used both for a person or an object. Note how they have to agree with the person or object referred to:

> *È libero* **il bagno? No,** *è occupato.*
> Is the bathroom free? No, it's occupied.

> **La linea** *è occupata.* **Può attendere in linea?**
> The line is busy. Can you hold?

> **Il professore** *è impegnato* **in questo momento. Può richiamarLa quando** *sarà libero*?
> The professor is busy right now. Can he call you back when he's free?

11.6 Expressing 'some', 'any'

There are various ways of saying how much is available, and expressing 'some' in Italian, depending on whether we are referring to *countable* nouns or *uncountable* nouns.

A countable noun refers to people or things that can be counted; you can put a number in front of them. An uncountable noun *cannot* usually have a number before it and therefore is *normally* singular; examples would be **zucchero** 'sugar', **vino** 'wine' (although of course it is possible to talk about **i vini italiani** 'Italian wines').

11.6.1

Del, dei

Del, **dei**, etc. can be used with both *countable* nouns and *uncountable* nouns:

With countable nouns, we use plural forms **dei**, **delle**, **degli** (the form varies according to the noun which follows; see 1.3.2):

> **Ci sono** *delle* **sedie?**
> Are there any chairs?

> **Ci sono** *degli* **studenti italiani all'università.**
> There are some Italian students at the university.

With uncountable nouns, we use the singular forms **del**, **dello**, **della**, **dell'**:

> **C'è *del* vino?**
> Is there any wine?

> **Per colazione, c'è *della* marmellata d'arancia.**
> For breakfast, there is marmalade.

11.6.2 *Un poco di, un po' di*

This can be used in the singular, with *uncountable* nouns such as 'bread', 'butter', 'coffee', 'wine':

> **È rimasto ancora *un po'* di vino.**
> There's still a little wine left.

> **C'è *un poco* di caffè anche per me?**
> Is there some coffee for me too?

Or in the plural, with *countable* nouns:

> **Dammi *un po'* di monete!**
> Give me some coins!

11.6.3 *Qualche*

Qualche can only be used with *countable* nouns, *not* with uncountable nouns like 'sugar'. **Qualche** means 'a few', 'some' but despite its plural meaning, it must be used with nouns in the singular. Its form is the same for both masculine and feminine nouns:

> **C'è *qualche programma* interessante stasera?**
> Are there any interesting programmes on TV tonight?

> **C'è *qualche donna* manager che guadagna più degli uomini.**
> There are some women managers who earn more than men.

11.6.4 *Alcuni, alcune*

Alcuni/alcune can be used instead of **qualche**, with *countable* nouns, in the plural only, meaning 'some', 'a few':

> **In televisione, ci sono *alcuni* programmi educativi, ma i bambini preferiscono guardare i cartoni animati.**
> On television there are a few educational programmes, but children prefer to watch cartoons.

> **Ci sono *alcune* donne manager in Italia che guadagnano più degli uomini.**
> There are a few women managers in Italy who earn more than men.

With *ne*

Both **alcuni/alcune** and **un po'** (**di**) can be used on their own, with or without the particle **ne** (see below), meaning 'a few things', 'a few people', and 'a little':

> *Ci sono* dei ragazzi italiani al corso estivo? *Ce ne* sono *alcuni.*
> Are there any Italian kids on the summer course? There are a few (of them).

> *Avete* delle guide in italiano? Sì, *ne* abbiamo *alcune.*
> Do you have any guide books in Italian? Yes, we have a few.

> *C'è* del parmigiano? Sì, *ce n'è* un po'.
> Is there any parmesan? Yes, there's a bit.

11.7 *Specifying the quantity available*

With a number or other indication of quantity **rimanere**, **essere** or **avere** (see 11.2, 11.5) can be used:

> *Sono rimasti* solo due panini. Li buttiamo?
> There are only two rolls left. Shall we throw them away?

> Quanti giorni di vacanza *avete*? *Ho* trenta giorni all'anno.
> How many days' holiday do you have? I have 30 days a year.

> Da Roma a Napoli *ci sono* 190 chilometri.
> From Rome to Naples is 190 kms.

To refer to the number or the indication of quantity without repeating the noun previously mentioned, we use the pronoun **ne** (see Chapter 3). Before **ne** or another pronoun, **ci** becomes **ce**, as in **ce n'è** or **ce ne sono**:

> *Sono rimasti* dei panini? Sì, *ne sono rimasti* due.
> Are there any rolls left? Yes, there are two (of them) left.

> *C'erano* molti spettatori al cinema? Sì, *ce n'erano* almeno 300.
> Were there many spectators at the cinema? Yes, there were at least 300.

> *C'è* una banca? Sì, *ce ne sono due* in centro.
> Is there a bank? Yes, there are two (of them) in the centre.

> *C'è* del caffè? Sì, *ce n'è tanto.*
> Is there any coffee? Yes, there's lots (of it).

Ne can also be used when there is *no* indication of quantity, but this is less common and is shown below in brackets:

> *C'è* del latte? Sì, c'è. (Si, ce *n'è*.)
> Is there any milk? Yes, there is some.

Ci sono fichi? Sì, ci sono. (Sì, ce *ne* sono.)
Are there figs? Yes, there are some.

11.8 Expressing 'something/anything', 'someone/anyone'

While **qualche** (see 3.9.2 and 11.6.3) is always used with a noun, **qualcosa** 'something', 'anything' and **qualcuno** 'someone', 'anyone' are used on their own:

C'è *qualcosa* **da leggere?**
Is there anything to read?

C'è *qualcuno*?
Is anyone there?

We can add a 'qualifying' **che** clause ('someone/something', 'anyone/anything *that*...'). This can be followed by the *indicative* (particularly in spoken Italian or informal writing) or the *subjunctive*, if the chances of success seem lower (see 2.3.14 and 9.5). The English translation is the same in both cases:

Cerco *qualcuno* **che** *sa/sappia* **tradurre le lettere commerciali.**
I'm looking for someone who can translate commercial letters.

11.9 Specifying location, time or frequency

You can specify *where* something/someone is, or *when* or *how often* something happens.

11.9.1 Specifying location

You can indicate where the action is taking place, or where something is, by using adverbs or adverbial phrases referring to place (for example **vicino**, **lontano**) or position (for example, **dietro**, **davanti**):

La mia casa si trova *qui vicino*.
My house is near here.

La sede è *a due km dal centro*.
The head office is 2 km from the centre.

Nella riunione, il direttore era seduto *davanti a me*.
In the meeting, the manager was sitting in front of me.

Or phrases with prepositions such as:

C'è un ufficio cambio? Sì, ce n'è uno *in centro*.
Is there a bureau de change? Yes, there's one in the centre.

C'è un Consolato Britannico? Sì, ce n'è uno *a Roma*.
Is there a British Consulate? Yes, there's one in Rome.

Specifying time or date

You can indicate when the action takes place by adding an expression of date or time (see Chapter 36):

C'è un treno alle cinque.
There's a train at five o'clock.

C'è il Telegiornale stasera? Sì, c'è alle 8.00.
Is there a news bulletin this evening? Yes, there's one at 8 o'clock.

Quando si svolge il Palio? Si svolge a luglio e ad agosto.
When does the Palio take place? It takes place in July and in August.

Specifying frequency

You can indicate how often the event or action takes place with phrases of frequency (see Chapter 36):

una volta alla settimana 'once a week'
due volte al mese 'twice a month'
una volta all'anno 'once a year'
il martedì/ogni martedì 'on Tuesdays', 'every Tuesday'

C'è un servizio medico al campeggio?
Is there a medical service on the campsite?

Sì, c'è *due volte alla settimana*, il martedì e il venerdì.
Yes, there's one twice a week, on Tuesdays and Fridays.

Expressing non-existence or non-availability

Non

The easiest way of saying that something does not exist or is not available, is to add **non** to the verbs or phrases shown above:

***Non ci sono* serpenti velenosi in questa zona.**
There are no poisonous snakes in this area.

C'è il medico? No, mi dispiace. *Non c'è*.
Is the doctor here? No, I'm sorry. He isn't here.

***Non c'è rimasto* più niente.**
There's nothing left any more.

Mi dispiace, il direttore *non è disponibile* oggi.
I'm sorry, the manager is not available today.

No, *non è libero* questo posto.
No, this place isn't free.

Full details on negatives, including **nessuno**, **niente**, are found in 16.5, 16.6 and 16.7.

11.10.2

Mancare

The verb **mancare** means 'to be missing', 'to be short':

Vorremmo migliorare i nostri servizi, ma *mancano* i fondi.
We would like to improve our services, but funds are short.

L'ufficio rimarrà chiuso venerdì. *Manca* il personale.
The office will be shut on Friday. There is a shortage of staff.

Manca solo Giorgio.
Only Giorgio is missing.

Manchi solo tu.
Only you are missing.

Mancano i dati.
There are no facts or figures.

11.10.3

Essere assente

When a person is missing, or absent:

Chi *è assente* stamattina?
Who's absent this morning?

Someone who has sent his/her excuses and apologies in advance is called:

un assente giustificato
literally: an explained absentee

The noun **l'assente** can be a metaphor for 'the dear departed' (and see 11.10.8 below).

Note that the verb **partire** is used colloquially not only to express the idea of someone having left, but to express the idea that someone is 'not all there' mentally, i.e. is crazy:

È partito!   He's off his head!

11.10.4

Non ... più, essere esaurito, essere finito

When talking about supplies that are finished, or have run out:

Purtroppo *sono esaurite* le nostre scorte di candele.
Unfortunately, our supplies of candles have run out.

È finita la carta nella stampante.
The paper in the printer is finished.

Non c'è più **posto per stasera.** *È* **tutto** *esaurito.*
There's no more room for tonight. It's all sold out.

11.10.5 *Sparire, scomparire*

The verbs **sparire** and **scomparire** both mean 'to disappear', but can also convey other meanings, such as to 'disappear from the earth'. Of the two, **sparire** is more colloquial.

Sono scomparse **le chiavi di casa.**
The house keys have disappeared.

I dinosauri *sono spariti* **dalla terra milioni di anni fa.**
The dinosaurs disappeared from the earth millions of years ago.

11.10.6 *Sradicare*

The passive form of the verb **sradicare** is most often used when talking about a disease or other evil which has been eradicated:

Il morbillo *è stato* **quasi completamente** *sradicato* **negli USA.**
Measles has been almost completely eradicated in the USA.

But we can also use **scomparire**:

Il morbillo *è* **praticamente** *scomparso* **dagli USA.**
Measles has practically disappeared from the USA.

11.10.7 *Estinguersi, spegnersi*

When talking about a species that has died out, we can use the verb **estinguersi**. Note that **estinto** when used as a noun means dead but not necessarily extinct! (See 11.10.8.)

Fra 500 anni, alcune specie di animali potrebbero *estinguersi.*
In 500 years time, some species of animals could die out.

Both **estingueri** and **spegnersi** can be used with their basic meaning of 'to be extinguished', so are often used of fires, volcanoes, and – metaphorically – of the fires of love:

L'amore *si spegne* **e la passione si raffredda.**
Love burns out and passion grows cold.

11.10.8 **Euphemisms for death**

A reluctance to mention the word 'death' has led Western languages to produce a wide range of euphemisms to express the concept of death and dying. Italian is no exception. Any of the following verbs can be used: **mancare**, **scomparire**, **estinguersi**, **spegnersi**.

The participle **scomparso** is the form most often used in death announcements:

È *scomparso* **il nostro caro Alfredo.**
Our dear friend Alfredo has passed away.

The noun **la scomparsa** is also often seen in this connection:

> **Nel terzo anniversario della *scomparsa* di *Carlo*, la mamma lo ricorda con grande amore.**
> On the third anniversary of the death of Carlo, his mother remembers him with love.

The verb **spegnersi** 'to be extinguished' can be used as a euphemism for **morire**:

> **Il conte *si spense* a mezzanotte, con i familiari attorno al letto.**
> The count died at midnight, with his family around the bed.

So can **mancare**:

> **È improvvisamente *mancato* all'affetto dei suoi cari Marco Strada.**
> Marco Strada has suddenly been lost to the affection of his dear ones.

Note the use of these participles:

> **l'assente** 'the absent one' (literally)
> **il caro estinto** 'the dear departed'

12 *Talking about the present*

12.1 *Introduction*

Situations, actions and events are expressed by the use of verbs (see Chapter 2).

Here we look at how to describe situations, actions and events taking place at the *present* time (i.e. in the same period of time when we are speaking or writing). The verb tense most commonly used for this is the *present indicative*, as shown in our examples. The examples here are mainly in the affirmative; interrogative and negative statements are covered more fully in Chapters 15 and 16 respectively.

12.2 *Describing present situations, actions and events*

A present fact, situation, description, action or event is one that is in effect or taking place at the present time, although not necessarily at the exact moment when we speak or write.

12.2.1 Facts

L'avv. Bianchi *lavora* **alla FIAT.**
Mr Bianchi, the lawyer, works at FIAT.

Questo film *dura* **due ore.**
This film lasts two hours.

Molti italiani *amano* **il calcio.**
Many Italians love football.

Mi piace **molto passeggiare.**
I like walking a lot.

12.2.2 Situations

Mia madre *è* **malata.** *Ha* **una malattia cardiaca.**
My mother is ill. She has a heart disease.

Le autostrade *sono* invase da turisti stranieri che *vengono* in vacanza in Italia.
The motorways are invaded by foreign tourists who come on holiday to Italy.

Il turismo in Calabria *è poco* sviluppato.
Tourism in Calabria is not very developed.

12.2.3   Descriptions

Il tempo *è* brutto.
The weather is bad.

I gemelli non *sono* identici.
The twins are not identical.

12.2.4   Actions
Single actions

Perché *non telefoni* all'Ufficio Vendite?
Why don't you phone the Sales Department?

Oggi *cucina* Walter.
Today Walter is cooking.

Single or regular actions

In Italian, there is no difference in the way we describe facts or events which are happening at the time we speak or write ('Isabella is teaching this morning'), and those that may not be happening *right now*, but are a habit or regular occurrence ('Isabella teaches every Tuesday'). All these actions or events are expressed by the present tense of verbs:

Isabella *insegna* stamattina. / Isabella *insegna* ogni martedì.
Isabella is teaching this morning. / Isabella teaches every Tuesday.

L'infermiera non *viene* oggi. / L'infermiera non *viene* il giovedì.
The nurse isn't coming today. / The nurse doesn't come on Thursdays.

Regular actions

The only feature that distinguishes *habitual* actions from *single* actions is the adverb or phrase used. Words or phrases that convey the notion of *habit* include:

di solito 'usually'
generalmente 'generally'
normalmente 'normally'
ogni 'every'
tutti i, tutte le 'every'

Ogni mese, **andiamo a trovare i parenti in campagna.**
Every month, we go to see our relatives in the country.

Tutte le settimane **facciamo la spesa al Centro Commerciale 'Globus'.**
Every week we do the shopping at the 'Globus' shopping centre.

Normalmente **mio marito torna a casa prima di me.**
Normally my husband comes home before me.

With days of the week, use of the article **il, la** conveys the idea of a regular weekly action:

Il venerdì **mangiamo il pesce.**
Every Friday we eat fish.

La domenica **mia madre va a messa.**
On Sundays my mother goes to Mass.

Other phrases of frequency and repetition can be found in 36.6.

12.2.5
Events: single events, regular events
Again, Italian makes no distinction between a regular event ('The Boat Show takes place every year') and an event taking place *this* week/month/year ('The Boat Show is taking place this week'):

Il Salone Nautico *si svolge* **questa settimana a Genova.**
The Boat Show is taking place this week in Genoa.

Il Salone Nautico *si svolge* **ogni anno ad aprile.**
The Boat Show takes place every year in April.

12.3 Expressing ongoing actions

If you need to express something more immediate, or an action that is still going on at the present time and is not yet completed, you can use the *progressive* form of the present tense. The *progressive present* (see 2.3.28), similar to the English 'to be doing something', is formed by using the present tense of the verb **stare** together with the *gerund* of the verb expressing the action (**lavorando, leggendo, partendo**):

I ragazzi *stanno leggendo.*
The boys are reading.

Il signor Rossi *sta partendo.*
Mr Rossi is just leaving.

Stiamo lavorando.
We are working.

Note that **stare** and the *gerund* cannot be used to translate the English 'to be doing' construction when it refers to the future, even if it's the very near future. For this you use the regular present indicative or the future:

> **Il dott. Cuomo *arriva* fra mezz'ora.**
> Dr Cuomo is arriving in half an hour.

> **Dove *andrete* domani?**
> Where are you going tomorrow?

12.4 *Words and phrases indicating present time*

The present time can be indicated by using adverbs or phrases specifying time, as well as the verb in the present tense. (For more complex time contexts, see Section IV.) Here are some examples:

Ora, adesso 'now':

> **È tardi. *Ora* andiamo a casa.**
> It's late. Let's go home now.

> **Scusami, *adesso* non voglio parlare.**
> Sorry, I don't wish to talk now.

> **Ho cambiato ufficio. *Adesso* lavoro al terzo piano.**
> I've changed my office. I'm working on the third floor now.

Subito, immediatamente 'right now', 'immediately':

> **Vieni *subito* qua!**
> Come here right now!

> **Attenda un attimo, per favore. Le passo *immediatamente* il direttore.**
> Hold on a second, please. I'll put you through to the manager immediately.

Oggi 'today':

> **Oggi mi sento felice!**
> I feel happy today!

> **Oggi è sabato.**
> Today is Saturday.

Ancora 'still':

> **È *ancora* presto per partire.**
> It's still early to be leaving.

> **Ho *ancora* fame!**
> I am still hungry!

Questo 'this':

Questo can be used to refer to the present year, month, week or part of the day:

>*Quest'anno* **le vendite vanno bene.**
>This year the sales are going well.

>*Questa settimana* **lavoro fino a tardi.**
>This week I'm working till late.

>*Questo pomeriggio* **fa freddo.**
>It's cold this afternoon.

Note the shortened forms **stasera, stanotte**:

>*Stasera* **Monica è nervosa.**
>Tonight Monica is edgy.

>*Stanotte* **non riesco a dormire.**
>I can't sleep tonight.

12.5   Dialogo

In this dialogue the different forms of the present are highlighted.

Mario Adinolfi *è* impiegato alla Camera di Commercio di Bari, ma in questi giorni *sta lavorando* a Roma per organizzare la partecipazione di alcune industrie romane alla Fiera del Levante di Bari. La Ditta Cosmetici 2000 Spa *vuole* presentare alla Fiera un nuovo prodotto per la cura dei capelli e il sig. Luca Violli, Direttore delle Vendite, *incontra* il sig. Adinolfi per chiedere informazioni sui servizi della Fiera. Ecco un brano della loro conversazione:

VIOLLI: **Quanto *costa* l'affitto di un ufficio per il periodo della Fiera?**
ADINOLFI: **Quest'anno *abbiamo* uffici attrezzati con servizi di segreteria, che *costano* 3 milioni per 5 giorni.**
VIOLLI: **Quando *posso* visitare gli uffici?**
ADINOLFI: **Gli uffici *si possono* visitare dopo il 10 settembre. *Ora stiamo ancora completando* i lavori, ma Lei *può* fare una prenotazione adesso. *Deve* solo riempire questo modulo.**
VIOLLI: **Va bene. Chi *deve* firmare il modulo?**
ADINOLFI: **Può firmare Lei, o un altro responsabile della ditta, come *preferisce.***

Dialogue
Mario Adinolfi is an employee at the Chamber of Commerce in Bari, but at present he is working in Rome making arrangements for several Roman companies to take part in the 'Fiera del Levante' Trade Fair in Bari. The company 'Cosmetics 2000' Ltd wants to present its new hair care product and Mr Luca Violli, Director of Sales, meets Mr Adinolfi to ask for information on the

services offered by the Fair. Here is a snatch of their conversation.

VIOLLI: How much does it cost to rent an office for the duration of the Fair?

ADINOLFI: This year we have ready-equipped offices with secretarial services, which cost three million lire for five days.

VIOLLI: When can I visit the offices?

ADINOLFI: After the 10th September. We are just finishing the work, but you can book now. You only need to fill in this form.

VIOLLI: All right. Who needs to sign the form?

ADINOLFI: You can sign it, or else some other representative of the company, as you prefer.

13 Speaking/writing about the past

Introduction

When speaking or writing about the past in Italian we generally use two different verb forms: a *perfect* form and an *imperfect* form. These two forms are two different *aspects* of Italian verbs in the past – two different *points of view* – and it is essential to distinguish between them.

The *perfect* aspect is used when we talk about the past from the point of view of the present. The *imperfect* aspect looks at the past from the point of view of the past; it is used to talk and write about past events from 'inside' the past itself.

To describe what we or someone else did, we can use any of the following:

The perfect *form*:

> **Ieri *ho lavorato* fino alle 5.00 e poi *sono andata* al bar.**
> Yesterday I worked until 5 and then I went to the bar.

The imperfect *form*:

> **Gli impiegati *lavoravano* tutta la mattina e poi *andavano* al bar.**
> The employees worked all morning and then they went to the bar.

A combination of both:

> **Quando *lavoravo* lì, *sono andata* molte volte nell'ufficio del direttore.**
> When I worked there, I went several times to the manager's office.

In the next few pages, we look first at the *perfect* aspect (in its two different forms: compound and simple) then at the *imperfect* aspect, and finally at the two aspects used together.

All the examples here are of verbs in the *indicative* mood; for examples of perfect and imperfect in the *subjunctive* mood, see Chapter 2 for the verb forms and Chapters 25–7, 29–33, 35–6 and 38–9 in particular for examples of how they are used.

The perfect aspect: introduction

When talking about events in the past, regarded as complete, Italian uses the *perfect* tense. There are two forms of *perfect* tense: the *simple perfect* (**passato remoto**) and the *compound perfect* (**passato prossimo**). Their forms are described in Chapter 2.

The **passato prossimo** is a *compound* tense formed of an auxiliary and participle, while the **passato remoto** is not a compound form, so can be defined as the *simple perfect.* (The latter is also known in English as the *past historic,* which has led to misunderstandings over its use.)

The *perfect* tense most frequently used is the *compound* form, the **passato prossimo**:

> *Sono arrivato* **la settimana scorsa.**
> I arrived last week.

> **Ieri** *ho comprato* **una camicia rossa.**
> Yesterday I bought a red shirt.

> **Ti** *è piaciuto* **il film?**
> Did you like the film?

> *Avete conosciuto* **il direttore?**
> Have you met the manager?

The *simple perfect* form (**passato remoto**) can also be used. Here are the same examples as above, this time using the **passato remoto**:

> *Arrivai* **la settimana scorsa.**
> I arrived last week.

> **Ieri** *comprai* **una camicia rossa.**
> Yesterday I bought a red shirt.

> **Ti** *piacque* **il film?**
> Did you like the film?

> *Conosceste* **il direttore?**
> Have you met the director?

It is clear that the difference between the two sets of examples is *not* one of *time,* as suggested by traditional grammar terminology, which makes a distinction between **passato remoto** or 'far-off' past, and **passato prossimo** or 'near' past. This is the reason why these two tenses are best defined in English as *simple* and *compound* perfect (in Italian **passato semplice, passato composto**), so as not to stress any difference in 'time setting'.

The sentences in the second set above, although perfectly correct, are unlikely to be used in everyday conversation, at least in northern or central Italy (see

13.4.3). The different functions and uses of the two past tenses are best explained by example.

The **passato remoto** (see Chapter 2) is much less frequently used than the **passato prossimo**. Its main function is to represent events in the past which have *no connection with the present*, i.e. with the time when the sentence is spoken or written. So, when talking about the date someone was born, we can use the **passato remoto** if that person is no longer alive:

> **Dante *nacque* nel 1265. *Visse* per molti anni a Firenze.**
> Dante was born in 1265. He lived for many years in Florence.

> **Pier Paolo Pasolini *nacque* nel 1922. *Fu* uno dei più famosi scrittori del Neorealismo.**
> Pier Paolo Pasolini was born in 1922. He was one of the most famous Neorealist writers.

However, if we want to stress the relationship of those personalities with the present, in other words their influence on today's readers, we use the **passato prossimo**:

> **Dante *è nato* nel 1265, e oggi si festeggia l'anniversario della nascita.**
> Dante was born in 1265, and today we celebrate the anniversary of his birth.

> **Pier Paolo Pasolini *è nato* nel 1922, e i suoi film più famosi sono ancora molto popolari.**
> Pier Paolo Pasolini was born in 1922, and his best-known films are still very popular today.

The **passato prossimo** is always used if the person is still alive at the present time:

> **Mio figlio *è nato* nel 1983.**
> My son was born in 1983.

<h2>13.3   Using the passato prossimo</h2>

This form is very similar to the English present perfect ('I have eaten', etc.); however they do not always correspond exactly in their use, as shown below:

> **Gli *ho parlato* apertamente.**
> I have spoken openly to him.

> ***Siamo partiti* alle 5.00.**
> We left at 5 o'clock.

Here is an example of a passage in which you will recognize many verbs used in the compound form of the perfect. Some of the participles shown do not follow a regular pattern; for more information, see Chapter 2:

Sono uscito alle 9.00 per andare a far spese e *ho incontrato* un vecchio amico che non vedevo da molto tempo. *Abbiamo deciso* di fare le spese insieme e *siamo andati* prima alla Rinascente e poi da UPIM. Alle 11.00 *abbiamo bevuto* un aperitivo al bar e quindi *abbiamo comprato* verdura e carne per preparare il pranzo. *Siamo arrivati* a casa a mezzogiorno e *abbiamo cucinato* e *mangiato* con appetito. Alle 2.00 il mio amico *è tornato* a casa sua, perchè aveva un appuntamento.

I went out at 9 o'clock to go shopping and I met an old friend whom I hadn't seen for a long time. We decided to go shopping together and we went first to 'Rinascente' and then to 'Upim'. At 11 o'clock, we drank an aperitif at the café and then we bought vegetables and meat to make lunch. We arrived home at midday and we cooked and ate hungrily. At 2 o'clock my friend went back home, because he had an appointment.

13.4   *Using the* passato remoto

Although the **passato remoto** is much less frequently used than the **passato prossimo**, there are certain contexts in which it is used to describe events or actions:

In an historical context

The **passato remoto** is used frequently in historical narration as can be seen from this example, taken from a history textbook for primary schools (*Strumenti*, Alfio Zoi, ed., Editrice La Scuola, 1991, pp.188–9):

Quando nel 1152, Federico I detto Barbarossa *divenne* re di Germania, *decise* di sottomettere i Comuni ribelli. *Compì* cinque discese in Italia: nella prima (1154) *soffocò* la ribellione di Roma e *si fece* incoronare imperatore; nella seconda *conquistò* Milano e *riaffermò* solennemente i diritti dell'Imperatore sui Comuni (1158); nella terza *assediò* e *distrusse* Milano (1163); nella quarta *occupò* Roma (1168) e nella quinta *fu sconfitto* a Legnano dalla Lega Lombarda (alleanza tra i Comuni, decisa a Pontida nel 1167, e appoggiata dal Papa Alessandro III). Per questo *dovette* riconoscere la libertà dei Comuni con il trattato di pace di Costanza (1183).

When, in 1152, Frederick I, known as Redbeard, became King of Germany, he decided to suppress the rebellious City States. He carried out five raids in Italy: in the first (1154) he suppressed the rebellion in Rome, and had himself crowned emperor; in the second he conquered Milan and with due ceremony reaffirmed the rights of the emperor over the city states (1158); in the third he besieged and destroyed Milan (1163); in the fourth he

occupied Rome (1168) and in the fifth he was defeated at
Legnano by the Lombard League (an alliance between the City
States, set up in Pontida in 1167, and supported by Pope
Alexander III). For this reason he was forced to recognize the
freedom of the City States, with the peace treaty of Constance
(1183).

Note however that when historical events are seen in their relevance to the
present time, again the **passato prossimo** is more likely to be used, even if the
events happened a long time ago. Here is another example, again from the same
textbook *Strumenti* (p.248):

> **La storia moderna di Roma *è iniziata* nel 1870 quando la città *è
> diventata* capitale del giovane Regno d'Italia. Allora Roma contava
> appena 200.000 abitanti ed anche il suo aspetto urbanistico non
> era molto diverso da quello dei secoli precedenti . . . .**
>
> **Anche nel nostro secolo, e in particolare negli ultimi decenni,
> Roma *ha continuato* a espandersi per l'afflusso di lavoratori
> provenienti da tutto il Lazio e dalle regioni centro-meridionali.**

> The modern history of Rome began in 1870 when the city
> became the capital of the young Kingdom of Italy. At that time
> Rome counted scarcely 200,000 inhabitants, and as a town it did
> not appear very different from in previous centuries . . . .
>
> In our own century, and particularly in the last few decades,
> Rome has continued to grow, because of the influx of workers
> coming from all over Lazio, and the central and southern
> regions.

Here the events described, some of which happened more than 100 years ago,
are relevant to today's situation (Rome is still the capital of Italy and its
population is still expanding because of the influx of immigrants).

13.4.2
In a narrative
The **passato remoto** is in general the 'perfect' form most often used in the
narrative register and is therefore more frequently found in *written* than in
spoken language.

Here is another example of the use of the **passato remoto**, this time not in an
historical context but in a narrative literary passage:

> **E allora vieni avanti, *disse* la voce di Tadeus, ormai la casa la
> conosci. *Chiusi* la porta alle mie spalle e *avanzai* per il corridoio. Il
> corridoio era buio, e *inciampai* in un mucchio di cose che *caddero*
> per terra. *Mi fermai* a raccogliere quel che avevo sparso sul
> pavimento: libri, un giocattolo di legno, un gallo di Barcelos, la
> statuetta di un santo . . . .**

> (from the novel *Requiem*,
> by Antonio Tabucchi, Feltrinelli, 1992, p.37)

So, come on through, said Tadeus' voice, you know the house by now. I shut the door behind me, and started off along the corridor. The corridor was dark and I stumbled into a pile of things which fell on the ground. I stopped to pick up what I had spread over the floor: books, a wooden toy, a Barcelos cock, the statuette of a saint . . . .

— **13.4.3** —
In spoken Italian

The **passato remoto** used as an historical or narrative tense is most frequently found in written texts. The use of this tense in spoken conversational Italian is rare and restricted to the southern regions of Italy. So the examples of spoken Italian seen in 13.2 above, using the **passato remoto**, are very unlikely to be heard in central and northern Italy, but quite acceptable, for example, in Sicily.

13.5 *Expressing the imperfect aspect*

The imperfect aspect of actions or events in the past is conveyed by the **imperfetto** in Italian. (For further information on the **imperfetto** and its forms, see Chapter 2.)

This section of the chapter looks at the use of the imperfect aspect by itself, while 13.6 considers its use together with the perfect.

The general function of the *imperfect* aspect is to represent past events and actions as if seen from *within* the past itself.

The following two sentences illustrate how the same fact, happening at the same time, can be seen from two different points of view, in other words from two *aspects*:

> **Ieri *faceva* molto caldo a Napoli.**
> Yesterday it was very hot in Naples.

> **Ieri *ha fatto* molto caldo a Napoli.**
> Yesterday it was very hot in Naples.

The first example (the *imperfect* aspect) talks about the hot weather as the condition experienced by people *during* that particular span of time; it could be said, for instance, by someone who was actually in Naples yesterday and wants to talk about his/her own experience of the weather.

The second example (the *perfect* aspect) sees yesterday's weather from *outside*; it could be said, for example, by someone who was not in Naples (e.g. a weather forecaster) and who wants to tell someone else about the weather with a certain detachment.

The following paragraphs consider the main uses of the **imperfetto** or imperfect aspect.

13.5.1

Parallel events or actions

Two past actions or events can be viewed in a symmetrical relationship, taking place within the *same time span*:

> **Mentre *lavorava,* Anna *pensava* alle vacanze in Sardegna.**
> While she was working, Anna was thinking about the holidays in Sardinia.

> **Il direttore *parlava* e gli invitati *ascoltavano* annoiati.**
> The director was talking and the guests were listening, bored.

These are parallel actions that take place at the *same* time and are part of the *same* situation, described as if seen from within the situation itself, rather than a set of events viewed in relation to the present time (the time when we are speaking or writing):

$$\longrightarrow$$

$$\longrightarrow$$

13.5.2

Habitual or repeated actions

In the following examples, the actions are not separate actions taking place at the same time; because of their repetition, they are seen not as individual actions but as the general state or situation of the subject, at the period of time when they happened. In English, this situation can be expressed with the form 'used to'.

> **A Roma *andavo* tutti i giorni a mangiare in trattoria.**
> In Rome I went to eat in a trattoria every day.

> **Da ragazzo *facevo* molto sport.**
> When I was a boy, I used to play lots of sport.

13.5.3

Describing past events or situations

> **All'università *c'era* una gran confusione. Gli studenti, che *volevano* iscriversi, *cercavano* di capire che cosa fare mentre gli impiegati della Segreteria non *riuscivano* a farsi sentire nel gran chiasso. *Faceva* molto caldo e molti *si riparavano* all'ombra degli alberi nel cortile.**
> At the university, there was a great deal of confusion. The students, who wanted to enrol, were trying to find out what to do, while the staff in the Administration Office couldn't make themselves heard in the racket. It was very hot, and many people took refuge in the shade of the trees in the courtyard.

Here we have a *picture* of a situation where the verbs are the elements *inside* the picture, rather than the *whole* of an event or an action.

Compare the situation above with a narrative description, which uses the perfect aspect if the facts take place one after the other, i.e. when they are not seen as details inside a picture, but as a sequence of single separate actions:

$$| \longrightarrow | \longrightarrow | \longrightarrow | \longrightarrow | \longrightarrow |$$

> **Ieri *sono andato* all'università e *ho trovato* una gran confusione. *Ho chiesto* informazioni in Segreteria e mi *hanno detto* di aspettare. Faceva molto caldo e *mi sono riparato* sotto gli alberi nel cortile.**
> Yesterday I went to the university and I found a great deal of confusion. I asked for information in the Administrative office and they told me to wait. It was very hot, and I took refuge under the trees in the courtyard.

Each of these actions had to be carried out before the following one could take place:

$$| \text{ ho chiesto } | \text{ hanno detto } | \text{ mi sono riparato } |$$

13.5.4

Narrative using imperfect

Here is a passage from a novel which uses almost entirely verbs in the *imperfect*. Note how the description below ends with two verbs in the simple perfect, **finì, girò**:

> **Era entrata nella stanza adiacente dove adesso i giornali *toccavano* il soffitto o comunque la *sovrastavano* pencolanti e minacciosi. *Era* una vera e propria foresta di carta con scricchiolanti sottoboschi in fondo ai quali vide farsi largo la luce del giorno e lei, la vecchia striminzita imbacuccata in un mucchio di stracci maschili e di coperte. *Era* in piedi davanti alla finestra rotta e le *presentava* la schiena. *Stava* incollando con impasto di acqua e farina bianca un foglio di giornale sul riquadro senza vetro. E contemporaneamente lo *stava* bisbigliando dalla a alla zeta. *Doveva* certo essere così assorta da non averla sentita, non *si decideva* a girarsi. Brunilì *finì* con calma il duplice lavoro e poi *si girò*....**
>
> (from *La Delfina Bizantina*, by Aldo Busi, Mondadori, 1992, p.53)

She had gone into the adjacent room, where the newspapers now touched the ceiling, or at least towered over her, swaying and threatening. It was an absolute forest of paper, with creaking undergrowth at the other side of which she saw the light of day penetrating, and then her, the shabby old woman all muffled up in a heap of tattered men's clothes and blankets. She was standing in front of the broken window with her back turned. She was gluing – with flour and water paste – a sheet of newspaper on the windowless frame. And at the same time she was whispering it to herself from cover to cover. She must have been so absorbed that she hadn't heard her, she didn't give any sign of turning around. Brunilì calmly finished her two-fold task, and then turned around ....

13.5.5
Progressive imperfect (*stare* + gerund)

One very common form of the *imperfect aspect* is the *progressive* form. This is formed using the imperfect of the verb **stare** together with the gerund of the main verb. This form is fairly familiar to English speakers, being similar in form and use to the English 'to be -ing'.

> **Che cosa *stavate facendo* ieri sera?**
> What were you doing yesterday evening?

> ***Stavo lavorando* quando mi ha telefonato Andrea.**
> I was working when Andrea called me.

The progressive form expresses an action in progress, i.e. not completed, at a certain moment in time. It cannot be used to convey, for example, the aspects of repetition or description of past events, as in the paragraphs above, where the simple imperfect is used instead. The *progressive* aspect in Italian, as in English, can be used not only in the past, but also in the present and future (see Chapters 12 and 14 respectively).

13.6   *Combinations of perfect and imperfect aspects*

13.6.1
Scene-setting: introduction

In the paragraphs above, we saw how the *imperfect* expresses the elements of a past situation, in contrast with the *perfect* tenses, which see actions or events in their entirety and 'separateness'. To understand more clearly how the two aspects interact to depict the past we can use the metaphor of a play seen at the theatre:

The *scenery* or *stage set* is the *background* of the play and is represented by the *imperfect*. The *actors*, their **actions**, and the *events* of the play are in the *foreground* and represented by the *perfect*.

Scene-setting in novels

A traditional technique of novelists is to set a scene, using the *imperfect*, and to let the characters act within it, using the *perfect*. In each of the following two passages, taken from Leonardo Sciascia's *Il Giorno della Civetta*, Einaudi, 1981, p.9 and p.57, it is easy to identify the two aspects, perfect and imperfect:

(a) L'autobus *stava* per partire, *rombava* sordo con improvvisi raschi e singulti. La piazza *era* silenziosa nel grigio dell'alba.... Il bigliettaio *chiuse* lo sportello, l'autobus *si mosse* con un rumore di sfasciume.... *Si sentirono* due colpi squarciati... Il bigliettaio *bestemmiò*: la faccia gli era diventata colore di zolfo, *tremava*....
The bus was about to leave; it was giving out a dull roar, with sudden rasping and hiccupping noises. The square was silent, in the grey dawn ... the conductor shut the door, the bus moved off with a disintegrating noise ... then two shots were heard to rip the air ... the conductor swore: his face turned the colour of sulphur, he shook....

(b) Il corpo di Parrinieddu *era* ancora sul selciato, coperto da un telo azzurrastro. I carabineri di guardia *sollevarono* il telo: il corpo *era* contratto come nel sonno prenatale, nella oscura matrice della morte.
Parrinieddu's body was still on the asphalt, covered by a blueish sheet. The policemen on duty lifted the cloth: the body was drawn up as if in a prenatal slumber, in the dark womb of death.

Scene (an event or action already in progress) and action or event

A less obvious example of scene-setting is the way in which Italian, even in everyday speech or writing, distinguishes between actions in the past, using the imperfect to describe certain actions that are seen as a background to others. Here are a few examples, where the pattern is that of an *action/event* happening at a certain moment, set against the *background* of something that was going on in the same moment (but also before and possibly after):

Paola *è arrivata* (*event*), mentre *preparavo* la cena (*scene*).
Paola arrived (*event*) while I was preparing dinner (*scene*).

Gli impiegati *lavoravano* (*scene*) quando *è suonato* l'allarme (*event*).
The staff were working (*scene*) when the alarm went (*event*).

Passeggiavamo (*scene*) tranquillamente, ma all'improvviso *è scoppiato* (*action*) un temporale.
We were walking along quietly (*scene*), when suddenly a storm broke (*action*).

13.6.4

Scene (a situation) and action or event

Erano le 5.25 quando *è esplosa* la bomba.
It was 5.25 when the bomb went off.

Sono arrivato alla stazione proprio quando il treno *partiva*.
I arrived at the station just when the train left.

In both these examples, the **imperfetto** represents a fact that, although instantaneous, is seen as the situation, context or background in which something happened.

13.6.5

Cause and effect

Non *sono venuto* a trovarti perché *avevo* troppo lavoro da fare.
I didn't come to see you, because I had too much work to do.

Avevamo fame e *abbiamo deciso* di fare due spaghetti.
We were hungry and (so) we decided to cook a bit of spaghetti.

In these sentences the role of the **imperfetto** is clearly that of the background to, or cause of, an event.

All the examples given above can be illustrated with the following pattern:

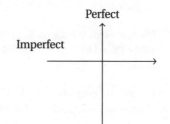

13.6.6

Examples of different patterns

Here are examples of how the same two verbs can be used in three different patterns as described above (see 13.5.1, 13.5.3 and 13.6.4):

Parallel actions:

Mentre io *riposavo* Sandro *telefonava* a sua sorella.
While I was resting, Sandro was on the phone to his sister.

Sequence of actions:

Ho riposato e poi *ho telefonato* a Sandro.
I rested and then I telephoned Sandro.

Situation + event:

> Mentre *riposavo* mi *ha telefonato* Sandro.
> While I was resting, Sandro telephoned me.

— 13.6.7 — **Further examples of imperfect/perfect aspects**

Here are some further examples illustrating the different functions of *imperfect* and *perfect*; see if you can link them to the explanations above:

> *Ho ordinato* gli articoli che mi *interessavano*.
> I ordered the items that I was interested in.

> Ieri sera *pensavo* a quello che mi *hai detto* e *ho capito* che *avevi* ragione.
> Yesterday evening I was thinking about what you said to me, and I realized that you were right.

> Mi dispiace, non *volevo* offenderti quando ti *ho rimproverato*.
> I'm sorry, I didn't want to offend you when I told you off.

> *Ho visitato* Firenze con quell'amico che *lavorava* al museo.
> I visited Florence with that friend who worked in the museum.

> *Abbiamo imparato* l'italiano con un professore che non *diceva* nemmeno una parola d'inglese.
> We learnt Italian with a teacher who didn't speak a word of English.

> Quando *abitavo* a Napoli *ho visitato* tre volte il Museo Nazionale.
> When I lived in Naples, I visited the National Museum three times.

> Per quanto tempo *hai vissuto* in Cina?
> How long did you live in China for?

> *Ho vissuto* a Shanghai per tre anni.
> I lived in Shanghai for three years.

> Quando *vivevo* in Cina *mangiavo* il riso tre volte al giorno.
> When I lived in China, I ate rice three times a day.

> Ieri *ho mangiato* riso tre volte.
> Yesterday I ate rice three times.

— 13.6.8 — **Imperfect/perfect aspect: modal verbs *volere, dovere, potere***

With certain verbs, particularly the modal verbs **dovere**, **potere**, **volere**, the choice of tense can be even more important, since it may alter the meaning. Use of the imperfect tense suggests that the intention was not fulfilled (the action was not completed). In sentences of this kind, the past conditional may also be used (see 2.3.13).

Volevo **andare in banca, ma era chiusa.**
I wanted to go to the bank, but it was shut.
(*So I couldn't go after all.*)

Ho voluto **andare in banca.**
I wanted to go to the bank.
(*The implication is that I did go there.*)

Dovevano **venire ieri, ma c'era sciopero dei treni.**
They should have come yesterday, but there was a train strike.
(*They should have come but they didn't.*)

Hanno dovuto **introdurre un nuovo prodotto per competere con i francesi.**
They had to introduce a new product to compete with the French.
(*They had to introduce one – and they did.*)

Sapevamo **che lui era disposto a trattare.**
We knew that he was prepared to negotiate.

L'*abbiamo saputo* **troppo tardi.**
We found it out too late.
(**Sapere** *in the* **passato prossimo** *generally means 'to learn', 'to find out'.*)

La nostra azienda non *conosceva* **il mercato inglese.**
Our firm was not familiar with the English market.

Ho conosciuto **il direttore di marketing alla Fiera di Genova.**
I met the director of marketing at the Genoa Trade Fair.

The tense used with **potere** is generally whichever tense would have been used with the verb expressing the action if **potere** had not been present:

Non *hanno potuto* **salvare il ragazzo.**
They were not able to save the boy.
(*One action is implied*: **Non hanno salvato il ragazzo.**)

Non *potevano* **fare quello che volevano perché il padre non glielo permetteva.**
They were not able to do what they wanted, because their father would not allow them.
(*Long-term state or condition implied*: **Non facevano quello che volevano.**)

13.7   *Present tense expressing past*

There are two situations in which past events are not expressed either by *imperfect* or *perfect* but by the *present* indicative tense:

When the event in question is still going on

13.7.1

When the event, action or situation in question is still going on, the present tense is used with **da**, the equivalent of the English 'since':

> *Studio* l'italiano *da* 5 anni.
> I have been studying Italian for 5 years.
> (*implication: And I'm still trying!*)
> (*literally*: I study Italian since 5 years.)

Compare this with the following example:

> *Ho studiato* l'italiano *per* 5 anni.
> I studied Italian for 5 years.
> (*implication: But now I've given up!*)

For dramatic effect

13.7.2

For example reporting events in newspapers:

> Fuori dal bar *si accende* un furibondo litigio. Un signore, in giro
> con il cane, *vede* i due sudamericani che *si rincorrono.*
> Outside the bar a furious quarrel started up. A man, out walking
> his dog, saw the two South Americans chasing each other.

Or in historical descriptions:

> Nel settembre 1939 la Germania *invade* la Polonia, e Francia e
> Gran Bretagna *dichiarano* la guerra. L'Italia *rimane* fuori del
> conflitto fino al 1940.
> In September 1939, Germany invaded Poland, and France and
> Great Britain declared war. Italy stayed out of the conflict until
> 1940.

13.8   *Indicators of time*

Time indicators

13.8.1

To say how long ago the action took place, use **fa** 'ago' and the appropriate length of time:

> **due giorni fa** 'two days ago'
> **un mese fa** 'a month ago'
> **poco tempo fa** 'a short time ago'

To express 'last' meaning 'the one just past', use the adjectives **scorso** or **passato** (note that while **scorso** can come before or after the noun, **passato** can only come after):

> **la scorsa settimana** 'last week'
> **il mese scorso** 'last month'
> **l'anno passato** 'last year'
> **l'estate passata** 'last summer'

Here are some common time phrases which can be used to refer to the past:

> **ieri** 'yesterday'
> **l'altro ieri** 'day before yesterday'
> **ieri mattina** 'yesterday morning'
> **ieri sera** 'yesterday evening'
> **stamattina** 'this morning'

13.8.2

Negative time indicators

When the double negative phrases: **non ... ancora; non ... mai; non più** (see 16.3) are used with the **passato prossimo**, **non** goes before the whole verb, but the second negative element will normally go *before* the participle:

> **La consegna *non* è *ancora* arrivata.**
> The delivery hasn't arrived yet.
>
> ***Non* è *più* venuto.**
> He didn't come any more.
>
> ***Non* c'è *mai* stata la pace in quel paese.**
> There has never been peace in that country.

The second negative element can also be placed *after* the verb:

> **La consegna *non* è arrivata *ancora*.**
> The delivery hasn't arrived yet.
>
> ***Non* è venuto *più*.**
> He didn't come any more.
>
> ***Non* c'è stata *mai* la pace in quel paese.**
> There has never been peace in that country.

14 Talking about the future

Introduction

English speakers often assume that when talking about future events, actions or situations Italian always uses the future tense of verbs (see Chapter 2). This is not always the case. As we can see in the following examples, we can use either the *future* tense or the *present* tense, to refer to the same event or facts. We can also use a different verb or verb phrase when talking about the *very near future*.

14.2 Using the future tense

In the examples below, the *future tense* of the verbs is used to imply firm intention or plans or a certain future event:

> **La settimana prossima *partirò* per gli Stati Uniti.**
> Next week I'll leave for the USA.

> ***Arriveremo* non appena possibile.**
> We'll arrive as soon as possible.

> **Spero che tu non *cambierai* idea.**
> I hope you *won't change* your mind.

> **Fra pochi giorni *saremo* in Francia.**
> In a few days we *'ll be* in France.

14.3 Using the present tense

The future tense is not very much used in colloquial Italian. The *present tense* can be used in its place in almost every situation, just as it can in English:

> **Domani *parto* per Genova.**
> Tomorrow I'm leaving for Genoa.

> **A che ora *arriva* l'aereo?**
> What time *is* the flight *arriving*?

> **La settimana prossima *cambiamo* ufficio.**
> Next week we are changing office.

> **Fra poco *siamo* in Francia.**
> Soon we*'ll be* in France.

 With a time indicator

Even events in the *distant* future can be expressed using the present. However, when using the present, some explicit indication placing the events firmly in the future (such as **la settimana prossima, l'anno prossimo, fra un mese**, etc. . . .) helps to avoid misunderstanding, as in the following examples:

> **L'anno prossimo *passiamo* le vacanze a New York.**
> Next year we are spending the holidays in New York.

> **Fra un mese *siamo* in Italia.**
> In a month we'll be in Italy.

The future tense is generally preferable when speaking or writing in a more formal context.

14.4 Expressing the immediate or very near future

There are two particular ways of talking about actions that are imminent or 'about to happen':

14.4.1 *Stare per*

The expression **stare per** is used with the *verb infinitive*:

> **Stiamo per partire.**
> We are about to leave.

> **La conferenza *sta per* cominciare.**
> The talk will begin soon.

> **Attenda un attimo. La sua fattura è quasi pronta. *Sto per* finire di scriverla.**
> Please wait a second. Your invoice is almost ready. I am just finishing writing it.

14.4.2 *Essere sul punto di*

The expression **essere sul punto di . . .** approximately corresponds to the English 'to be on the verge of . . .':

> **Il professore *è sul punto di* avere un esaurimento nervoso.**
> The teacher *is on the verge of* a nervous breakdown.

> **Attenzione! Il treno *è sul punto di* partire!**
> Attention! The train *is just about* to depart!

14.5 *Expressing the English 'going to'*

The English 'going to' can sometimes be a way of expressing the future, or an intention. Occasionally it literally means 'going to'. You have to know which meaning it conveys before you can translate it into Italian:

Future or intention:

> When I'm on holiday, I'm going to learn Italian.
> **Quando *sarò* in vacanza, *imparerò* l'italiano.**

or   ***Ho intenzione di* imparare l'italiano.**

Literally 'going':

> Tomorrow I'm going shopping.
> **Domani *vado a* fare le spese.**

For other examples of future planning and intention, see 14.9 below.

14.6 *The 'past in the future'*

Sometimes when we talk about a point in the future, we need to describe events/actions that have not yet happened but that will have happened *by then*.

1	2	3
Now	*	Future
(moment of speaking)	(action or event)	(point referred to)

> **Oggi i giornali *dicono* che il Governo *avrà deciso* il bilancio prima di *agosto*.**
> Today the papers say the Government will have decided on the budget before August.

> **Franco *dice* che *avremo già finito* il lavoro quando *arriverà* lo stipendio.**
> Franco says that we will have finished the work before the salary arrives.

This reference to *the past in the future* – often called the *future perfect* in English – is expressed in Italian by a tense called **futuro anteriore**. Here are some examples:

> **Domani l'ufficio chiuderà alle 12. A quell'ora *avremo* già *finito* la nostra relazione.**
> Tomorrow the office will close at 12 o'clock. By then we'll already have finished our report.

> **È tardi. Quando arriveremo allo stadio, la partita *sarà* già *iniziata*.**
> It's late. When we reach the stadium, the match will already have started.

> **Nel 1997 il Consiglio d'Europa *avrà deciso* i modi dell'unificazione monetaria.**
> By 1997 the Council of Europe will have decided the modalities of monetary union.

> **Soltanto dopo che *avrai migliorato* il tuo italiano potrai superare l'esame.**
> Only after improving your Italian, will you be able to pass the exam.

For other examples of how the past and future are linked, see 30.5.2 and 31.3.1.

14.7 *The future seen from the past*

We do not just talk of future events with reference to the actual moment when we are speaking or writing ('the present'). We may be talking *now* about a point in the *past*, when the particular events referred to were still in the *future*.

How to express this situation in Italian depends on the *sequence of events* and on the probability of their happening. We can use a variety of verb tenses/moods:

Simple future

When the future moment has not yet come, and it is still possible that Carlo will pass by:

> **Carlo ha detto che *passerà* più tardi.**
> Carlo said he will pass by later.

> **Carlo ha detto che *passa* più tardi.**
> Carlo said he will pass by later.

14.7.2 The *condizionale al passato* 'past conditional':

The past conditional (see Chapter 2) indicates the future *from a past point of view*. (See also 30.5.2.) It is generally used after the moment has passed, regardless of whether Carlo actually came or not:

> **Carlo ha detto che *sarebbe passato* (ed è venuto).**
> Carlo said he would pass by later (and he did).

> **Carlo ha detto che *sarebbe passato* (e non è venuto).**
> Carlo said he would pass by later (and he didn't).

14.7.3

The *imperfetto* 'imperfect':
More colloquially, it is possible to use the *imperfect* (see Chapter 2) to replace the compound conditional:

> **Carlo ha detto che *passava* più tardi.**
> Carlo said he would pass by later.

For more examples of putting events in a time context, and the sequence of tenses, see 30.4.

14.8   Some expressions of time in the future

Here are a few words frequently used to indicate future time:

Prossimo 'next':

> **Domenica *prossima* andiamo al mare.**
> Next Sunday we'll go to the sea.

> **Dovremo lavorare molto nei *prossimi* mesi.**
> We'll be very busy in the next few months.

> **Le telefonerò il mese *prossimo*.**
> I'll phone you next month.

Fra (tra) 'within a certain time':

The prepositions **fra/tra** are identical in meaning. (For this and other uses, see 4.3.8.)

> **Ci vediamo *fra* una settimana.**
> We'll see each other in a week.

> **Sandro deve partire *tra* poco.**
> Sandro has to leave in a moment.

> **Mi scusi, sono occupata. La richiamo *fra* cinque minuti.**
> Excuse me, I'm busy at the moment. I'll call you back in five minutes.

Presto 'soon', 'early', 'quickly':

> ***Presto* cambieremo casa.**
> We'll soon move house.

> **Le manderò *presto* una risposta.**
> I'll send an answer to you soon.

(**Presto** can also be used to mean 'at an early hour', as in **È presto!** 'It's early', or 'at a fast pace', as in **Fa' presto!** 'Hurry up!')

Poi 'then':

> **Prima parleremo della riunione *poi* passeremo all'argomento principale.**
> First we'll speak about the meeting, then we'll go on to the main subject.

Dopo 'after', 'later':

> **Andiamo a fare una passeggiata e *dopo* andiamo a casa tua.**
> Let's go for a walk and after we'll go to your place.

Domani 'tomorrow':

> ***Domani* porto Filippo dal pediatra.**
> Tomorrow I'm taking Filippo to the paediatrician.

Dopodomani 'the day after tomorrow':

> ***Dopodomani* l'ufficio rimarrà chiuso.**
> The day after tomorrow the office will be closed.

Stasera 'this evening', 'tonight':

> ***Stasera* alle 19.30 si trasmetterà la prossima puntata di *Ispettore Derek*.**
> This evening at 7.30 p.m., will be shown the next episode of *Inspector Derek*.

Alla fine 'at the end':

> **Il vertice durerà cinque giorni; *alla fine* verrà offerto un pranzo dall'ambasciatore britannico.**
> The summit will last five days; at the end there will be a dinner given by the British ambassador.

Prima o poi 'sooner or later':

> ***Prima o poi* riusciranno a risolvere il problema.**
> Sooner or later they'll manage to solve the problem.

> **Verrò a trovarti, *prima o poi*!**
> I'll come to see you, sooner or later.

D'ora in poi 'from now on':

> ***D'ora in poi* non mi sentirò più sola. Ci sei tu.**
> From now on I won't feel lonely. You're here.

14.9 *Expressing intention and future plans*

As seen above, the English 'going to' can be expressed by Italian **aver intenzione di**:

> *Ho intenzione di* **noleggiare una macchina.**
> I'm going to hire a car.

Other expressions of intention and planning for the future include:

> **decidere di** 'to decide to'
> **promettere di** 'to promise to'
> **decidersi a** 'to make one's mind up to'
> **fare progetti per** 'to make plans for'
> **aver in progetto di** 'to have planned to'
> **desiderare** 'to wish', 'desire'
> **non vedere l'ora di** 'to not be able to wait for'
> **aspettare** 'to expect'
> **aspettarsi (di/che)** 'to expect'

> *Mi sono decisa* **a passare le feste natalizie in famiglia.**
> I've made up my mind to spend the Christmas celebrations with my family.

> **Gli studenti** *stanno facendo progetti per* **venire a studiare in Inghilterra.**
> The students are planning to come and study in England.

> **Il professore** *si aspetta di* **ricevere i nostri compiti domani.**
> The lecturer expects to receive our homework tomorrow.

> **I bambini** *non vedono l'ora* **di andare in vacanza.**
> The children can't wait to go on holiday.

See also Chapter 26 and Chapter 33.

15 Asking questions

15.1 Introduction

There is no specific verb form in Italian to distinguish a statement from a question, such as the English question form 'Does he ...?' 'Is he ...?' In Italian the form of the verb and the word order of the sentence generally remain the same:

> **Devo chiudere la porta. Devo chiudere la porta?**
> I must shut the door. Should I shut the door?

15.2 Asking a question using interrogative intonation

Very often the only difference between a statement and a question is the intonation of the voice, which therefore becomes particularly important in getting our message through. The pitch of the voice is raised on the word that is the *main point* of the question. In the sentence above we may raise the voice on any one of its components, depending on what the main focus of our question is:

> **Devo chiudere *la porta*? (o la finestra?)**
> Should I shut the door? (or the window?)

> **Devo *chiudere* la porta? (o devo aprirla?)**
> Should I shut the door? (or should I open it?)

> **_Devo_ chiudere la porta? (o non devo?)**
> Should I shut the door? (or should I not?)

15.3 Asking a question using interrogative words

When we ask questions about somebody or something, we usually use *interrogative* words (details on the forms of these are found in 3.6).

We now look at some of the words used to ask questions about (1) *identification* (2) *quantity* or (3) other details about something or somebody.

Questions about identification (of people or things)

Chi? che cosa? quale? che?:

(a)   **Pronto,** *chi* **parla?**
        Hello, who's speaking?

(b)   ***Chi* ha scritto questa lettera?**
        Who wrote this letter?

(c)   **Buongiorno,** *che cosa* **desidera?**
        Good morning, how can I help you? (What would you like?)

(d)   ***Che cosa* facciamo stasera?**
        What shall we do tonight?

(e)   ***Chi* devi vedere stasera?**
        Who will you see tonight?

(f)   ***Per chi* è questo pacco?**
        Who is this parcel for?

(g)   ***Di chi* è questa giacca?**
        Whose jacket is this?

(h)   ***Di che cosa* parliamo con l'avvocato?**
        What shall we talk about with the solicitor?

(j)   ***Quale* computer devo usare?**
        Which computer should I use?

(k)   ***Qual* è la mia penna?**
        Which one is my pen?

(l)   ***Che* ora è?**
        What time is it?

In spoken Italian, **quale** – when used as in example (j) – can be replaced by **che**:

        ***Che* computer devo usare?**
        Which computer should I use?

Quale is abbreviated before the verb form **è**, but never uses an apostrophe:

        ***Qual* è il tuo indirizzo?**
        What is your address?

Chi is *invariable* (see 3.5.4 and 3.6): unlike English 'who', 'whom', 'whose', it does not change form regardless of whether it is the *subject* of the verb (as in examples (a), (b)), the *direct object* (as in example (e)), or preceded by a preposition (as in examples (f), (g)).

In Italian prepositions (**di**, **per** ...) always come *before* **chi** or **che cosa**.

We can also use just **che** or **cosa** instead of **che cosa**, especially in a more familiar or informal context:

>*Che* vuoi? *Che* fai? 'What do you want?' 'What do you do?'
>*Cos'*è questo? 'What is this?'
>*Cosa* stai mangiando? 'What are you eating?'
>*Di cosa* ti occupi? 'What is your occupation?'
>*Di cosa* sta parlando? 'What is he talking about?'

15.3.2 Questions about quantity
Quanto? quanti?:

When used as adjective with the meaning 'how much', 'how many', **quanto** changes its ending to agree with the noun, as in examples (d), (e), (f), (g) (see 3.6):

(a) *Quanto* costa? *Quant'*è?
     How much is it?

(b) *Scusi, quanto* ci vuole per Palermo?
     Excuse me, how long does it take to Palermo?

(c) *Quanto* l'hai pagato?
     How much did you pay for it?

(d) *Quante* stanze ci sono in questa casa?
     How many rooms there are in this house?

(e) *Quanto* zucchero vuole nel caffè?
     How much sugar do you want in your coffee?

(f) *Di quanta* carta ha bisogno?
     How much paper do you need?

(g) *Fra quanti* giorni sarai a Roma?
     In how many days' time will you be in Rome?

15.3.3 Other types of questions
Here are some other words commonly used to introduce questions. These usually come immediately before the verb.

Perché? *why?*

>*Perché* non vai in ufficio?
>Why don't you go to the office?

>*Perché* Teresa piange?
>Why is Teresa crying?

Note that **perché** also means 'because', and can be used to answer a question as well as to ask it:

> *... perché* ho mal di testa.
> ... because I have a headache.
>
> *... perché* ha fame.
> ... because she is hungry.

Come mai? (similar to the conversational English 'how come?') is very often used, instead of **perché**, in a familiar context:

> *Come mai* torni a casa così presto?
> How come you're going home so early?
>
> *Come mai* non c'è più pane?
> How come there is no bread left?

Quando? when?

Quando comincia la scuola?	When does school begin?
Quando è arrivato questo fax?	When did this fax come?
Quando verrai in Italia?	When will you come to Italy?

Dove? where?

Dove va Paolo in vacanza?	Where does Paolo go on holiday?
Scusi, *dov'*è il bagno?	Excuse me, where is the toilet?
Dove hanno trovato il corpo?	Where did they find the body?
Dove compreranno una casa?	Where will they buy a house?

Come? how?

Buongiorno, *come* sta?	Good morning, how do you do?
Come si dice 'today' in italiano?	How do you say 'today' in Italian?
Come avete fatto a ...?	How did you manage to ...?
Come faremo a ...?	How will we manage to ...?

15.4   Dialogo

Un esame di storia

PROFESSORE:	Si accomodi. Cominciamo con una domanda generale. *Che cosa* è il Risorgimento italiano?
CANDIDATO:	È il movimento di indipendenza e unità nazionale dell'Italia.
PROFESSORE:	E *quando* è avvenuto questo movimento?
CANDIDATO:	Nel XIX secolo.
PROFESSORE:	Mi dica ... *chi* era Giuseppe Mazzini?
CANDIDATO:	Mazzini è stato un grande leader democratico e repubblicano. Insieme a Giuseppe Garibaldi lottò per realizzare la partecipazione popolare al movimento nazionale.
PROFESSORE:	*Quali* sono stati gli altri grandi protagonisti del Risorgimento?
CANDIDATO:	I più importanti sono stati Camillo Cavour, il Re Vittorio

	Emanuele II, il Papa Pio IX ... e tanti altri....
PROFESSORE:	Senta ... saprebbe dirmi *come* e in *quale* anno Roma divenne capitale d'Italia?
CANDIDATO:	Nel 1870. Roma fu presa con la forza.
PROFESSORE:	*Perché* fu necessaria la forza?
CANDIDATO:	Perché il Papa non voleva perdere la sua autorità politica e la sovranità su Roma.
PROFESSORE:	Per concludere ... *come mai* Garibaldi ebbe il soprannome di 'eroe dei due mondi'?
CANDIDATO:	Perché aveva combattuto sia in Italia che in America Latina per la causa della libertà e indipendenza dei popoli.
PROFESSORE:	Bene, complimenti! Si accomodi pure, l'esame è finito.

A history exam

PROFESSOR:	Sit down. Let's begin with a general question. *What* is the Italian Risorgimento?
CANDIDATE:	It was the movement for independence and national unity in Italy.
PROFESSOR:	And *when* did this movement take place?
CANDIDATE:	In the nineteenth century.
PROFESSOR:	Tell me ... *who* was Giuseppe Mazzini?
CANDIDATE:	Mazzini was a great democratic and republican leader. Together with Giuseppe Garibaldi he fought to achieve popular participation in the national movement.
PROFESSOR:	*Who* were the other great characters in the Risorgimento?
CANDIDATE:	The most important were Camillo Cavour, King Vittorio Emanuele II, Pope Pius IX ... and many others....
PROFESSOR:	Listen ... could you tell me *how* and in *what* year Rome became capital of Italy?
CANDIDATE:	In 1870. Rome was taken by force.
PROFESSOR:	*Why* was force necessary?
CANDIDATE:	Because the Pope didn't want to lose his political authority and sovereignty over Rome.
PROFESSOR:	To conclude ... *how come* Garibaldi was known as the 'hero of the two worlds'?
CANDIDATE:	Because he had fought both in Italy and in Latin America for the cause of freedom and independence for the people.
PROFESSOR:	Good, well done! You may go, the exam is finished.

16 Negative sentences

Forming a negative sentence: introduction

The most common way to make a negative statement, or question, is to use **non** *immediately before* the verb. There is usually no specific word order, to distinguish a negative sentence from an affirmative one.

> **Sono stanca.**
> I'm tired.

> *Non* **sono stanca.**
> I am not tired.

> **Potete venire alla festa?**
> Can you come to the party?

> *Non* **potete venire alla festa?**
> Can't you come to the party?

> **C'erano molti studenti in aula?**
> Were there many students in the classroom?

> **No.** *Non* **ce n'erano molti.**
> No. There weren't many.

When answering a question negatively, **no** is used. Generally we do not repeat the verb used in the question, as English often does, although we can do so if we include a pronoun object (here **li, la**):

> **Hai diecimila lire?** *No!* **(No, non le ho.)**
> Have you got 10,000 lire? No, I haven't.

> **Sa guidare la macchina?** *No!* **(No, non la so guidare.)**
> Can you drive a car? No, I can't.

Reinforcing a negative statement

There are several other words expressing negation that can be used to reinforce the negative concept introduced by **non**. All negation words are generally used together with **non** – except when the word order is reversed – so in Italian we often have a *double negative* (two negative words in the same sentence):

16.2.1

Affatto, per niente, mica

A negative statement can be *reinforced* by using **affatto**, **per niente**, **mica** (the last is rather colloquial):

> *Non* ho *affatto* **paura!**
> I am not afraid at all!

> **Il film** *non* **era** *per niente* **interessante!**
> The film was not at all interesting!

> *Non* sono *mica* **scema!**
> I am not stupid!

Notice how all the reinforcing adverbs are used *after* the verb.

16.2.2

Neanche, nemmeno, neppure

These adverbs are used to *reinforce* or, rather, *expand* a negative statement, with the meaning of 'not even', 'not either':

> *Non* ho *neanche* **una lira!**
> I haven't got even a penny!

> **Non mi piace la TV.** *Non* **guardo** *nemmeno* **il telegiornale.**
> I don't like TV. I don't even watch the news.

16.3 *Expressing negation with reference to time*

The following are used to specify negation, with reference to *time*:

Non ... mai 'never', **non ... più** 'no longer'

> *Non* leggiamo *mai* i giornali.
> We never read the newspapers.

> *Non* sono *mai* stato in America.
> I've never been to America.

> *Non* lavorava *più* alla FIAT.
> He didn't work at FIAT any longer.

> *Non* c'è *più* benzina.
> There isn't any more petrol.

16.4   *Expressing negation using* né . . . né

When we have to make a negative statement about two (or more) related words or sentences they are introduced by **né . . . né**, used after **non**. These correspond to the English 'neither . . . nor'.

> **Sto bene.** *Non* **ho** *né* **fame** *né* **sete.**
> I'm fine. I'm neither hungry nor thirsty.

> **Di domenica** *non* **voleva** *né* **lavorare** *né* **studiare.**
> On Sundays he didn't want either to work or to study.

> **Il direttore ha troppi impegni.** *Non* **può vederLa in ufficio,** *né* **può venire a casa Sua.**
> The director is too busy. He can't see you at the office or come to your house.

> **Questo bicchiere** *non* **è** *né* **mio** *né* **tuo, è di Andrea.**
> This glass is neither mine nor yours. It's Andrea's.

Like other negative phrases (see examples below) **né . . . né** can also stand on its own at the beginning of a sentence or clause.

> *Né* **Marco** *né* **Luisa** *sapevano* **come far funzionare la fotocopiatrice.**
> Neither Marco nor Luisa knew how to make the photocopier work.

> *Né* **io** *né* **lui** *sapevamo* **dove andare.**
> Neither I nor he knew where to go.

16.5   *Expressing negation using* niente, nulla

Niente (and the less common **nulla**) mean 'nothing' and are normally used together with **non**:

> *Non* **ho** *niente* **da dire.**
> I have nothing to say.

> *Non* **vedo** *niente.*
> I can't see anything.

> *Non* **c'è** *nulla* **di buono da mangiare.**
> There isn't anything good to eat.

When **niente, nulla** come first in the sentence, the **non** is not needed. This is however a rather dramatic style of writing, although in Sicily and the south this word order can be heard in spoken Italian too:

Niente **succede.**
Nothing happens.

Nulla **lo preoccupa.**
Nothing worries him.

16.6 Expressing negation using the adjective nessun/o/a

We can reinforce the idea that a person or object is not available by adding the negative adjective **nessun/o/a** 'no', 'not any'. **Nessun/o/a** follows the pattern of **un, una** (see 1.3.2).

Non c'è nessuna **guida.**
There is no guidebook.

Non c'è nessun' **automobile disponibile.**
There are no cars available.
(*literally*: There is no car available.)

Non c'è nessun **posto.**
There is no place free.

Non c'era nessuno **scrittore italiano presente.**
There were no Italian writers present.

Nessun/o/a can also come first in the sentence, in which case **non** is omitted:

Nessun **compito gli era difficile.**
No task was too difficult for him.

Nessuna **guida ti spiega queste cose.**
No guidebook explains these things to you.

16.7 Expressing negation using the pronoun nessuno/a

Nessuno is a negative *pronoun*, standing on its own; it has a masculine form **nessuno** (occasionally abbreviated to **nessun**) and feminine form **nessuna**. **Nessuno** is usually found with **non**, but if it comes before the verb, **non** is not needed (see also 16.5). **Nessuno** is more commonly found in this position than **niente** is:

Nessun **dorma!**
Let nobody sleep!

Nessuno **viene dopo le 16.00.**
No one comes after 4 p.m.

A questo numero *non* risponde *nessuno*.
Nobody answers on this number.

In casa *non* c'è *nessuno*.
There isn't anybody at home.

When **nessuno, niente** are followed by a clause that more closely defines or specifies the negative ('no guidebook . . . that explains clearly') Italian uses **che**, normally followed by the subjunctive:

Non c'è nessuna guida *che spieghi* la storia della città in modo chiaro.
There is no guide that explains the history of the town clearly.

Non c'è nessuno *che sappia* fare la pizza come mia cugina.
There is no one who can make pizza like my cousin.

Non c'è niente *che possa* soddisfarlo.
There's nothing that can satisfy him.

16.8   *Reinforcing negation*

There are other ways in which you can be emphatic in expressing the negative concept:

***Non* c'è *alcun* motivo per offendersi.**
There's absolutely no reason to take offence.

***Non* ha *la minima intenzione* di finire quel progetto.**
He hasn't the slightest intention of completing that project.

***Non* ho *la più pallida idea* di quello che sta facendo.**
I haven't got the faintest idea what he's doing.

17 Comparisons and degrees of intensity

17.1 Making comparisons: introduction

When we make comparisons between objects or people, or situations, we define the relationship of one to the other in terms of 'more', 'less' or 'the same as'.

In Part A the comparative forms of adjectives (Chapter 1) and adverbs (Chapter 6) are illustrated. Here we look at the ways in which these forms are used, and at other ways of expressing degrees of intensity.

17.2 Using comparative adjectives and adverbs

17.2.1 'More'

La situazione economica è *più grave* in Italia che in Inghilterra.
The economic situation is more serious in Italy than in England.

Si mangia *meglio* in Italia che in Inghilterra.
One eats better in Italy than in England.

17.2.2 'Less'

Enrico era *meno intelligente* di Enrica.
Enrico was less intelligent than Enrica.

Bisogna andare *meno velocemente* del solito.
You should go more slowly than usual.

17.2.3 'Same as'

Non troverà mai una moglie *tanto* comprensiva *quanto* Angelica.
He will never find a wife as understanding as Angelica.

Non guidi *così* attentamente *come* me.
You don't drive as carefully as me.

The first words of each pair can be omitted:

Non troverà mai una moglie comprensiva *quanto* Angelica.
He will never find a wife as understanding as Angelica.

> **Non guidi attentamente *come* me.**
> You don't drive as carefully as me.

17.3 *Expressing 'than'*

English 'than' is translated by **di** or by **che** (see examples in 17.2) according to which two elements are being compared, and their position in the sentence:

17.3.1 Comparing two nouns

When comparing two nouns or two proper names, we normally use **di** (although see 17.3.3 below):

> **L'ipotesi di Biagi è più valida *di* quella di Goldoni.**
> Biagi's hypothesis is more valid than Goldoni's.

> **In classe, i maschi sono meno estroversi *delle* ragazze.**
> In class, the males are less extrovert than the girls.

> **Luciano scrive più lentamente *di* Alessandra al computer.**
> Luciano writes more slowly than Alessandra on the computer.

17.3.2 Comparing two pronouns

As with nouns, we use **di** when comparing pronouns.

Personal pronouns:

> **Isabella è meno stressata *di* te.**
> Isabella is less stressed than you.

> **Lui guida più velocemente *di* te.**
> He drives more quickly than you.

*Demonstrative pronouns **questo**, **quello*** (see 3.8):

> **Questa stanza è più spaziosa *di* quella.**
> This room is more spacious than that one.

> **Questo è più saporito *di* quello.**
> This one is more tasty than that one.

*Possessive pronouns **il mio**, **il tuo*** (see 3.7):

> **Lo stipendio di mio marito è più basso *del mio*.**
> My husband's salary is lower than mine.

> **La nostra automobile è meno comoda *della vostra*.**
> Our car is less comfortable than yours.

17.3.3

Comparing two adjectives

When comparing two adjectives that refer to the *same person* or *same thing*, it is more normal to use **che**:

> **I genitori del bambino rapito erano più preoccupati *che* arrabbiati.**
> The parents of the snatched child were worried more than angry.

> **Questi mobili sono più vecchi *che* antichi.**
> This furniture is not so much antique as old.

And the same can apply when two nouns are compared, if both refer to the *same person or thing*:

> **Il mulo è più asino *che* cavallo.**
> The mule is more donkey than horse.

17.3.4

Comparing two verbs

When comparing two verbs, use **che**:

> **Andare a ballare è più divertente *che* andare al cinema.**
> Going dancing is more fun than going to the cinema.

> **Spendere è più facile *che* guadagnare.**
> Spending is easier than earning.

17.3.5

Comparing phrases of time and place

When comparing *adverbs* of time/place, use **di**:

> ***Ora* mi stanco più *di prima.***
> Now I get more tired than before.

But use **che** if the adverbs are next to each other, separated only by **che** 'than':

> **Sono più stanca *adesso che prima.***
> I am more tired now than before.

When at least one of the terms of comparison is a prepositional phrase of time/place, use **che**:

> **Si sta meglio *adesso che negli anni Cinquanta.***
> People are better off now than in the fifties.

> **I turisti si divertirebbero più *a Napoli che a Roma.***
> The tourists would enjoy themselves more in Naples than in Rome.

17.3.6

Comparing two elements separated by 'than'

In fact, the rules given above can be simplified by remembering that when 'than' comes *directly between* the two elements compared, it is always translated by **che**:

Fa meno freddo oggi *che* **ieri.**
It is colder today than yesterday.

Mia madre era più preoccupata *che* **arrabbiata.**
My mother was worried more than angry.

Comparing with one's expectations

To compare an actual state of affairs with what we thought, expected or imagined beforehand, we use the construction **di quanto** or **di quel che** along with either the imperfect indicative (e.g. **pensavo**) or the imperfect subjunctive (e.g. **pensassi**) according to whether we are using a formal or informal register:

Il corso d'italiano era più facile *di quel che pensavo.*
The Italian course was easier than I thought.

or

Il corso d'italiano era più facile *di quanto pensassi.*

or

Il corso d'italiano era più facile *di quanto non pensassi.*

17.4 *Expressing 'which'*

Use the interrogative **quale** (Chapter 3) to express English 'which':

Quale **città è più interessante, Roma o Firenze?**
Which city is more interesting, Rome or Florence?

Quali **fichi sono più dolci, quelli bianchi, o quelli neri?**
Which figs are sweetest, the white ones or the black ones?

17.5 *Expressing different degrees of intensity*

Adjectives: relative superlative

When the person/object has more of a particular quality than all the others, we use the *relative* superlative (the most in relation to others):

I ragazzi italiani sono *i più viziati* **d'Europa.**
Italian kids are the most spoilt in Europe.

È stato *il più bel* **viaggio della mia vita.**
It was the best trip of my life.

Per me, venerdì è *il giorno meno complicato* **della settimana.**
For me, Friday is the least complicated day of the week.

17.5.2

Adjectives: absolute superlative

When no comparison is being made, we use the absolute superlative:

> **I vestiti di Armani sono costos*issimi.***
> Armani clothes are really expensive.

> **Il viaggio è stato bell*issimo.***
> The trip was really wonderful.

Often Italians prefer not to use this **-issimo** form, but to use a simple qualifying adverb such as **molto, tanto, così,** or an adverb such as **estremamente, veramente:**

> **Sono *tanto stanca.***
> I'm so tired.

> **Le sono *estremamente grato.***
> I'm extremely grateful to you.

17.5.3

Adjectives: diminishing the intensity

The opposite effect can be conveyed by using the adverb **poco:**

> **Ha fatto una mossa *poco intelligente***
> He made a not very intelligent move.

17.5.4

Adjectives: moderate intensity

The adverbs **piuttosto** and **abbastanza** express only a moderate degree of intensity:

> **Il processo elettorale è *piuttosto lento.***
> The electoral process is rather slow.

> **Siamo *abbastanza soddisfatti* del suo lavoro.**
> We are quite satisfied with his work.

17.5.5

Numbers and placing

Note how the superlative form is used with ordinal numbers (**primo, secondo**):

> **Milano è *la seconda città più grande* d'Italia.**
> Milan is the second biggest city in Italy.

17.5.6

Adverbs

With adverbs, the superlatives are less commonly used.

The English 'as ... as possible' is expressed as shown:

> **Per favore, parla *il più lentamente possibile.***
> Please, speak as slowly as possible.

> **Ho fatto *il meglio possibile.* Speriamo bene.**
> I've done as well as I could. Let's hope things go well.

When no comparison is being made, we can express the absolute superlative by using the qualifying adverbs **molto, tanto, così, veramente, estremamente** as for the adjectives:

> **Ha guidato** *molto attentamente.*
> He drove very carefully.

Again, the opposite effect can be conveyed by use of the word **poco**:

> **Ha seguito** *poco attentamente* **in classe.**
> He followed not very attentively in class.

Often adverbs are replaced anyway in Italian with a phrase such as **con** or **in maniera**. In this case the comparative and superlative are formed in a different way:

> **Ha suonato la chitarra** *con tanta passione.*
> He played the guitar with great passion/very passionately.

> **Ha parlato** *nella maniera più calma possibile.*
> She spoke in the calmest way possible.

> **Ha studiato** *con poco impegno.*
> He studied with little commitment.

18 Referring to objects and persons

18.1 Introduction

When talking or writing, we often need to refer to something or somebody
without naming them, usually because they have already been mentioned
earlier and we want to avoid repeating the name or object; references to 'this' or
'that', 'he' or 'she', 'him' or 'her', and 'it', are the connecting thread of any
discourse.

18.2 Using a pronoun to refer back

Pronouns are the instrument that allow us to perform the vital function of
referring back. There are many different kinds of pronoun (indefinites,
demonstratives, relatives, interrogatives, possessives) and all of them can be
used to refer to a noun. Here we look in detail at *personal pronouns*, the
pronouns that describe persons and also objects. For details on all the pronoun
forms (stressed, unstressed, combined) see Chapter 3.

18.3 Using a pronoun: referring to the subject of an action

In Italian when talking about the person or thing carrying out an action, we do
not usually need the subject pronoun, as we do in English; the verb ending tells
us who or what is carrying out the action (see Chapter 2). But sometimes we
want to emphasize who is carrying out an action, to distinguish him/her from
someone else or to emphasize the contrast:

> *Io* vado a scuola, *lui* va a lavorare.
> I'm going to school, he's going to work.

> *Noi* andiamo al cinema. *Voi* dove andate?
> We're going to the cinema. Where are you going?

18.4 | *Using a pronoun: referring to someone other than the subject*

When we want to refer to somebody who is *not* the subject of the action, avoiding the use of a noun, we use an *object* pronoun (English 'me', 'you', 'her', 'him', 'us', 'them').

In Italian we can choose either an *unstressed* object pronoun (**mi**, **ti**, **lo**, **la**, **gli**, **ci**, **vi**, **li**, **le**) or the more emphatic *stressed* object pronoun (**me**, **te**, **lui**, **lei**, **Lei**, **noi**, **voi**, **loro**).

18.4.1

Using stressed pronouns

When we want to emphasize the identity of the person we are referring to, we use the *stressed* or *emphatic* pronouns. We also use them if we want to contrast or compare, or to distinguish him/her from somebody else. The three sets of examples below show the different emphasis given, depending on whether we use an unstressed pronoun (examples A) or a stressed pronoun (examples B):

A   **Dov'è Paola? *La* chiamo e non risponde.**
     Where is Paola? I call her and she doesn't answer.

B   **Dov'è Paola? Chiamo *lei* e risponde Anna.**
     Where is Paola? I call her and Anna answers instead.

A   **Guarda*mi*!**
     Look at me!

B   **Guarda *me*, non *lui*.**
     Look at me, not him.

A   **La mia amica mi ha invitato a cena. *Le* porto dei fiori.**
     My friend has invited me for dinner. I'll bring some flowers for her.

B   **La mia amica mi ha invitato a cena. Porto dei fiori *a lei* e del vino a suo marito.**
     My friend has invited me for dinner. I'll bring some flowers for her and some wine for her husband.

After a *preposition* (**con**, **di**, **da**, **a**, **per** . . ., etc.) the stressed forms are the only type of pronoun that can be used:

     Ho parlato *di voi* con la dott.ssa Prati.
     I talked about you with Dr Prati.

     Ho telefonato *a te* prima che a Sandra.
     I rang you before I called Sandra.

> **Questa lettera è *per lui*.**
> This letter is for him.

> **Ti ho visto *con lei*.**
> I saw you with her.

Stressed pronouns are used mainly to refer to persons. They are rarely used to refer to animals and even more rarely for inanimate objects; if we use **lui**, **lei**, **loro** for 'it', 'them' to refer to animals – or even more so to things – it endows the objects or animals with a 'human' personality. **Questo**, **quello** can be used instead.

Here, in this news item, the motorcyclist whose life has been saved is grateful to the helmet for protecting him and thinks of it almost as a friend, hence the use of **lui**.

> **Io devo la mia vita a questo casco. È grazie *a lui* che sono vivo.**
> I owe my life to this helmet. It's thanks to it (him) that I'm alive.

18.4.2

Using unstressed pronouns

The most common way of all to refer to somebody or something – when no particular emphasis is required – is to use unstressed pronouns.

The pronouns can be *direct object* pronouns (used when the action directly involves or affects the person or thing):

> **Conosci Paola? Sì, *la* conosco.**
> Do you know Paola? Yes, I know her.

> **Pronto, *mi* senti? No, non *ti* sento bene!**
> Hello, can you hear me? No, I can't hear you very well!

> **Mi piace il caffè italiano, *lo* bevo tutti i giorni.**
> I like Italian coffee, I drink it every day.

> **Hai la chiave? Sì, ce *l'*ho.**
> Have you got the key? Yes, I've got it.

Alternatively, they can be *indirect object pronouns* (used when the action is aimed *at* or directed *to* them). Common verbs which often use indirect pronouns include:

dare 'to give'	**dire** 'to say', 'tell'
inviare 'to send'	**mandare** 'to send'
offrire 'to offer'	**passare** 'to pass'
presentare 'to present'	**prestare** 'to lend'
raccontare 'to tell'	**regalare** 'to give'
scrivere 'to write'	**spedire** 'to send'
telefonare 'to telephone'	

> **Paola è rimasta senza soldi. Domani *le* mando un assegno.**
> Paola's got no money left. Tomorrow I'll send a cheque to her.

> **A che ora *gli* telefoni? Ciao. Scrivi*mi* presto!**
> At what time will you call (to) him? Bye. Write to me soon.

> **Di*mmi*!**
> Tell me!

> **Da*mmi* lo zucchero!**
> Give (to) me the sugar!

Both types of pronoun can be found in the same sentence:

> ***Mi* piacciono le poesie di Montale. *Le* ho lette tutte.**
> I like Montale's poems. I've read them all.

They can even be combined:

> **Se vedi Anna, di*lle* di telefonar*mi*. Va bene, *glielo* dirò, non preoccuparti.**
> If you see Anna, tell her to ring me. All right, I'll tell her, don't worry.

Remember that occasionally the correct pronoun might not be the one you think. An English 'it' might well be plural **li**, **le** in Italian, if it refers to a plural noun; an English 'them' might on the other hand be singular **lo**, **la** in Italian:

> **Odio questi mobili. *Li* brucerei.**
> I hate this furniture. I'd burn it.

> **Tutta questa gente. Io *la* manderei via.**
> All these people. I would send them all away.

One of the main sources of difficulty for English speakers is remembering that the unstressed pronouns *usually come before the verb.*

— 18.4.3 —
Direct or indirect?

Another problem for English speakers is knowing when to use the indirect pronoun in Italian. This is because often in English direct and indirect object are not easily distinguishable. Sometimes the English sentence uses the word 'to' before the pronoun, for example 'I'll give the parcel to him. He lent the novel to me.' But it is equally possible to say in English: 'I'll give him the parcel; he lent me the novel.'

Look at these examples, where Italian distinguishes between *direct* and *indirect* object pronouns, depending on the choice of verbs, but where English uses identical pronouns ('him', 'them') in each case:

Direct: **Li accompagno all'aeroporto.**
                I'll take them to the airport.

| *Indirect*: | **Gli do un passaggio.** (*unstressed form*) |
| | I'll give them a lift. |

Do un passaggio *a loro*. (*stressed form*)
I'll give them a lift.

Direct: **Chiama*lo* subito.**
Call him now.

Indirect: **Telefona*gli* subito.** (*unstressed form*)
Ring him now.

Telefona *a lui* subito. (*stressed form*)
Ring him now.

Special cases: *piacere, servire*

Remember that with **piacere** (see Chapter 28), the person who likes something is expressed by the indirect pronoun **mi** (*literally*, 'Music pleases (to) me, the shoes please (to) me'). So if we want to avoid repeating the name of the person or thing liked (music, shoes), we simply miss it out:

Ti piace la musica moderna? Sì, mi piace.
Do you like modern music? Yes, I like it. (*literally*: It pleases me.)

Ti piacciono queste scarpe? Sì, mi piacciono.
Do you like these shoes? Yes, I like them. (*literally*: They please me.)

Similarly when we use **servire** (literally 'to be of use to') or similar verbs, the object needed (**le forbici**) is the subject of the verb (the scissors are of use to me), while the person in need is expressed by the indirect pronoun, either stressed or unstressed. When we want to refer to the objects without mentioning them again, we simply miss out **le forbici** or **la calcolatrice**:

Ti servono le forbici? (*unstressed form*) **Sì, mi servono (le forbici).**
Le forbici servono *a te*? (*stressed form*)
Do you need the scissors? Yes, I need them (the scissors).

Signora, *Le* serve la calcolatrice?
(*unstressed*) **Sì, mi serve (la calcolatrice).**
La calcolatrice serve *a Lei*, signora? (*stressed*)
Do you need the calculator, signora? Yes, I need it (the calculator).

18.5   *Referring to someone or something using* questo, quello

The demonstrative pronouns **questo**, **quello** can also be used to avoid naming or repeating the object or person (see 3.8). Often the use of **quello**, **quella** without naming the person involved indicates dislike or contempt:

> **Non c'è nessuno più egoista di *quella*.**
> There is no one more self-centred than that woman.

> **È *questo* il tuo nuovo amico?**
> Is this your new friend?

> **Non ho mai mangiato una torta come *questa*.**
> I've never eaten a cake as good as this one.

> **Hai visto *quello*?**
> Did you see that man?

> ***Questo* è il mio tavolo.**
> This is my desk.

> **Ti servono dei fogli? Prendi *quelli*.**
> Do you need some sheets of paper? Take those.

The English 'the former ... the latter' can be conveyed by using **quello** and **questo** respectively, but only in written texts. Sometimes 'the latter' is conveyed by **quest'ultimo**.

18.6 *Using indefinites to refer to someone/something*

Often *indefinite pronouns* such as **alcuni**, **certi**, **altri**, **ognuno** (see 3.9) can be used to refer to something or someone previously mentioned:

> **Abbiamo parlato con i prigionieri di guerra. *Alcuni* di loro erano stati presi all'inizio del conflitto.**
> We spoke to the prisoners of war. Some of them had been taken at the beginning of the conflict.

> **Avevamo invitato una ventina di bambini alla festa. *Ognuno* di loro ha ricevuto un regalino prima di andare a casa.**
> We invited around twenty children to the party. Each of them received a small present before going home.

> **La sala d'attesa era piena di viaggiatori pallidi e stanchi. *Alcuni* sfogliavano giornali, *altri* sonnecchiavano.**
> The waiting room was full of pale, tired travellers. Some were flicking through newspapers, others were dozing.

18.7 *Referring to something or someone mentioned*

The words **simile**, **tale** can be used when referring to something or someone already mentioned:

Nell'incidente sono morti cinque giovani tutti di Cornate. Al paese non era mai accaduta *una tale* tragedia.
In the accident, five young people died, all from Cornate. A similar tragedy had never happened in the village.

In un paese abruzzese una volpe veniva regolarmente al bar a mangiare le brioche.... *Una cosa simile* si vedeva a Opicina (vicino Trieste) dove un cane di nome Lucky era un cliente abituale del Bar Centrale.
In a village in Abruzzo, a fox came regularly to the bar to eat brioches.... Something similar used to be seen in Opicina (near Trieste) where a dog called Lucky was a regular customer of the café Centrale.

18.8 Referring to what has been said or will be said

Particularly in business or formal letters, use is made of expressions such as **come sopra, sopraindicato, sopraccitato, sopraddetto**, referring back, or **il seguente, come segue, quanto segue**, to refer forward:

Per eventuali chiarimenti, si prega di telefonare al numero *sopraindicato*.
If any clarification is needed, you are asked to telephone the above number.

Prima di accendere il vostro frigorifero, vi suggeriamo di leggere *il seguente*....
Before turning on your fridge, we suggest you read the following....

19 *Focusing on the action*

19.1 *Focusing on the action: introduction*

Sometimes we want to focus on the *action*, or on the *person or thing affected* by the action, rather than on the person carrying the action out. In Italian there are various ways in which we can do this.

19.2 *Focusing on the action using the passive*

Normally, the grammatical subject of the verb is the person carrying out an action; the verb form is therefore an active verb form:

> **I camerieri *hanno servito* la cena.**
> The waiters served dinner.

One way of focusing on the action or on the person/thing affected, is to use a passive verb form (see Chapter 2) and to make the person or thing affected by the action the grammatical subject of the verb instead, so that it becomes more important than the 'doer':

> **La cena *è servita* alle ore 20.00.**
> Dinner is served at 8 p.m.

19.2.1 — With *essere*

The passive is normally formed with **essere** and the past participle. It has a full range of tenses in the same way as the active verb does. There may or may *not* be an agent (person carrying out the action) mentioned, but even when there is, the agent is at the end of the sentence, in a *secondary* position compared to the action or person affected:

Agent not mentioned:

> **Le destre *sono state fermate*.**
> The Right has been stopped.

> **La merce *era stata scaricata* a Genova.**
> The goods had been unloaded at Genoa.

Agent mentioned:

> **Stamattina il Vesuvio *è ricoperto* da un candido manto di neve.**
> This morning Vesuvius is covered by a snow-white mantle of snow.

> **Ogni mattina, quando mi alzo, i bagni *sono* sempre *occupati* dai miei figli.**
> Every morning, when I get up, the bathrooms are always occupied by my children.

> **Domani la Principessa *sarà ricevuta* dal Papa.**
> Tomorrow the Princess will be received by the Pope.

> **Nel 1944 Napoli *è stata bombardata* dagli Alleati.**
> In 1944 Naples was bombarded by the Allies.

> **I ladri *furono scoperti* dalla guardia mentre entravano da una finestra.**
> The thieves were discovered by the guard as they came in through a window.

> **I risultati delle elezioni *erano attesi* da una grande folla per le strade della città.**
> The results of the elections were awaited by a great crowd in the streets of the city.

> **Mentre rientravano negli spogliatoi gli atleti *erano assediati* dai giornalisti.**
> While they were going back into the dressing rooms, the athletes were besieged by journalists.

> **Se avessi più pazienza, forse *saresti ascoltato* di più dai tuoi figli.**
> If you had more patience, perhaps you would be listened to more by your children.

> **Secondo i giornali, i quadri *sarebbero stati rubati* da una banda di ladri professionisti.**
> According to the newspapers, the pictures were stolen by a band of professional thieves.
> (*Note*: For this use of the conditional to express report or rumour, see Chapter 31.)

19.2.2 — **With *venire***

In the examples above, the *passive* construction is formed with the verb **essere** and the past participle. You can also use **venire** instead of **essere**. This is used only in a more formal register and only in the simple tenses: present, imperfect, **passato remoto**, future, conditional. **Venire** tends to express the idea that a regular action is involved.

> **Gli studenti *verranno ammessi* solo se muniti di tessera.**
> Students will be admitted only if in possession of a membership card.

> **La cena *viene servita* da camerieri vestiti di giacca bianca.**
> Dinner is served by waiters dressed in white jackets.

> **Gli ordini ci *venivano trasmessi* dai nostri rivenditori italiani.**
> The orders were sent on to us by our Italian dealers.

> **Le lezioni *vengono impartite* in italiano.**
> The lessons are given in Italian.

The other reason for using **venire** is to avoid ambiguity. The passive, used with certain verbs, e.g. **chiudere**, **aprire** can sound as though it is 'static' ('the door is already closed') rather than expressing an action ('the door is being closed'); this is particularly true when there is no agent mentioned, as shown by the examples below:

> **La porta *è chiusa* da Marco.**
> The door is shut by Marco. (*action*)

> **La porta *è chiusa.***
> The door is shut/is being shut. (*action or state: ambiguous*)

This ambiguity can be avoided by using the verb **venire**:

> **La porta *viene chiusa.***
> The door is being shut/gets shut. (*action*)

19.2.3 | With *andare*

The passive can also be formed with **andare**, in which case it has a prescriptive sense: this is how things *should* be done:

> **Eventuali riparazioni *vanno effettuate* solo dai nostri tecnici qualificati.**
> Any repairs should be carried out only by our qualified technicians.

> **Il vino bianco *va servito* fresco, mentre il vino rosso *va servito* a temperatura ambiente.**
> White wine should be served chilled, while red wine should be served at room temperature.

19.2.4 | In scientific papers, news reports, etc.

While Italians tend to avoid the use of passive sentences in everyday speech, there are certain special contexts where it is preferred, for example *scientific papers and news reports* and *bureaucratic language* where it is used to express detachment and impartiality.

Sometimes the passive is used without mention of any agent, because the agent is not known, has already been mentioned, is unimportant, or is too obvious to be stated.

Scientific papers
In the case of scientific papers, the intention is to stress the objectivity of experimental procedures; a passive sentence puts emphasis on the results of an action, rather than on the person who has carried it out. When scientific observations are described, the 'agent' (i.e. the person or institution that carries them out) is omitted, to stress the objective nature of the findings:

> **Il nuovo vaccino contro l'Aids** *è stato sperimentato* **presso l'Università di Pisa.**
> The new Aids vaccine has been tested at Pisa University.

> **L'eclissi** *è prevista* **alle 15.23 del 10 agosto.**
> The eclipse is expected at 15.23 on 10 August.

> **Il tasso medio di inflazione** *è calcolato* **sulla base di rilevazioni che** *vengono effettuate* **nelle principali città.**
> The average inflation rate is calculated on the basis of surveys which are conducted in the main cities.

There can be exceptions where the discovery has made the scientist or inventor famous:

> **La penicillina** *fu scoperta* **da Fleming nel 1928.**
> Penicillin was discovered by Fleming in 1928.

News reports
Passive statements are widely used in the reporting of news by the press. Again this is due to the need to present events as facts and to suggest they are true, impartial and accurately verified:

> **La legge finanziaria** *è stata approvata* **dal Parlamento.**
> The budget bill has been approved by Parliament.

> **I due ostaggi** *saranno liberati* **domani.**
> The two hostages will be released tomorrow.

Media headlines often omit the **avere/essere** part of the passive and use the subject and the past participle only:

> *Liberati* **i due ostaggi.**
> The two hostages freed.
> (Italian daily newspaper)

> *Aggredita* **da africano tredicenne lo picchia.**
> Attacked by an African, a thirteen-year-old girl beats him up.
> (*Televideo,* 24 August 1995)

Bureaucratic language

Legal and bureaucratic language also uses passive statements to emphasize the impersonality of rules and duties (see 40.6):

> **Il biglietto deve *essere timbrato* all'inizio del viaggio.**
> Tickets must be stamped at the beginning of the journey.

> **Ogni cambiamento di indirizzo dovrà *essere comunicato* per iscritto.**
> Any change of address should be reported in writing.

19.3 *Situations when the passive is* not *used*

19.3.1 Verbs with an indirect object only

Many English verbs differ from their Italian counterparts. Only a transitive verb (verb taking a direct object) can be turned into a passive in Italian, as shown below:

In English the active sentence

> Anna *told* Franco to call the plumber.

. . . can be rephrased using the passive:

> Franco *was told* by Anna to call the plumber.

In Italian we can use the active form:

> **Anna *ha detto a Franco* di chiamare l'idraulico.**

but we cannot turn this sentence round into a passive construction.

We can only turn a sentence into the passive when there is a *direct* object which can become the subject of the action. An *indirect* object (English '*to* Franco', '*to* her') cannot be turned into the grammatical subject. Verbs which take an indirect object include **telefonare, dire, raccontare** where the action does not affect the person directly, but indirectly ('to telephone *to me*', 'to say *to him*', 'to tell *to them*').

Here are some more examples where an English passive sentence cannot be translated directly into a passive form in Italian, because the person affected is *not* the direct object. No agent is mentioned, so Italian uses the 'anonymous' *third person* verb form, for example **hanno telefonato** '*they* phoned' (see 19.3.3):

> **Mi *hanno telefonato* a casa.**
> I was telephoned at home.

> **Gli *hanno detto* di sbrigarsi.**
> He was told to hurry up.

19.3.2

Verbs with a direct and indirect object

In the case of verbs such as **dare, dire, inviare, mandare, passare, presentare, prestare, raccontare, regalare, spedire,** there is often a direct object *and* an indirect object.

The direct object – often a thing – *can* become the subject of a passive verb:

> Mi *è stato rubato* l'orologio.
> I've had my watch stolen.
> (*literally*: My watch has been stolen from me.)

Alternatively, you can use the third person active verb form (see 19.3.3):

> Mi *hanno rubato* l'orologio.
> I've had my watch stolen.
> (*literally*: They have stolen my watch from me.)

But you cannot make 'I' the subject in Italian, as it is in English ('I've had my watch stolen').

> Gli *hanno offerto* un buon posto.
> Gli *è stato offerto* un buon posto.
> He was offered a good job.

> Durante la riunione, ci *hanno passato* un messaggio del direttore.
> Durante la riunione, ci *è stato passato* un messaggio del direttore.
> During the meeting, we were passed a message from the manager.

Note in the last example how mention of an agent would require the preposition **da**:

> Durante la riunione, ci *è stato passato* un messaggio *dal* direttore.
> During the meeting, we were passed a message by the manager.
> (*literally*: During the meeting a message was passed to us by the manager.)

19.3.3

Use of third person plural instead of passive

In Italian we use the passive construction only very sparingly. In everyday language an Italian speaker would almost always prefer to use the corresponding active sentence, if at all possible. Often the third person verb forms are preferred, even where the passive would technically be possible.

So instead of using the passive construction:

> *Sono stata invitata* a una festa.
> I've been invited to a party.

> *Sono state mandate* dieci casse di spumante.
> Ten crates of spumante were sent.

Italians would prefer to use the active construction:

> *Mi hanno invitata* **a una festa.**
> They (some unspecified people) have invited me to a party.

> *Hanno mandato* **dieci casse di spumante.**
> They sent ten crates of spumante.

19.4 Focusing on the action using si passivante (passive form with si)

Another way of emphasizing the action rather than the subject of it, is to use the **si passivante**, where the pronoun **si** is added to the active form to give the verb (in this case, **possono vedere**) a passive meaning. This is only possible with the third person, singular or plural.

The **si passivante** can be used only when there is no mention of the *agent* or author of the action. This construction is very common in Italian, because of the reluctance to use the plain passive forms, especially in the more colloquial register.

Like the passive, **si passivante** can only be used with verbs taking a direct object.

So instead of the passive construction:

> **Da Manfredonia, le isole Tremiti** *possono essere viste.*
> From Manfredonia, the Tremiti islands can be seen.

we can use the **si passivante**:

> **Da Manfredonia** *si possono vedere* **le isole Tremiti.**
> From Manfredonia, the Tremiti islands can be seen.

When the object or person affected is *plural*, we use a *plural verb*:

> **Qui** *si parla* **italiano.**
> Italian is spoken here.

> **In Alto Adige** *si parlano* **sia l'italiano che il tedesco.**
> In Alto Adige both Italian and German are spoken.

> **In quel concessionario Lancia** *si vendono* **25 automobili al giorno.**
> At that Lancia dealer, 25 cars are sold every day.

> **Le vendite** *si registrano* **su questo libro.**
> Sales are recorded in this book.

> **In questo club** *si deve mettere* **la cravatta.**
> In this club a necktie must be worn.

Al centro di Milano, *si vende* un appartamento di quattro vani per lo stesso prezzo di una villa.
In the centre of Milan, a four-room apartment is being sold for the same price as a villa.

Often in the 'small ads' a reverse combination of verb + **si** is used. In the plural form, the final vowel is dropped (affittano > **affittan**):

**Vendesi *appartamento di quattro vani.*
Four-room apartment for sale.

Affittasi* monolocale.
One-room apartment for rent.

Affittansi* camere.
Rooms for rent.

19.5   Si impersonale *(impersonal* si)

Often confused with the **si passivante**, is the very similar **si impersonale** 'impersonal **si**' equivalent of English 'one'. Whereas the **si passivante** is always used with a *transitive* verb, and has both singular and plural, the **si impersonale** is used with an *intransitive* verb and is found only in the singular. Often the **si impersonale** is not really impersonal but is used as a substitute for 'we':

Domenica *si va* al mare.
On Sundays we go to the seaside.

In genere, *si parte* presto quando *si va* all'aeroporto.
In general, one leaves early when one is going to the airport.

Both past participle and adjectives, when used with **si impersonale**, are plural. The compound tenses take **essere**:

La sera dopo una giornata di lavoro, *si è stanchi.*
In the evening, after a day at work, one is tired.

***Si è partiti* la mattina presto, e *si è arrivati* la sera tardi.**
One (we) left in the morning early, and one (we) arrived in the evening late.

19.6   *Focusing on the object of the action*

Italian has more freedom to change word order (see also Appendix IV). The normal order of *subject, verb, object* can be reversed; we can emphasize the *object* of an action (rather than the *subject*, or author, of it) by keeping the active form of the sentence, but placing the object in a more prominent position before the verb. The pronoun (in this case, **lo**) is used as well (see Chapter 3) to reinforce the object:

Emphasizing the subject:

(Subject – verb – object)

> **Il *direttore* ha già firmato il contratto.**
> The director has already signed the contract.

Emphasizing the object:

(Object – pronoun – verb – subject)

> **Il *contratto lo* ha già firmato il direttore.**
> The contract has already been signed by the director.

II Actions affecting ourselves and others

20 Social contacts

20.1 Greeting, welcoming

Saying 'hello' and 'goodbye':

Buon giorno	used to greet people during the day time.
Buona sera	used to greet people in the evening (approximately after dark or after siesta time in the south).
Buona notte	used only when taking leave of one's companions to go to bed or go home at the end of the evening.
Ciao	a more informal, and extremely popular, way to say 'hello' as well as 'goodbye'.
Salve	another informal greeting, used only when meeting somebody, but less common and limited to certain regions and certain social contexts.

When enquiring about someone's state of health, use the verb **stare**:

Come stai? or **Come va?** is used when addressing somebody with the familiar **tu**:

> **Ciao Paolo,** *come stai?*
> Hello Paolo, how are you?

Come sta? is used with the formal **Lei** (see Chapter 1), both for men and women:

> **Buon giorno dott.ssa Serra,** *come sta?*
> Good morning Dr Serra, how are you?

A normal reply might be one of the following (providing some brief information about one's physical or psychological state):

> **(Molto) bene, grazie; e tu/Lei?**
> Very well, thank you. And you?

> **Bene grazie, non c'è male.**
> Thanks, not bad.

> **Insomma ... non c'è male.**
> Not bad (*but said doubtfully*).

> **Non molto bene purtroppo.**
> Not very well, unfortunately.

Benvenuto means welcome, but is used mainly on relatively formal occasions.

When welcoming someone into a room, Italians often say:

> **Si accomodi, signora.**
> Please come in, signora.
> (*literally*: Make yourself comfortable.)

> **Accomodati/Accomodatevi.**
> Come in (familiar form of address, using **tu/voi**)

> **Avanti!**
> Come in! (*literally*: Forward!)

When inviting guests to sit down, you can use **accomodarsi** again, or else **sedersi**:

> **Prego, si sieda signora.**
> Please take a seat, madam.

> **Siediti, Angela.**
> Sit down, Angela.

> **Sedetevi, voi due.**
> Sit down, you two.

When passing on greetings from someone else, use the verb **salutare**:

> **Mio marito La saluta.**
> My husband sends (you) best wishes.

> **Giorgio ti saluta.**
> Giorgio sends (you) best wishes.

And when someone wants to pass on their greetings to your family, they say:

> **Mi saluti Sua madre.**
> Say 'hello' to your mother for me.

> **Salutami la tua mamma.**
> Say 'hello' to your mum for me.

20.2 Introducing oneself and others

When meeting someone we don't know, we need a few words to introduce each other, or to introduce someone else. Here are the phrases most commonly used, with approximate translations:

> **Permette ...?**
> Allow me ... (rather formal, used as a first approach, and followed by one's name).

Mi chiamo Peter Green.
My name is Peter Green. (*literally*: I call myself . . .)

Piacere, Sally Parker.
My name is Sally Parker. It's a pleasure to meet you.

Molto lieta/o.
Glad to meet you.

Here are two examples of typical introductions, the first rather formal (e.g. business situation), the second more informal (e.g. two young students):

Dialogue 1:

A: *Permette?* . . . **Vorrei presentarmi** . . . *mi chiamo* **William Hughes.**
B: *Molto lieto* . . . **io sono Andrea Fulgenzi . . . sono l'agente della ditta Duemila.**
A: *Molto lieto,* **ho sentito parlare spesso di Lei. Io lavoro per il Ministero degli Esteri canadese.**
B: **Questo è il mio** *biglietto da visita.*
A: **Grazie, ecco il mio. . . .**

A: Excuse me! . . . I'd like to introduce myself . . . my name is William Hughes.
B: Very pleased (to meet you) . . . I'm Andrea Fulgenzi . . . I'm the agent for the Duemila company.
A: Very pleased (too), I've often heard speak of you. I work for the Canadian Ministry of Foreign Affairs.
B: This is my card.
A: Thanks, here's mine. . . .

Dialogue 2:

A: **Ciao, come ti chiami?**
B: **Mi chiamo Sandra, e tu?**
A: **Io mi chiamo Luigi.** *Piacere!*
B: *Piacere!*

A: Hi, what's your name?
B: My name's Sandra, and yours?
A: My name's Luigi. Pleased (to meet you)!
B: Pleased (to meet you)!

When introducing a third person, we may say:

Le presento **l'avvocato Negri.**
Can I introduce Mr Negri (to you)? (*literally*: Lawyer Negri)

Posso presentarLe **l'avvocato Negri?**
Can I introduce Mr Negri (to you)?

Ti presento **il mio amico Luigi.**
This is my friend Luigi.

Notice that in Italy professional titles or qualifications such as **dottore**, **professore**, **ingegnere**, **direttore** are commonly used when addressing or introducing somebody, where we would not use them in English. The same applies to **signora** 'madam' or **signore** 'sir' (see 20.9).

20.3   *Taking leave*

'Goodbye' in Italian is either **arrivederci** or (with friends) **ciao**.

More formal is **arrivederLa**, although **arrivederci** is appropriate in almost all circumstances.

Other very common familiar forms of leave-taking are:

> **ci vediamo** 'see you'
> **a presto** 'see you soon'
> **a domani** 'see you tomorrow'
> **di nuovo** 'see you again' (*less familiar*)
> **buona notte** 'good night' (used only when taking leave at the end of an evening)

20.4   *Wishes*

Here is a series of expressions used as good wishes in various circumstances. These may be exchanged both when meeting and when leaving people:

> **auguri** 'best wishes' (used in virtually all situations: birthdays, Christmas, but not before exams ... see below)
> **buon viaggio** 'bon voyage'
> **buone vacanze** 'have a nice holiday'
> **buon Natale** 'merry Christmas'
> **buon Anno** 'happy New Year'
> **Felice Anno Nuovo** 'happy New Year' (on Christmas cards, etc.)
> **buona Pasqua** 'happy Easter'
> **in bocca al lupo** 'good luck' (idiomatic, literally means 'in the mouth of the wolf', used before exams or other difficult tests or competitions. In such circumstances **auguri** is considered not appropriate and even ominous. The traditional reply is **Crepi!** 'May the wolf die!'
> **buona fortuna** 'good luck' (generic)
> **buon divertimento** 'enjoy yourself'
> **salute** 'bless you' (after a sneeze)
> **cin cin** or **salute** 'cheers' (raising glasses for a toast)
> **alla tua, alla vostra** 'your health' (as a toast)
> **buon appetito** 'enjoy your meal' (very common before beginning a meal, both in formal and in informal situations: as a reply we

may say: **grazie altrettanto** although often **buon appetito** is repeated instead)

Expressing and receiving thanks, appreciation

Saying thank you:

> **grazie** 'thanks'
> **molte grazie** 'many thanks'
> **grazie mille** 'many thanks'
> **ti ringrazio, Paola** '(I) thank you, Paola'
> **La ringrazio, Professore** '(I) thank you (teacher)'

Receiving thanks:

> **prego** 'you are welcome'
> **di niente** 'don't mention it'
> **non c'è di che** 'don't mention it'
> **per carità, non è nulla** 'don't even mention it', 'it's nothing'

Expressing a more intense appreciation:

> **grazie, molto gentile** 'thank you', 'very kind of you'
> **molto gentile da parte Sua** 'how kind of you'
>
> **La ringrazio molto per la Sua ospitalità.**
> Thank you very much indeed for your hospitality.
>
> **Le sono molto grata/o per l'assistenza che ho ricevuto.**
> I am very grateful to you for the assistance I received.
>
> **Ho apprezzato molto il Suo regalo.**
> I much appreciated your present.
>
> **Ho gradito molto i Suoi fiori.**
> I very much appreciated your flowers.
>
> **Ancora mille grazie. Lei è stata/o veramente gentile.**
> Thank you again. You have been extremely kind.

20.6 *Compliments*

Here is a list of expressions that can be used to convey our compliments to somebody in various circumstances.

> **bravo/a** 'well done' (friendly and informal)
> **complimenti** 'congratulations'
> **complimenti per la laurea** 'congratulations on your degree'
> **congratulazioni** 'congratulations' (more formal)
> **felicitazioni** 'congratulations' (especially on marriage and new babies)

Che bello!
How beautiful!

Che bel vestito!
What a nice dress!

Che begli occhi che hai!
What beautiful eyes you have!

Come sei elegante!
How elegant you are!

Le sta molto bene questa giacca.
This jacket looks really good on you.

Come nuota bene tuo figlio!
How good your son is at swimming!

Come parli bene l'italiano!
How good your Italian is!

20.7 *Making and accepting excuses, apologies*

These are the most usual ways to say 'excuse me' or 'sorry' in Italian:

Using **Lei**:

mi scusi 'excuse me'
scusi 'excuse me'
chiedo scusa 'I apologize'

La prego di scusarmi.
I beg your pardon.

La prego di accettare le mie scuse.
I hope you will accept my apologies. (with more formality)

Sono *spiacente* **che non ci sia abbastanza caffè per tutti.**
I regret there is not enough coffee for everybody. (very formal)

Using **tu**:

scusami 'excuse me'
mi dispiace/mi spiace 'I'm sorry'
spiacente 'I'm sorry' (formal)

To accept someone's apologies we may say:

per carità 'you don't need to apologize' (*literally*: 'for pity's sake')
non si preoccupi 'don't worry'
non fa niente 'it doesn't matter'
prego 'it's all right'

20.8   *Expressing commiseration, sympathy*

To express sympathy for someone's death, speaking or in writing, we can use:

condoglianze 'condolences', 'sympathy'

Desidero esprimere le mie *condoglianze* per la perdita di Suo marito.
I wish to express my sympathy for the loss of your husband.

Some common expressions of commiseration or regret are the following:

(Che) peccato!
What a pity! It's a shame!

***Peccato* che lei sia arrivata in ritardo.**
It's a pity that she arrived late.

È un *peccato* che non abbiate visto quel film.
It's a pity you haven't seen that film.

Poveretto/a!
Poor him/her!

Povero Mario!
Poor Mario!

Che pena!
What a shame!

***Poveretti*, mi fanno pena!**
Poor things. I feel sorry for them.

Mi dispiace che abbiate avuto questo brutto incidente.
I'm sorry you had this bad accident.

20.9   *Using titles, salutations*

As mentioned above (20.2) in Italy professional titles and qualifications are commonly used when addressing somebody, either speaking or in writing. Failing to do so, or using the wrong title, may result in embarrassment or upset.

Here we present the titles most commonly used. In Chapter 41 you will find abbreviations and other conventional forms used in correspondence.

The titles most frequently used are those shown immediately below; they are general forms of address used when the person has no special title, but also when we don't know whether the person addressed has other titles or not. Italians would tactfully try to find out whether any other title is appropriate, before addressing somebody with **signor(e)**. A title may be used on its own or followed by the person's surname, in which case the final **-e** is dropped from the masculine form, for example **signore** is abbreviated to **signor** (*signor* **Rossi**):

> **signore** 'Mister'
> **signora** 'Madam'
> **signorina** 'Miss' (if unmarried)

The final **-e** is also dropped before a surname with many of the following (as indicated by the brackets):

> **dottor(e)** 'Doctor' (used both for medical doctor and for anybody with a university degree, also when there is not a more specific professional title)
> **dottoressa** 'Doctor' (female equivalent of above)
> **professor(e)** 'Professor' (used for university and secondary school male teacher)
> **professoressa** 'Professor' (female equivalent of above)
> **avvocato** 'lawyer', 'solicitor' (**avvocatessa** exists but see p.228)
> **ingegner(e)** 'engineer' (only if holding a university degree)
> **ragionier(e)** 'accountant'
> **architetto** 'architect'
> **maestro** 'Master' used for all male *artists* (it is used in southern Italy also for highly skilled manual labourers and artisans)
> **onorevole** 'Member of Parliament'
> **ministro** 'Minister'
> **padre** 'Father' (for priest)
> **madre/sorella** 'Mother/Sister' (for nun)
> **monsignor(e)** 'Monsignor' (used for high-ranking Catholic priest)

Generally used on its own, not with surnames is:

> **direttore** 'Director' (or other high-ranking official or manager)

In some professions (such as military or diplomatic), the specific title indicating the rank should be used:

> **generale** 'General'
> **capitano** 'Captain'
> **ambasciatore** 'Ambassador'

In some cases, but not always, there are both masculine and feminine forms. A list of the most common titles or professions with distinct feminine equivalents is given in Chapter 1. Where there is no feminine form, women should be addressed with the same title as their male counterparts: **ingegner Maggioni, avvocato Parma.**

While some of the titles shown here and in Chapter 1 are widely used to denote the female professional (for example **professoressa, dottoressa**), in other cases the feminine forms follow the rather old-fashioned tradition of indicating the *wife* of the professional person: **ambasciatrice** 'the ambassador's wife',

presidentessa 'the president's wife'. In these cases, it is common practice not to use the feminine form but to use the masculine form to indicate women working in this profession as well, with the feminine article where available:

> *La presidente* della Camera Irene Pivetti. . . .
> The speaker of the House Irene Pivetti. . . .

Generally speaking, when there is a choice of forms, the use of the masculine form is perceived as putting less emphasis on the gender aspect and more on the profession of the person, and is therefore seen as less sexist.

The masculine form is used for all those professions for which there is no commonly used feminine form, such as those listed above:

> *Il ministro* degli esteri Susanna Agnelli . . .
> The Minister for Foreign Affairs Susanna Agnelli . . .

The use of feminine titles newly created because of the recent increase of women entering traditionally male-only jobs, such as **avvocatessa**, **soldatessa**, **poliziotta**, **vigilessa** is perceived as ironical and patronising.

Note: The basic formalities used in *correspondence* are illustrated in Chapter 41.

21 Getting other people to do things

21.1 *Making requests and giving commands*

Possibly the most important 'transactional' function in any language, is to get people to do things, either by giving an order or by making a request. Indeed one of the first words a child learns – apart from 'mummy' or **mamma** – is often 'Give!' or **Dammi.**

There are various degrees of urgency and authority, from a request to a friend **Passami il sale!** to a more formal command, albeit at the simplest level, used to call the waiter in the restaurant or bar **Senta! Mi porti il conto!**

One way to get someone to do something is to use the *imperative* (order or command) form of the verb (see Chapter 2). Another way is to use the indicative, in question form.

21.1.1 *Lei*

For a command addressing someone formally, the **Lei** form of the *imperative* is used (see Chapter 2). Here are some frequently used verbs in command form:

> **Senta!**
> Excuse me! (*literally*: Listen!)
>
> **Scusi!**
> Excuse me!
>
> **Si accomodi!**
> Come in/make yourself comfortable!
>
> **Mi *dia* il passaporto, signora.**
> Give me your passport, madam.

If we prefer to make a request rather than issue a command, we would use the present indicative, or sometimes the verb **volere** 'to wish to':

> **Mi *dà* il passaporto, signora?**
> Would you give me your passport, madam?
>
> ***Vuole accomodarsi*, signora?**
> Would you like to sit down, madam?

We can also make a polite request by use of the phrase **Le dispiace ...?** (see also Chapter 22) and verb infinitive:

> *Le dispiace* **aprire la finestra?**
> Would you mind opening the window?

Tu

To give a command or instruction to someone you are on familiar terms with, you use the **tu** form of the imperative:

> *Mangia***!**
> Eat up!

> *Vieni* **a casa mia alle 6.00.**
> Come to my house at 6 o'clock.

> *Siediti* **qui accanto a me.**
> Sit here next to me.

> *Dagli* **un colpo di telefono!**
> Give him a call!

> *Fa'* **quello che vuoi!**
> Do what you want!

As seen above, the imperative form is sometimes replaced by the less abrupt indicative form (the 'normal' form) of the verb. This gives the effect of the speaker making a request rather than giving an order:

> *Mangi* **un altro po' di dolce?**
> Would you eat another little bit of cake?

> **Mi** *passi* **il pane, per favore?**
> Would you pass me the bread?

> **Mi** *dai* **un passaggio?**
> Would you give me a lift?

This is particularly common where the one-syllable imperatives of the verbs **andare, dare, fare, stare, dire** (**va', da', fa', sta', di'**) are concerned (see Chapter 2). These are often replaced with the indicative:

> *Dai* **retta a me.**
> Listen to me.

> *Fai* **come vuoi.**
> Do as you please.

Here too a polite request can be made using **ti dispiace ...** (see also Chapter 22):

> *Ti dispiace* **prestarmi la giacca da sci?**
> Would you mind lending me your ski jacket?

— 21.1.3 —
Voi

To give a command or instruction to more than one person, use the **voi** form of the imperative:

> *Mangiate*, ragazzi!
> Eat up, kids!

> *Venite* a cena da me sabato prossimo!
> Come to dinner at my house next Saturday!

— 21.1.4 —
Loro

There is a polite form of 'you' (corresponding to singular **Lei**) in the plural as well: **Loro** is however less used than **Lei**, being largely used by waiters or hotel staff to address customers. **Loro**, like **Lei**, takes a third person verb form:

> *Si accomodino*, signore.
> Make yourselves comfortable, ladies.

> *Vengano* di qui, signori.
> Come this way, ladies and gentlemen.

— 21.1.5 —
Noi

When we are personally involved in the action, we use a proposal or exhortation rather than a command:

> *Controlliamo* questi conti adesso.
> Let's have a look at these accounts now.

> **Usciamo.**
> Let's go out.

21.2 Making negative requests and giving negative commands

All the imperative forms shown above (21.1) can be expressed in a negative form, to tell someone *not* to do something (see Chapter 2):

Lei:

> **Non si preoccupi!**
> Don't worry!

tu:

> *Non fumare*, Walter.
> Don't smoke so much, Walter.

voi:

> *Non andate* lontano, ragazzi.
> Don't go far, kids.

loro:

> *Non si stanchino,* signorine.
> Don't get tired, ladies.

noi:

> *Non usciamo* stasera, restiamo a casa.
> Let's not go out tonight, let's stay in.

When it comes to the present *indicative* forms, adding **non** doesn't make any real difference to the meaning of the request, except to try and sound more persuasive:

> *Non* mi *porti* a cena?
> Aren't you taking me to dinner?

> *Non andiamo* al cinema?
> Aren't we going to the cinema?

21.3   *Asking someone to do something*

An alternative to the imperative forms shown above is a strongly worded request – one that you expect to be met – using a verb such as **chiedere**, **volere**:

Chiedere with *di*:

Chiedere can be linked to the action (what is being asked) by **di**, in which case the second verb will be in the infinitive. The person asked will be expressed by a noun (introduced by **a**) or by an indirect pronoun:

> *Bisogna chiedere agli studenti* italiani *di* stare un po' più zitti.
> We have to ask the Italian students to keep a little quieter.

> *Le chiedo di* rispettare l'orario di lavoro.
> I ask you to respect working hours.

Chiedere with *che*

Chiedere can also be followed by **che** and then the subjunctive:

> *Chiedo* soltanto *che* Lei rispetti l'orario di lavoro.
> I only ask that you respect working hours.

Volere with *che*

Volere – like **chiedere** – can also be followed by **che** and then the subjunctive (see Chapter 2). The present indicative (**voglio**) is used to make a strong request, while the present conditional (**vorrei**) sounds more polite. Note the different tenses of the subjunctive depending on which tense of **volere** is used:

> *Voglio che tu faccia* **uno sforzo per ricuperare il tempo perso.**
> I want you to make an effort to recover the time lost.

> *Vorrei che tu facessi* **uno sforzo per ricuperare il tempo perso.**
> I would like you to make an effort to recover the time lost.

21.4 Giving an order using 'command' verbs

More explicit command forms such as **comandare, ordinare** as well as **dire** can also be used, as an alternative to the imperative forms or the verbs shown above. Some or most take an indirect object (noun governed by **a** or indirect object pronoun):

> **I carabinieri** *hanno comandato* **ai mafiosi di venire fuori dalla casa.**
> The police commanded the Mafia men to come out from the house.

> **La padrona di casa ci** *ha ordinato* **di pulire le scale.**
> The landlady ordered us to clean the stairs.

> **Gli** *ho detto* **di sbrigarsi.**
> I told him to hurry up.

21.5 Far fare, lasciar fare

When asking someone to *do* something, we frequently use the verb **fare** 'to make' with another verb expressing the action you are making the person carry out. The person carrying out the action can be the direct *or* indirect object, expressed by a noun or pronoun (see Chapter 3):

When there is *no other object* in the sentence, the noun or pronoun is the direct object:

> *Faccio venire* **Isabella.**
> I'll call Isabella.

> **Abbiamo bisogno di Isabella.** *La faccio venire.*
> We need Isabella. I'll have her come.

> *Ha fatto entrare* **il poliziotto.**
> He let the policeman in.

When the second verb also has an object, the person (whether noun or pronoun) who is being made to do something becomes the *indirect* object:

> **Ho** *fatto riparare* **il computer** *al* **fidanzato di Giovanna.**
> I got Giovanna's boyfriend to repair the computer.

> *Gli* ho *fatto riparare* il computer.
> I got him to repair the computer.

Similarly, to allow someone to do something is expressed by **lasciar fare** (or **lasciare** + any other verb), again with the person as direct object, or as indirect object if there is a second object:

> **Sono tornati gli operai.** *Li lascio entrare?*
> The workmen are back. Shall I let them in?

> **Non** *lo lascia parlare.*
> She doesn't let him speak.

> **Ho lasciato fare quel lavoro a mio marito.**
> I let my husband do that job.

When the person involved is the indirect object, either the stressed or the unstressed form of indirect object pronoun (see 3.3 and 3.4) can be used:

> *Ho lasciato fare* quel lavoro *a lui.*
> (*Gli ho lasciato fare* quel lavoro.)
> I let him do that job.

> **Il capo** *ha lasciato scrivere* la relazione *a me.*
> (**Il capo** *mi ha lasciato scrivere* la relazione.)
> The boss let me write the report.

21.6   *Using persuasion*

Other ways of getting something done include invitation, encouragement, begging, and gentle persuasion.

Using *invitare* 'to invite', *incoraggiare* 'to encourage'
These verbs use a direct object (person or pronoun), and a verb in the infinitive, linked by **a**:

> **Il preside** *invitò i ragazzi a* **riflettere sulle loro azioni.**
> The headmaster invited the boys to reflect on their actions.

> **Il mio supervisore** *mi ha incoraggiato a* **finire la mia tesi.**
> My supervisor encouraged me to finish my thesis.

Using *persuadere, convincere* 'to persuade'
These verbs also use a direct object (person or pronoun), and a verb in the infinitive, linked by **a**:

> **Mio marito cerca di** *persuader mi ad* **andare in vacanza invece di finire il libro.**

My husband is trying to persuade me to go on holiday instead of finishing the book.

Convincerò Donatella *a* cambiare idea.
I'll persuade Donatella to change her mind.

Using *pregare* 'to beg'

Pregare uses a direct object (person or pronoun) and a verb in the infinitive, linked to it by **di**:

Il direttore *mi pregò di* sedermi.
The manager begged me to sit down.

Mia madre *ha pregato mia sorella di* rimanere ferma.
My mother begged my sister to stay still.

Signora, *La prego di* ricordarsi della patente.
Madam, I beg you to remember your licence.

21.7   Monologo

And finally, since imperative verb forms (see Chapter 2 and 21.1.2, 21.1.3 above) are quite commonly used in the relationship between adults and children, we reproduce two typical, if somewhat exaggerated, 'conversations' between a mother and a group of children, adapted from *Il Libronuovo*, by B. Reggiani and A. Salvatore, IGDA, Novara,). The first takes place on the beach, in summer, and, the second is in the winter, getting ready for school. The imperative forms are in bold italic, to help the reader identify them:

Mia moglie, d'estate, è così:

Valentina, *spogliati*. Franco *non buttarti* in acqua vestito. Roberta *lascia* stare il secchiello e togliti le scarpe. Roberta *sta'* ferma, Franco dov'è? Franco *vieni* a spogliarti, Valentina *metti* il costumino a Lorenzo, Franco dov'è? Roberta, *vieni* qui, il bagno si fa più tardi! Franco, dov'è Franco? Valentina *acchiappa* Roberta che si butta in acqua! Franco, perché hai fatto il bagno? Lorenzino di mamma sua, non si mangia la sabbietta, brutta la sabbietta! Franco, non vedo più Franco! Franco! *Torna* indietro, sennò niente gelato! Valentina *corri* a prendere Franco. Roberta *non ti muovere*! Franco, dov'è Franco?

D'inverno, invece, è così:

Valentina, *svegliati*, Roberta *svegliati*. . . . Franco *salta* giù dal letto. Ragazzi sono le sette e cinque! Franco, presto, *vai* a fare la doccia. Valentina *vestiti*. Sono le sette e dieci! Ragazzi, il caffelatte è pronto! Franco hai fatto la doccia? *Asciuga* per terra. Roberta, perché piangi? Valentina, avanti, *falle* mettere la gonna gialla. Sono le sette e un quarto! Insomma, venite o no a prendere il caffelatte? Si sta freddando tutto! Roberta se piangi ancora vengo di là e ti ammazzo! Francooooooo! Dov'è Franco? Roberta *non piangere, vatti* a pettinare invece. Sono le sette e mezzo. Perderete l'autobus. Ma *dimmi* tu che razza di figli!

In the summer, my wife sounds like this:

Valentina, get undressed. Franco don't jump into the water with your clothes on. Roberta leave the bucket alone and take your shoes off. Roberta keep still, where's Franco? Franco come and get undressed, Valentina put Lorenzo's costume on, where's Franco? Roberta, come here, you can go swimming later! Franco, where's Franco? Valentina grab hold of Roberta, she's jumping into the water! Franco, why did you go swimming now? Lorenzino, mummy's treasure, you mustn't eat the sand, nasty sand! Franco, I can't see Franco any more! Franco! Come back, otherwise no ice cream! Valentina run and get Franco. Roberta don't move! Franco, where's Franco?

But in winter she sounds like this:

Valentina, wake up, Roberta wake up. . . . Franco get out of bed. Kids, it's five past seven! Franco, quick, go and have a shower. Valentina get dressed. It's ten past seven! Kids, your *caffelatte* (milk with coffee in it) is ready! Franco have you had a shower? Dry the floor. Roberta, why are you crying? Valentina, come on, let her put your yellow skirt on. It's quarter past seven! Come on, are you coming to have this *caffelatte* or not? It's all getting cold! Roberta if you keep on crying, I'll come over there and kill you! Francooooooo! Where's Franco? Roberta don't cry, go and comb your hair, instead of crying. It's half past seven. You'll miss the bus. Honestly, tell me, what kind of kids have I got!

22 Permission and possibility

In English, the verb 'can' may convey many different meanings, for example: possibility, permission, ability or opportunity. A similar function is expressed in Italian by the verb **potere**, seen in several different situations below, along with other expressions of similar meaning.

22.1 Asking or granting permission

Using *potere*

> *Posso* **andare in bagno?**
> Can I go to the bathroom?

> *Potete* **andare a giocare fuori, bambini.**
> You can go and play outside, kids.

> *Puoi* **lasciare qui la giacca, se vuoi.**
> You can leave your jacket here, if you want.

The examples illustrated above use the *present indicative* of **potere** 'to be able to', but to formulate a request more politely, the *conditional* is often used:

> *Potrei* **andare in bagno?**
> Could I go to the bathroom?

22.1.2
Using *è possibile*
Potere can often be replaced by the impersonal expression **è possibile** followed immediately (without prepositions such as **d**, **i** or **a**) by a verb in the infinitive:

> *È possibile* **lasciare qui la giacca?**
> Is it possible to leave one's jacket here?

> *È possibile* **andare in bagno?**
> Is it possible to use the bathroom?

22.1.3
Using *permettere*
Another way of asking or granting (*someone*) permission to (*do something*) is to use the verb **permettere a** (**qualcuno**) **di** (**fare qualcosa**). The person being allowed to do something – or not – is the indirect object of the verb **permettere** while the second verb, always in the infinitive, is linked by the preposition **di**.

> **La legge non *ci permette di* importare i prodotti direttamente dalla Tailandia.**
> The law does not allow us to import the products directly from Thailand.

22.1.4

Granting permission, using *pure*

Pure – best translated by the English expression 'by all means' – can be added to an imperative to imply not only permission, but encouragement to do something:

> **Posso dire qualcosa? Dica *pure*!**
> Can I say something? Go ahead, (speak) by all means.

> **Faccia *pure*!**
> Go ahead, do it! (Be my guest!)

Prego! also invites someone to do just what they have requested:

> **Posso andare in bagno? *Prego*, si accomodi.**
> May I use the bathroom? Please, go ahead.

22.1.5

Asking permission <u>not</u> to do something

If you *don't* want to do something, use the verb **dovere** and the intensifier **proprio**:

> ***Devo proprio* andare a letto?**
> Do I really have to go to bed?

22.1.6

Granting permission <u>not</u> to do something

You can use a negative imperative, along with the phrase **se vuoi/se volete** 'if you want':

> **Non andate, *se volete*.**
> Don't go, if you want (if you don't want to).

Or you can use the negative infinitive **non andare**, etc.:

> **Puoi non andare, *se vuoi*.**
> You can not go, if you want.

22.2 *Denying permission*

22.2.1

Using *vietare* or *proibire*

Denying someone permission to do something is a similar grammatical construction as allowing (see 22.1.3): a verb such as **vietare** or **proibire** combined with a person (expressed by noun or indirect pronoun) and verb in the infinitive, linked by **di**:

> *Gli ho proibito di firmare* le lettere per conto mio.
> I have forbidden him to sign letters on my behalf.

> I bambini *mi hanno proibito di mangiare* il loro cioccolato.
> The children have forbidden me to eat their chocolate.

> La polizia *ha vietato ai non residenti di parcheggiare* in questa
> strada.
> The police have banned non-residents from parking in this
> street.

22.3 Speaking about the ability or opportunity to do something

Using *potere*

Potere expresses the ability or the opportunity to do something:

> *Puoi* arrivare per le sette?
> Can you arrive by 7 o'clock?

> *Potete* vedere ancora oggi la grotta dove viveva San Paolo.
> You can still see the cave where Saint Paul lived.

Omission of potere *with certain verbs*
Sometimes the verb **potere** is omitted, when the English 'can' means 'to be able to', especially when used with verbs of seeing, hearing, feeling:

> Ci *vedi*?
> Can you see? (*literally*: 'there')

> Si *sente* la musica dal giardino?
> Can one hear the music from the garden?

Using *è possibile*

Here too, **potere** can be replaced by the impersonal expression **è possibile**:

> *È possibile* prendere l'autobus per andare all'aeroporto?
> Is it possible to get the bus to go to the airport?

> A Malta, *è possibile* vedere le catacombe di San Paolo.
> In Malta, it is possible to see the catacombs of Saint Paul.

Using *sapere*

The English 'can', 'to be able to' can very often be translated by the verb **sapere** in Italian, which does not express permission or possibility, but rather *knowledge* or *ability* to do something, referring to a learnt skill:

> *Sai* nuotare?
> Can you swim? (Do you know how to swim?)

> **Il direttore non *sa* parlare inglese, e quindi si deve rivolgere all'interprete.**
> The manager can't speak English, and so he has to use the interpreter.

The choice of **sapere** rather than **potere** changes the meaning of a phrase entirely:

> ***Sai* fare questo esercizio?**
> Do you know how to do this exercise?

> ***Puoi* fare questo esercizio?**
> Can you do this exercise? (i.e. do you have time or energy to do it?)

22.3.4 Using *essere in grado di*

The expression **essere in grado di** implies the meaning 'to be up to' or 'to be fit to':

> **Non *è in grado di* gestire l'ufficio da solo.**
> He's not up to managing the office on his own.

> **Non *eravamo in grado di* prendere una tale decisione.**
> We weren't able to make such a decision.

22.4 Making a request

22.4.1 Using *potere*

Either the present or the conditional of **potere** can be used:

> ***Può* indicarmi la fermata del tram?**
> Can you show me the tram stop?

> ***Potrebbe* aiutarmi a portare giù i bagagli, per favore?**
> Could you help me to take the luggage down, please?

22.4.2 Using *si può, è possibile*

A more formal or general request, not necessarily referring to one specific person, is sometimes expressed using the impersonal form **si può** 'one can' / 'can one?' or again **è possibile**:

> ***Si può* prenotare?**
> Can one book?

> ***Si può* partire adesso?**
> Can one (we) go now?

> ***È possibile* prenotare?**
> Is it possible to book?

È possibile **telefonare in Inghilterra?**
Is it possible to phone England?

Using *Le/ti/vi dispiace*

A more formal or polite request can be expressed by the verb **dispiace/dispiacerebbe**, **se** or **(Le) dispiace** + infinitive (see also Chapter 21), both used with the appropriate indirect pronoun:

Le dispiace **se fumo?**
Do you mind if I smoke?

Le dispiacerebbe **aprire la finestra?**
Would you mind opening the window?

Ti dispiace **se vado via un po' prima?**
Do you mind if I leave a little earlier?

Ti dispiace **darmi una mano?**
Would you mind giving me a hand?

Vi dispiace **aspettare cinque minuti?**
Would you mind waiting five minutes?

23 Expressing need, obligation or desire

23.1 Need v. Want

Sometimes in Italian, as in other languages, there is little to distinguish a desire, expressed by the verb **volere**, and a need, expressed by the phrase **aver bisogno di** or similar expression:

> *Ho bisogno di* **un caffè.**/*Voglio* **un caffè.**
> I need a coffee./I want a coffee.

23.2 Expressing wants

23.2.1

Using *volere*

The verb **volere** (see Chapter 2) can be used both with a noun (something or someone you want) and with a verb (something you want to do):

> **Gli operai** *vogliono* **un aumento di stipendio.**
> The workmen want a wage increase.

> *Volete* **parlare del contratto?**
> Do you want to talk about the contract?

> *Vuoi* **andare a cena?**
> Do you want to go to dinner?

> *Vuoi* **una mano?**
> Do you want a hand?

Using the *present indicative* form of **volere** can sometimes sound rather demanding, or even discourteous, especially in the first person 'I':

> *Voglio* **un francobollo.**
> I want a stamp.

> **Il direttore** *vuole* **parlarLe.**
> The manager wants to speak to you.

A request or wish can be expressed less urgently and more politely by using the *conditional* rather than the present indicative of **volere**:

> *Vorrei* **due biglietti per stasera, per favore.**
> I would like two tickets for tonight, please.

> **La signora Giannini** *vorrebbe* **parlarLe.**
> Signora Giannini would like to speak to you.

> *Vorrei* **un appuntamento per domani.**
> I would like an appointment for tomorrow.

23.2.2

Using *aver voglia di*

Another way of expressing 'want' is the phrase **aver voglia di**, used either with a *verb* or a *noun*:

> **Gli studenti** *avevano voglia* **di andare a casa.**
> The students wanted to go home.

> **Non** *ha voglia* **di scherzare.**
> He's not in the mood for joking.

> *Ho voglia* **di un gelato.**
> I fancy an ice-cream.

23.2.3

Using *mi va*

A very idiomatic way of saying what you want to do or feel like doing is to use the verb **andare** and an indirect pronoun, either with a *noun* or with a *verb infinitive*, linked by **di**:

> *Ti va* **un gelato?**
> Do you fancy an ice-cream?

> **Non** *mi vanno* **queste domande.**
> I don't like these questions.

> *Ti va di* **mangiare la pizza?**
> Do you feel like (having) a pizza?

> **Non** *gli andava di* **seguire le mie istruzioni.**
> He didn't want to follow my instructions.

23.2.4

Using *me la sento*

Another idiomatic way to say what you feel like doing is **sentirsela** (the verb **sentire** used in a phrase with a reflexive pronoun and the pronoun **la**, here invariable); again it can be linked to a verb infinitive by **di**:

> **Faccio i compiti domani. Non** *me la sento* **stasera.**
> I'll do my homework tomorrow. I don't feel like it tonight.

> **Non** *se l'è sentita di* **assumere la responsabilità.**
> He didn't feel like taking on the responsibility.

23.2.5

Making a request in a shop

One of the most common ways of requesting something in a shop or restaurant is to use **vorrei** as seen above, or else **Mi dà ...** 'please give me ...':

Mi dà **un pacchetto di Marlboro, per favore.**
Would you give me a packet of Marlboro, please.

23.3 *Expressing needs*

Using *bisogna*

The verb **bisogna** 'it is necessary' can be used with a *verb* in the infinitive, or with **che** and the subjunctive:

Bisogna farlo **subito.**
One must do it straightaway. (It must be done straightaway.)

Bisogna vedere **qual è la soluzione migliore.**
We'll have to see what the best solution is.

Bisogna che **tu capisca la situazione.**
You have to understand the situation.

Using *aver bisogno di*

The phrase **aver bisogno di** 'to have need of' can be used with either a *noun* or a *verb* infinitive:

Ho bisogno di **tempo per studiare.**
I need time to study.

Avete bisogno di **me?**
Do you need me?

Aveva bisogno di **riposare.**
He needed to rest.

Using *c'è bisogno*

The phrase **c'è bisogno di** 'there is need of' can be used with a noun (object or person); a verb infinitive linked by **di**; or **che** + subjunctive:

Ci sarà bisogno di **un interprete. Il direttore parla solo italiano.**
We will need an interpreter. The manager only speaks Italian.

Non *c'era bisogno di* **spiegare. Avevamo già capito.**
There wasn't any need to explain. We had already understood.

Non *c'è bisogno che* **Lei mi accompagni. Penso di trovare l'ufficio senza problemi.**
There's no need for you to accompany me. I think I can find the office without any problem.

23.3.4
Using *dovere*

The verb **dovere** 'to have to' expresses a personal obligation as well as a need:

> *Devo* prendere il treno delle 5.00 per arrivare in tempo per la riunione.
> I have to get the 5 o'clock train to arrive in time for the meeting.

> Gli studenti *devono* impegnarsi di più.
> The students must make more of an effort.

Used in the conditional, it expresses what one *ought* to do, rather than what one *must* do:

> *Dovremmo* organizzare la prossima riunione prima di Natale.
> We ought to organize the next meeting before Christmas.

23.3.5
Using *servire, occorrere*

To express *need*, the verbs **servire** and **occorrere** are used. **Occorrere** is often found in recipes.

Both verbs are used in their third person form (**serve**, **servono**). The person needing something is expressed by an indirect pronoun ('to me', 'to you ...') while the object needed is the grammatical subject, in a similar way as with **piacere**:

> *Mi serve* un cacciavite.
> I need a screwdriver.

> Quanti fogli *ti servono*?
> How many sheets do you need?

> *Occorrono*: 6 uova
> Needed: 6 eggs

The verbs are also used *impersonally* (meaning 'it is necessary') followed by a verb infinitive, or by **che** + subjunctive. **Occorrere** tends to be used in more formal contexts, while **servire** is more widely used:

> *Occorre controllare* prima di consegnare la traduzione.
> You/one should check before handing in the translation.

> *Occorre che* lei mi dia un documento.
> She has to give me a document.

> Non *mi serve imparare* l'italiano.
> It's not much use to me learning Italian.

When used impersonally, as here, both **servire** and **occorrere** can be replaced by the phrase **è necessario**.

24 Suggesting, proposing, advising and recommending

24.1 *Giving advice*

There are lots of ways of giving advice, some formal, some informal. Advice can range from encouragement to an order or warning. Here we look at some ways of giving advice in Italian.

24.1.1

Using *consigliare*

In the act of advising or recommending, there are usually two people involved: the person giving advice and the person receiving it. **Consigliare** is most commonly used with an indirect object (the person receiving the advice), governed by **a** when necessary, and linked by **di** *to the verb that follows*:

> **Gli addetti consolari consigliavano *agli* italiani *di* lasciare il paese al più presto possibile.**
> The consular officials were advising Italians to leave the country as soon as possible.

Sometimes the person(s) receiving advice is represented by a *pronoun*, normally an unstressed *indirect* object pronoun such as **mi, ti, gli** (see 3.4.2):

> **Gli addetti consolari *gli* consigliavano *di* lasciare il paese al più presto.**
> The consulate officials were advising them to leave the country as soon as possible.

> **Mia madre *mi* ha consigliato *di* sposare un inglese.**
> My mother advised me to marry an Englishman.

Occasionally there might be a reason for emphasizing the person who is receiving the advice, or contrasting with another person; in this case the emphatic stressed forms of indirect pronouns such as **a me, a te, a lui** (see 3.3.2) are used:

> **Mia madre ha consigliato *a me di* sposare un inglese, ma *a mio fratello di* sposare un'italiana!**
> My mother advised me to marry an Englishman, but (advised) my brother to marry an Italian girl!

The verb **consigliare** is not only used with another verb but is also linked to a *noun direct object* (the thing advised or recommended), with the meaning 'to recommend' or 'to advise':

> **Mi può *consigliare* un buon ristorante?**
> Can you recommend (to me) a good restaurant?

> **I nostri avvocati *hanno consigliato* la massima cautela.**
> Our lawyers recommended/advised the utmost caution.

24.1.2 Using *raccomandare*

Raccomandare is almost synonymous with **consigliare** and can be used in a similar way, i.e. with a person or personal pronoun as *indirect object* and followed by a *verb* infinitive linked by **di**:

> ***Mi* ha raccomandato *di* andare a parlare con il contabile.**
> He advised me to go and speak to the accountant.

Like **consigliare**, it can also be used with a person as indirect object (**gli**) and a noun as direct object (**prudenza**) as below:

> ***Gli* hanno raccomandato *prudenza*.**
> They advised him to be prudent.

24.1.3 Using *raccomandarsi*

Raccomandarsi is difficult to translate. Used by the parents of toddlers and teenagers throughout Italy, it means something like 'If you don't do what you're told . . .', or else 'I'm warning you' or 'Listen to me'. It is used either:

(a) With imperative (but not dependent on it):

> ***Mi raccomando,* non fate tardi!**
> Listen to me, don't be late!

(b) Directly followed by **di** + verb infinitive:

> **Si è *raccomandato di* fare attenzione.**
> He warned (them) to be careful.

Note: This verb should not be confused with the phrase **dare/fare una raccomandazione** or with the verb **raccomandare**, both of which have come to mean 'recommending someone for a job'.

24.2 Making or receiving a suggestion

24.2.1 Using *suggerire*

The verb **suggerire** can be used in a similar way to **consigliare**. Again, in most cases, the person giving advice is the grammatical *subject* of the verb **suggerire**, the person receiving it is the *indirect object* (preceded if necessary by **a**) while any verb following is in the infinitive, linked by **di**:

> **Le compagnie aeree** *suggeriscono ai passeggeri di* **non portare troppi bagagli a mano.**
> The airlines suggest to passengers that they should not bring too much hand luggage.

Again, the person or persons receiving advice is/are represented by *indirect object pronouns*:

(a) By the *unstressed* forms **mi**, **ti**, **gli**, etc. (see 3.4.2):

> **Il suo capo** *le ha suggerito di* **fare una breve pausa.**
> Her boss suggested she take a short break.

> **L'impiegata** *ci ha suggerito di* **prenotare subito il traghetto per la Sardegna, perché non c'erano tanti posti disponibili.**
> The sales assistant suggested we should book the ferry for Sardinia straightaway because there weren't so many places left.

(b) By the *stressed* (*emphatic*) forms **a me**, **a te**, **a lui**, etc. (see 3.3.2):

> **Il capo** *ha suggerito a lei* **di fare una breve pausa, ma ha detto agli altri di continuare a lavorare.**
> The boss told her to have a short break but he told the others to carry on working.

Consigliare, suggerire + subjunctive

Both **consigliare** and **suggerire** can be used with **che** + subjunctive:

> **La consulente** *ha consigliato che* **il direttore** *si informasse* **sul mercato prima di lanciare il nuovo prodotto.**
> The consultant advised the manager to find out about the market before launching the new product.

> **Il capo** *ha suggerito che* **lei** *facesse* **una breve pausa.**
> The boss suggested she have a short break.

Using *proporre*

The verb **proporre** 'to propose', 'to suggest', can be used with two slightly different meanings:

(a) When someone suggests that he/she and others do something together (using a similar structure to **consigliare**, **suggerire** in 24.2.2):

> **Antonio** *mi ha proposto di* **fare una passeggiata lungo il fiume.**
> Antonio suggested (to me) taking a walk along the river.

> *Vorrei proporre agli azionisti di* **accettare l'offerta.**
> I would like to suggest to the shareholders that we accept the offer.

(b) When someone or something else is involved (using **che** + subjunctive):

> *Propongo che* l'ufficio *rimanga* chiuso per due giorni prima dell'ispezione.
> I propose that the office stays closed for two days before the inspection.

Using *dire*

Even the verb **dire** 'to say' can be used to give advice. Used in the conditional, it sounds like advice rather than an order:

> *Ti direi di* portare l'impermeabile.
> I would say (to you) to take a raincoat.

> *Direi che sia* meglio rinviare a domani.
> I would say that it is better to postpone until tomorrow.

> *Direi che* Giovanni *debba* impegnarsi di più.
> I would say that Giovanni needs to show more commitment.

24.3 *More expressions of advising or suggesting*

24.3.1 Giving or asking for advice using *dare indicazioni, dare suggerimenti*

The expression **dare un'indicazione** means to give advice or information, usually on one particular thing; **un'indicazione** is one piece of advice, whereas **delle indicazioni** means advice in general:

> Vorrei trovare un albergo vicino al centro. Mi può *dare qualche indicazione*?
> I would like to find a hotel near the centre. Can you give me some suggestions?

> Il mio collega mi *ha dato delle indicazioni* per il congresso.
> My colleague gave me some suggestions for the conference.

Almost synonymous are **dare suggerimenti/un suggerimento** and **dare consigli/un consiglio**.

24.3.2 Giving advice using *fare una proposta*

The phrase **fare una proposta**, depending on the context, can mean either a business proposition or similar, or occasionally a proposition of a less welcome kind:

> L'azienda aveva delle difficoltà economiche, e il direttore *ha fatto una proposta* di riorganizzazione finanziaria all'assemblea generale.
> The company had some economic difficulties and the director made a proposal for financial reorganization at the general meeting.

Preferirei non stare nello stesso albergo di lui. L'altra volta mi *ha fatto una proposta*.
I would prefer not to stay in the same hotel as him. The last time he propositioned me.

24.3.3 **Giving advice stressing personal point of view**

In spoken Italian, advice is often preceded by the expression **Se (io) fossi in te** 'if I were you':

Se io fossi in te, farei la domanda per aver quel posto a Milano.
If I were you, I would apply for that post in Milan.

The same thing can be expressed more plainly and less emphatically:

Per me, è pericoloso.
(If you want to know what I think) it's dangerous.

Secondo te, non dovrei chiedere un aumento di stipendio?
In your opinion, shouldn't I ask for a rise?

(See also Chapter 27 on expressing an opinion.)

24.4   *Advising someone not to do something, giving a warning*

When advising someone *not* to do something, use **avvertire**. With this verb, the person being warned or advised is the *direct* object:

Il portiere *mi ha avvertito che* l'acqua non è potabile.
The porter warned me that the water is not drinkable.

La maestra dovrebbe *avvertire i ragazzi che* domani non c'è scuola.
The teacher should warn the children that tomorrow there is no school.

Warning people to be careful, use **stare attento**:

Gli operai dicono al pubblico di *stare attenti* a non cadere.
The workmen are telling the public to be careful not to fall.

Note in the example above how an impersonal statement requires a plural adjective (**attenti**); see also Chapter 19.

Or use **Attenzione!**

Attenzione a non bruciare la cravatta con la candela.
Watch you don't burn your tie on the candle.

Or **fare attenzione**:

Faccia attenzione **al semaforo.**
Look out for the traffic light.

24.5 *Asking for advice*

All the verbs seen above can be used to *ask for* advice:

Cosa *mi consiglia di* **fare?**
What do you advise me to do?

And:

Cosa *faccio*?
What shall I do? (*literally*: What do I do?)

Cosa *devo fare*?
What shall I do? (*literally*: What must I do?)

Secondo te, *cosa dovrei fare*?
In your opinion, what should I do?

24.6 *Other ways of making suggestions*

Another way to propose something for yourself and others is to use **perché non?**:

Perché non **facciamo una gita in montagna?**
Why don't we have a trip into the mountains?

Or an imperative verb form:

Vieni a **prendere un caffè a casa mia!**
Come and have a coffee at my house!

III Expressing emotions, feelings, attitudes and opinions

25 Expressing emotions: positive, negative, neutral

25.1 Introduction

The ways in which emotion can be expressed vary from straightforward *vocal interjections* (brief utterances) **Ah, oh, ahimé . . .** to *exclamations* **Che bello!** or **Quanto mi piace!** 'That's lovely!' or 'I like him so much!', through to more *complex statements*, for example: **Mi dispiace che tu abbia avuto questi problemi** 'I'm sorry that you've had these problems'.

Here are some of the ways in which we use language to express emotion in Italian:

25.2 Interjections (positive, negative, neutral)

Emotions can often be conveyed with very simple utterances, which have no specific meaning in themselves, but can be inserted at any point in the conversation and can express a variety of emotions according to the context. These include:

Simple vowel sounds, in general expressing surprise, amazement, shock or horror:

> **Ah! Oh! Eh! Uh!**

Sounds indicating doubt, uncertainty, embarrassment:

> **Mah! Boh! Ehm! Beh!**

> **Di chi è questa macchina?** *Boh*?
> Whose car is this? Who knows?

> *Beh*! **Cosa volete?**
> So? What do you want?

Painful feelings (physical or psychological):

> **Ahi! Ahimè! Ohimè!**

> *Ahi*! **Mi sono scottato!**
> Ouch! I've burnt myself!

> *Ahi* **serva Italia, di dolore ostello,**
> Alas Italy enslaved, wherein dwells grief,
> (*Purgatorio*, Dante, Canto VI, v. 76)

> *Ahimè* **è finito il vino!**
> Oh no, the wine is finished!
> (*literally*: Alas!)

Boredom, impatience, irritation:

> *Uffa!* **Non ce la faccio più!**
> (...) I can't stand it any longer!
> (No real translation in English)

25.3 *Expressing positive emotions*

Exclamations

Common adjectives can be used to form exclamations, expressing for example *pleasure, admiration, enthusiasm, approval, gratitude.* Obviously there is a whole range of adjectives, only a few of which are shown here:

Bello!	**Bravo! Bravissimo!**
'Beautiful!'	'Well done!'
Che bello!	
'How nice!' 'How lovely!'	

Ottimo!	**Eccellente!**	**Perfetto**
'Very good!'	'Excellent!'	'Perfect!'
Fantastico!	**Eccezionale!**	**Magnifico!**
'Fantastic!'	'Exceptional!'	'Magnificent!'
Che bellezza!	**Che gioia!**	**Che piacere!**

(All roughly translated as: 'Great!')

Buona idea!	**Ottima idea!**
'Good idea!'	'Wonderful idea!'
Caspita!	

(Untranslatable, but expresses admiration as well as amazement)

Adjectives can be used with the verb **essere** to convey positive feelings about someone or something:

> **È magnifico!**
> It's magnificent!

> **È un regalo stupendo!**
> It's a splendid present!

Adjectives can often be used in combination with **che**:

> **Che bravo!**
> How clever!

> **Che bel bambino!**
> What a beautiful child!
>
> **Che serata perfetta!**
> What a perfect evening!

They can also be used in combination with **quanto** or **come**:

> **Quant'è bravo quello studente!**
> How clever that student is!
>
> **Come sei furbo!**
> How crafty you are!

Satisfaction, admiration, happiness, pleasure

Using **essere** *or* **rimanere**
The verbs **essere** and **rimanere** can both be used with a past participle or adjective to express how one feels about something:

> **Il direttore era molto soddisfatto del mio lavoro.**
> The manager was very satisfied with my work.
>
> **Siamo rimasti veramente ammirati della nuova casa.**
> We really admired the new house.
>
> **Sei rimasta contenta dei voti che hai preso?**
> Were you happy with the marks you got?
>
> **I ragazzi erano contenti dei regali che gli ho portato dagli USA.**
> The kids were pleased with the presents I brought them from the USA.

Contento, felice, soddisfatto

The adjectives **contento**, **felice**, **soddisfatto** can either be followed by **di** and the verb infinitive, or by **che** normally followed by the subjunctive, at least in a more formal context:

> **Era contento di venire con voi.**
> He was happy to come with you.
>
> **Sono contento che vieni anche tu stasera.**
> I'm happy you're coming too tonight.
>
> **Sono felice che Lei possa venire alla conferenza.**
> I'm glad you can come to the conference.
>
> **Gli studenti erano soddisfatti di aver superato gli esami.**
> The students were satisfied at having got through the exams.

Fare piacere

The phrase **fare piacere**, literally 'to make pleasure for someone' can be used with a noun, a verb infinitive or **che** and the subjunctive, in each case acting as the subject of the sentence. The person affected by the event or action is indicated by a noun, name (with **a**), or *indirect* object pronoun.

In the examples below, the subject of the sentence is shown in italic.

> *Questa notizia* farà molto piacere a Marco.
> This news will make Marco very happy.

> Gli ha fatto piacere *sentire le tue notizie.*
> He was happy to hear your news.

> Ci fa piacere *che i ragazzi stiano tutti bene.*
> We're happy that the kids are all well.

See also Chapter 28.

25.3.3 **Approval, appreciation, gratitude**

Simple phrases

D'accordo!	**(Va) Bene!**	**Benissimo!**	
Agreed!	*Good!*	*Very good!*	
Giusto!	**Certo!**	**Esatto!**	**Chiaro!**
Right!	*Sure!*	*Precisely!*	*Of course!*

Sono cinquemila lire. Va bene così?   **Sì, esatto!**
That's five thousand lire. Is that all right?   *Precisely!*

Fare bene

The phrase **fare bene** addressed to someone expresses satisfaction or approval with their action:

> *Hai fatto bene a* dirmelo.
> You did well to tell me.

> *Daniela ha fatto bene a* scegliere l'Università di Viterbo.
> Daniela did well to choose the University of Viterbo.

25.3.4 **Relief**

Meno male!	**Grazie al cielo!**
Just as well!	Thank Heavens!

> *Per fortuna!*
> Luckily!

> *Meno male che* tu ti sei informato.
> Just as well that you took the trouble to find out.

> *Per fortuna* è arrivato subito il medico.
> Luckily the doctor arrived straight away.

— 25.3.5 —

Pity

Pity for others is conveyed by **fare pena** 'to make one pity' or **far pietà**:

> Questi bambini mi *fanno pena.*
> I feel sorry for these children.

> *Faceva pena* vedere i mendicanti per la strada.
> It was pitiful to see the beggars on the street.

> I profughi *fanno pietà* a tutti.
> Everyone feels sorry for refugees.

The exclamation **Poveretto!** also expresses pity, as does the adjective **povero** used with a noun or pronoun:

> La professoressa ha lavorato anche durante l'intervallo. *Poveretta!*
> The teacher worked during the interval as well. Poor thing!

> *Povero Mario,* gli va tutto storto.
> Poor Mario, everything goes wrong for him.

> *Povero me!* Devo preparare due conferenze in una settimana.
> Poor me! I have to prepare two talks in a week.

— 25.3.6 —

Support

> **Evviva!** 'Hooray!'
> **Viva . . .!** 'Long live . . .!'

— 25.3.7 —

Trust

Phrases conveying trust include: **avere fiducia (in)**, **fidarsi (di)**:

> *Mi* posso *fidare di* lui?
> Can I trust him?

> Non *hai fiducia in* me.
> You don't have any confidence in me.

— 25.3.8 —

Interest or enthusiasm

> *Ti interessa* il tuo lavoro?
> Does your work interest you?

> Gli studenti non *sono interessati alla* politica.
> The students are not interested in politics.

> Alfredo non *si è mai interessato del* corso.
> Alfredo never cared about the course.

Sono interessanti i lavori di quest'artista, ma non mi piacciono.
The works of this artist are interesting, but I don't like them.

I turisti sono sempre *entusiasti* di Venezia.
Tourists are always enthusiastic about Venice.

Dopo un mese *mi sono* veramente *entusiasmata* del mio lavoro.
After a month I got really enthusiastic about my work.

Bisogna *essere motivati* per fare il dottorato di ricerche.
You have to be motivated to do a Ph.D.

Gianni e Luisa *sono appassionati* di mobili antichi.
Gianni and Luisa are passionate about antique furniture.

25.4 *Expressing negative emotions*

Regret, sorrow, unhappiness

Purtroppo expresses regret at a fact:

Purtroppo il treno è in ritardo.
Unfortunately the train is late.

The verb **dispiacere** can be used with an indirect object noun or pronoun, indicating the person who is expressing regret. It is normally followed by the subjunctive in formal language:

Ci dispiace che tu non abbia avuto il posto.
We're sorry that you didn't get the job.

Mi dispiace che tu la pensi così.
I'm sorry you feel like that.

You can also use the expression (È un) **peccato che**, again followed by the subjunctive in formal language:

Peccato che voi dovete studiare.
Pity you have to study!

È un peccato che i suoi genitori abitino così lontano.
It's a pity that her parents live so far away.

Desperation

Sono disperata, è partito il mio fidanzato per un viaggio di 6 mesi.
I'm in despair, my fiancé has left for a six-month long journey.

Non so più come fare. Non ce la faccio più.
I don't know what to do. I can't go on.

25.4.3 Disappointment

Simple expressions of disappointment include:

Che delusione!	**Che disastro!**	**Per amor del cielo!**
'How disappointing!'	'What a disaster!'	'Heaven forbid!'

Deludere is the verb used when we want to articulate this feeling more clearly:

> *Sono veramente delusa* **del tuo comportamento.**
> I'm really disappointed with your behaviour.

> **Mi** *hai* **proprio** *deluso.*
> You've really disappointed me.

The verb **dispiacere**, seen above, can also be used to express disappointment:

> *Sono proprio dispiaciuto* **che i nostri amici non siano (sono) venuti.**
> I'm really upset that our friends didn't come.

> *Che dispiacere* **mi ha fatto vederlo così mal ridotto!**
> What a disappointment to see him in such a bad shape!

25.4.4 Dissatisfaction

Expressions of dissatisfaction include:

> **Così non va bene.**
> That won't do.

> **Il tuo supervisore** *non è molto soddisfatto* **del tuo lavoro.**
> Your supervisor isn't very satisfied with your work.

> **A volte i clienti** *rimangono insoddisfatti* **della qualità del prodotto.**
> Sometimes customers are dissatisfied with the quality of the product.

25.4.5 Disapproval, disagreement

Expressions of disapproval include **non . . . approvare, essere contrario, fare male a:**

> *Sono contrario all'***idea di andare al mare solo per la giornata.**
> I'm against the idea of going to the seaside just for the day.

> *Hai fatto male a* **scegliere Giurisprudenza.**
> You made a mistake choosing law.

Further expressions of disagreement are shown in Chapter 27.

25.4.6 Irritation, annoyance, displeasure

Irritation, annoyance or displeasure can be expressed by any of the following:

Basta!	**Non va!**	**Non mi va!**
That's enough!	It doesn't work!	I don't like it!
	It's no good.	

Non *mi piace* il tuo comportamento.
I don't like your behaviour.

Il mio amico era proprio *seccato* con me.
My boyfriend was really fed-up with me.

Se mia madre venisse a sapere, sarebbe *furiosa.*
If my mother were to find out, she would be furious.

**I professori sono *furibondi* con gli studenti che non hanno
partecipato al seminario.**
The lecturers are furious with the students who didn't take part
in the seminar.

Quando ha saputo della macchina, *è andato su tutte le furie.*
When he found out about the car, he went wild.

25.4.7   Boredom

Boredom is expressed by words such as **noioso, noia**:

È un libro veramente *noioso.*
It's a really boring book.

È *noioso* imparare i verbi irregolari.
It's boring learning irregular verbs.

Che noia!
What a bore!

Other more colloquial expressions corresponding to the English 'How boring!'
include:

Che barba!
What a bore!

Che palle! (rather vulgar)
What a bore!

25.4.8   Anger

Anger can be conveyed with stronger language such as these *interjectional
expressions* (used as isolated utterances at any point in a discourse). These sorts
of words do not always have an exact translation:

Mannaggia!	**Accidenti!**	**Porca miseria!**

There is an infinite variety of curses and swearwords used by Italians of different age groups and different regions and dialects. We leave it to the reader to investigate further.

Less harsh but more explicit ways of expressing anger include:

Che rabbia!	**Che nervi!**
That's really infuriating!	It gets on my nerves!

Mi fa una rabbia pensare che ha vinto lui invece di me.
It makes me angry to think that he won instead of me.

Le fanno venire i nervi tutti questi spostamenti.
All these moves get on her nerves.

25.4.9   Antipathy, hostility

Again a variety of idiomatic expressions can be used to represent the speaker's antipathy towards somebody.

Mild dislike can be expressed thus:

Non mi piacevano gli amici di mia madre.
I didn't like my mother's friends.

Non ci va il nuovo Preside.
We don't like the new headmaster.

Alfredo le *è* sempre *stato antipatico.*
She's always disliked Alfredo.

Non lo *trovi* un po' *antipatico*?
Don't you find him rather unlikeable?

Se viene Caterina, io non vengo. Non la *sopporto.*
If Caterina is coming, I'm not coming. I can't stand her.

See also 28.3.

Speakers can express hostility by cursing someone:

Al diavolo!	**Va al diavolo!**
To hell!	Go to hell!

Che gli venga un accidente!
Damn him!

Other more picturesque or violent ways to express hostility are left to individual preferences and creative fantasy.

Sei proprio *antipatico. Vattene.*
You're really horrible. Go away.

Leonardo è una persona molto *aggressiva.*
Leonardo is a really aggressive person.

> **A volte gli inglesi possono sembrare addirittura *ostili*.**
> Sometimes the English can actually seem hostile.

When a certain degree of courtesy and formality is needed, the following might come in useful:

> **Per favore, *mi lasci in pace. Si accomodi fuori*!**
> Please, leave me alone. Leave the room now.

Disgust

Disgust is usually conveyed by the following expression, rather vulgar, but very common in a familiar context:

> **Che schifo!**   **Mi fa schifo!**
> Disgusting!   I am disgusted! It makes me
>   sick.

> **Mi fa schifo dover lavorare con gente del genere!**
> It's sickening having to work with these sorts of people!

> **Questi episodi di razzismo *fanno schifo*.**
> These espisodes of racism are sickening.

25.5   *Expressing neutral emotions*

Indifference

Ways of expressing indifference to a person, object or proposal include the following:

> ***A me non interessa* se vieni o no. Fai *come vuoi*.**
> I don't care if you come or not. Do what you want.

> **Se *per te è uguale*, partiamo il 15 dicembre.**
> If it's all the same for you, we'll leave on 15 December.

> **Scegli quello che vuoi, tanto per me *è lo stesso*.**
> Choose what you want, it's all the same for me anyway.

> ***Fa lo stesso se* viaggiamo in treno o in macchina.**
> It's the same whether we travel by train or by car.

> **Che lui venga o no *per me fa lo stesso*.**
> Whether he comes or not, it's the same for me.

> ***Non importa se* finisci l'esercizio o no.**
> It doesn't matter if you finish the exercise or not.

> ***Non mi importa niente della* tua vita personale.**
> I don't care about your personal life.

> **I voti che danno i professori** *non importano a* **nessuno.**
> The marks the teachers give don't matter to anyone.

> **Scusa,** *che t'importa di* **quello che dice lui?**
> Excuse me, what do you care about what he says?

> **Mangiamo dove vuoi tu,** *per me è indifferente.*
> Let's eat where you want, for me it's all the same.

> **Quello che pensano loro** *non mi interessa.*
> I don't care what they think.

To express straightforward indifference without a particular focus, we can say:

> **Non me ne importa niente.**
> I don't care a bit about it.

> **Non ha importanza.**
> It doesn't matter.

> **Non fa nessuna differenza.**
> It doesn't make any difference.

The *lack* of positive qualities such as interest and enthusiasm (see 25.3.8) can also convey indifference:

> **Gli** *manca* **proprio l'entusiasmo.**
> He's really lacking enthusiasm.

> **Non** *ha interesse* **(***nel* **suo lavoro).**
> He has no interest (in his work).

> **Gli studenti** *sono poco motivati.*
> The students are not very motivated.

Or, more forcefully:

> **Non gliene frega niente.**
> He couldn't give a damn.

> **Chi se ne frega?**
> Who cares?

In the expression **non mi importa niente**, **niente** can be replaced by **un corno/un fico (secco)**, both very colloquial expressions:

> **Non me ne importa un fico (secco).**
> (*literally*) I don't care a (dried) fig.

25.5.2 **Resignation**

When you are resigned to a situation, or feel you can do little about it:

> **Pazienza!**
> Never mind! (*literally*: Patience!)

Non importa!
It doesn't matter.

Mi dispiace, sono finite le lasagne.
Sorry, the lasagne is finished.

Fa lo stesso. **Prendo i tortellini.**
It doesn't matter. I'll have the tortellini.

Non c'è niente da fare.
There's nothing to be done.

Cosa vuoi! **Hanno sedici anni.**
What do you expect? They're sixteen years old.

Puzzlement, perplexity

Cosa faccio?
What shall I do now?

Non so (più) cosa fare.
I don't know what to do (now).

Positive and/or negative emotions

Expressions which are not neutral, but can express *either* positive or negative
emotions according to the context are:

Surprise, shock, amazement

Che sorpresa!
What a surprise!

Che bella sorpresa!
What a nice surprise!

Che brutta sorpresa!
What a horrible surprise!

Il suo comportamento mi ha fatto impressione.
His behaviour amazed me.

Nooo!	**Davvero?**
No!	Really?
Veramente?	**Mamma mia!**
Really?	(Untranslatable)
Non ci credo!	**Perbacco!**
I don't believe it!	(Untranslatable)

Two expressions of amazement used particularly in the north of Italy are:

Perdinci!   Perdiana!
(Both are untranslatable ...)

25.6.2 ## Patience, impatience, expectation

Pazienza!
Have patience!

(And see also 25.5.2 Resignation.)

Non vedo l'ora di **finire questo libro!**
I can't wait to finish this book!

I bambini *non vedono l'ora* **di andare in vacanza.**
The children can't wait to go on holiday.

26 Expressing emotions: hope, fear, doubt

26.1 Introduction

Hope, fear and doubt are probably the most frequently expressed emotions. Like the other subjective utterances, they are often represented by a verb construction requiring the subjunctive.

26.2 Expressing hope

26.2.1

Sperare

The verb **sperare** is used to express 'hope', either followed by **di** and a verb infinitive or by **che** and a subjunctive.

The construction **di** + verb infinitive can only be used where the subject or implied subject is the same in both parts of the sentence:

> *Spero di vederti domani.*
> I hope to see you tomorrow.
> (I hope that I will see you tomorrow.)

Otherwise, when the two verbs have a different subject, the construction **spero che** must be used, followed by the subjunctive:

> *Spero che tua madre si senta meglio adesso.*
> I hope your mother feels better now.

Speriamo is often used as a kind of imperative form (meaning 'let's hope' rather than 'we hope'), and conveys a certain *anxiety*, or almost pessimistic expectation:

> *Speriamo di farcela!*
> Let's hope we can manage it! (but it's going to be hard!)

> **Arriverai in tempo?** *Speriamo di sì!*
> Will you arrive in time? Hopefully yes! (or I'll be in trouble)

> **Sta finendo la benzina?** *Speriamo di no!*
> Are we running out of petrol? Let's hope not!

26.2.2

Augurarsi

In formal conversation and greetings we can use **mi auguro** instead of **spero** to convey a combination of hope and wish.

> **ArrivederLa.** *Mi auguro* **che faccia un buon viaggio.**
> Goodbye. I hope you'll have a nice journey.

> *Mi auguro* **che il vostro progetto abbia successo.**
> I hope/wish your project will be successful.

26.2.3

Magari

This is a very common exclamation used to express hope combined with a strong desire. With this meaning it can be used with a verb in the imperfect subjunctive, or alone as an *interjection*.

> **Ti piacerebbe avere una casa sul mare?** *Magari*!
> Would you like to have a home at the seaside? If only it could be true!

> *Magari* **vincessi la Lotteria di Capodanno!**
> If only I could win the National Lottery!

26.3 Expressing fear

Both **avere paura** and **temere** express fear. The first is more commonly used as the equivalent of the English 'to be afraid'. Both are also used when the meaning is not literally intended (conveying regret rather than real fear). When used in combination with another verb they use the constructions **di** + infinitive or **che** + subjunctive.

26.3.1

Real fear

> **Ho paura dei temporali.**
> I am scared of thunderstorms.

> **Mio figlio** *ha paura* **dei fantasmi.**
> My son is afraid of ghosts.

> **Mia nonna** *teme* **anche le più piccole malattie.**
> My grandmother is afraid of even the slightest illness.

26.3.2

Pessimism

> *Ho paura di* **non riuscire a finire in tempo.**
> I am afraid I won't finish on time.

> **Gli studenti** *temono che* **il professore sia arrabbiato con loro.**
> The students are afraid that the teacher is angry with them.

Anxiety

> *Speriamo* **che non succeda niente di brutto.**
> Let's hope nothing awful happens.

See also 26.2.1 for further examples of how **sperare** can express anxiety.

Polite expression of regret

In the following examples **temere** and **avere paura** are used, as the English 'to be afraid', as a polite expression of regret rather than real fear:

> *Temo di* **disturbare.**
> I am afraid I am disturbing (you).

> **Si è rotta la macchina?** *Ho paura di sì*!
> Is the car broken down? I am afraid it is!

> *Ho paura* **che sia troppo tardi per disdire l'appuntamento.**
> I am afraid it is too late to cancel the appointment.

Terror, panic

Stronger feelings of terror are represented by nouns as:

> **terrore** 'terror'
> **panico** 'panic'
> **spavento** 'fright'
> **fifa** 'fear' (this rather ironical)

> **Il mio collega ha il** *terrore* **della possibilità di prendere malattie.**
> My colleague is terrified by the possibility of catching illnesses.

> **Tutti gli studenti hanno una** *fifa* **eccessiva degli esami.**
> All students have an exaggerated fear of exams.

> **A grandi altezze** *mi prende il panico.*
> I'm scared of heights.

> **Che spavento!**
> What a fright!

> **Che fifa!**
> How frightening! (said scathingly)

or verbal expressions as:

> **essere terrorizzato** 'to be terrorized/terrified'
> **prendere uno spavento** 'to get a fright'
> **essere in preda al panico** 'to be in the grip of panic'

> **Mia moglie è** *terrorizzata* **dai topi.**
> My wife is terrified of rats.

Quando l'aereo è atterrato nella tempesta *ho preso uno spavento che non dimenticherò mai più!*
When the plane landed in the storm, I was so scared that I'll never forget it!

Durante i bombardamenti la popolazione *era in preda al panico.*
During the bombardments, the population was in a panic.

Non *lasciarti prendere dal panico.*
Don't panic.

26.4　*Expressing doubt*

26.4.1　With the subjunctive

As we have seen in several parts of this book, the use of verbs in the *subjunctive mood*, as an alternative to the *indicative mood*, is the most common way to express doubt or uncertainty in Italian. The subjunctive is frequently found linked with verbs indicating doubt, opinion, guessing, possibility such as **credere, pensare, dubitare, ritenere, sembrare, immaginare:**

Ritengo che Luigi *potrà* laurearsi il prossimo luglio.
I believe that Luigi will be able to graduate next July. (Certain)

Ritengo che Luigi *possa* laurearsi il prossimo luglio.
I believe that Luigi might be able to graduate next July. (Probable)

Immagino che *sei* stanco.
I imagine that you are tired. (Certain)

Immagino che tu *sia* stanco.
I imagine that you must be tired. (Probable)

Information on the forms of the subjunctive can be found in Chapter 2, while other examples of how it is used will be found throughout Sections III and IV.

26.4.2　With the future

The *future indicative* is also often used to give to the fact or action expressed by a verb the aspect of doubt. It is quite common when the verb is not depending on a main verb such as those shown above (and see Section IV throughout).

Non ho l'orologio. *Saranno* quasi le 8.
I don't have a watch. It must be almost 8 o'clock.

Che bella macchina. *Costerà* un occhio della testa.
What a beautiful car. It must cost a fortune.

Marco non c'è. *Sarà uscito.*
Marco's not there. He must have gone out.

With specific verbs such as *dubitare*

The verb **dubitare** expresses doubt in an explicit way. It is used with **che** and the subjunctive, or with **di** and infinitive (see above 26.2.1).

> *Dubita che* il problema si risolva così facilmente.
> He doubts whether the problem will be solved so easily.

> *Dubito di* poter risolvere facilmente il problema.
> I doubt whether I'll be able to solve the problem easily.

Forse, possibilmente, probabilmente, eventualmente

These adverbs (see Chapter 6) can be used to imply an element of doubt in anything we say.

Forse is the most colloquial and also generic in meaning. **Possibilmente** is similar in meaning but less used. **Probabilmente** implies something more likely to happen.

Eventualmente expresses an option or alternative. It must not be confused with the English 'eventually' (with its reference to an 'eventual' or final time). It means in Italian that something may or may not happen, and is closer to the meaning of the English 'possibly'.

> Non so se avrò tempo. *Eventualmente* passerò a salutarti verso le 5.
> I don't know whether I'll have time. Possibly (if I have the time) I'll pop in to say hello around 5 o'clock.

> In frigorifero non c'è quasi nulla. *Eventualmente* possiamo uscire a mangiare una pizza.
> There is almost nothing in the fridge. We might (if thought desirable or necessary) go out for a pizza.

 ### *Può darsi*

This is another expression indicating doubt or possibility. It is followed by **che** + (usually) subjunctive, or used alone as an answer without certainty.

> Non rispondono al telefono. *Può darsi che siano usciti.*
> They're not answering the phone. They might have gone out.

> *Può darsi che* stasera *venga/verrà* Marinella a cena.
> It's possible that Marinella will come for dinner tonight.

> Ci sarà *la Divina Commedia* in biblioteca?
> *Può darsi!*
> Do you think there is a copy of Dante's *Comedy* in the Library? It's possible!

26.4.6

Chissà se ...

This expression means 'who knows whether . . .' and is followed by a verb in the indicative. It carries a strong sense of doubt.

> *Chissà se* **c'è ancora qualcuno in ufficio?!**
> Is it possible that someone is still in the office?

> *Chissà se* **sono già partiti?!**
> Could they have already left?

Chissà is also used as a highly doubtful answer to a question:

> **Pensi che ci pagheranno in tempo?** *Chissà?!*
> Do you think they will pay us in time? Who knows!!

27 Expressing an opinion or belief, agreement or disagreement

27.1

Expressing or seeking an opinion or belief

There are many ways of expressing your own opinion, either hesitantly or forcefully. You can also seek someone else's opinion using a similar range of expressions.

Pensare, credere

The verb **pensare** can be used in three different ways to express an opinion or belief.

Pensare di + *noun*:

> **Cosa *pensate di* questo cantante?**
> What do you think of this singer?

Pensare di + *verb infinitive*:

> **Pensate di essere infallibili?**
> Do you think you are infallible?

Pensare che and the subjunctive:

> **I clienti *pensavano che* il direttore fosse molto in gamba.**
> The customers thought that the manager was very bright.

Where **pensare** has the meaning 'to think', 'to believe' (not 'to think of') it can be replaced by **credere**:

> **Lo *credevano* un genio.**
> They thought he was a genius.

> **I clienti *credevano che* il direttore fosse onesto.**
> The customers thought the director was honest.

27.1.2

Credere expressing a belief

Credere can also be used to convey religious, political, ideological or other strong belief. In this context, it is generally used with **in**:

Credo in **Dio Padre onnipotente, creatore del cielo e della terra.**
I believe in God the Father almighty, creator of heaven and earth.
(From the Creed)

I Buddisti *credono nella* **reincarnazione dell'anima.**
Buddhists believe in the reincarnation of the soul.

I Musulmani *credono nella* **rivelazione del Corano.**
Muslims believe in the revelations of the Koran.

Se non *credi in* **te stesso non raggiungerai mai il tuo scopo.**
If you don't believe in yourself, you will never reach your goal.

Molti italiani *credono in* **un sistema educativo pubblico e gratuito.**
Many Italians believe in an education system that is public and free.

Sembrare, parere

The verbs **sembrare**, **parere** are used impersonally ('it seems . . .') with an indirect object or object pronoun to express an opinion. They are slightly more tentative – less forceful – than **pensare**, **credere**:

Ci sembra **che sia una iniziativa valida.**
It seems to us that this is a worthwhile initiative.

Ti pare **giusto escludere Teresa?**
Do you think it's fair to exclude Teresa?

Used on its own, **(ti)** **pare** is used to express disbelief or incredulity.

Ma, ti pare!
Really?!

As well as this impersonal use, they can also be used with a person or thing to say how he/she/it seems to you:

Il suo ragionamento non *mi è sembrato* **molto valido.**
His reasoning didn't seem very sound to me.

Come *ti sembra* **questo progetto?**
What do you think of this project?

Come vi *è parso* **il direttore d'orchestra?**
How did the conductor seem to you?

I bambini non *mi sembravano* **molto contenti.**
The children didn't seem very happy to me.

il/un parere

Parere can also be used as a noun meaning 'opinion'. Near synonyms of **parere** are: **il giudizio, la valutazione, l'opinione:**

Vorrei conoscere *il Suo parere* **sulla qualità dei nostri prodotti.**
I would like to know your opinion of the quality of our products.

Qual è la tua *valutazione* **della situazione?**
What is your evaluation of the situation?

Essere del parere:

Mio marito *è del parere* **che dovremmo andare a sciare nelle Dolomiti quest'anno.**
My husband is of the opinion that we ought to go skiing in the Dolomites this year.

Noi siamo *del parere* **opposto.**
We are of the opposite opinion.

A mio parere, secondo me, per me:

The phrase **a mio parere** and the similar phrases **secondo me** and **per me** act as an adjunct to the main message of the sentence, serving to convey the fact that it is a personal opinion. The *conditional* is sometimes used to convey the same message.

A mio parere, **Berlusconi è molto abile nel manipolare l'opinione pubblica.**
In my opinion Berlusconi is very skilled at manipulating public opinion.

Al parere del mio professore **di storia, il Risorgimento è il periodo più interessante della storia italiana.**
In my history teacher's opinion, the Risorgimento is the most interesting period in Italian history.

Secondo mio padre **i genovesi** *sarebbero* **tirchi.**
According to my father the Genoese are mean.

Per me, **non ci sono alternative.**
In my opinion there are no alternatives.

Secondo can be used not only with a personal opinion, but also with a saying, a tradition or legend:

Secondo la leggenda, **nel castello girerebbe il fantasma di un soldato austriaco morto in modo violento.**
According to legend, the castle is haunted by the ghost of an Austrian soldier who died violently.

Secondo un detto popolare, **'chi dorme non piglia pesci'.**
According to a popular saying, he who sleeps doesn't catch fish.

27.1.5

Making a point: *dico*

To express your opinion more strongly, use **dico che**:

Dico che **è ora di finirla con queste menzogne.**
I say it's time to finish with these lies.

See also 42.2.2.

27.2 *Expressing agreement, disagreement*

An important linguistic function in any language is to be able to express or indicate agreement or disagreement with a person or statement. Not surprisingly, there are many ways of doing this in Italian. Some are more polite than others.

27.2.1

Expressing agreement

Simple expressions of agreement include:

> **OK** 'OK'
> (**essere**) **d'accordo** '(to be) agreed'/'in agreement'
> **essere favorevole** 'to be in favour (of)'
> **va bene** 'all right'
> **è vero/è giusto** 'that's true'/'that's correct'

Note how these expressions are used:

> *È vero* **quello che dici tu.**
> What you say is true.

> *Era vero che* **c'erano pochi dipendenti disposti a lavorare anche il sabato.**
> It was true that there were few employees willing to work on Saturdays too.

> *Sono d'accordo che* **bisogna cambiare la struttura del reparto.**
> I agree that we need to change the structure of the department.

Essere d'accordo can be followed by **in** or **di** with a verb in the infinitive, or by **in**, **di**, **su** or **con** with a noun:

> **Eravamo d'accordo di votare sì.**
> We were in agreement in voting yes.

> **I clienti** *sono d'accordo sul* **prezzo.**
> The customers are in agreement on the price.

> **I dipendenti** *saranno d'accordo con* **la decisione del sindacato.**
> The employees will agree with the decision of the trade union.

When expressing agreement *with a person,* **con** is used:

> *Sono d'accordo con* lui.
> I agree with him.

Other ways of expressing agreement, particularly in the spoken language, include:

> **Hai proprio ragione.**
> You're absolutely right.
>
> **Sì, anch'io la vedo così.**
> Yes, I see it like that too.
>
> **Naturalmente.**
> Naturally. (Of course.)

27.2.2

Expressing disagreement

Expressions of disagreement include:

> **sbagliare** 'to be wrong'
> **per niente** 'not at all'
> **non è vero** 'it's not true'
> **non essere d'accordo** 'to not agree'
> **non condividere (una scelta)** 'to not agree with (a choice)'

Here are some examples of how these expressions are used:

> *Non condivido* la tua scelta di partner.
> I don't agree with your choice of partner.
>
> **Su questo aspetto del Trattato di Maastricht gli Eurodeputati inglesi non sono mai** *stati d'accordo* **con gli Eurodeputati francesi.**
> On this aspect of the Treaty of Maastricht the English Euro MPs have never been in agreement with the French Euro MPs.
>
> *Non eravamo d'accordo di* fare lo sciopero.
> We were not in agreeement to strike.
>
> **Sbagli. Vincerà la Juventus, non il Glasgow.**
> You are wrong. Juventus will win, not Glasgow. (football teams)

The phrase **non è vero** can be used to correct a statement or deny an accusation. In formal written language, the construction **non è vero** takes the verb in the subjunctive:

> *Non è vero* che l'abbiano licenziato. È stato lui a dare le dimissioni.
> It's not true that they've fired him. It was he who resigned.

Often in less formal language, the indicative is used instead:

> *Non è vero* che Marco è stato fuori per una settimana.
> It's not true that Marco has been away for a week.

Another way of disbelieving the truth of a report is:

> **Non ci credo per niente.**
> I don't believe a word.

27.2.3

Agreeing in part: *non dico che*

> *Non dico che* vada bene il suo comportamento, ma lo capisco.
> I'm not saying that his behaviour is all right, but I can understand it.

28 Indicating preference, likes and dislikes

28.1 Introduction

One of the communicative functions that we need to master in Italian is how to express our likes, preferences, and, on occasions, our dislikes. Some of the ways of expressing likes or dislikes are more appropriate for people, others for objects.

28.2 Expressing likes

28.2.1

Things and people, using *piacere*

Probably the commonest way of expressing likes or dislikes is to use the verb **piacere**. **Piacere** means literally 'to please' so the phrase 'I like music' has to be translated into Italian as **la musica mi piace** or, more emphatically, **la musica piace a me** 'music is pleasing to me' in which the English structure is reversed, so that the thing or person giving pleasure is the *subject* of the sentence and the person receiving pleasure is the *indirect object*:

Italian: **Mi piace la musica**

(Music pleases to me)
English: I like music

Piacere is equally suitable for people, objects and activities, but note that if the person or thing liked is plural, the verb must be plural too:

Ci piacciono gli spaghetti.
We like spaghetti.

Piacere can be used in a full range of tenses, and uses **essere** in all compound tenses.

The indirect object (the person receiving pleasure) can be a noun governed by **a**:

Il caldo *piace* solo *alla gente* che è in vacanza.
Only people who are on holiday like the heat.

***Ai ragazzi* italiani *piacciono* le magliette americane.**
Italian kids like American T-shirts.

> *A* Marco *piaceva* andare in bicicletta.
> Marco used to like going by bike.

Alternatively, an indirect object pronoun (see Chapter 3) can be used instead of the person:

> Quella ragazza *mi* è piaciuta un sacco.
> I really liked that girl.

> Come può piacer*ti* una persona così superficiale?
> How can you like such a superficial person?

> *Vi* sono piaciuti i cannelloni fatti con spinaci?
> Did you like the cannelloni made with spinach?

> *A noi* piaceva fare delle lunghe passeggiate, *a loro* piaceva stare fermi.
> We liked going for long walks; they liked staying still.

Piacere can also be qualified with the words **molto, tanto**, etc.:

> Mi piace *molto* questo paese.
> I like this village a lot.

> Gli piaceva *tanto* andare in barca.
> He used to love going in the boat.

28.2.2
Liking a person

Because likes and loves are the subject of much discussion in everyday life, phrases on the topic abound:

> **volere bene a** 'to love, like'
> **trovare simpatico** 'to find someone pleasant, likeable'
> **prendere la cotta per** 'to get a crush on'
> **amare** 'to love'

While the first two expressions can equally well be used for a non-romantic friendship or any friendly relationship, the second last one has a romantic/sexual connotation:

> *Vogliamo bene a* tutti i nostri figli.
> We love all our children.

> Ho conosciuto il nuovo insegnante; l'*ho trovato* molto *simpatico*.
> I've met the new teacher; I found him very nice.

> Pino mi ha telefonato di nuovo stasera; *ha* proprio *preso una cotta*.
> Pino rang me again tonight; he's really got it bad.

> *Ti amo* più di ieri, meno di domani.
> I love you more than yesterday, less than tomorrow.
> (Often found on the back of medallions or inside lockets.)

28.2.3

Liking a thing, activity

Apart from **piacere**, we can use one of the following expressions to say what we like or what we like doing:

> **amare** 'to love'
> **andare bene** 'to be all right, OK, acceptable'
> **gradire** 'to please' (no longer very common, mainly used for offering food and drinks)

Like **piacere**, **andare bene** can be used with an indirect object pronoun, referring to the person, and a noun or verb infinitive, linked by **di**, to say what one might like:

> *Ti va bene* **questo posto?**
> Is this place all right for you?

> **Non** *mi va di* **mangiare fuori stasera.**
> I don't feel like eating out tonight.

> *Gradisce* **un aperitivo?**
> Would you like an aperitif?

> **I miei genitori** *amano* **la musica; infatti si sono conosciuti ad un concerto di musica classica.**
> My parents love music. In fact they met at a concert of classical music.

For forms of entertainment, we often use verbs such as:

> **godersi** 'to enjoy'
> **divertirsi** 'to enjoy oneself'

> *Vi siete divertiti* **a Londra?**
> Did you enjoy yourselves in London?

> *Ti diverti* **a giocare a carte?**
> Do you enjoy playing cards?

> **I ragazzi** *si sono goduti* **le vacanze al mare.**
> The boys enjoyed their holiday at the seaside.

28.3 Expressing dislikes

Most of the expressions conveying dislike can be used equally for a person, object, event or activity.

28.3.1

Non ... piacere

If you really don't like something or someone, you can of course say so, just by using **piacere** and adding **non**:

Non mi è piaciuto **il tuo comportamento.**
I didn't like your behaviour.

Gli spinaci *non piacevano ai* **ragazzi.**
The boys didn't like spinach.

Al **direttore** *non piace* **scrivere delle relazioni.**
The manager doesn't like writing reports.

Non mi piacciono **le persone maleducate.**
I don't like bad-mannered people.

Note that **dispiacere** is not the exact opposite of **piacere**; it does not mean 'to dislike' but expresses apologies or a request, as in **ti dispiace passarmi il sale? Mi dispiace** means literally 'It is displeasing to me', in other words 'I am sorry'.

The construction is similar to that of **piacere**; the indirect pronoun **mi, ti, gli,** etc. indicates the *person* who is apologizing:

Scusi, *mi* **dispiace disturbarla.**
Excuse me, I'm sorry to disturb you.

See Chapters 20 and 42.

See Chapters 20 and 42.

28.3.2 Conveying mild dislike
Sometimes it is better to be tactful and tell someone that you 'don't like something very much' by using **poco**:

Le piace **questo libro? A me piace poco.**
Do you like this book? I don't like it very much.

The word **abbastanza** in Italian expresses a distinct lack of enthusiasm:

Le piacciono **le vongole? Abbastanza.**
Do you like clams? A bit (*literally*: enough)

28.3.3 Other expressions of dislike
trovare antipatico 'to find unpleasant'
(non) andare 'to be not all right'

The expression **non andare** 'to be not all right or acceptable' is more commonly used with an object or activity, but can also be used with a person:

Non gli va bene **Marco al posto di Giorgio.**
He's not happy about Marco, in place of Giorgio.

28.3.4 Conveying strong dislike
Here are some stronger ways of conveying dislike, of a person or thing:

non sopportare 'to not be able to stand'
non tollerare 'to not be able to stand'

non potere vedere 'to not be able to bear'
odiare 'to hate'
detestare 'to hate'
fare schifo a qualcuno 'to make somebody sick'
fare effetto a qualcuno 'to make somebody sick' (mainly used with a thing)

Non sopporto il mio collega, lo *trovo* proprio *antipatico.*
I can't bear my colleague, I find him really unpleasant.

Il direttore *non può* **vedere Berlusconi.**
The manager can't stand Berlusconi.

Mio padre *detesta* **i fannulloni.**
My father detests layabouts.

Non mi piacciono le vongole. Mi *fanno effetto.*
I don't like clams. They make me want to throw up.

Vedere le mosche sulla carne *mi ha fatto schifo.*
Seeing the flies on the meat made me feel sick.

Odio **gli spinaci.**
I hate spinach.

28.4   *Expressing a preference*

Unsurprisingly, to express a preference, you can use **piacere** again, with the words **di più** 'more' or **di meno** 'less':

Noi andiamo al mare quest'estate, ma *ci piacerebbe di più* **andare in montagna.**
We're going to the sea this summer, but we would prefer to go to the mountains.

Secondo un sondaggio recente sui personaggi famosi, sono i politici che *piacciono di meno* **alla gente.**
According to a recent survey on famous people, it's the politicans who are less popular.

You can also use a 'dedicated' verb, **preferire** 'to prefer':

Oggi si *preferisce* **mangiare meno carne, più verdura e frutta fresca.**
Today people prefer eating less meat, and more vegetables and fresh fruit.

I professori *preferiscono* **gli studenti che si impegnano di più.**
Lecturers prefer students who are more committed.

29 Expressing certainty and knowledge

Introduction

In this section of the book we describe various states of mind and emotions. Other personal feelings which are to some extent subjective include feelings of knowledge and certainty. How to express various degrees of certainty, including knowing, remembering and forgetting, is described in this chapter, while in Chapter 32, we describe more objective, less personal ways of expressing certainty or uncertainty.

29.2 Sapere

'Knowing' can be conveyed by the verb **sapere**. Sapere can be used with a noun or a verb (infinitive or introduced by **che** or **se**):

With a noun or noun equivalent (a fact):

> **Lei *sa* quanto è il cambio con la sterlina?**
> Do you know how much the exchange with sterling is?

> **Bisogna *sapere* queste date a memoria.**
> These dates must be known by heart.

> **Cosa ne *sai* tu di queste cose?**
> What do you know about these things?

> **Non *so* niente di questo.**
> I don't know anything about this.

With a verb infinitive:

> **Per chi *sa* scrivere a macchina, è facile usare il computer.**
> For those who know how to type, it's easy to use the computer.

With a verb introduced by se:

> ***Sai se* arrivano oggi i nostri amici?**
> Do you know if our friends are arriving today?

*With a verb introduced by **che**:*

> **Sapevamo *che* lui veniva, ma non l'ora precisa del suo arrivo.**
> We knew he was coming, but not the precise time of his arrival.

Normally, with **se** or **che**, **sapere** is followed by a verb in the indicative:

> **Il direttore *sa che c'è* ancora molto da fare.**
> The manager knows there's still a lot to do.

> **Noi *sappiamo che* tu *sei* onesto.**
> We know that you are honest.

When **sapere** is negative, it is often followed by the subjunctive to stress *uncertainty* (see also 32.3). However this is not essential in informal conversation or writing:

> **Non sapevo che tu *cantassi* così bene.**
> I didn't know you could sing so well.

> **Non so se si *possa* rimborsare il biglietto.**
> I don't know if the ticket can be refunded.

> **Il mio collega *non sa che sta* per essere licenziato.**
> My colleague doesn't know he's about to be sacked.

> **Non so se questa *sia* una mossa intelligente.**
> I don't know if this is an intelligent move.

At the end of the sentence, we can add the phrase **o no**:

> **Non so se questa *sia* una mossa intelligente, *o no*.**
> I don't know if this is an intelligent move, or not.

29.3   Essere certo, sicuro, convinto

Certainty or uncertainty can be expressed using the verb **essere** and one of the following adjectives:

> **certo** 'certain'
> **sicuro** 'sure'
> **convinto** 'convinced'

(The last adjective – **convinto** – is the past participle of the verb **convincere**.)

The message that follows can either be introduced by **che**, or by **di** + infinitive.

The construction **di** + infinitive can be used *only* if the subject of the two parts of the sentence is the same:

> **Siete sicuri *di* trovare la strada?**
> Are you sure you'll find the road?

> *Siete sicuri che* questa *sia/è* la strada giusta?
> Are you sure this is the right road?

Che can introduce either the indicative or the subjunctive. We use the *indicative* when we are certain of something. If the sentence is negative, or interrogative, the *subjunctive* can be used to express doubt or uncertainty, although it is often replaced by the indicative in conversation or informal writing:

Essere certo:

> *Sono certo* che *hanno* già ricevuto la merce.
> I am certain they have already received the goods.

> *Non sono certo* che *abbiano* ricevuto il nostro fax.
> I'm not certain if they have received our fax.

Essere sicuro:

> *Sono sicura che* questa *è* la casa di Cristina.
> I'm certain that this is Cristina's house.

> *Non sono sicura che* questa *sia* la casa di Cristina.
> I'm not certain that this is Cristina's house.

> *Sei sicura che* questa *è* la casa di Cristina?
> Are you sure that this is Cristina's house?

> *Lei è sicura che* questa *sia* la casa di Cristina?
> Are you sure that this is Cristina's house?

In the second example above, **se** could be used instead of **che**:

> *Non sono sicura se* questa *sia* la casa di Cristina.
> I'm not certain if this is Cristina's house.

When a fact that we are certain of at the time is later disproved, then the subjunctive is essential:

> *Eravamo convinti* che la merce *fosse* in magazzino ma ci
> sbagliavamo. L'avevano rubata.
> We were convinced that the goods were in the warehouse, but
> we were wrong. They had been stolen.

To see how **certo** and **sicuro** are used to express *possibility* and *probability*, in a more impersonal way, see Chapter 32.

29.4   Non certo, poco certo, incerto

Lack of certainty can be expressed *either* by using **non** (**non certo**) *or* by using **poco** (**poco certo**):

> **I ragazzi *sono poco sicuri di* trovare la strada.**
> The boys are not at all certain of finding the way.

> **Il cliente *non era certo di* ricevere l'ordine.**
> The customer was not certain of receiving the order.

The adjective **incerto**, on the other hand, can apply not only to personal feelings, but to a situation:

> ***Sono* un po' *incerta* sul da farsi.**
> I'm a bit uncertain as to what to do.

> **È una situazione un po' *incerta*.**
> It's an uncertain situation.

29.5 Pensare, credere; sembrare, parere

Verbs of *thinking* (**pensare, credere; sembrare, parere**) can also express certainty and uncertainty (see 27.1.1 and 27.1.3):

> **(mi) sembra/pare che** 'it seems (to me) that'
> **pensare/credere che** 'to think that'

> **Mia madre *pensa che* io *sia* troppo vecchia per sposarmi.**
> My mother thinks that I am too old to get married.

> ***A me sembrava* che mia madre *fosse* troppo vecchia per fare figli.**
> I thought that my mother was too old to have children.

29.6 Ricordare, dimenticare

'Remembering' and 'forgetting' are expressed in Italian by the verbs **ricordare** and **dimenticare** respectively. **Ricordare** can express both the English 'to remember' and 'to remind':

29.6.1

Ricordare

When **ricordare** conveys 'to remember', it can be used with or without the reflexive pronoun depending on how involved the person is (see also Chapter 2). It can be followed by the person or thing remembered or by a verb (**di** + infinitive, or **che** + indicative):

> **I professori *ricordano* solo gli studenti più bravi.**
> The teachers only remember the cleverest students.

> **Daniela ha aspettato mezz'ora davanti all'università perché non *ci siamo ricordati di* lei.**
> Daniela waited half an hour in front of the University because we didn't remember her.

Non *ti ricordi* dove hai messo quella cartella?
Don't you remember where you put that file?

Ricordati di comprare il giornale.
Remember to buy the newspaper.

Il vigile *si ricordava di* aver visto la macchina parcheggiata vicino all'incrocio.
The traffic warden remembered seeing the car parked near the crossroads.

Mia moglie *si è ricordata che* io avevo lasciato i biglietti sul comò.
My wife remembered that I had left the tickets on the bedside cabinet.

When **ricordare** conveys the concept of 'reminding', the person reminded is expressed by an indirect object noun or pronoun. If followed by a verb (to remind someone to do *something*), the verb infinitive is preceded by **di**:

Questa casa ci *ricorda* le vecchie case di montagna.
This house reminds us of the old houses in the mountains.

Il direttore *ha ricordato* agli impiegati la riunione generale alle 6.00.
The manager reminded the employees of the general meeting at 6 o'clock.

Stasera cambia l'ora. *Ricordami di* aggiustare l'orologio.
Tonight the clocks change. Remind me to adjust my watch.

Un ricordo conveys the idea of nostalgia rather than a practical reminder:

Questo orsacchiotto è *un ricordo* della mia infanzia.
This teddy bear is a reminder/souvenir of my childhood.

Finally **ricordare** can also be used with the sense of 'to commemorate':

Oggi *ricordiamo* il nostro caro compagno Enrico.
Today we remember our dear companion Enrico.

─ 29.6.2 ─

Dimenticare

Like **ricordare**, **dimenticare** can be used, with or without a reflexive pronoun, with a noun (to forget something or someone) or a verb (**di** + infinitive or **che** + indicative):

Scusi, ho dimenticato il Suo nome.
I'm sorry, I've forgotten your name.

Marco, non *dimenticare di* prendere le chiavi.
Marco, don't forget to take your keys.

Oh Carla, *ti sei dimenticata di* comprare la carta igienica.
Oh Carla, you forgot to buy toilet paper.

> **Mio marito *si era dimenticato* che oggi è il nostro anniversario.**
> My husband had forgotten that today is our anniversary.

It can also mean 'to leave something behind':

> **Mia moglie *ha dimenticato* la borsa in ufficio.**
> My wife forgot her briefcase in the office.

Lastly, verbs of *remembering* and *forgetting* (**ricordarsi**, **dimenticare**) can also convey uncertainty, by use of the subjunctive or conditional:

> ***Non mi ricordo se* Carlo *abbia* già compiuto 40 anni.**
> I don't remember if Carlo has already reached 40 or not.

> **La direttrice *aveva dimenticato che* la segretaria *sarebbe stata* in vacanza.**
> The manager had forgotten that the secretary would be on holiday.

IV Putting in context

30 Combining messages

30.1 Introduction

Many of the previous sections show how we can get our message across: communicating information, completing a transaction, expressing a feeling or emotion.

In this section, 'Putting in context', we deal with the various ways of conveying a more complex message, of combining more than one message, and of putting our message in a context, e.g. of time.

Some chapters look in detail at *specific* contexts, such as relating or reporting, expressing certainty, purpose, reason, result or time. However, in this introductory chapter, 'Combining messages', we look at some *general* points that need to be borne in mind when conveying a complex message: for example, the structure of the sentence and the tenses and moods of the verbs used.

Not surprisingly, when the message is more complex, the sentence structure also tends to become more complex. The possible sentence structures can be summarized in *two* broad-ranging categories: sentences where there are two or more clauses of equal weight, and sentences where there is a *main* clause and one or more *dependent* (or *subordinate*) clauses.

30.2 Combining messages of equal weight and/or importance

Two messages of equal importance are conveyed by use of two clauses or groups of words of equal importance. These can be completely *separate sentences*:

> **Le truppe di Zagabria sono entrate stamane a Petrinja. Lo ha annunciato Radio Zagabria.** (*Televideo, 6/8/95*)
> Zagreb's troups entered Petrinja this morning. This was announced by Radio Zagreb.

Alternatively they can be separate clauses linked by coordinating conjunctions such as **e, ma**, in which case they are known as *coordinated clauses*:

> **Prosegue l'avanzata delle truppe croate *ed* appare imminente la conquista del parco nazionale di Plitvice.** (*Televideo*, 6/8/95)
> The advance of the Croatian troops continues and the conquest of the national park of Plitvice appears imminent.

30.3 *Combining messages of unequal weight*

When there are two messages which are *not* of equal importance, one message usually expresses a main event or action, while the other expresses an action or event linked to it. The main action or event is normally expressed by a *main clause* (one that could stand on its own without another clause) while the linked action or event is expressed by a clause that cannot stand on its own but is *dependent* or *subordinate* to the main clause. There are many types of *dependent* clause.

> **Alla cerimonia di Hiroshima, cui hanno assistito 100 mila persone, non erano presenti rappresentanti del Governo americano, né di altri paesi.** (*Televideo*, 6/8/95)
> (Main clause **... non erano presenti**, dependent relative clause **cui hanno assistito ...**)
> At the ceremony of Hiroshima, which 100,000 people attended, there were no representatives of the American Government, nor of other countries.

This combination of main/dependent clauses is used to express many different relationships, many of them illustrated in other chapters in Section IV.

30.4 *Setting events in a time context: introduction*

30.4.1 Simple time relationship

When facts or events are related only to the moment of speaking or writing, the time relationship is simple. Section I gives more examples of these simple time relationships: the *present* (Chapter 12); the *past* (Chapter 13); the *future* (Chapter 14). Usually the verb tense alone (present, past, future) is enough to indicate the time when the action took place, although the sentence sometimes includes an *adjunct of time* (phrase, adverb or noun group) which is more specific:

> **(*Oggi*) è il compleanno di Marta.**
> (Today) it is Marta's birthday.

> **Siamo andati a Londra *(la settimana scorsa)*.**
> We went to London (last week).

> **(*L'anno prossimo*) ci trasferiremo negli Stati Uniti.**
> (Next year) we will be moving to the USA.

30.4.2 ## Complex time relationship

In a complex sentence, where messages are combined, the verbs used are closely interlinked, in a *relationship of time* which determines the *tense and mood* of the verb used.

(a) *Main clause and dependent clause*:

When the sentence is composed of main clause and dependent clause, the choice of verb tense and mood in the dependent clause is determined by the verb in the *main* clause. Italian has a set of 'rules' (the *sequence of tenses*) which demonstrate this, shown in a schematic way in Appendix III, and illustrated below in 30.5. These are only guidelines, and how rigidly they are applied depends on the *type* of dependent clause; they are particularly important when the clause acts as *object* of a verb (for example **Spero che *tu possa venire*, lui dice *che partiranno più tardi***) or as *subject* (as in **Mi sembra assurdo *che tu debba fare il lavoro della segretaria***) and hence many of the examples chosen illustrate this.

(b) *Series of main clauses*:

When the sentence is composed of a series of main clauses, these rules do not apply so rigidly, and the choice of verb tense and mood is much wider.

In both types of sentences (main/main and main/dependent), the choice of verbs used depends on the relationship between the events referred to: this may be *same time context* (both events taking place in the same time context), *earlier time context* (one event earlier than the other) or *later time context* (one event taking place later than the other). Events can be described as taking place earlier or later not just in relation to the point of speaking or writing, but in relation to another point in time (in past or in the future) mentioned.

Here we show how these guidelines work in practice, with some general examples in *this* chapter, and some specific examples in the other chapters (for example, Chapter 31 illustrates time relationships in the context of *relating* or *reporting* an event or action, while Chapter 36 illustrates sentences where there is a *specific time reference*).

Where possible, we have used extracts from the newspaper *La Repubblica* to illustrate the different time relationships with examples taken from two separate days of reporting on the war in Bosnia (27 and 31 July 1995): in some cases they have been adapted. The widely varying contexts and styles of writing (diary, report, 'action') affect the mood and tense used.

30.5 Relationship of main clause and dependent clauses

Here we illustrate the way in which the 'sequence of tenses' (see Appendix III) works in different time contexts, taking as our starting point the *choice of verb in the main clause*. We have chosen examples where the relationship *main verb/dependent verb* is illustrated most clearly.

With a present tense in the main clause, the dependent verb can be:
(a) Indicating same time context
Indicative or *conditional*: present. *Subjunctive*: present or imperfect. *Infinitive* or *gerund*: present.

(b) Indicating earlier time context
Indicative: simple or compound perfect, imperfect. *Conditional*: past. *Subjunctive*: past or imperfect. *Infinitive, gerund, participle*: past.

(c) Indicating later time context
Indicative: simple future (or present). *Subjunctive* or *conditional*: present (no future tenses). *Infinitive, gerund*: present.

(a) Same time context
The *indicative* expresses certainty or objectivity:

> **I giornalisti *sanno* che *è* pericoloso lavorare in Bosnia.**
> The journalists know that it is dangerous working in Bosnia.

The *conditional* (see Chapter 2) is used where a condition is either present or implied. It is also used to indicate a report which has not been confirmed (see also Chapter 31) in which case it is translated into English by a simple present indicative:

> **I tecnici *dicono* che la situazione a Bihac *sarebbe* più complicata che a Gorazde, perché l'area è più grande e confina con la Croazia.**
> The experts say that the situation at Bihac is more complicated than at Gorazde, because the area is bigger and borders Croatia.

The *subjunctive* (see Chapter 2) indicates a relationship of uncertainty or 'subjectivity':

> ***Pare* che il governo britannico *sia* disposto ad accogliere altri 500 profughi della ex-Iugoslavia.**
> It seems the British Government is prepared to welcome another 500 refugees from ex-Yugoslavia.

When the main verb is in the *present conditional*, the dependent verb indicating a fact in the same time context will be in the *imperfect subjunctive*:

> **Il governo bosniaco *preferirebbe* che le Nazioni Unite *avessero* più risorse per l'assistenza ai rifugiati.**
> The Bosnian Government would prefer that the UN had more resources to assist the refugees.

> ***Vorrei* che tu *fossi* meno prepotente.**
> I'd like you to be less domineering.

(b) Earlier time context
In the example below, the actions which happened earlier are expressed by the
compound perfect:

> **Dalla notte scorsa i civili musulmani di Zepa hanno cominciato a
> lasciare l'enclave per il loro viaggio verso l'ignoto. *Sappiamo* che il
> primo gruppo di civili, circa 1400 persone, *è partito* martedì sera a
> bordo di una ventina di mezzi serbo-bosniaci ed *ha raggiunto* ieri
> mattina all'alba la linea del fronte.**
> Since last night, the Muslim civilians of Zepa have begun to leave
> the enclave, for their journey towards the unknown. We know
> that the first groups of civilians, around 1,400 people, left on
> Tuesday evening aboard around twenty Bosnian Serb vehicles,
> and yesterday morning at dawn reached the front line.

In the second example, the action is again in the past in relation to the moment
of writing, but this time the verb **sembrare** requires a *past subjunctive* (**abbia
voluto**) in the dependent clause:

> *Sembra* **che il generale Ratko Mladic *abbia voluto* usare maniere
> più civili per quella che resta comunque un'operazione di pulizia
> etnica.**
> It seems that General Ratko Mladic wanted to act in a more civil
> fashion for what is, however, nothing other than an operation of
> ethnic cleansing.

(c) Later time context
The action that will happen *later* than the moment in time of the main clause
(**non importa**) is expressed by a *simple future* (**metteremo**):

> **"Ci riprenderemo con le armi Glamoc e Grahovo", tuonava il
> generale Manojlo Milovanovic, capo dello Stato maggiore di Pale.
> "Non *importa* quanto ci *metteremo*, ma ci riusciremo."**
> 'We will take back Glamoc and Grahovo by force', thundered
> General Manojlo Milovanovic, head of the Pale armed forces. 'It
> doesn't matter how long we take, but we will succeed.'

> **"*Bisogna chiedersi* se il Congresso *resterà* a guardare la sconfitta
> del governo bosniaco", ha dichiarato il Segretario di Stato
> Christopher.**
> 'We have to ask ourselves whether Congress will just sit back and
> watch the defeat of the Bosnian Government,' said Secretary of
> State Christopher.

It is also quite common to use the *present indicative* instead of the future tense,
especially (but not only) when talking of the very near and immediate future:

> **La Croce Rossa *sta preparando* l'accoglienza per i profughi che
> *arrivano* domani dalla Bosnia.**
> The Red Cross is getting ready to receive the refugees who will
> arrive tomorrow from Bosnia.

There is no future tense for the conditional and the subjunctive. With verbs such as **sperare**, which require the subjunctive, and where the action happens *later*, the *present subjunctive* is used instead:

> **I bosniaci *sperano* che il voto americano si *traduca* in realtà e *venga tolto* l'embargo sulla vendita delle armi.**
> The Bosnians hope that the American vote will become reality, and that the embargo on arms sales will be lifted.

With a past tense in the main clause, the dependent verb can be:
(a) Indicating same time context
Indicative or *subjunctive*: imperfect.

(b) Indicating earlier time context
Indicative or *subjunctive*: pluperfect. *Infinitive, gerund* or *participle*: past.

(c) Indicating later time context
Conditional: past (or imperfect indicative). *Indicative*: simple future.

(a) Same time context

> **La popolazione di Sarajevo *ha trovato* rifugio negli scantinati, mentre le bombe *cadevano* sulla città.**
> The people of Sarajevo took shelter in the cellars, while the bombs fell on the city.

(b) Earlier time context

> **Il presidente della Croce Rossa *ha rivelato* che almeno seimila persone *erano fuggite* dalla città nella notte del 6 agosto.**
> The president of the Red Cross has revealed that at least six thousand people had fled the town on the night of 6 August.

In the following example the dependent clause contains a pluperfect subjunctive (**fosse terminato**), which depends on **attendeva** in the main clause. The use of the pluperfect tense implies that the bombing has to be finished *before* people would go out on the street:

> **A Sarajevo la gente *attendeva* che *fosse terminato* il bombardamento prima di uscire per strada.**
> In Sarajevo people waited for the bombing to finish before going out in the street.

(c) Later time context
When events or actions are viewed as happening later than a point of reference in the past, but are still seen as previous to the actual moment of speaking, Italian uses the *past conditional* (which depends on the main verb in a past tense):

Il Presidente Clinton *ha dichiarato* che *avrebbe posto* il veto a una decisione del Congresso in favore dell'abolizione dell'embargo.
President Clinton declared that he would impose a veto if Congress were to decide to lift the embargo.

Gli americani *speravano* che la conferenza di Londra si *sarebbe conclusa* con un maggior impegno militare dell'Europa in Bosnia.
The Americans hoped that the London conference would end with Europe having a greater military involvement in Bosnia.

Sometimes the past conditional is replaced, in more colloquial fashion, by the *imperfect indicative*:

Mia madre mi *aveva promesso* che *veniva* (or *sarebbe venuta*) a trovarmi ieri sera.
My mother had promised me that she would come to see me yesterday evening.

Note, however, that if the events will take place in the *future* with respect to the *actual moment of speaking*, the simple future indicative is used, even when the verb depends on a main clause in a past tense:

Mia madre mi *ha promesso* che *verrà* a trovarmi domani mattina.
My mother has promised me that she will come to see me tomorrow morning.

30.5.3 — **With a future tense in the main clause, the dependent verb can be:**
(a) Indicating same time context
Indicative: simple future. *Conditional* or *subjunctive*: present. *Infinitive* or *gerund*: present.

(b) Indicating earlier time context
Indicative: future perfect. *Infinitive, gerund* or *participle*: past.

(c) Indicating later time context
Indicative: future. *Conditional* or *subjunctive*: present.

(a) Same time context

Pagheremo quando *riceveremo* la merce.
We'll pay when we (will) receive the goods.

Le *dirò* che *sarebbe* meglio *lavorare* in gruppo.
I'll tell her that it would be better to work in a team.

(b) Earlier time context

Partiremo per le vacanze solo dopo che *avremo finito* di scrivere il libro.
We'll go on holiday only after we finish writing the book.

> *Partiremo* per le vacanze solo dopo *aver finito* di scrivere il libro.
> We'll go on holiday only after finishing writing the book.

> *Avendo finito* di scrivere il libro, la settimana prossima *potremo partire* per le vacanze.
> Having finished writing the book, next week we'll be able to go on holiday.

(c) Later time context

> Gli *comunicheremo* con un telegramma che *dovrà* pagare entro una settimana.
> We'll inform him with a telegram that he will have to pay within one week.

> *Dovremo* completare il lavoro prima che il personale *parta* per le vacanze.
> We'll have to complete the work before the staff leave for the holidays.

30.6   *Relationship of tenses in other complex texts*

Sometimes the link between main and dependent clauses is not so obvious.

Here we look at some longer extracts from *La Repubblica* which illustrate the different ways in which time relationships are expressed in current journalistic Italian, and which expand the network of relationships. In these examples, we look at the *time context* first rather than the choice of verb in the main clause.

Here, some of the dependent clauses are of a different type from those illustrated above, some of the sentences contain only main clauses, and in some of the sentences a main verb is implied but not stated. However, note that the same basic 'rules' of the sequence of tenses (see Appendix III) still apply, in these more complex situations.

30.6.1   Same time context

Present
In this example, all the verbs are in the *present indicative*, whether main verbs (**devi, barattiamo, manca, aiutano, sono**) or verbs in dependent clauses (**perché ..., manca, di cui ... riesci**):

> *Devi* cercare il cibo in campagna perché in città *manca* la farina, il latte, le uova ... *barattiamo* scarpe, vestiti, tv, tutto quello di cui *riesci* a fare a meno ... spesso *manca* l'acqua potabile.... Tutti però *aiutano* tutti: l'amicizia e la solidarietà *sono* le uniche risorse rimaste.

> ('Diario di guerra di Ivan', *La Repubblica*, 27/7/95)

You have to search for food out in the country because in town there are shortages of flour, milk, eggs . . . we barter shoes, clothes, TVs, anything you can do without . . . often there is no drinking water. . . . But everyone helps everyone else: friendship and solidarity are the only resources left.

('War Diary of Ivan')

This next example shows how present tenses are used in the dependent time clauses (**Mentre si sentono . . . mentre piovono . . . e si contano**), in the dependent relative clause (**che mordono . . .**) and again in the main clause (**ci si interroga . . .**) to express simultaneous events. The *present conditional* (**sarebbe**) is used to express what the effect *would be* if Bihac were to fall:

> *Mentre si sentono* **le sirene d'allarme,** *mentre piovono* **le granate serbe** *che mordono* **rabbiose il selciato e i tetti delle case, e** *si contano* **i colpi di mortaio,** *ci si interroga* **sulla sorte della lontana Bihac: perché, dopo Srebrenica, dopo Zepa, la perdita di Bihac** *sarebbe* **un disastro.**

> (B. Valli, *La Repubblica*, 27/7/95)

> While the sirens are sounding, while the Serbian grenades rain down, biting furiously into the tarmac and roofs, and people count the number of mortar strikes, questions are being asked about the fate of far-off Bihac: because after Srebrenica, after Zepa, the loss of Bihac would be a disaster.

Past

Here the actions or events in the main clause are expressed by a past tense, and the tenses and moods used in the dependent clauses, to express simultaneity, are the *imperfect indicative* or the *imperfect subjunctive*.

As seen elsewhere (Chapter 13) the compound perfect in the main clause (**è avvenuto**) expresses the *event*, while the imperfect indicative in the time clause (**mentre . . . leggevano . . . accusavano**) forms the *background* to it:

> **Il voto** *è avvenuto* **in un'atmosfera infuocata,** *mentre* **alcuni senatori** *leggevano* **le ultime notizie sulle atrocità serbe in Bosnia, altri** *accusavano* **Clinton. . . .**

> The vote took place in a heated atmosphere. While some senators were reading the latest news on Serbian atrocities in Bosnia, others were accusing Clinton. . . .

Again here, the first clause (**è diventato . . . hanno abbattuti**) expresses the events, while the second (**in uno di questi c'era**) expresses the background; the two clauses are coordinated and linked by **e**:

> **I bombardamenti non smettono mai. Anche l'elicottero** *è diventato* **pericoloso: ne** *hanno abbattuti* **due negli ultimi tempi,** *e* **in uno di questi** *c'era* **il ministro degli Esteri bosniaco Irfan Ljubjankic. . . .**

The bombing never stops. Even helicopters have become dangerous, two have been shot down recently, and in one of these was the Bosnian Minister for Foreign Affairs Irfan Ljubjankic.

Future
When the time referred to is the future, a variety of verb moods can be used to express related actions taking place in the same time context. If the indicative mood is used, it will be in the *future* tense. If the conditional or subjunctive moods are used, they will be in the *present* tense, since they have no future tense.

In this first example, the present conditional (**dovrebbero**) expresses what *would* happen if the decision were to be adopted, while **lasciare che** introduces a present subjunctive (**dilaghi**). Note how Italian sometimes uses a future tense after **se** (and see Chapter 38).

> *Se* la decisione del Congresso *dovrà* essere adottata dal presidente Clinton e *sarà applicata*, Francia e Inghilterra *dovrebbero* ritirare le proprie truppe dalla Bosnia, vale a dire abbandonare a se stessa la guerra civile, lasciare che essa *dilaghi*, senza più le fragili dighe dei caschi blu.
>
> If the decision of Congress is to be adopted by President Clinton and applied, France and England would have to withdraw their troops from Bosnia, in other words abandon the civil war to its own devices, let it spread, no longer retained by the fragile dams of blue berets.

Using the infinitive or the gerund
Both present infinitive and gerund can be used to express simultaneous actions and situations in a dependent clause, whatever the tense of the main verb (present, future or past):

> "La missione delle Nazioni Unite è fallita", ha detto Dole. "Dobbiamo avere il coraggio di *riconoscer*lo e *incoraggiare* i nostri amici francesi e britannici a lasciare la Bosnia. *Togliendo* l'embargo daremo la possibilità ai musulmani di *difender*si dall'aggressione serba."
>
> 'The UN mission has failed', said Dole. 'We have to have the courage to recognize this, and encourage our French and British friends to leave Bosnia. By lifting the embargo, we will give the Muslims the chance to defend themselves against Serbian aggression.'

> Susanna Agnelli *ha voluto sottolineare* l'aspetto 'umanitario' dell'impegno italiano in Bosnia *andando* a *visitare* la base operativa di Spalato della Cooperazione e *dando* simbolicamente il 'via' a un nuovo convoglio di aiuti per i profughi.

> Susanna Agnelli wanted to underline the 'humanitarian' aspect of Italian involvement in Bosnia, by going to visit the Cooperazione operations base at Split and by symbolically starting off a new aid convoy for refugees.

Earlier time context

Earlier than the time of speaking/writing
In this example, the event clearly takes place *earlier* than the time of writing. In Italian, a *past conditional* is used in the main clause (**avrebbero espugnato**) to express the idea that it is *report* or *hearsay*; English simply uses the past tense ('have taken over') but qualifies it by use of the word 'apparently':

> **Nelle ultime ore i bosniaci *avrebbero espugnato* alcune trincee serbe sulle alture di Sarajevo e lo scambio di colpi è piuttosto intenso tra la città e i suoi assedianti che contrattaccano.**
> In the last few hours, the Bosnians have apparently taken over some Serbian trenches above Sarajevo, and the exchange of fire is quite intense between the town and its besiegers who are counter-attacking.

Earlier than a past time referred to
When the time setting talked or written about is already in the past, and the actions or events described had already taken place *before* those described in the main clause, or implied, the time relationship can be described as the '*past of the past*'.

The tenses of Italian verbs specifically used to represent this time context are the *pluperfect* (**trapassato** in Italian), either *pluperfect indicative* or *pluperfect subjunctive*. The conditional and other verbal moods have no specific pluperfect tense so they use the more common past tenses.

In the following example, all the main clauses use the pluperfect indicative (**erano state, aveva delineato**) to express something that *had already* been said and was previous to the event described earlier (**avvertiva ...**):

> **"Trattative di pace entro 24 ore, o sarà guerra", *avvertiva* oggi Franjo Tudjman, il presidente croato ... Ben più esplicite *erano state* le parole dei ministri degli Esteri nella riunione di ieri notte ... il capo della diplomazia di Zagabria, Mate Granic, *aveva* già *delineato* la linea di condotta croata.**
> 'Peace negotiations within 24 hours, or it will be war', warned Franjo Tudjman, the Croatian president, this afternoon.... Much more explicit had been the words of the Foreign Ministers in last night's meeting ... the head of the diplomatic service in Zagreb, Mate Granic, had already set out the Croatian line.

The next example shows a main verb (**abbiamo finito**) with a second main event (**si erano dimenticati**) which had taken place earlier; the dependent clause also uses the pluperfect indicative (**laddove avevamo cominciato**) to show that the action had taken place earlier:

> *Abbiamo finito* laddove *avevamo cominciato*: in chiesa ... "c'era una volta un paese", diremo un giorno, noialtri incomodi testimoni di qualcosa che ci sfugge e che ci angoscia, non abbiamo visto morti e neanche i vivi – una lunga macchia di sangue, questa l'ho vista: *si erano dimenticati* di lavare l'asfalto – volevamo soltanto "sapere", non abbiamo saputo proprio nulla.
>
> (L. Cohen, *La Repubblica*, 31/7/95)
>
> We finished where we had begun: in church ... 'once upon a time there was a country ...' we will say one day, we the uncomfortable witnesses to something which evades us and which tortures us, we haven't seen the dead, we haven't seen the living either – what I saw was a long stain of blood: they had forgotten to wash the tarmac – we only wanted to 'learn', but we really haven't learnt anything.

Earlier than a future point in time

Sometimes an action will take place after an action *has taken place* at a certain point in time which itself is yet to come. The action which still has to take place (but will take place before the 'main' event/action) is expressed by the *future perfect* tense (**futuro anteriore**):

> Solo *dopo che* le parti *avranno trovato* un accordo politico, la guerra potrà concludersi.
>
> Only after the parties have reached a political settlement, will the war end.

> Il piano d'azione elaborato dai militari verrà sottoposto agli ambasciatori, quando *sarà stato convocato* il Consiglio di Sicurezza.
>
> The action plan drawn up by the military will be submitted to the ambassadors when the Security Council has been convened.

Using past infinitive, past participle and gerund

In the dependent clause, the *past infinitive, past participle* and *past gerund* of the verbs are often used, whatever the time context (present, past and future).

When using the infinitive or the gerund, the subject of the dependent clause must be *the same as* that of the main clause:

> Dopo *avere concordato* l'intensificazione delle azioni della NATO ... gli alleati *stanno approntando* i piani operativi per la difesa di Bihac.
>
> After agreeing on intensification of NATO action ... the Allies are preparing operation plans to defend Bihac.

> *Avendo ricevuto* la delega dalle Nazioni Unite, il generale Smith
> *potrà* dirigere le operazioni di appoggio alle truppe dell'Onu in
> Bosnia.
> Once he has received the authority from the UN, General Smith
> can direct support operations for the UN troops in Bosnia.

30.6.3 **Later time context**

Later than the time of writing/speaking
Events or actions which will take place later than the time of writing or speaking
are generally expressed in the *future*. Sometimes the *present* tense is used to
express the near *future*:

> Domani *arriva* a Udine il vescovo di Sarajevo per partecipare alle
> Festa della pace che si *celebra* domenica prossima.
> Tomorrow the Bishop of Sarajevo arrives in Udine to take part in
> the Festival of Peace, which will be celebrated next Sunday.

The expression **stare per** (see Chapter 14) is used to refer to events just about to
happen:

> *Sta per accadere* a Bihac quello che è accaduto a Srebrenica? La
> viltà internazionale *trionferà* un'altra volta?
> Is what happened at Srebrenica about to happen at Bihac? Will
> international cowardice triumph again?

In the next example, the main verb (**afferma**) supports a future (**non permetterà**)
in the dependent clause, itself followed by a dependent clause where the
present conditional (**rappresenterebbe**) expresses what would happen if the
enclave were to fall:

> Zagabria *afferma* che non *permetterà* la caduta dell'enclave
> "perché ciò *rappresenterebbe* una minaccia per la sicurezza della
> Croazia".
> Zagreb states that it will not allow the enclave to fall, 'because
> that would represent a threat for the security of Croatia'.

Later than a past point in time
In this example, the time referred to is the past (**voleva**, **passavano**) but the
action or event expressed in the second and third sentences (**sarebbe morto**) is
clearly one that will take place *later* than this point in time.

> "Il figlio di una nostra amica a 14 anni voleva combattere. La
> madre tremava come una foglia: gli anni dell'assedio passavano e
> lui si avvicinava ai fatidici 18." ('Diario di guerra di Ivan', *La
> Repubblica*, 27/7/95). Quel ragazzo *sarebbe morto* a 16 anni,
> ucciso da una granata. *Sarebbe morto* senza andare in guerra.

'The son of a friend of ours at age 14 wanted to fight. His mother was trembling like a leaf: the years of siege went by, and he was getting ever closer to the fateful age of 18.' ('War Diary of Ivan', *La Repubblica*, 27/7/95). That boy would die at age 16, killed by a grenade. He would die without even going to war.

31 Quoting or reporting events and hearsay

31.1 Reporting what someone says: introduction

There are two main ways of reporting what somebody has said (and indeed what we ourselves may have said on a previous occasion):

(a) Direct speech:

> **Il direttore mi ha detto: "*Può andare a casa*".**
> The manager said to me: 'You can go home'.

> **Gli ho chiesto: "*Quando mi restituisci i soldi?*"**
> I asked him: 'When are you giving me back the money?'

> **Il principe Carlo, ospite di Caprarola, in provincia di Viterbo ha ricevuto un'accoglienza strepitosa. Sua Altezza mastica un po' d'italiano e ha chiesto a una donna ottuagenaria: "*Molti dolori?*"**
> **... Dopo una cena all'Accademia di Santa Cecilia, un addetto all'organizzazione è finito in una vasca della fontana e il principe, incuriosito, ha esclamato: "*Per fortuna non è accaduto a me!*"**
> (*La Repubblica*, 6/8/95)
>
> Prince Charles, guest of Caprarola, in the province of Viterbo, received an enthusiastic welcome. His Royal Highness can mumble a few words of Italian and he asked an eighty-year-old woman: 'Many pains?' ... After a dinner at the Academy of Santa Cecilia, an employee of the organization fell into the basin of a fountain, and the prince, intrigued, exclaimed 'Luckily it didn't happen to me!'

(b) Indirect speech:

> **Il direttore mi ha detto *che potevo andare a casa*.**
> The manager said to me that I could go home.

> **Gli ho chiesto *quando mi avrebbe restituito i soldi*.**
> I asked him when he would give me back the money.

> **Il principe Carlo ha chiesto a una donna ottuagenaria *se aveva molti dolori*. Dopo la cena ha esclamato *che per fortuna non era accaduto a lui* di cadere in una vasca della fontana.**

Prince Charles asked an eighty-year-old woman if she had many pains. After the dinner, he exclaimed that luckily he hadn't been the one to fall into the fountain.

31.2 Quoting direct speech

The form of *direct speech* is used for all kinds of quotations, whenever we want to report something that has been said or written, with exactly the same words used by the quoted person or text. It is very common in newspaper titles (here are a few examples from the sports page of *La Repubblica*, 6/8/95):

> **Maradona: "Ferlaino è la rovina del Napoli."**
> Maradona: 'Ferlaino is Napoli's downfall.'
>
> **Avellino, il giudice ordina: "Fate giocare Lupo."**
> Avellino, the judge orders: 'Let Lupo play.'
>
> **La May subito qualificata nella corsa sui 100 metri. "Ma di questo paese capisco poco."**
> May qualifies straightaway in the 100 metres. 'But I can't understand this country very well.'
>
> **Arbitri: "Vogliamo più soldi."**
> Referees: 'We want more money.'

In written Italian, we normally use two **virgolette** (" ... ") to open and close a quotation. Sometimes, however, writers use pairs of **frecce** («...») as shown below. When the quotation is interrupted by a phrase such as 'he said' or 'they asked', the convention is to use a pair of dashes or hyphens:

> **«Bene – ha detto Marco – andiamo a letto.»**

Written texts, too, are often quoted directly. This is very common not only in essays and scientific literature, but also in everyday language, in business correspondence and again in newspapers:

> **Ho ricevuto una cartolina di Venezia con un bel cuoricino rosso e la scritta: "Manchi solo tu".**
> I got a postcard of Venice with a lovely little red heart on it and the words 'All it needs is you'.
>
> **Nel suo libro *Gli Inglesi* (Rizzoli, 1990) Beppe Severgnini afferma che: "Gli anni Ottanta sono stati per la Gran Bretagna gli anni di Margaret Thatcher, come gli anni Sessanta furono gli anni dei Beatles."**
> In his book *The English* (Rizzoli, 1990) Beppe Severgnini states that 'The eighties were for Great Britain the years of Margaret Thatcher, just as the sixties were the years of the Beatles.'

Il sindaco di Carloforte ha emanato un'ordinanza che vieta a tutti di girare senza camicia o maglietta: "Nel periodo estivo – *si legge nell'ordinanza* **– il centro urbano è invaso da bagnanti che girano a torso nudo e in costume da bagno. . . . È quindi severamente vietato circolare in queste condizioni, pena una sanzione amministrativa che varierà dalle 50 alle 500 mila lire." E le prime multe sono cominciate a fioccare.**

(*La Repubblica*, 6/8/95)

The Mayor of Carloforte has issued a decree which forbids anyone to go around without a shirt or a T-shirt: 'In the summer – the decree reads – the town centre is invaded by bathers who wander around with bare torsos and in swimming costumes. . . . It is therefore strictly forbidden to walk around in this condition, on pain of a fine which will vary from 50 to 500,000 lire.' And the first fines are starting to rain down.

Notice how, when quoting a regulation or law (as in the last example above), an impersonal expression (see 19.5) such as **si legge** can be used to stress the objective nature of its content rather than its 'author'. This, and other impersonal expressions, are often used when a quotation is included in formal or legal reports and correspondence, as below:

Nella Vostra lettera del 15 maggio u.s. *si dichiarava* **quanto segue: "La consegna della merce avverrà entro e non oltre il 10 giugno p.v.".**

In your letter of 15 May last, the following was stated: 'The delivery of the goods will take place by and no later than 10 June.'

Nella circolare del 6/7/94 *si fa riferimento* **a "tutte le competenze spettanti all'interessato" e** *si assicura* **che "saranno liquidate entro trenta giorni dalla data dell'assunzione in servizio".**

In the circular of 6/7/94, reference is made to 'all the charges relating to the person concerned' and assurance is given that 'these will be paid within 30 days of the date of starting employment'.

Note that when quoting from a newspaper, when the title includes **il**, **la**, etc., the article is sometimes combined with a preceding preposition, but sometimes left separate. The second solution reflects spoken usage and is therefore more natural.

Sul *Messaggero* **di oggi abbiamo visto un annuncio per una casa al mare.**

In today's *Messaggero* we saw an advertisement for a house by the sea.

> **Su La Repubblica dell'8 agosto 1995** *si afferma che*: **"L'inflazione in luglio si è attestata al 5,6 per cento rispetto allo stesso mese del '94."**
> In *La Repubblica* of 8 August 1995, it is stated that 'Inflation in July was shown to be running at 5.6 per cent compared to the same month in 1994.'

See also the use of the impersonal expression **si dice** in 31.4.

31.3   *Reporting indirect speech*

When using *indirect speech* to quote somebody, note how the reported discourse is often introduced by the conjunction **che**:

> **Le previsioni del tempo dicono** *che* **oggi farà caldo.**
> The weather forecast says that today it will be hot.

> **Il governo di Zagabria ha dichiarato** *che* **è possibile una soluzione pacifica del conflitto con la Serbia.**
> The Government of Zagreb has stated that a peaceful resolution of the conflict with Serbia is possible.

When referring to something that one has been told, using the first person 'I' in English, it is not always possible in Italian to use a passive construction similar to the English 'I have been told . . .' (see Chapter 19). The following expressions may be used instead:

> *Mi hanno detto che* **dovevo rivolgermi a questo ufficio per il rinnovo del passaporto.**
> I've been told that I should apply to this office for the extension of my passport.

> *Mi hanno comunicato* **in ritardo che la data della partenza era stata cambiata.**
> I was informed too late that the departure date had been changed.

An indirect quotation of the kind shown in the examples above is usually composed by a main clause containing the verb of 'saying', 'stating', etc. (for example **dicono, hanno detto, mi hanno comunicato**) and a dependent clause, introduced by **che**.

When using a verb such as **informare** which takes a direct object, the passive construction can be used:

> *Sono stata informata* **che la mia patente è scaduta.**
> I have been told (informed) that my driver's licence has expired.

31.3.1

Choosing the verb tense

When deciding which tense to use for the dependent verb, it is important to take into account the tense/time of the main verb, and to apply the guidelines of the sequence of tenses, illustrated in Appendix III and Chapter 30.

Let's see some examples of how to transform a direct quotation into an indirect quotation, applying the sequence of tenses:

Main clause		Dependent clause	
Present	Present	Past	Future
Mario dice	**"Finisco all'una"**	**"Ho finito all'una"**	**"Finirò all'una"**
Mario dice che	finisce all'una	ha finito all'una	finirà all'una
Past			
Mario ha detto	**"Finisco all'una"**	**"Ho finito all'una"**	**"Finirò all'una"**
Mario ha detto che	finiva all'una	aveva finito all'una	avrebbe finito/finiva all'una

When transforming somebody's speech into the indirect form, other components of the discourse must change, together with the tenses of the verbs. Note the change of *subject* (**io** > **lui**) in the dependent clause in the examples above:

> **Mario dice: "(*Io*) finisco all'una".**
> Mario says 'I finish at 1 o'clock'.

> **Mario dice che (*lui*) finisce all'una.**
> Mario says that he finishes at 1 o'clock.

Also any time or place indications, and any demonstratives (**questo, quello**) need to be adapted to the form of indirect speech, as in the following examples:

> **Il ministro ha dichiarato: "L'accordo sarà firmato *domani*".**
> The Minister stated: 'The agreement will be signed tomorrow'.

> **Il ministro ha dichiarato che l'accordo sarebbe stato firmato *il giorno dopo*.**
> The Minister declared that the agreement would be signed the next day.

> **Mia madre mi ha chiesto: "Hai letto *questo* libro di Eco?"**
> My mother asked me: 'Have you read this book by Eco?'

> **Mia madre mi ha chiesto se avevo letto *quel* libro di Eco.**
> My mother asked me if I had read that book by Eco.

Here is a brief list of the time specifications used in indirect speech:

Direct speech	Indirect speech
Mario ha detto "Parto *oggi*"	**Mario ha detto che partiva *quel giorno***
"Sono partito *ieri*"	**era partito *il giorno prima***
"Partirò *domani*"	**sarebbe partito *il giorno dopo***
"*Questo mese/quest'anno* ho fatto buoni affari"	***quel mese/quell'anno* aveva fatto buoni affari**
"*Il mese/l'anno scorso* ho fatto buoni affari"	***il mese/l'anno precedente* aveva fatto buoni affari**
"*Il mese/l'anno prossimo* farò buoni affari"	***il mese/l'anno successivo* avrebbe fatto buoni affari**

31.4 *Reporting information or hearsay*

Reporting information or quoting hearsay may be done with a greater or lesser degree of certainty and/or objectivity. For this purpose different moods of verbs can be used: *indicative* to show objectivity, *conditional* and *subjunctive* to show uncertainty or subjectivity.

The following example shows how an established fact of an accident is reported in the *indicative*, while something less certain, such as the possible cause of an incident, is expressed in the *conditional*. In English, a plain indicative tense is used, sometimes accompanied by a word such as 'apparently' to indicate lack of proof or certainty:

> **È *annegato* davanti a Capo Ferrato Giuseppe Puddu, guardia giurata di 30 anni, di Maracalagonis, durante una battuta di pesca subacquea. La causa della morte *sarebbe* un malore che *avrebbe colto* il giovane durante l'immersione.**
>
> (*La Repubblica*, 6/8/1995)
>
> A guard aged 30, from Maracalagonis, Giuseppe Puddu, drowned off Capo Ferrato, while underwater fishing. The cause of death was, apparently, a sudden bad turn which the young man suffered while diving.

> **Per i tabloid inglesi Will Carling *sarebbe* il nuovo fidanzato della principessa Diana. Lui: "*Penso* solo a mia moglie".**
>
> (*La Repubblica*, 8/8/1995)
>
> The English tabloids say that Will Carling is Princess Diana's new boyfriend. He says: 'I only care about my wife'.

Hearsay or highly doubtful information is usually introduced by such verbs as **pare che ... sembra che ... si dice che ...** and the subjunctive. These verbs, being impersonal, convey information without referring to its source:

> **Il capitano della nazionale inglese, che *pare abbia incontrato* per la prima volta la principessa in una palestra, ha cercato di mantenere un certo distacco, di reagire con calma.... *Pare che* l'ex**

moglie del principe di Galles, da cui è separata legalmente, *abbia accolto* le ultime rivelazioni sulla sua vita privata con un sospiro di rassegnazione.

(*La Repubblica*, 8/8/1995)

The captain of the English national team, who apparently met the princess for the first time in a gym, tried to keep his cool, and react calmly. It appears that the ex-wife of Prince Charles, now separated from him, greeted the latest revelations on her private life with a sigh of resignation.

Sembra che la regina Elisabetta *abbia detto* di no al progetto di vacanze del principe Edoardo con la fidanzata Sophie.

(*La Repubblica*, 31/7/1995)

It seems that Queen Elizabeth has said no to the holiday plans of Prince Edward with his girlfriend Sophie.

Si dice che Paul Gascoigne *sia riuscito* già a dividere i tifosi del Glasgow.

People say that Paul Gascoigne has already managed to split Glasgow fans.

When we want to refer to the source of information, without endorsing its content, we use the word **secondo** ... followed by the indication of the source. In this case too the option of using the indicative or the conditional allows us to indicate the different degrees of certainty of the information. When used to express one's own opinion too (**secondo me**, **secondo noi**), using the *conditional* softens the forcefulness of our opinion and sounds more polite (see also 27.1.4).

Secondo il giornale *News of the World*, **Lady Diana *avrebbe dato* al giocatore anche il numero segreto del suo telefono cellulare.**

(*La Repubblica*, 8/8/1995)

According to the *News of the World*, Lady Diana also gave the player the secret number of her cellphone.

... e secondo te tutte queste notizie *sarebbero* vere?

... and in your opinion, are all these news stories true?

Secondo me i giornalisti *dovrebbero* controllare meglio le informazioni.

In my opinion, the journalists should have better control over information.

Secondo me faresti bene a prenderti una vacanza.

In my opinion, you would be better having a holiday.

The use of the *indicative*, on the other hand, conveys strong conviction or belief, presented as a fact:

Secondo me tutte queste notizie *sono* false.
In my opinion, all these news stories are false.

Secondo fonti attendibili della Banca d'Italia l'inflazione *è diminuita* dello 0,5 per cento nel primo trimestre del 1995.
According to reliable sources in the Banca d'Italia, inflation has fallen by 0.5 per cent in the first three months of 1995.

Secondo quanto accertato dalla polizia stradale, prima dello scontro, la Renault 5 *viaggiava* ad oltre 150 chilometri all'ora e il guidatore *ha battuto* la testa morendo sul colpo.
                                                              (*La Repubblica*, 6/8/95)
According to the findings of the traffic police, before the crash the Renault 5 was travelling at over 150 kms per hour, and the driver struck his head, dying instantly.

Secondo un sondaggio 8 italiani su 10 *tradiscono* il coniuge; e gli stessi naturalmente non *credono* che si possa rimanere fedeli.
                                                              (*La Repubblica*, 31/7/1995)
According to an opinion poll, eight Italians out of ten betray their partner, and these same eight, naturally, believe that it is not possible to stay faithful.

Another very simple way to convey an opinion is to use **per**, with the *indicative* or the *conditional*:

Per me, *hai* torto.
In my opinion, you are wrong.

Per me, Andreotti ha commesso un errore.
In my opinion, Andreotti made a mistake.

Per la stampa italiana, la situazione economica del paese *sarebbe* in via di miglioramento.
According to the Italian press, the economic situation is improving.

Per gran parte del pubblico americano, O.J. Simpson non *avrebbe commesso* nessun delitto.
According to a large sector of the American public, O.J. Simpson did not commit any crime.

32 Expressing possibility and probability

32.1 Introduction

This section looks at ways of putting our message in context, in a complex sentence. One important context is that of *possibility* and *probability*: saying how certain or how likely it is, that something has happened/is happening/will happen.

On the whole, we can separate statements of possibility or probability into two broad categories: those which represent a *personal opinion* or *subjective* point of view ('I think', 'we believe'), and those which represent a *general state of affairs*, or **objective** point of view, whether fact or fiction ('it seems', 'it is likely').

The first category – personal opinion or subjective viewpoint – is covered in Chapter 27, illustrating the use of verbs such as **sapere**, **credere**, **pensare**, **ricordare**, **sembrare**, and Chapter 29, illustrating the personal use of **essere certo**, **sicuro**, etc. In this chapter we look at the second category, the *objective* or *impersonal* point of view.

32.2 Certainty, uncertainty

The adjectives **certo**, **sicuro** can be used impersonally, to express the English 'it is certain' (compare with the personal use illustrated in 29.3):

> *È certo che* **la vita è più cara in Italia.**
> It's certain that life is dearer in Italy.

> *Non è sicuro che* **il posto lo** *prenda* **lui.**
> It's not certain that he will get the job.

È certo che, **è sicuro che** can be replaced by the adverbs or adverbial phrases **certamente**, **sicuramente**, **di sicuro**:

> *Certamente* **la vita è più cara in Italia.**
> Certainly life is dearer in Italy.

> *Sicuramente/ Di sicuro* **il posto non lo** *prende* **lui.**
> Certainly he won't get the job.

Note the difference in degree of certainty between the two negative statements: **Non è sicuro che il posto lo prenda lui**, where the subjunctive expresses doubt, and **Sicuramente il posto non lo prende lui**, in which no doubt is expressed, and the indicative is used.

32.3 Knowing, not knowing

Verbs of knowing can also be used with an impersonal subject **si** 'one', as in the expression **si sa** (see also Chapter 3). Again uncertainty is expressed by the use of the subjunctive:

> *Si sa* che gli inglesi *sono* molto riservati.
> It is generally known that the English are reserved.

> *Non si sa se* gli ostaggi *siano* ancora vivi.
> It is not known if the hostages are still alive.

32.4 Possible or impossible, probable or improbable

Certain adjectives can be used with the verb **essere** to form so-called impersonal phrases in which no specific person or object is mentioned:

> *È impossibile* imparare l'italiano.
> It's impossible to learn Italian.

These adjectives can also be used personally, referring to a person or object: **è un compito impossibile** 'it is an impossible task'; **è una persona difficile** 'she is an impossible person'. The most common examples are:

> **è possibile** 'it's possible'
> **è impossibile** 'it's impossible'
> **è probabile** 'it's probable/likely'
> **è improbabile** 'it's improbable/unlikely'
> **è facile** 'it's easy/likely'
> **è difficile** 'it's difficult/unlikely'

These phrases can be followed either by the verb infinitive, or by **che** and a clause.

When the statement is a general one and no individual subject is mentioned, we use these phrases with the verb infinitive:

> *È possibile vedere* il mare?
> Is it possible to see the sea?

> *È possibile mangiare* fuori?
> Is it possible to eat outside?

> *È facile imparare* l'italiano.
> It's easy to learn Italian.

> *È impossibile completare* questi ordini prima della fine del mese.
> It's impossible to complete these orders before the end of the month.

When a *specific subject* needs to be mentioned (for example 'I', 'you', 'the hotel') we use **che**, introducing a verb in the subjunctive to express uncertainty:

> *È possibile che tu abbia dormito* fino a mezzogiorno?
> Is it really possible that you slept to midday?

> *È probabile che* l'albergo *sia* pieno.
> It is likely that the hotel will be full.

> *È poco probabile che* lui *l'abbia rubato.*
> It's not very likely that he stole it.

> *È impossibile che* i conti *siano* sbagliati.
> It's impossible that the accounts are wrong.

English speakers may find it strange that the phrases **è facile che/è difficile che**, as well as meaning 'it's easy'/'it's difficult' can also be used with the meaning of 'likely'/'unlikely':

> *È facile che* il contabile *sbagli.*
> It's easy (likely) for the accountant to make mistakes.

> *È difficile che* loro *arrivino* prima di pranzo.
> It's unlikely that they will arrive before lunch.

The expressions **si dice/dicono** 'one says'/'it is said', 'they say' are used to report what someone said, either likely or just hearsay, and are studied more fully in Chapter 31:

> *Si dice* che Joan Collins abbia fatto il *lifting* varie volte.
> They say that Joan Collins has had several facelifts.

32.5   *Evident, obvious*

Expressions which convey certainty include:

> **è chiaro** 'it's clear'
> **è evidente** 'it's evident', 'obvious'
> **è ovvio** 'it's obvious'

These expressions, by their very nature, always express certainty, so are always followed by the indicative:

È chiaro che l'autore *scrive* di una sua esperienza personale.
It is clear that the author is writing about a personal experience.

Era evidente che l'impiegato non *era* in grado di svolgere quella funzione.
It was obvious that the employee was not able to carry out that function.

33 Purpose

Stating purpose: introduction

Purpose involves an element of premeditation; it tells us what the speaker's *intention* or *purpose* is, or was, in advance of the action. Both 'reason' clauses and 'purpose' clauses are introduced by conjunctions or other connecting words. Generally, clauses of reason have a verb in the *indicative*, while clauses of purpose have a verb in the *subjunctive*. The difference between them is best illustrated in the case of **perché**, which is used for both *reason* and *purpose*:

Reason:

> **Ho parlato lentamente *perché* l'interprete doveva tradurre.**
> I spoke slowly because the interpreter had to translate.

Purpose:

> **Parlerò lentamente *perché* l'interprete possa tradurre.**
> I will speak slowly so that the interpreter can translate.

Note that, when referring to *cause* or *reason*, an event may not have had a human cause or agent, but may have been caused by 'events outside our control', for example an 'act of God' or a natural disaster. A *sense of purpose*, on the other hand, is almost always limited to humans:

> **A *causa del* temporale, la partita è finita presto.**
> Because of the storm, the match ended early.

> **Mi sono alzata presto *per* prendere il treno delle 5.00.**
> I got up early to catch the 5 a.m. train.

In *grammatical* terms, the most important factor in expressing *purpose* is to determine whether another person or object is involved in, or affected by, the action, apart from the original subject (subject of the main verb).

33.2 Purpose involving only the subject of the action

In Italian, when the aim or purpose expressed involves *only the subject of the action*, it is expressed by either:

(a) *Preposition and infinitive*

The prepositions used to express purpose are **per** 'in order to', **a** 'for (the purpose of)':

> **Lucia è andata a Londra *per/a* comprare dei libri alla Libreria Italiana.**
> Lucia went to London to buy some books at the Italian Bookshop.

(b) *Prepositional phrase + infinitive*

The phrases used to express purpose include:

> **allo scopo di (con lo scopo di)** 'with the aim of'
> **al fine di** 'with the aim of'
> **onde** 'so that'

> **Lucia è andata a Londra *allo scopo di* comprare dei libri alla Libreria Italiana.**
> Lucia went to London to buy some books at the Italian Bookshop.

In all the cases mentioned, the verb that follows is in the *infinitive*:

> **Lo facciamo *per* risparmiare tempo.**
> We are doing it to save time.

> **Chiudi la porta *per non* far entrare il gatto.**
> Shut the door so as not to let the cat in.

> **Abbiamo lanciato il nuovo prodotto *al fine di* conquistare il mercato italiano.**
> We have launched the new product with the aim of conquering the Italian market.

Other phrases expressing future intention can be found in 14.9.

A sense of near-desperation is implied by use of the phrase **pur di** 'only to':

> **È disposto a tutto *pur di* non fare il servizio militare.**
> He's willing to do anything just to get out of military service.

> **La signora Ferri avrebbe fatto di tutto *pur di* essere invitata al ricevimento all'ambasciata.**
> Signora Ferri would have done anything to be invited to the reception at the embassy.

With verbs expressing *movement*, such as **andare, venire, correre**, there is a choice of using **a** or **per**. Whereas **a** tends to focus on *where* you are going, **per** has more of a sense of purpose and indicates *for what reason* you are going there:

I turisti vanno a Roma *per* vedere il Papa.
Tourists go to Rome to see the Pope.

Mentre eravamo a Roma, siamo andati *a* vedere il Papa.
While we were in Rome, we went to see the Pope.

Devo andare a Londra *per* rinnovare il passaporto al Consolato.
I have to go to London to renew my passport at the Consulate.

I ragazzi sono andati a casa di Edoardo *a* guardare una videocassetta.
The boys went to Edoardo's house to watch a video.

Teresa veniva da me *per* fare lezioni d'italiano.
Teresa used to come to me to do Italian lessons.

33.3 *Purpose involving someone or something else*

In Italian, where the aim or purpose expressed involves another person, or object, other than the one carrying out the original action (the subject of the main verb), it is necessary to use a *conjunction* to introduce a subordinate clause in which the person involved or affected is the subject of a verb in the *subjunctive.*

33.3.1 Conjunctions

Examples of conjunctions and phrases used to introduce a purpose clause are:

(The most common) **perché** 'in order that', **affinché** 'in order that' (and) **in modo che** 'in such a way that', **in maniera che** 'in such a way that'.

The *subjunctive* is used after these conjunctions because it is not certain that the aim can be achieved. The tense can be either *present* (when the main verb is present or future) or *imperfect* (when the main verb is in a past tense or present conditional):

Il governo si impegnerà *affinché* la guerra in Bosnia non *diventi* un massacro.
The government will take steps so that the war in Bosnia does not become a massacre.

Volevamo organizzare il congresso per settembre *in modo che venissero* tutti i rappresentanti.
We wanted to organize the congress for September so that all the representatives would come.

The normal order in sentences of this kind is to have the main clause followed by the subordinate clause (the purpose clause). But it is possible to reverse the order:

> *Perché* gli handicappati *possano venire ospitati* in albergo, chiediamo agli albergatori di mettere a disposizione alcune camere al pianterreno.
> So that the disabled can be put up in hotels, we ask hotel-owners to put at their disposal a few rooms on the ground floor.

33.3.2 Alternatives to a purpose clause

In everyday speech, and writing, Italians will sometimes prefer to avoid a 'heavy' construction such as those above, and will find alternative ways of expressing the same thing:

Relative pronoun expressing purpose
Where another person (or an object) is involved, we can use a relative pronoun to express what our intention is for that person, i.e. what we want him/it to do. The 'purpose' significance is marked by the use of the subjunctive:

> **Facciamo venire un meccanico *che* ripari la lavatrice.**
> We'll call a mechanic who (so that he) can repair the washing machine.

> **Volevamo prenotare una vacanza al sole *che* ci permettesse di rilassarci e di visitare dei posti d'interesse.**
> We wanted to book a holiday in the sun which would allow us to (so that we could) relax and to visit some places of interest.

> **Il direttore cerca un'assistente *che* possa tradurre le lettere commerciali e mandare dei fax in inglese.**
> The manager is looking for an assistant who can translate commercial letters and send faxes in English.

In spoken Italian, when the objective is more likely to be met, an *indicative* verb is sometimes used:

> **Chiamiamo il camieriere *che* ci porta una bella bibita fresca.**
> Let's call the waiter, who'll bring us a nice cool drink.

Fare + infinitive:
Another way to mention or bring into the conversation the person affected by the plans, is to use **fare**, with a direct or indirect object pronoun identifying the person affected either directly or indirectly. Study the examples below:

> **Telefoniamo alla Reception, *per farci* portare la colazione in camera.**
> Let's ring Reception to have breakfast brought to us in the room.

> **Valentina ha chiamato il fidanzato *per farlo* venire alle 7.00.**
> Valentina called her boyfriend to have him come at 7 o'clock.

> **Valentina ha chiamato il fidanzato *per fargli* portare la macchina.**
> Valentina called her boyfriend to have him bring the car.

To summarize, the same concept can be expressed in three different ways, depending on the register used. In order of formality they are:

> **Chiamo mia figlia** *perché prepari* **la cena.**
> I'll call my daughter so that she can make supper.

> **Chiamo mia figlia** *per farle preparare* **la cena.**
> I'll call my daughter to get her to make supper.

> **Chiamo mia figlia** *che prepari* **la cena.**
> I'll call my daughter who will make supper.

33.4 *Purpose attached to a person/object*

33.4.1 Per

As well as its use depending on a verb as shown above, **per** can also express the purpose of an object, or person, for example:

> **Questo è un nuovo prodotto** *per* **liberare il bagno dagli scarafaggi.**
> This is a new product to free the bathroom of cockroaches.

> **Gli studenti hanno formato un'organizzazione** *per* **proteggere i diritti delle minoranze etniche.**
> The students formed an organization to protect the rights of ethnic minorities.

> **Adesso che ho deciso di tornare al lavoro, devo trovare una persona** *per* **tenermi la bimba.**
> Now that I've decided to go back to work, I have to find someone to look after the child for me.

33.4.2 Da

Da can be used to express the purpose or use of an object in the passive sense (in these examples 'a magazine to read', 'something to eat' actually means 'a magazine *to be read*', 'something *to be eaten*'):

> **Vorrei comprare una rivista** *da* **leggere sul treno.**
> I'd like to buy a magazine to read on the train.

> **Dopo averci fatto aspettare 12 ore all'aeroporto, finalmente ci hanno offerto qualcosa** *da* **mangiare.**
> After making us wait 12 hours at the airport, they finally gave us something to eat.

34 Causes and reasons

34.1 Introduction

Frequently we need to explain an event or action, or to justify our actions or those of someone else. There are various ways in which we can do this in Italian. Sometimes one person or thing is responsible, sometimes there is a factor or set of circumstances.

34.2 Specific people, factors or events responsible

Sometimes the cause of an event can be attributed to one person, or group of people, or to one factor or set of factors (expressed by a noun or pronoun), in which case one of the following *prepositional phrases* can be used:

> **grazie a** 'thanks to'
> **a causa di** 'because of'
> **per via di** 'because of'

> È *grazie a* **Federico che mio figlio è ancora vivo oggi.**
> It's thanks to Federico that my son is still alive today.

> È *grazie agli impiegati* che l'azienda ha avuto tanto successo.
> It's thanks to the employees that the firm has been so successful.

> *A causa degli* **scioperi, l'aereo è arrivato a Milano con due ore di ritardo e abbiamo perso il volo per Catania.**
> Because of the strikes, the plane was two hours late arriving in Milan, and we missed the plane for Catania.

> *Per via del* **traffico, siamo arrivati a casa stanchi e nervosi.**
> Because of the traffic, we arrived home tired and edgy.

34.3 General cause or reason

Sometimes the cause of an event or action is a situation or combination of factors. There are several ways of expressing such a cause:

── 34.3.1 ──
Using a causal clause

A conjunction or similar phrase can be used to introduce a *causal clause* (*clause of reason*). The most common conjunctions are:

perché 'because'	**poiché** 'since'
giacché 'since'	**siccome** 'since'
dato che 'given that'	**visto che** 'seeing as'
in quanto 'inasmuch as'	**considerato che** 'considering that'
per il fatto che 'for the fact that'	
per il motivo che 'for the reason that'	
dal momento che 'since'	

The most commonly used of these is **perché** (compare with **perché** expressing 'purpose' – see 33.1), followed by **poiché**, **giacché**, with **siccome** frequent in the spoken language. Unlike the conjunctions introducing *purpose*, these conjunctions require the *indicative*. (See examples and also the *Note* p.325). Note how the *position* of the 'since'/'because' clauses differs according to the conjunction used:

A clause introduced by **perché** always comes after the main clause:

> **Sono stata bocciata *perché* non avevo studiato per niente.**
> I failed because I didn't study at all.

Clauses introduced by other conjunctions/phrases are more flexible, and can come before or after the main clause:

> ***Poiché* non avevano il capitale per formare una società, hanno deciso di cercare collaboratori.**
> Since they didn't have enough capital to form a company, they decided to look for collaborators.

> **Ci metteremo subito al lavoro, *giacché* abbiamo cominciato con un po' di ritardo.**
> We will start work straightaway, since we began a little late.

> ***Siccome* sei stato tu a voler comprare i calamari, adesso li puoi preparare.**
> Since it was you who wanted to buy the squid, now you can prepare it.

> ***Dato che* la situazione in Bosnia peggiorava, l'ONU ha deciso di ritirare le sue truppe.**
> Since the situation in Bosnia was getting worse, the UN decided to withdraw its troops.

Sometimes **perché** is substituted by the shortened form **ché**, considered rather old-fashioned, but still seen in modern texts:

> **Non far rumore, *ché* ho mal di testa.**
> Don't make a noise because I've got a headache.

Also used, in informal spoken language, is the less specific **che**, which can be used, as here, with a causal meaning:

> **Vieni con me,** *che* **vado a vedere cosa succede.**
> Come with me (since) I'm going to see what's happening.

The phrases **visto che, considerato che, in quanto** tend to be used particularly in bureaucratic or legal language:

> *Visto che* **non si è concluso niente, sarebbe meglio rimandare la riunione a domani.**
> Since nothing has been decided, it would be better to put off our meeting until tomorow.

> *Visto e considerato che* **non sono stati rispettati i termini del contratto, possiamo procedere all'annullamento dello stesso.**
> In view of the fact that the terms of the contract have not been fulfilled, we can proceed to the annulment of the same.

> **È in parte responsabile il direttore di marketing** *in quanto* **non aveva pensato a come realizzare il progetto.**
> The director of marketing is partially responsible in that he hadn't thought about how to put the plan into effect.

Note that **in quanto** can also be used *without* a verb, for example:

> **Dopo il disastro, l'ingegnere è stato criticato** *in quanto* **responsabile della manutenzione della diga.**
> After the disaster, the chief engineer was criticized as the person responsible for the upkeep of the dam.

Note: When saying that something is *not* the real reason behind an event or action, **non perché** or **non ché** are often followed by the subjunctive (although the indicative is frequently used in everyday speech). The *real* reason is often given as well, and this is in the indicative:

> **Il capo vuole mandarla via,** *non perché* **gli** *sia* **antipatica, ma** *perché* **proprio non** *sa* **fare il suo lavoro.**
> The boss wants to get rid of her, not because he doesn't like her, but because she really doesn't know how to do her job.

> *Non perché* **ti voglia offendere, ma forse la danza classica non è il tuo forte.**
> Not that I want to offend you, but perhaps classical dance isn't your strong point.

34.3.2 ## Using *per* + infinitive

When the *same person* is the subject of both cause and effect, **per** and an infinitive (usually past) can be used:

> **Un nostro collega fu licenziato *per aver portato* a casa un computer.**
> A colleague of ours was sacked for having taken a computer home.

Per can be expanded into **per il fatto di**:

> **Mio fratello è rimasto stupito *per il fatto di aver vinto* il premio.**
> My brother was amazed at having won the prize.

> **Il direttore è arrabbiato *per il fatto di dover riprogrammare* tutto.**
> The manager is angry at having to reschedule everything.

> **Il ragazzo viene giudicato male *per il fatto di essere* timido.**
> The boy is judged harshly because of being shy.

Using the gerund

The gerund (present or past) can also have a '*causal*' meaning. The subject of the gerund should also be the subject of the 'result' clause ('we' . . . 'we') or should be mentioned explicitly, as in the last example:

> ***Sapendo* che saremmo tornati a Natale, abbiamo lasciato gli sci a casa dei nostri amici.**
> Knowing that we would be coming back at Christmas, we left our skis at our friends' house.

> ***Avendo* già *chiesto* il prezzo della camera all'ufficio turistico, abbiamo capito subito che la padrona di casa ci faceva pagare troppo.**
> Having already asked the price of the room at the tourist office, we realized immediately that the landlady was charging us too much.

> ***Essendo* chiuso *il negozietto*, abbiamo comprato il latte al bar.**
> Since the corner shop was shut, we bought milk from the café.

Using the past participle

Similarly, even the past participle can express a reason or cause. As seen in 34.3.2 and 34.3.3, the subject of the participle must be that of the main verb, or, if someone or something other than the subject of the main verb, it must be specifically expressed:

> ***Laureato* con 110 e lode, Marco pensò di trovare subito un posto, ma non era così facile.**
> Having graduated with top marks, Marco thought he would find a job straightaway, but it wasn't so easy.

> ***Partiti* i genitori, i ragazzi hanno organizzato una festa in casa.**
> With their parents gone, the kids organized a party at their house.

34.4   Il motivo, la causa, la ragione

Italian, as English, has several nouns denoting 'cause' or 'reason' such as **la ragione**, **la causa** or **il motivo**, already seen above. Note how they are followed by the relative **per cui** or **per il/la quale** 'the reason ... for which' rather than the more generic **perché** 'the reason ... why' when asking or giving the reason:

> *Il motivo per cui* **abbiamo scelto questa casa è la posizione tranquilla.**
> The reason we have chosen this house is its quiet position.

> *La ragione per la quale* **non sono venuti è che avevano dei compiti da finire.**
> The reason why they didn't come is that they had homework to finish.

> *Che ragioni* **aveva per agire in questo modo?**
> What reasons did she have to act in this way?

> **Il disaccordo tra i soci è stato** *la causa* **del fallimento dell'azienda.**
> The disagreement between the shareholders was the cause of the company's bankruptcy.

> *Per quale motivo* **bisogna fare il check-in due ore prima del volo?**
> Why does one have to check-in two hours before the flight?

The reasons can be specified with an *adjective*, for example:

> **per ragioni familiari** 'for family reasons'
> **per motivi finanziari** 'for financial reasons'
> **per motivi economici** 'for economic reasons'

34.5   *Verbs meaning 'to cause'*

Verbs meaning to cause include **causare, portare a, produrre, provocare, stimolare, suscitare** (see also 35.5.2):

> **Una sigaretta buttata per terra** *ha provocato* **l'incendio.**
> A cigarette thrown on the ground caused the fire.

All these verbs can be used in a passive construction:

> **La sua malattia era** *causata* **dallo stress.**
> His illness was caused by stress.

> **Le proteste erano** *provocate* **dall'inerzia delle autorità.**
> The protests were caused by the inertia of the authorities.

34.6   Dovere, dovuto

The verb **dovere** can have the meaning 'to be due to' and can be used to express cause:

> *Si deve* **al tuo lavoro se abbiamo ottenuto buoni risultati.**
> If we have had good results, it's due to your work.

The past participle **dovuto** is the form of **dovere** most commonly used to express cause, but it *must refer to one specific noun*, with which it agrees. The participle **dovuto** can only be used in a *passive* construction like those below:

> **Il problema del traffico a Napoli** *è dovuto* **alla struttura della città.**
> The traffic problem in Naples is due to the structure of the city.

> **Abbiamo incontrato delle code sull'autostrada** *dovute* **a una manifestazione dei camionisti.**
> We met queues on the autostrada (motorway) due to a demonstration of lorry drivers.

Where the reason is not one single thing, but a whole set of circumstances, the phrase **il fatto che** 'the fact that' can be used to introduce it:

> **Marisa non si decideva a buttarsi in acqua. La sua indecisione era** *dovuta al fatto che* **non sapeva nuotare.**
> Marisa couldn't make up her mind whether to jump into the water. Her indecision was due to the fact that she couldn't swim.

34.7   *Asking why*

The question 'why' can of course also be asked by using **come mai** or **perché**:

> *Come mai* **non sei venuto stasera?**
> How come you didn't come tonight?

> *Perché* **non mi rivolge la parola?**
> Why isn't she speaking to me?

And asking the reason:

> *Qual è il motivo* **della sua gelosia?**
> What is the reason for her jealousy?

> *Qual è la spiegazione* **di questo comportamento?**
> What is the explanation for this behaviour?

> *Come si può spiegare* **questo fenomeno?**
> How can one explain this phenomenon?

34.8 Using the imperfect tense to give reason

Often the *imperfect* tense (see Chapter 2 and 13.6.5) is used to supply the background to an action or event, usually expressed in the compound perfect. With or without a specific conjunction of *cause*, the 'reason' aspect is clear from the context:

> **Siamo andati a casa. (perché) Eravamo stanchi.**
> We wanted to go home. (because) We were tired.

35 Result, effect and consequence

35.1 Introduction

In narrative, and in everyday conversation, events can be seen as a sequence of purpose–action–result. In Chapters 33 and 34 we looked at purpose and reasons respectively. Here we look at how to express results, consequences and effects in Italian.

35.2 Result or consequence

Clauses of *consequence* or *result* can be introduced by simple coordinating conjunctions or other phrases which link an action or event to its end result. In this case the two clauses (parts of the sentence) are of *equal importance*. Examples are:

> **così** 'thus'
> **in questo modo** 'in this way'
> **perciò** 'therefore'
> **quindi** 'therefore'

> **Mi hanno rubato la borsetta con tutte le carte di credito e i soldi** (action or event) *e così* **mi sono trovata senza soldi** (end result).
> They stole my handbag with all my credit cards and cash and so I found myself without any money.

> **Ti sei comportato malissimo alla festa** (action/event). *In questo modo* **non avrai più amici** (end result).
> You behaved really badly at the party. If you carry on like this, you won't have any more friends.

> **La ditta versava in condizioni economiche disastrose e** *perciò* **ha licenziato più di 200 impiegati.**
> The company was in a disastrous economic condition and therefore they sacked more than 200 employees.

> **Non ho potuto fare una vacanza quest'anno e** *quindi* **mi sento veramente stanca.**
> I wasn't able to have a holiday this year, so I feel really tired.

35.3 Result introduced by 'so', 'so much'

Consequence or result can also be expressed by a sequence of *main* clause (the original action) and *dependent* verb construction (the consequence). In this case, the original action or event forms the *main* clause, while the *consequence* is either an *infinitive*, introduced by **da** or **per**, or a clause of consequence, introduced either by **che** (or **perché**), or a phrase such as **di modo che**, **in modo che**.

Often the main clause contains a word expressing *excess* or *extent*, such as those shown below. Adverbs such as **tanto**, **troppo** can be used either on their own or modifying an adjective or another adverb (see 6.2.2).

Adverbs:

> **così** 'so', 'so much so (that)'
> **talmente** 'so', 'so much so (that)'
> **tanto** 'so', 'so much (that)'
> **troppo** 'too', 'too much (for)'

Adjectives:

> **tale** 'of such a kind (that, as to)'
> **tanto** 'so much', 'so great (that)'
> **troppo** 'too much (for)'

35.3.1 Da, per + infinitive

Tale ... da + *infinitive*:

> **La sua intelligenza è *tale da* far paura.**
> His intelligence is so great as to be frightening.

Tanto ... da + *infinitive*:

> **È cambiato *tanto da* non essere più riconoscibile.**
> He's changed so much as to have become unrecognizable.

Troppo ... per + *infinitive*:

> **Il direttore è *troppo* impegnato *per* riceverla oggi.**
> The manager is too busy to see you today.

> **Ha bevuto *troppa* birra *per* potere guidare la macchina.**
> He has drunk too much beer to be able to drive the car.

35.3.2 Che, perché, di modo che, in modo che followed by a verb

The verb expressing the result or consequence is normally in the indicative or conditional:

Così ... che

> **Eravamo *così* stanchi *che* non riuscivamo a tenere gli occhi aperti.**
> We were so tired that we couldn't keep our eyes open.

Sometimes **così (sì)** and **che** combine to form a single word **cosicché, sicché**:

> **La strada era bagnata *cosicché* quando mio marito ha frenato, la macchina ha sbandato.**
> The road was wet, so that when my husband braked, the car skidded.

Tale ... che + *conditional*:

> **Provo una *tale* antipatia per Carlo *che* vorrei ucciderlo.**
> I dislike Carlo so much that I could kill him.

Talmente ... che + *conditional*:

> **La soluzione mi sembra *talmente* facile *che* potrei anche cominciare domani.**
> The solution seems to me so easy that I could even start tomorrow.

Tanto ... che + *indicative*:

> **Mi sento *tanto* male *che* non riesco a stare in piedi.**
> I feel so ill I can't stand up.

However the verb may be in the subjunctive, if the result is seen as unlikely or unreal:

Troppo ... perché + *subjunctive*:

> **Gli studenti sono *troppo* giovani *perché* possano capire i nostri problemi.**
> The students are too young to be able to understand our problems.

Di modo che, in modo che do not need an expression of 'excess' in the first part of the sentence. Because the consequence is somewhat uncertain and hypothetical, the subjunctive is used in the example below:

> **Ha versato da bere *in modo che* non vedessimo quello che faceva.**
> He poured the drinks in such a way that we didn't see what he was doing.

35.4   *Result introduced by 'only ... to'*

Occasionally the effect of an action uses a conjunction or preposition normally used to express *purpose* (see Chapter 33). In the example below, **perché** followed by the subjunctive, which normally means 'so that', 'in order to', is used to express the *effect* of an action. Note the word **basta** 'it is enough ... to' in the first part of the sentence:

> **Ci sono la radio, la televisione, *basta* aprirle per un secondo *perché* il male ci raggiunga, ci entri dentro.**
> There is the radio, the television. You only have to switch them on for the evil to reach us, to enter into us.
>
> (*Va dove ti porta il cuore,*
Susanna Tamaro, Baldini & Castoldi, 1994)

The preposition **per** can be used to similar effect after **basta** or **solo**:

> ***Devi solo* leggere i giornali *per* capire i problemi del mondo.**
> You only have to read the newspapers to understand the problems of the world.

> ***Basta* un minimo di intelligenza *per* imparare una lingua straniera.**
> One only needs a minimum of intelligence to learn a foreign language.

35.5   *Words expressing result, effect*

35.5.1

Nouns which express result, effect, consequence include:

> **il risultato** 'result'
> **l'effetto/gli effetti** 'effect(s)'
> **l'impatto** 'impact'
> **la conseguenza** 'consequence'
> **la conclusione** 'conclusion'

> **L'iniziativa ha avuto *risultati* inattesi.**
> The initiative had unexpected results.

> **La mancanza di azione da parte dell'ONU ha avuto *conseguenze* disastrose per la popolazione.**
> The lack of action on the part of the UN had disastrous consequences for the population.

> **Questa medicina può avere *effetti collaterali*. Leggere attentamente le istruzioni.**
> This medicine can have side effects. Read the instructions carefully.

> ***L'effetto* dello sciopero è stato minimo.**
> The effect of the strike was minimal.

35.5.2

Verbs which express cause:
These verbs are also illustrated in 34.5 and include

provocare 'to cause'   causare 'to cause'
portare a 'to lead to'   produrre 'to produce'
stimolare 'to provoke', 'stimulate'
suscitare 'to provoke', 'arouse'

L'intervento di Bossi *ha suscitato* un dibattito molto acceso.
Bossi's speech provoked a very lively debate.

La tossicodipendenza può *portare a* conseguenze ancora più gravi.
Drug addiction can lead to even more serious consequences.

35.5.3 Extent

The *extent* of the effect or consequence is expressed by adjectives such as
rilevante, importante, notevole, or phrases such as **di lunga portata, di rilievo**, if
stressing its importance; if stressing its insignificance, use adjectives such as
irrilevante, minimo, insignificante, or phrases such as **di nessun rilievo, di
nessuna importanza**:

Il terremoto aveva provocato poche morti, ma aveva avuto
conseguenze economiche *di lunga portata*.
The earthquake had caused few deaths, but had had
far-reaching economic consequences.

In Italia, la recessione ha avuto un impatto *notevole*.
In Italy, the recession had a considerable impact.

Secondo il Governo francese, gli effetti degli esperimenti nucleari
a Mururoa sarebbero *di nessuna importanza*.
According to the French Government, the effects of the nuclear
experiments at Mururoa are of no importance.

35.5.4 Surveys, opinion polls

The results of surveys, opinion polls, etc. are often expressed by the verbs
risultare, emergere:

Risulta da un sondaggio della DOXA che il 70% dei milanesi è
favorevole al divieto di fumare nei ristoranti della città.
A survey by DOXA shows that 70 per cent of the Milanese favour
a ban on smoking in restaurants in the city.

Emerge un quadro generale della situazione che non è molto
positivo.
A general picture emerges of the situation which is not very
positive.

36 *Specifying time*

36.1   *Introduction*

When we need to indicate explicitly the time context in which different actions or events take place, or in which different facts are set, we use *time clauses* and/or *adjuncts of time* (phrases which specify a time context).

Adjuncts of time may be adverbs such as **oggi** or **domani**, adverbial phrases such as **fra dieci giorni**, **un anno fa**, or *conjunctions* such as **quando**, **mentre**, **appena**.

Time clauses are dependent clauses (see 30.3) and their function is to expand the content of a main clause with a specification of time. They are usually introduced by an adjunct of time such as **quando**, **mentre**, **dopo**. When using dependent clauses, the tenses of main and dependent verbs must follow the rules of the *sequence of tenses* (see Appendix III for the basic 'rules' and 30.4 for a fuller illustration of how these rules are applied).

We have divided our examples into three time settings: *simultaneity, actions happening earlier, actions happening later*. In all three time contexts, the relationship of one event to another can either be that of two or more linked main clauses (see 30.2) or of main/dependent clause (see 30.3).

36.2   *Expressing same time context*

Actions happening at the same time as those of the main clause are generally marked by words such as those below, followed by a verb in the *indicative*:

> **quando** 'when'
> **mentre** 'while'
> **al tempo in cui** 'at the time when'
> **nel momento in cui** 'at the moment when', 'just as', 'when'

36.2.1

Quando 'when':
This is by far the most frequently used specification of time:

> *Quando* **ero ragazzo giocavo a pallacanestro.**
> When I was a boy I used to play basket-ball.

> **Ho visitato Siena** *quando* **sono stato in Italia.**
> I visited Siena when I was in Italy.

Quando ci hai telefonato stavamo cenando.
When you phoned us we were having dinner.

36.2.2 — *Mentre* 'while':

Cerco di lavorare un po' *mentre* i bambini giocano in giardino.
I'm trying to do a little work while the children are playing in the garden.

Mentre tu eri al telefono sono arrivati due clienti.
While you were on the telephone two clients arrived.

La folla gridava senza sosta *mentre* i giocatori si preparavano a iniziare la partita.
The crowd was shouting continuously while the players got ready to start the match.

36.2.3 — *Al tempo in cui* 'at the time when':

Al tempo in cui noi abitavamo a Trieste, loro abitavano a Venezia.
At the time when we were living in Trieste, they were living in Venice.

36.2.4 — *Nel momento che/in cui* 'at the same time as', 'just as', 'just when', 'when':

Il direttore mi ha chiamata proprio *nel momento in cui* stavo per uscire.
The manager called me just when I was about to go out.

In the next example Italian uses the future tense after **nel momento in cui**, while English uses the present after 'when' (the same applies to other time clauses in the future tense):

Pagheremo in contanti *nel momento in cui* riceveremo la merce.
We'll pay in cash when we receive the goods.

Come 'as', 'when', 'just as':

Although less common, **come** can be used with the sense 'as soon as' or 'just as':

Come sono arrivata a casa, ho fatto una doccia.
As soon as I arrived home, I took a shower.

36.3 Expressing earlier time context

An earlier time context is often indicated by the word **prima**:

36.3.1 — *Prima* 'earlier':
When the time relationship of one event happening earlier than another is represented by two clauses, or groups of words, of equal weight, it is often expressed by **prima** 'first', followed by **poi** 'then', 'after', 'later':

Prima **ho fatto la spesa e poi sono tornata a casa.**
First I did some shopping and then I went back home.

Prima **andremo a Monaco e poi visiteremo Salisburgo.**
First we'll go to Munich and then we'll visit Salzburg.

Prima **mangerei un gelato, e poi andrei volentieri a letto.**
First I'd (like to) eat an ice-cream, then I'd happily go to bed.

Bisogna andare *prima* **al supermercato e poi dal fruttivendolo.**
One has to go first to the supermarket and then to the greengrocer.

È meglio che parliate *prima* **con l'agenzia di viaggio e che poi compriate i biglietti alla stazione.**
It's better if you speak first to the travel agency and then buy the tickets at the station.

36.3.2

Prima di, prima che 'before'

When the time relationship is represented by a combination of *main* clause and *dependent* clause, with one fact, action or event happening *earlier* than the other, the action which takes place later is introduced by **Prima di** or **prima che**. **Prima di** and the present infinitive can only be used when the subject of main and dependent clause are the same person ('*I* came to the office,' '*I* visited my cousin'):

Devo fare la spesa *prima di tornare* **a casa.**
I have to do some shopping before going back home.

Prima di venire **in ufficio sono andata a trovare mia cugina.**
Before coming to the office I went to visit my cousin.

Prima di essere nominata **preside, la dottoressa Baldoni aveva insegnato al liceo 'Parini'.**
Before being appointed headmistress, Dr Baldoni had taught at the 'Parini' High School.

Prima che 'before':

Prima che introduces a dependent time clause containing a *subjunctive*. This construction is generally used when the two parts of the sentence have a different subject:

Prima che Lei arrivasse **in ufficio ha telefonato il dott. Rosi.**
Before you arrived in the office Dr Rosi phoned.

Devo informare Lucio di quello che è successo *prima che sia* **troppo tardi.**
I must inform Lucio of what happened before it is too late.

36.4 Expressing later time context

A later time context can be marked by using words such as **dopo**, **più tardi** or **poi**:

Dopo, poi, più tardi 'after'/'afterwards', then', 'later'

When the time relationship of one event happening later than another is represented by two clauses, or groups of words, of equal weight, it can be indicated by words such as **dopo** 'afterwards', **più tardi** 'later' or **poi** 'then', 'afterwards', 'later':

> **Prima ho fatto lezione e *più tardi* sono andata in biblioteca.**
> First I taught and later I went to the library.

> **Prima andremo al mare e *poi* andremo in montagna.**
> First we'll go to the seaside and then we'll go to the mountains.

> **Per cambiare valuta estera, bisogna andare prima allo sportello no. 6 e *dopo* alla cassa.**
> To change foreign currency, one has to go first to window no. 6 and afterwards to the cash desk.

> **È meglio che lei parli prima con la segretaria e che *dopo* chieda di parlare con il direttore.**
> It's better if you speak first to the secretary and then afterwards ask to speak to the manager.

Dopo, dopo che 'after', 'afterwards'

When the time relationship is represented by a combination of *main* clause and *dependent* clause, with one fact, action or event happening *later* than the other, the action which took place earlier is introduced by **dopo** or **dopo che**:

Dopo can be followed by a *past infinitive*:

> **Dopo aver cenato faremo una passeggiata.**
> After having dinner we'll have a walk.

> **Andammo tutti insieme al cinema *dopo essere stati* da Franco un'ora.**
> We went all together to the cinema after staying an hour at Franco's.

Dopo che is followed by a verb in the *indicative*:

> **Partirò solo *dopo che avrò finito* il mio lavoro.**
> I'll leave only after I've finished my work.

> **Vieni a trovarmi *dopo che hai finito* il tuo lavoro.**
> Come to see me after you've finished your work.

> **Andrea è venuto a trovarmi *dopo che aveva finito* il lavoro.**
> Andrea came to see me after he had finished his work.

36.4.3

Appena, non appena 'as soon as'

These are used to indicate that the action of the main clause happens *immediately after* something else. Note the optional use of **non**:

> **Telefonami** *(non) appena hai finito.*
> Ring me as soon as you have finished.

> *Appena sei partito* **ci siamo acccorti che avevi dimenticato le chiavi.**
> As soon as you left, we realized that you had forgotten the keys.

Note the use of the **futuro anteriore** (see Chapter 2) in the following example:

> **Ti telefonerò** *non appena sarò arrivato* **a Tokyo.**
> I'll ring you as soon as I have arrived in Tokyo.

Note in the following example the use of the **trapassato remoto**, generally only used in written texts, and only when there is a **passato remoto** in the main clause:

> **Non** *appena ebbe visto* **l'orologio, corse via senza dire una parola.**
> As soon as he caught sight of the clock, he ran off without saying a word.

36.5 *Defining the limits of a period: 'since'/'until'*

We can also define the period of time in which several facts happened, by specifying the moment when the period began (*time from when*) and the moment when it ended (*time until when*), as in the examples below:

36.5.1

Time from when (since):

> **(fin) da** 'since'
> **da quando** 'since when'
> **dal momento in cui** 'since the moment when'

> *Fin dal momento in cui* **ti ho conosciuta ho sempre pensato che tu fossi la persona ideale per me.**
> Since the moment I first met you I've always thought you to be the ideal person for me.

> *Da quando* **sono arrivata ho già letto la corrispondenza, risposto a due lettere, ricevuto due clienti, e ho perfino avuto il tempo di prendere il caffè con Sara.**
> Since I arrived I've already read the mail, answered two letters, received two clients, and I've even had the time to have a coffee with Sara.

> *Dal* **1990 abbiamo già cambiato tre macchine.**
> Since 1990 we have already changed car three times.

>**Lavoro alla FIAT** *da* **cinque anni.**
>I've been working at FIAT for five years.

Note the use of the present tense, with **da**, in the last example, where English uses the perfect continuous ('I have been working'). The present is used to stress that the action is still going on, or the situation still applies (see 2.3.3).

Similarly, **da** can be used with the imperfect tense to show that the action *was* still going on at that time:

>*Vivevo* **in Italia già** *da* **due anni, quando ho conosciuto Carlo.**
>I had been living in Italy for two years when I met Carlo.

— 36.5.2 —
Time until when

We can also define how long a period of time lasts, by specifying the moment *up to when* the actions or events referred to continue/will continue/have continued, by using one of the following:

>**fino a** 'until'
>**finché (non)** 'until', 'as long as'
>**fino a quando** 'up to the moment when'

Finché is normally followed by **non** when it expresses the meaning of 'until something happens':

>**Rimarremo in ufficio** *finché non* **avremo finito il nostro lavoro.**
>We'll stay in the office until we finish the job.

It can be followed by a verb in the subjunctive rather than the more normal indicative form, but this tends to convey doubt as to whether the event or action will ever be complete:

>**Dovremo fare economie,** *finché* **la nostra situazione finanziaria**
>*non sia* **più sicura.**
>We will need to cut back, until our financial situation becomes more certain.

Finché can convey the meaning of 'during the length of time that' or 'during the whole period that':

>*Finché* **l'avvocato Prati ha lavorato con noi non abbiamo mai avuto problemi e gli affari sono andati a gonfie vele.**
>In all the time Mr Prati worked with us, we had no problems and business was booming.

>**Ho lavorato in questo ufficio** *fino al* **1994 e ho realizzato molti progetti collaborando con numerose ditte e clienti.**
>I worked in this office up until 1994 and I carried out many projects collaborating with several companies and clients.

Note how when the starting and finishing point of the time context are specified (as in the last examples), the verbs are in the perfect rather than the imperfect, even when the facts took place over a long span of time. In fact, as shown in 13.2, the perfect aspect stresses the completion of an action rather than its duration.

36.5.3
Duration of time

The phrase **tutta la giornata** expresses an action or event that went on *all* day. In fact the use of the feminine form ending in **-ata** tends to convey the meaning of a long period of time: **una serata** 'an evening out', 'an evening together', **una mattinata** 'a whole morning':

> **Abbiamo passato una bellissima *serata*.**
> We spent a beautiful evening.

> **Ci aspetta una *mattinata* di lavoro.**
> We've got a morning of work ahead of us.

36.6   *Specifying repetition and frequency*

There are various ways to indicate the repetition of a fact or action in certain circumstances.

36.6.1
Ogni volta che, tutte le volte che

Repetition can be indicated by adding a dependent time clause introduced by one of the following:

> **ogni volta che** 'every time'
> **tutte le volte che** 'every time'
> **ogni qual volta (che)** 'every time'

> **Non rimproverarmi *ogni volta che* accendo una sigaretta.**
> Don't tell me off every time I light a cigarette.

> ***Tutte le volte che* andavamo a Londra, trovavamo sempre traffico.**
> Every time we went to London, we always used to find traffic.

> ***Ogni qual volta* ho avuto bisogno di aiuto, ho sempre trovato la massima collaborazione dei miei colleghi.**
> Every time I needed some help, I always had the greatest support from my colleagues.

> **Venga pure a trovarmi *ogni volta che* avrà bisogno di una mano.**
> Come and see me any time you need a hand.

36.6.2
Ogni

Ogni followed by a time specification can indicate the frequency of repetition as in:

> *ogni* **giorno** 'every day'
> *ogni* **mese** 'every month'
> *ogni* **cinque minuti** 'every five minutes'
>
> **Ogni giorno riceviamo almeno venti telefonate.**
> We receive at least twenty telephone calls every day.
>
> **Il telefono suona *ogni* cinque minuti.**
> The telephone rings every five minutes.
>
> **Dose prescritta: due pillole *ogni* quattro ore.**
> Prescribed dose: two tablets every four hours.

For more details on the use of **ogni** as indefinite adjective see 3.9.2.

36.6.3 ### Other expressions of frequency

Tutti/e + *article **i**, **gli**, **le***:

> *tutti i* **giorni** 'every day'
> *tutti gli* **anni** 'every year'
>
> **Vado a scuola *tutti i* giorni.**
> I go to school every day.
>
> **Abbiamo pagato regolarmente le tasse *tutti gli* anni.**
> We paid taxes regularly every year.
>
> **Prendo lezioni d'italiano *tutte le* settimane.**
> I take Italian lessons every week.

Un giorno sì e un giorno no '*every other day*':

> **Da ragazzo andavo al cinema *un giorno sì e un giorno no*.**
> When I was a teenager I used to go to the cinema every other
> day.

36.7 Other expressions of time

Other expressions of time with particular reference to the *present, past* or *future* can be found in the relevant chapters.

Some expressions of time which are not specifically related to any one time context are:

> **man mano (che)** 'gradually as'
> **subito** 'immediately'

Man mano che i lavori procedevano, il costo aumentava
vertiginosamente.
As the works went on, the cost went soaring up.

Ha capito *subito* cosa volevo.
He understood immediately what I wanted.

37 *Place and manner*

37.1 *Introduction*

Chapter 36 showed how to put events in a time context, by saying *when* something happened. Other ways of setting an action or event in context are to say *where* it happened or *how* it happened, in other words to indicate *place* and *manner*.

37.2 *Place*

Expressions of place can indicate the place *where* an action or event happens, the place *to where* an action or a person is directed, and the place *from where* something originates. The most common way to express *place* is using a *preposition*.

Prepositions: introduction

Full information on each specific preposition and on the forms when combined with the definite article (**al**, **nel**, **dal**, **sul**, etc.) can be found in 4.2.

37.2.2

To a place

Prepositions which express movement *to* a place or other kinds of destination include **a**, **in**, **per**, **da**, **verso**, **su**:

> **Vorrei andare *a* Venezia per Carnevale.**
> I would like to go to Venice for the Carnival.
>
> **A maggio si sono trasferiti *negli* Stati Uniti.**
> In May they moved to the USA.
>
> **Domani devo partire presto *per* Roma.**
> Tomorrow I have to leave early for Rome.
>
> **È arrivato un fax *per* Lei.**
> There is a fax for you.
>
> **L'aereo stava scendendo *verso* l'aeroporto quando è caduta a terra una porta.**
> The plane was descending towards the airport when a door fell to the ground.

> **Il passeggero ha cercato di saltare *sull'*autobus che però era già in partenza.**
> The passenger tried to jump onto the bus, which however was already leaving.

Da can indicate movement *to* somewhere, normally the place (shop, studio, surgery, house) of an individual indicated by name or by trade:

> **Devo accompagnare i bambini *dal* dentista.**
> I have to take the children to the dentist.

From a place

Prepositions which express movement from a place include **da** and less frequently **di**:

> **Il treno *da* Trieste arriverà al binario 10.**
> The train from Trieste will arrive on platform 10.

> **Per arrivare alle 7.00 all'aeroporto, bisognerà uscire *di* casa alle 6.00.**
> To get to the airport by 7 o'clock, we will have to leave the house at 6 o'clock.

> **Vai via *di* qua, brutto cane.**
> Go away from here, ugly dog.

In or at a place

Prepositions which indicate *being in* or *at a place* include **a, da, in, tra/fra, su, sopra, sotto, davanti, dietro, dentro, fuori**:

> **Ho fatto i miei studi *a* Padova.**
> I carried out my studies at Padova.

> **Abbiamo mangiato benissimo *da* Gianni.**
> We ate really well at Gianni's.

> **Una grande percentuale dei lavoratori lavora *in* centro ma abita *in* periferia o anche *in* campagna.**
> A large percentage of workers work in the centre but live in the suburbs or even in the country.

> **La mia macchina è parcheggiata *tra* due camion. Non si vede da qui.**
> My car is parked between two lorries. You can't see it from here.

> **Quando vengono i nipoti, metto i vasi di porcellana *sullo* scaffale più alto.**
> When my grandchildren come, I put the china vases on the highest shelf.

Mia madre nascondeva i regali per Natale *sopra* l'armadio nella
sua camera.
My mother hid the Christmas presents on top of the cupboard in
her bedroom.

I gattini dormono *sotto* il letto.
The kittens sleep under the bed.

La macchina era parcheggiata *davanti* alla casa.
The car was parked in front of the house.

Il portafogli è caduto *dietro* all'armadio.
The wallet has fallen behind the cupboard.

Ci sono dei negozi anche *dentro* la galleria, ma sono costosi.
There are some shops inside the galleria as well, but they're
expensive.

La chiesa era affollatissima, c'erano dei fedeli che ascoltavano la
messa *fuori* della chiesa.
The church was packed out, there were some worshippers who
were listening to the mass outside the church.

37.3   *Manner*

Introduction

The most straightforward way of stating *how* an action is carried out, is to use
an adverb. Full details of the formation and use of *adverbs* are found in Chapter
6. Here we look at other ways to specify or state how an action is carried out, for
example adverbial phrases.

Adverbial phrases

An adverbial phrase is a phrase composed of preposition and noun, which has
the meaning of an adverb. Some common adverbial phrases are formed with
con, a, in, senza.

With **con**:

Mariolina suonava il violino *con* molto entusiasmo ma con poca
accuratezza.
Mariolina played the violin with great enthusiasm but with little
accuracy.

With **a**:

I bambini dormivano e noi parlavamo *a* bassa voce.
The children were asleep and we were speaking in a low voice.

I treni Interregionali corrono *a* grande velocità.
The Inter-regional trains run at high speed.

With **in**:

> **Guardavano il programma *in* silenzio e senza commentare.**
> They watched the programme in silence and without commenting.

> **Ho preso un basso voto perché ho fatto il compito *in* fretta.**
> I got a low mark because I did the work in a hurry.

With **senza**:

> **Ha fatto l'esame di guida cinque volte *senza* successo.**
> She's taken the driving test five times without success.

With **maniera, modo**:

More specifically, an adverbial phrase formed with **maniera** and **modo** is used to indicate the way or manner in which something is done:

> **Nell'ultimo anno, le vendite dei computer portatili sono aumentate *in una maniera incredibile*.**
> Over the last year, sales of portable computers increased in an unbelievable manner.

> **Non parlarmi *in questo modo*.**
> Don't speak to me in this way.

Adverbial adjective

The so-called 'adverbial adjective' – an adjective used with the force of an adverb, for example **parlare chiaro** (= **chiaramente**) – is becoming more and more common, for example, in advertising language. The masculine singular form is the form always used:

> **Mangiare *sano*. Mangiare Yoplait.**
> Eat healthy. Eat Yoplait.

> **Abbiamo lavorato *sodo* per una settimana.**
> We worked solidly for a week.

> **Chi va piano va *sano* e va lontano.**
> He who goes slowly goes safely (*lit.* healthily) and goes far.

Benino, benone

Some common adverbs such as **bene** can also have suffixes such as **-ino**, **-one** added (see 6.2.4) to give the forms ben*ino*, ben*one* 'quite well', 'very well'.

Other adverbial forms

Unusual adverbial forms include those ending in **-oni**. Examples include:

carponi 'crawling', 'on all fours'
penzoloni 'dangling'
bocconi 'face down'

Describing an action using *come* or *da*

Camminava con la testa alta, *come* una giraffa.
She walked with her head high, like a giraffe.

Si è comportato *da* pazzo.
He behaved like a lunatic.

38 Expressing a condition or hypothesis

38.1 Expressing conditions: introduction

We express a condition, in English, by using the word 'if': '*If* you are good, I will buy you an ice-cream' (a distinct possibility), or '*If* we win the Lottery, we will buy a house in Tuscany' (possible but unlikely) or '*If* you had drunk less wine, you wouldn't have crashed the car' (too late, no longer a possibility). The second half of the sentence expresses what *will/ would* happen if the condition is met, or what *would have* happened if it had been met.

Similarly, in Italian, **se** 'if' can introduce a hypothesis or condition, or **periodo ipotetico**. Conditional sentences are traditionally divided into three types: real or probable, possible and impossible. This is a slightly artificial division. In reality there are only two main types of conditional sentence: those which are *a possibility*, and those which are *unlikely* or *impossible*.

38.2 Expressing a real possibility

Here the 'condition' is either likely to be met or may even be a *fact*. The verb in the **se** clause is in the *indicative* (*present, future* or *past* or a combination of more than one tense), to express certainty or reality. The *imperative* may also be . used. Most of the time, the **se** clause comes first in the sentence, but it can also come *after* the 'result' clause.

The choice of verbs used depends on the *degree of probability*, in other words, on how likely it is that the condition will be met. If we are expressing a near-certainty, rather than a condition – for example we may already know that our friends are going to Italy in October – we use a verb in the *indicative* for the **se** clause, and another *indicative* for the 'result' clause, in whatever tense is appropriate.

Present + present:

> **Se c'è qualche problema, mi *puoi chiamare* con il cellulare.**
> If there's a problem, you can call me on the mobile phone.

> **Se piove, entra l'acqua.**
> If it rains, the water gets in.

Present + imperative:

> **Se *decidi* di andare via, *lasciami* la chiave.**
> If you decide to go away, leave me the key.

> ***Chiudi* la porta, *se esci*.**
> Shut the door if you go out.

Present + future:

> **Se *c'è* un problema, mi *potrai chiamare* con il cellulare.**
> If there's a problem, you'll be able to call me on the mobile phone.

> **Se tu *sei* intelligente, non *avrai* difficoltà a imparare l'italiano.**
> If you're clever, you won't have any trouble learning Italian.

Past + future:

> **Se l'aereo non *ha fatto* un ritardo, lui *sarà* già all'aeroporto.**
> If the plane hasn't arrived late, he will be at the airport already.

Future + future:

> **Se voi *sarete* in Italia ad ottobre, *potrete partecipare* alla vendemmia.**
> If you are in Italy in October, you can take part in the grape-picking.

38.3   Expressing a condition unlikely to be met or impossible

Where there is little chance of the conditions coming true (for example in the case of the Lottery), we are more likely to use the *present conditional* to express what *would* happen, if the condition were met, while the condition or **se** clause uses the *imperfect subjunctive*, to express the hypothetical nature of the situation or the impossibility of the condition coming true:

> **Se noi *vincessimo* la lotteria, *compreremmo* una seconda casa, magari al mare.**
> If we were to win the Lottery, we would buy a second home, maybe at the seaside.

(Note the use of **magari** 'perhaps' in the example above.)

The example shown in 38.2 above can be expressed in a way that suggests you are *not* expecting any problems:

> *Se ci fosse* qualche problema, mi *potresti chiamare* con il cellulare.
> If there were any problem, you could call me on the mobile phone.

In present time context

> *Se* io *fossi* in te, non *accetterei* quell'incarico.
> If I were you, I wouldn't accept that job.

In past time context

This combination uses the *past* conditional to express what could or would have happened, if the condition had been met, while the conditional or *se* clause uses the pluperfect subjunctive. Clearly in this situation, the condition can no longer be met.

> *Se* il direttore *fosse stato* più gentile, non *avrebbe licenziato* il nostro collega in questo modo.
> If the manager had been kinder, he wouldn't have sacked our colleague in this way.

> *Se* tu me l'*avessi detto, avrei potuto* aiutarti.
> If you had told me, I could have helped you.

Occasionally, it is possible to have a combination of a condition which can no longer be met (*past* subjunctive) and a *present* conditional:

> *Se* io *avessi* sposato un inglese, *sarei* più felice oggi.
> If I had married an Englishman, I would be happier today.

In *spoken* language – rarely in written – the pluperfect subjunctive in the **se** clause is quite often replaced by the *imperfect indicative*. Compare the example below with the same sentence expressed more formally above:

> *Se* tu me lo *dicevi, avrei potuto* aiutarti.
> If you had told me, I could have helped you.

The past conditional in the result clause can also be replaced by the imperfect indicative:

> *Se* tu me lo *dicevi*, ti *potevo* aiutare.
> If you had told me, I could have helped you.

The choice of pluperfect subjunctive + past conditional, imperfect + past conditional, imperfect + imperfect depends very much on the register (spoken or written, formal or conversational). The same statement can be expressed in three different ways, all with the same meaning:

> Se tu *ti fossi comportata* meglio, ti *avrebbero invitata* alla festa.
> Se tu *ti comportavi* meglio, ti *avrebbero invitato* alla festa.
> Se tu *ti comportavi* meglio, ti *invitavano* alla festa.
> If you had behaved better, they would have invited you to the party.

As in other contexts, there is a general tendency for the language to become less formal, more colloquial, and the imperfect indicative is an easier verb form to use, even for Italians. In formal writing, it is usually preferable to use the first pattern shown above.

38.4 *Expressing conditions with other conjunctions*

Apart from **se**, there are several other conjunctions or phrases that can introduce a condition, such as:

> **nel caso (che)** 'if'
> **qualora** 'if (ever)'
> **posto che** 'given that'
> **ammesso che** 'given that'
> **a patto che** 'on condition that'
> **a condizione che** 'on condition that'
> **purché** 'provided that'
> **nell'eventualità che** 'in the event that'
> **nell'ipotesi che** 'in the event that'

Generally speaking, these phrases are used in the *possible* type of conditional sentences, with the *subjunctive*:

> *Nel caso che vi perdiate,* **chiedete informazioni ad un vigile.**
> If you get lost, ask a traffic warden for information.

Of similar meaning, but followed by a noun rather than a verb, is the prepositional phrase **in caso di** 'in case of':

> *In caso di incendio,* **rompete il vetro.**
> In case of fire, break the glass.

The conjunction **qualora** is used in a hypothetical clause; its nearest translation in English is 'if ever':

> *Qualora dovesse* **presentarsi l'occasione, Francesco e Chiara si trasferirebbero a Trieste.**
> If ever the occasion were to arise, Francesco and Chiara would move to Trieste.

Both **a patto che** and **a condizione che** express the more specific meaning 'on condition that' and are always used with the subjunctive:

> **Gli stiro le camicie** *a patto che* **lui lavi i piatti.**
> I iron his shirts on condition that (if) he washes the dishes.

> **La Madison firmerà il contratto solo** *a condizione che* **la commissione** *venga aumentata* **del 10%.**
> Madison will sign the contract only on condition that the commission goes up by 10 per cent.

The phrase **anche se** 'even if' acts like **se**; it can either express a *possible* condition (using the indicative) or an *improbable* condition (using the subjunctive):

> **Anche se lui mi *dice* che va bene, aspetterò di avere la conferma del direttore prima di procedere.**
> Even if he tells me that it is OK, I will wait to get confirmation from the director before going ahead.

> **Anche se tu mi *dovessi* pagare dieci milioni al mese, non accetterei di vendere i tuoi prodotti.**
> Even if you were to pay me ten million a month, I wouldn't agree to sell your products.

 ## 38.5 *Expressing conditions with other verb forms*

More unusually, instead of using a **se** clause, or any of the phrases shown above, one can express a condition by using one of the following verb forms. In each case, the subject of the main verb also has to be the subject of the other verb form or else be explicitly mentioned:

 ### Gerund

> **Andando in treno, si risparmierebbe un'ora.**
> If we (one) went by train, we (one) would save an hour.

Even when referring to a past context, only the present gerund can be used:

> **Guidando con più prudenza, non avresti preso la multa.**
> If you had driven more carefully, you wouldn't have got a fine.

38.5.2 Participle

With **se**

> **Se compilato con attenzione, il questionario può essere uno strumento utile per capire il carattere di una persona.**
> If compiled with care, the questionnaire can be a useful tool to understand someone's character.

Without **se**

> **Fatto in modo incompleto, il sondaggio non sarebbe molto valido.**
> (If it were) done in an incomplete fashion, the survey wouldn't be very valid.

 ### Infinitive

> **A guardarla bene, sembra più vecchia di lui.**
> If you look at her closely, she seems older than him.

A reagire in modo eccessivo, rischi di allontanare tuo figlio.
If you over-react, you risk alienating your son.

38.6 Unfinished conditional sentence

Sometimes in English we express a half-finished thought – for example a desire
or regret – with the words 'if'/'if only' ('If only I had listened to my teacher . . .').
A similar construction is possible in Italian, either with the imperfect
subjunctive or with the pluperfect subjunctive. Only the **se** clause is expressed,
while the 'consequence' or 'result' is left unspoken:

Se si potesse tornare indietro nel tempo . . . (si potrebbero evitare
tanti disastri).
If only one could turn the clock back . . . (so many disasters could
be avoided).

Se l'avessi saputo . . . (avrei fatto le cose in modo diverso).
If only I had known . . . (I would have done things differently).

Se mia madre avesse saputo . . . (mi avrebbe ammazzata).
If my mother had found out . . . (she would have killed me).

Sometimes **se** is replaced by **magari**:

Magari mi *avesse detto. . . .*
If he had only told me. . . .

Compare this use of **magari** with its use in 38.3 above.

Sometimes the half-finished thought is a tentative idea, a suggestion:

Se prendessimo il treno invece di andare in macchina?
What if we took the train instead of going by car?

Se gli *dicessimo* la verità?
What if we told him the truth?

38.7 Other uses of se

38.7.1

Contrast
In the examples below, we are referring to an action or event that clearly did
take place (a *fact* rather than a hypothesis). In this case **se** is not really
expressing a condition, but has a *contrasting* meaning, 'while', 'whereas':

Se lui *parlava* molto, sua moglie *parlava* due volte tanto.
If he spoke a lot, his wife spoke twice as much.

Se nell'Ottocento la gente *usava* ancora la carrozza, già agli inizi
del Novecento *si cominciava* ad andare in treno.

If in the nineteenth century people were still using carriages, already at the beginning of the twentieth century, they were starting to go by train.

Indirect questions

In an indirect question, **se** does not express a condition but means 'whether':

> **Voleva sapere *se* noi avevamo visto sua moglie.**
> He wanted to know if we had seen his wife.

For further examples of indirect questions, see 31.3.

39 Reservations, exceptions and concessions

39.1 Introduction

Whereas conditional sentences (see Chapter 38) talk about what will or will not take place *if* something happens, sentences expressing *reservation* talk about an action or event which will or will not take place *unless* something happens. Of similar type are those sentences which express *exception* ('except . . .'). Another type of sentence which balances one set of events against another is that which expresses *concession* ('although . . .'). Here we look at each type in detail.

39.2 Expressing reservation or exception

39.2.1 Conjunctions or phrases expressing reservation

Sometimes we speak about an event or circumstance that is true *except for* a particular detail, or which will take place *unless* a particular detail, circumstance or event prevents it. In other words, we are expressing a *reservation* ('unless . . .') or *exception* ('except . . .'). Words which express reservation or exception in Italian are:

> **se non che** 'except that'
> **a meno che (non)** 'unless'
> **eccetto che** 'except that'
> **tranne che** 'except', 'unless'
> **fuorché** 'except'
> **salvo (che)** 'save for', 'unless'

39.2.2 Phrases or conjunctions followed by *che* and a dependent clause

These phrases or conjunctions, with *che*, introduce a dependent clause (known as a *clause of exception*); the verb is usually in the *subjunctive*, but can be in the indicative if it expresses a reality rather than a possibility.

> **Il Ministro non darà le dimissioni, *tranne che* il Presidente del Consiglio non lo costringa a farlo.**
> The Minister won't resign unless the Prime Minister forces him to do so.

> **Dobbiamo spedire le lettere,** *salvo che* **non le abbia già spedite la segretaria.**
> We have to send the letters, unless the secretary has already sent them.

> **Avrei piacere di accompagnarti,** *se non che* **ho un appuntamento.**
> I would happily go with you, except that I have an appointment.

> **È tutto pronto per la cena,** *eccetto che* **non sono ancora arrivati gli ospiti.**
> Everything is ready for dinner, except that the guests haven't arrived yet.

Note the use of **non** after **a meno che**:

> **Domani mangiamo all'aperto** *a meno che* **non piova.**
> Tomorrow we will eat in the open air unless it rains/as long as it doesn't rain.

Phrases followed by a verb infinitive

The phrases **eccetto che, fuorché, tranne, salvo che** can also be followed by an infinitive:

> **Lei fa tutto** *fuorché* **aiutarmi.**
> She does everything except help me.

> **Chiedetemi qualsiasi cosa,** *tranne* **cantare!**
> Ask me anything, but don't ask me to sing!

Phrases followed by a noun or pronoun

Lastly, **tranne, salvo, eccetto, fuorché** can also be followed by a noun (object or person) or pronoun:

> **Non ho mangiato niente** *tranne* **quello che mi hai preparato tu.**
> I haven't eaten anything except what you made me.

39.3 *Modifying a statement by concession*

Introduction

Using a clause or phrase of concession means that we are *conceding* the existence of a possible factor which can alter circumstances, but saying that the event or action expressed in the main clause will take place despite it:

> **Per quanto tu possa lamentarti, non cambierai niente.**
> However much you complain, you won't change anything.

There are several ways in which a statement can be modified by an expression of concession in Italian (English 'although', 'even if', 'despite . . .', etc.): some are *explicit*, some are *implicit*, in other words the idea of *concession* is understood or implied from the context, even without a specific conjunction being used.

39.3.2

Conjunction or phrase of concession

Sometimes the expression of concession consists of a conjunction or phrase indicating concession:

benché 'although'	**sebbene** 'although'
nonostante 'despite'	**quantunque** 'however (much)'
malgrado 'in spite of'	**per quanto** 'however'
anche se 'even if'	**con tutto che** 'with all that'

Generally speaking, these conjunctions introduce a **che** clause, in the subjunctive:

> *Benché fosse* **tardi, voleva presentarmi tutti i suoi amici e parenti.**
> Although it was late, he wanted to introduce me to all his friends and relatives.

> *Malgrado* **la segretaria** *abbia lavorato* **fino alle 8.00 di sera, non è riuscita a completare la relazione.**
> Despite the secretary having worked until 8 o'clock in the evening, she wasn't able to finish the report.

> *Quantunque fosse* **preparato Marco, l'esame di guida si è rivelato più difficile di quanto si aspettasse.**
> However well prepared Marco was, the driving test turned out to be more difficult than he expected.

Nonostante is nowadays most commonly found with **che** omitted:

> *Nonostante (che) sia* **ancora piccolo, ha già cominciato a studiare il violino.**
> Despite being still little, he has already begun to study the violin.

Anche se can be followed by either the indicative *or* the subjunctive, depending on how probable or certain the situation is.

Probable:

> *Anche se* **tu sei la mia migliore amica, ci sono certe cose che non ti potrò mai raccontare.**
> Even though you are my best friend, there are certain things that I can never tell you.

Less probable:

> *Anche se* **fosse l'ultimo uomo su questa terra, non accetterei di uscire con lui.**
> Even if he were the last man on earth, I wouldn't agree to go out with him.

Con tutto che is also usually followed by the indicative:

> *Con tutto che* aveva da fare 200 chilometri in macchina, ha voluto
> accompagnarmi prima all'aeroporto.
> Despite the fact that she had 200 kms to drive, she wanted to
> take me to the airport first.

Sebbene:

> *Sebbene* non avessimo dormito tutta la notte, abbiamo deciso di
> andare a fare una passeggiata lungo il mare.
> Although we had not slept all night, we decided to go for a walk
> along the seafront.

 Prepositions

Malgrado, nonostante can also be used as prepositions, followed by a noun:

> *Malgrado* la nostra esperienza, torneremo in Calabria l'anno
> prossimo.
> Despite our experience, we will go back to Calabria next year.

> *Nonostante* tutto, è la compagnia aerea inglese più importante.
> Despite everything, it's the most important English airline.

Per … che + subjunctive

The combination of an adjective with **per … che** takes the subjunctive.

> *Per intelligente che sia*, non è stato promosso dalla terza alla
> quarta.
> Bright though he is, he didn't pass his exams to go from 3rd to
> 4th year.

> 'Casa mia, casa mia, *per piccina che tu sia*, tu mi sembri una
> badia.'
> 'Home sweet home, however small you are, to me you seem like
> a fortress.' (Italian saying)

A similar construction is possible with a verb, although less common:

> *Per studiare che lei faccia*, sarà bocciata agli esami.
> However she studies, she will fail the exams.

Chiunque, qualunque 'whoever', 'whichever'/'whatever':

For more details on indefinites, see 3.9.

> *Chiunque* lo veda, dice che sembra ringiovanito.
> Anyone who sees him, says he seems much younger.

> *Qualunque* risultato si ottenga, val la pena di provare.
> Whatever result is achieved, it is worth trying.

Past participle or adjective
A past participle or an adjective alone can have a concessive meaning, as shown below:

> *Nata* in Inghilterra, Giuseppina si sentiva tuttavia italiana al cento per cento.
> (Although) born in England, Giuseppina however felt 100 per cent Italian.

The optional **benché**, **anche se** can be added:

> *Anche se malato*, volle partecipare alla gara.
> Even though ill, he wanted to take part in the competition.

> *Benché invecchiato* un po', era ancora molto in forma.
> Although aged a little, he was still very fit.

Gerund *pur essendo, pur avendo*
Where the subject of the concessive clause is the same as that of the main verb, a gerund – normally present – can be used, preceded by **pur** 'although':

> *Pur avendo* pochi clienti, la commessa ci ha messo mezz'ora a servirmi.
> Although she had few customers, the shop assistant took half an hour to serve me.

> *Pur volendo* aiutarmi, mio padre non era in grado di finanziare i miei studi.
> Although wanting to help me, my father was unable to finance my studies.

Per essere, per avere
Per is generally used to express concession only with **essere** or **avere**, and only where the subject of both clauses is the same:

> *Per essere* così giovane, è proprio in gamba.
> Considering he's so young, he's really on the ball.

> *Per aver studiato* l'italiano cinque anni, non lo parla tanto bene.
> Considering he has studied Italian for five years, he doesn't speak it so well.

A costo di
This means literally 'at the cost of':

> All'età di 75 anni, insisté per fare un'ultima scalata del Monte Bianco *a costo di* rimetterci la pelle.
> At the age of 75, he insisted on making a last ascent of Mont Blanc even at the cost of losing his life.

39.3.10

Nemmeno, neanche, neppure a, manco a

These negative expressions can be followed by **se** and a verb (subjunctive) or by **a** and then the infinitive. The main clause has to be a negative statement.

> *Manco a* **fare la coda per 24 ore, non si trovano i biglietti per quel concerto.**
> Not even if one queues for 24 hours, can one get tickets for that concert.

> **Io non lo farei,** *neanche se* **tu mi pagassi.**
> I wouldn't do it, not even if you paid me.

> *Nemmeno a volerlo,* **non riuscirei a mangiare le lumache.**
> I couldn't eat snails even if I tried.

39.3.11

Tuttavia, nondimeno

Often the idea that the event will go ahead anyway is reinforced by the addition of **tuttavia** 'however' or **nondimeno** 'nonetheless' in the main clause:

> *Sebbene* **stanchi, volevamo** *tuttavia* **andare a vedere il centro.**
> Although (we were) tired, we wanted however to go and see the centre.

V Expanding the horizons

40 Formal registers and style

40.1 Introduction

Italy's long and complex history has left its distinctive mark on the Italian language. Used almost exclusively as a written and literary language up until the Unification of the 1800s, spoken by few people outside an educated elite, until recent years it has preserved unchanged many features of its far-off cultural origins: the aristocratic society of the late Middle Ages and the Renaissance.

That foundation, the fact that the literary language has existed side-by-side with a diversity of dialects, and the influence of foreign domination (particularly Spanish and French) have all contributed to the complexity of the syntactical structure, the richness of vocabulary, the variety of stylistic forms.

Today Italian is a modern and dynamic language, spoken by 60 million people, but still bears certain features of its literary and aristocratic tradition. In this section of the book, we will draw the reader's attention to a few of these features, although we cannot describe them all.

The Italian language has inherited a fondness for elegance and eloquence, a sometimes excessive search for a precise terminology (even to the detriment of clarity), an unabashed love of formality. These traditional characteristics of the language of the educated elite are still strong today in certain sectors of Italian life, although there is an opposing trend towards the modernization and simplification of language, which can be seen as part of the rise of mass culture.

40.2 Bureaucratic formality

Every day, Italians, as well as foreign visitors, are systematically confronted by the web of bureaucratic, highly technical, often mysterious, language used by Italian public administration – but often by private enterprise as well – in order to provide the public with 'information'.

The effect produced by this type of language is to make the man in the street feel like the accused in a Court of Law, under arrest and without the assistance of a lawyer, when in reality he is being given information as to where to insert his ticket before getting on a means of public transport.

To illustrate this well-known phenomenon, we have chosen just one original example from the funicular station in Mergellina, Naples.

> **Si informano i signori Viaggiatori che, ai sensi del D.P.R. n.2567 del 19/11/1973, essi devono munirsi di titolo di viaggio precedentemente all'ingresso sulle vetture della Funicolare. I titoli di viaggio vanno timbrati nelle apposite obliteratrici collocate nell'androne della Stazione.**

The approximate translation is:

> The esteemed passengers are informed that, as prescribed by the Decree of the President of the Republic n.2567 of 19/11/1973, travel documents must be purchased in advance of boarding the carriages of the funicular. The travel documents must be stamped in the specially provided obliterating machines, located in the entrance hall of the station.

The same concept could perfectly well be expressed by the simple words:

> **Timbrare il biglietto qui.**
> Stamp your ticket here.

(Perhaps with an arrow indicating where they should insert the tickets.)

This bureaucratic approach can be hard to accept for those not accustomed to it, but in Italy it is a fact of life, and anyone who needs or wants to establish a serious relationship with Italian society must be linguistically prepared to cope with it.

40.3 Hypertechnical language

Another feature, widespread in public administration, as well as in many professional areas (medicine, banks, schools) is the tendency to use a lavish sprinkling of obscure technical terminology. This applies not only to specialist texts or verbal communication between people working in a particular profession, but also to literature and communications intended to provide information for the general public.

Here are some examples. The first is taken from the reply to a letter to the health column of a newspaper, in which the reader asks about his nosebleeds:

> **La sintomatologia descritta è aspecifica e necessita di un inquadramento adeguato in quanto numerose possono essere le cause che fanno nascere una epistassi.**
>
> <div align="right">(<i>La Repubblica</i>, 18/11/95)</div>
>
> The symptomology described is aspecific and needs an adequate contextualisation, inasmuch as the causes that can produce a nosebleed are numerous.

The next example is taken from the 'information sheet' sent by a bank to a client, to explain the mechanism used to calculate the interest payable on his account. We have indicated in italic the words that even an Italian, without specialist knowledge in banking and finance, would find difficult to understand. Note too the length and complexity of the text. We have preferred not to attempt a translation.

> Questo è il *riassunto scalare* del suo conto: la sequenza dei *saldi* è ottenuta raggruppando giorno per giorno tutte le operazioni con eguale *valuta*; i numeri rappresentano il *prodotto*, diviso 1000, di ogni saldo per i giorni *intercorrenti* dalla *valuta* dello stesso alla *valuta* del saldo successivo. I tassi e i relativi *numeri* presi a base per il calcolo degli interessi, sono evidenziati nell'apposito spazio riservato all'indicazione degli *elementi* per il *conteggio* delle *competenze*. Gli importi degli interessi sono calcolati secondo l'*anno civile* ed il *tasso* applicato. La *dipendenza* presso la quale è aperto il suo conto è a disposizione per ogni ulteriore informazione e chiarimento.

Although examples such as this can be found in countries around the world, the extent to which the phenomenon has penetrated practically every area of life is perhaps unique to Italy. Road signs are one example (technical words in italic):

> Inizio *carreggiata* a traffico *canalizzato*. *Preselezionare* corsia. Get in lane.

40.4 Use of the Lei form

The use of the **Lei** courtesy form to address people is probably the most important characteristic inherited from the period of Spanish domination (the fifteenth to the eighteenth century). The **Lei** form is an indirect way of addressing a person using the *third person feminine* instead of the *second* person **tu** or **voi**, as if we were speaking not to 'you' but to 'her'.

The **Lei** form of address is one of the most difficult patterns of language for foreigners to learn, since it sounds 'unnatural' and confusing. It is particularly alien to English speakers, who are used to interacting with others in a simple, more direct fashion. Even students from an Italian background, who in their family situation have only ever used **tu**, sometimes find it difficult to use **Lei**.

Nonetheless the **Lei** form is an unavoidable part of everyday life and relationships in Italian society. Although the foreign learner will be treated with a certain amount of tolerance, failure to use it, amongst Italians, is perceived as an omission of a sign of respect and a serious infringement of good manners.

Here we draw the reader's attention to a few points that can cause difficulty when using the courtesy form.

Verb forms

All verb forms must be in the *third person*:

Tu	Lei
Prend*i* un caffè?	**Prend*e* un caffè?**
Would you like a coffee?	
***Hai* ragione!**	***Ha* ragione!**
You are right!	

Particular care should be taken over the imperative forms (see Chapter 2). The **Lei** form uses the present subjunctive:

Tu	Lei
Vieni. Accomodati.	**Venga. Si accomodi.**
Come in. Have a seat.	
***Dammi* quel libro.**	**Mi *dia* quel libro.**
Give me that book.	

The **Lei** forms of imperatives most commonly needed, even by tourists or visitors, are those used to attract someone's attention or ask a question:

Senta!	**Scusi!**
Listen!	Excuse me!

Possessives

The possessive used must be **suo** rather than **tuo**:

Tu	Lei
Dimmi il *tuo* nome.	**Mi dica il *suo* nome.**
Tell me your name.	
È *tua* questa giacca?	**È *sua* questa giacca?**
Is this your jacket?	

Pronouns

Personal pronouns must be in the *third person feminine*, both *direct* (**la**) and *indirect* (**le**):

Tu	Lei
Non *ti* sento.	**Non *la* sento.**
I can't hear you.	
***Ti* chiedo scusa.**	***Le* chiedo scusa.**
I apologize to you.	
***Ti* piace Mozart?**	***Le* piace Mozart?**
Do you like Mozart?	

The **Lei** form of *direct* and *indirect* pronouns often has to be used when speaking on the telephone, in a business situation:

> **Vuole che la faccia richiamare?**
> Do you want to be called back?

> **Vuole il catalogo? Glielo spedisco domani.**
> Do you want the catalogue? I'll send you it tomorrow.

40.5 Il sottoscritto

In formal bureaucractic language, the use of the *third* person is extended to refer to oneself, as though speaking of someone else, instead of using '*I*'.

This is done in applications, requests, declarations, and also often in *curricula vitae* addressed to an institution or public office, in order to stress the objectivity and impersonality of the information given. In such cases the formula used is **il sottoscritto** (for men) or **la sottoscritta** (for women), literally 'the undersigned'; all verbs used are in the *third* person, and are shown in italic in the text.

Here are some extracts from a real *curriculum vitae*, in which the writer attempts to use this formal style. Note the use of the rather old-fashioned **ivi** 'there' instead of **lì** or **ci**; **trascorrere**, **soggiornare** 'to sojourn' rather than the simpler **passare**; **in qualità di** 'in his capacity as' rather than **come**; **sopraindicati** 'the above-mentioned' and the extremely pompous **calandosi nelle realtà locali** 'immersing himself to the best of his ability in the local environment', and **riuscendo . . . ad allargare i propri orizzonti socio-culturali** 'succeeding in this manner to widen his social and cultural horizons'.

Curriculum Vitae di Policastri Carmelo

Il sottoscritto Carmelo Policastri, nato a Castellana Grotte il 16.01.1970 ed ivi residente alla Via della Mercanzia, numero civico 27, *ha conseguito* il Diploma di Maturità Scientifica nell'anno 1988, presso il Liceo Scientifico Statale di Putignano (Bari), riportando la votazione finale di 52/60.

Negli anni 1986 ed 1987 *il sottoscritto ha trascorso* entrambe le stagioni estive nell'Isola di Jersey (Channel Islands) al fine di approfondire e perfezionare la conoscenza della lingua inglese, l'estate del 1989 *ha soggiornato* invece a Hannover (Germania) per poter prendere dimestichezza con la lingua tedesca.

In ognuno dei periodi sopraindicati, *il sottoscritto ha* sempre *cercato* e *trovato* lavoro in campo turistico-alberghiero, *calandosi* al meglio delle proprie possibilità nelle realtà locali.

Guida-interprete, in qualità di lavoratore stagionale, già dal 1994, presso le Grotte di Castellana (Bari), *ha avuto* ulteriori possibilità di venire a contatto con turisti provenienti da ogni parte del mondo, riuscendo, così, ad allargare i propri orizzonti socio-culturali.

Castellana Grotte, 30.03.1995

Carmelo Policastri

40.6   *Using the passive*

As seen in Chapters 2 (2.1.7) and 19 (19.2), the passive form of verbs is a very common way to place less emphasis on the person who does something, and more on the action itself, or on its object. It is therefore very common to use passive constructions whenever the formality of a statement requires an impersonal approach.

One example has already been shown above (in 40.2) where a bureaucratic notice will state:

> *Si informano* **i signori Viaggiatori. . . .**
> The passengers are informed. . . .

Rather than:

> *Informiamo* **i signori Viaggiatori. . . .**
> We inform the passengers. . . .

Notice the use of the **si passivante** rather than the regular passive (**sono informati**) which is usually avoided in Italian whenever possible (see Chapters 2 and 19).

40.7   *Using the subjunctive*

Another marker of formality in Italian is the use of the subjunctive even in those cases where it is optional and not strictly required (see Sections III and IV throughout). The function of this verbal mood is to attenuate or soften all statements or represent doubt or uncertainty; it can also introduce a more literary style, markedly different from the spoken and informal register which normally uses the indicative.

Perhaps not surprisingly, the more traditionally minded sections of the Italian educated classes are today bemoaning the alleged '*death of the subjunctive*', often presented as a national disgrace, or as an alarming symptom of a decaying educational system. It is true that the more direct forms of communication encouraged by the technological era (from the telephone to fax or computer networks) favour the simpler, more accessible and standardized patterns of the spoken language.

Far from being dead, however, the subjunctive is still a widespread and irreplaceable form of expression in Italian (albeit a difficult one for the foreign student) as we have shown throughout this book. And fortunately its existence gives us the possibility either of achieving a higher degree of formality in our social intercourse, or a greater degree of subtlety in expressing our communicative functions.

41 Written correspondence

41.1 Introduction

Business letters are very important in the world of commerce, even more so now that fax communication has become the accepted means of communication, sometimes replacing the telephone call or telex.

There is a set form for business letters in Italian, which tend to be more formal than their English equivalent. Here we look at just a few important features of letters and faxes. For further information, students should use one of the many books on **corrispondenza commerciale** available on the market.

41.2 Layout of the letter

41.2.1

Heading
Most companies use headed paper, both for letters and for faxes. So generally there is no need to write the name or address of the company sending the letter.

41.2.2

Date
The name of the town or city is indicated top right, followed by the day (in figures), the month (written in full) and the year:

Milano, 14 ottobre 1996

This is often abbreviated in faxes and less formal letters to **Milano, 14/10/96**.

41.2.3

Name and address of the recipient/addressee
The name and address of the recipient can be written either on the left or on the right. On the first line of the letter is the name of the addressee, with the appropriate title in full or in abbreviated form. On the second line is the street, with street number following it; on the third line the name of the town or city, and **CAP** (**codice avviamento postale** or postcode). If the town is not the provincial capital, you may add in brackets the abbreviation for the province:

Egregio dott. Augusto Parente
Via G. Verdi, 42
47037 RIMINI (FO)

You may address a specific person within a company:

> **Ing. Carlo Biancardi**
> **Direttore Tecnico**
> **Palazzi S.p.A**

When replying to an Italian business letter, the title of the addressee must be used even if he/she hasn't used it when signing.

When writing to a company, the name of the company or organization is preceded by the abbreviation **Spett.** (**spettabile** 'worthy of respect'):

> **Spett. Bianchi S.p.A. (Società per Azioni 'PLC')**

or

> **Spett. Ditta Bianchi S.p.A.**

The name of the office or department can be given.

Either after the company name:

> **Spett. Bianchi S.p.A.**
> **Ufficio Contabilità**

Or as the addressee:

> **Spett. Ufficio Marketing**
> **Bianchi S.p.A.**

If you want to mark the letter for the attention of someone specific (English 'FAO'):

> **Alla cortese attenzione del sig. Di Giacomo**

or

> **Alla cortese attenzione dell'Amministratore Delegato**

Now see 41.3 for details on titles.

41.2.4 References

You might find the following *references* on a business letter:

> **Rif.** 'ref.'
> **Vs. Rif.** 'Your ref.'
> **Ns. Rif.** 'Our ref.'
> **Prot. N.** 'file number' (short for **protocollo**)

The word **oggetto** indicates what the letter or fax is about:

> **Oggetto: Richiesta di campione, prezzi e condizioni di pagamento.**
> Re: Request for samples, prices and terms of payment.

41.2.5

Salutation ('Dear . . .')

When addressing a letter to a company or organization, the equivalent of 'dear' is not used. The name and address is given at the top of the letter, as detailed above, and then is not repeated at the beginning of the letter.

41.2.6

Special annotations on the letter or envelope

riservata e personale 'private and personal'
raccomandata 'registered post'
per via aerea 'by air mail'
stampe 'printed papers'
mittente 'sender'
presso 'c/o'
pregasi rispedire 'please return to'

41.2.7

Some common abbrevations in commercial letters

all.	**allegato/i** 'enclosures'/'enclosed'
corr.	**corrente** 'current', 'this'
c.m.	**corrente mese** 'this month'
u.s.	**ultimo scorso** 'last (month)'
p.v.	**prossimo venturo** 'next (month)'
90/gg.	**90 giorni** '(payment in) 90 days'
c/c	**conto corrente** 'current account'
c/c/P	**conto corrente postale** 'post-office account'
C.P.	**casella postale** 'post box'
C.A.P.	**codice di avviamento postale** 'post code'
lett.	**lettera** 'letter'
p.c.	**(per conoscenza)** 'for information only'
p.c.c.	**(per copia conforme)** 'copy to'
p.es.	**per esempio** 'for example'
Racc.	**raccomandata** 'registered post'
n./N°	**numero** 'number'

41.2.8

Opening phrases

In risposta alla vostra (lettera)
Riguardo alla vostra (lettera)
In riferimento alla vostra del 10 c.m.

Abbiamo il piacere di informarvi
Ci permettiamo di scrivervi
Vi comunichiamo che
Ci dispiace dovervi informare

A seguito di quanto all'oggetto
In seguito ad aumento di costi

Siamo sorpresi per ciò che avete scritto

Siamo lieti di venir incontro alle sue esigenze

41.2.9   **Closing phrases**

Speriamo in una vostra sollecita risposta

In attesa di vostri ordini . . . siamo a vostra disposizione

Vi salutiamo distintamente

41.2.10   **Signature**

The signature at the bottom indicates the name and position of the writer. The signature itself is generally written by hand. The abbreviation **p** indicates that the person has been authorized to write on behalf of someone else.

41.3   *Academic, honorary and other titles*

For a fuller illustration of how to use these professional titles, see 20.9. Although there are English equivalents for the professions (lawyer, engineer, doctor, teacher, etc.), they are not generally used as titles in English. Apart from Doctor, English tends to address people as Mr, Mrs, Miss or Ms.

sig.	signore	e.g	sig. Carlo Rossi	Mr
sig.na	signorina		sig.na Carla Rossi	Miss
sig.ra	signora		sig.ra Celina Ginelli	Mrs
dott.	dottore		dott. Carlo Rossi	Doctor
dott.ssa	dottoressa		dott.ssa Gloria Parma	Doctor (female)
ing.	ingegnere		ing. Carlo Rossi	engineer
avv.	avvocato		avv. Francesco Baralle	lawyer
rag.	ragioniere		rag. Walter Maggioni	accountant
prof.	professore		prof. Augusto Parente	teacher (in secondary school, university)
prof.ssa	professoressa		prof.ssa Concetta Malorni	teacher (female)

If you know the name of the person, use the title along with their name:

Gentile signora Bianchi, Egregio signor Rossi

If you are addressing the director of a company or department but don't know their name, put:

Egregio direttore

If, on the other hand, you are sending a circular letter to teachers, you can address them as:

Egregio professore

Usually **Egregio** (abbreviated to **Egr.**) is used for a man, **Gentile** (abbreviated **Gent.**) for a woman, whether named or not named:

Egregio professore, Egregio dottore, Egregio signore
Gentile signora , Gentile dottoressa, Gentile professoressa

42 *Oral communication*

42.1 *Introduction*

Spoken Italian has certain features with which the foreign learner has to become familiar. One of them is the use of colloquialisms, for which use should be made of the many specific texts on **modi di dire**. Another is the use of specific techniques needed to get your message across.

42.2 *Techniques of oral communication*

Some examples of specific techniques needed in the spoken context are shown below.

Attracting attention
In a restaurant or shop situation, the most normal way of attracting a waiter's or assistant's attention is to use the verb **sentire** and say:

> **Senta, scusi!**   Excuse me, listen (*literally*)

In the same context, the shop assistant wishing to start off a dialogue, will say:

> **Dica, signora!**   Tell me, signora (*literally*)

Similar phrases can be used to initiate or to join in a conversation in a social situation:

> **Senti**   Listen (*literally*)

Interrupting and getting your point across
Getting your point across:

The phrases used in this situation can be found in Chapter 27.

Interrupting while acknowledging points made by others:

> **Ecco.** 'There!' (I *did* tell you . . .)
> **Vedi, io . . .** 'You see, I . . .'
> **Ho capito. Ma . . .** 'I've got the point, but . . .'

42.2.3
Asking/giving permission to speak

Asking permission:

> **permetti? permette?** 'may I speak?' (*literally*: 'Will you allow . . .?')
> **una parola?** '(may I have) a word?'

Giving permission or inviting to speak:

> **prego** 'please . . .' (*literally*)
> **dica (pure)** 'please speak (by all means).' (*literally*)

42.2.4
Clarifying or explaining what has been said

Explaining what you have said:

> **voglio dire** 'I mean'
> **cioè** 'that is'
> **mi spiego** 'I'll explain myself'

Checking someone has understood what you have said:

> **mi spiego?** 'am I explaining myself?'
> **è chiaro?** 'is that clear?'

Giving examples:

> **cioè** 'in other words'
> **per esempio** 'for example'

Asking someone to repeat what he/she has said:

> **può ripetere?** 'can you repeat?'
> **non ho capito** 'I didn't understand'
> **non ho sentito** 'I didn't catch what you said'
> **può spiegare?** 'can you explain?'

Summarizing:

> **insomma** 'in short'
> **allora** 'so'
> **in breve** 'in short'

Correcting oneself:

> **cioè, no** 'actually, no'
> **anzi** 'on the contrary'

43 Telephone skills

43.1 Introduction

At some time, you may have to make or receive a telephone call in Italian. This is probably one of the most difficult tasks for a non-native speaker to carry out, so it helps to have some standard phrases ready, and to know how to spell your name when asked.

43.2 Spelling on the telephone

When we speak on the phone, we often have to spell our name or the name of the place where we live. The alphabet, with the Italian names for letters, is given in full in Appendix I. However, on the telephone, Italians often use the names of cities to represent the sounds they wish to clarify: **A Ancona**, **G Genova**, and so on.

Some letters such as *J, K, X, Y* (**i lunga, cappa, ics, ipsilon**) do not exist in the Italian alphabet but can be used for spelling foreign names. Here is a list of the cities which are most often used for spelling; as you can see, there are no cities beginning with *H, Q* or *W*:

A	Ancona	N	Napoli
B	Bologna	O	Otranto
C	Como	P	Palermo
D	Domodossola	Q	cu/quaranta/Quarto
E	Empoli	R	Roma
F	Firenze	S	Salerno
G	Genova	T	Torino
H	hotel	U	Udine
I	Imola	V	Venezia
J	i lungo/Jolly	W	Washington
K	cappa/Kennedy	X	ics
L	Livorno	Y	ipsilon
M	Milano	Z	zeta/Zara

So to write the name *Jones* you would have to say: *J* – **I lunga**, *O* – **Otranto**, *N* **come Napoli**, *E* **come Empoli**, *S* **come Salerno**.

43.3 Telephone phrases

Initial greetings, saying goodbye:

Pronto	Hello.
Arrivederci.	Goodbye.

Asking to speak to someone:

Potrei parlare con il direttore?
Could I speak to the manager?

C'è il medico, per favore?
Is the doctor there, please?

Mi passa il dottor Caselli, per favore?
Could you pass me Dr Caselli, please?

Being put through:

Attenda un momento. Gliela passo.
Wait a minute. I'll put you through (to him/her).

Le passo la linea.
I'll put you through.

Se vuole attendere
If you hold on

Le faccio il nuovo interno.
I'll dial the new extension for you.

Mi potrebbe passare . . .
Could you put me through to . . .

Saying someone is not there/not available:

Mi dispiace, non c'è in questo momento.
I'm sorry. He's out at the moment.

È sull'altra linea.
He's on the other line.

È in riunione.
She/he's in a meeting.

Un momento. Non è in ufficio.
Just a minute. He's not in his office.

Credo che sia nel palazzo.
I think he's somewhere in the building.

Cercherò di rintracciarlo con l'intercom.
I'll try and page him on the intercom.

Vuole attendere?
Do you wish to hold?

Vuole provare più tardi?
Do you want to try later?

Non riesco a rintracciarlo.
I can't get hold of him.

Saying when someone is back:

Dovrebbe essere qui più tardi.
He/she should be back later.

Leaving a message:

Potrei lasciare un messaggio?
Could I leave a message?

Vuole lasciare un messaggio?
Would you like to leave a message?

Vuole ripetere il suo nome?
Could you repeat your name?

Come si scrive, per favore?
How is it spelt, please?

Dove posso rintracciarla?
Where can I get hold of you?

Va bene. Glielo dico.
I'll tell him.

Calling back:

Gli chiedo di chiamarLa appena torna (appena rientra).
I'll have him call you as soon as he gets back.

Vuole che la faccia richiamare?
Do you want me to have him call you back?

La faccio richiamare.
I'll have him call you back.

Può lasciare il suo numero?
Can you leave your number?

La richiamiamo appena possibile.
We'll get back to you as soon as possible.

Ho preso nota del suo numero.
I've made a note of your number.

Reasons for calling:

> **Chiamo per fissare un incontro.**
> I'm calling to arrange a meeting.

> **E il motivo della chiamata?**
> And the purpose of your call?

> **Qual è il motivo della chiamata?**
> What is the purpose of your call/what is it about?

> **Mi può dire il motivo della sua chiamata?**
> Can you tell me what it's about?

Fixing an appointment:

> **Le va bene domani a mezzogiorno?**
> Would tomorrow at midday suit you?

> **Adesso controllo i suoi impegni sull'agendina.**
> I'll just check his/her appointments in the diary.

> **Lei/lui sarà disponibile giovedì.**
> She/he'll be available on Thursday.

> **Facciamo alle due?**
> Shall we make it 2 o'clock?

> **Mi potrebbe chiamare per la conferma?**
> Will you call me back for confirmation?

> **Dovrei verificare.**
> I would need to check.

> **È abbastanza impegnato in questo periodo.**
> She/he's rather busy at the moment.

> **Non sarà possibile nei prossimi giorni.**
> It won't be possible over the next few days.

> **L'appuntamento fissato in precedenza non è più possibile/conveniente.**
> The appointment arranged earlier is no longer possible.

Other useful phrases:

> **numero interno** 'extension number'
> **contattare** 'to contact'
> **la linea è libera/occupata** 'the line is free/engaged'

43.4   *Telephone conversations*

Here are two examples of simple telephone conversations, the first using the polite **Lei** forms, the second using the familiar **tu**. On the use of professional titles, see 41.3.

Call A:

A: Pronto, sono Nicola Serra, vorrei parlare con l'avvocato Pira.
B: *Attenda* un attimo, glielo passo subito.
C: Pronto. *Con chi parlo?*
A: Buongiorno avvocato, sono Serra.
C: Buongiorno dottor Serra, *mi dica.*

A: Hello, it's Nicola Serra, I'd like to speak to (the lawyer) Mr Pira.
B: Wait a minute, I'll pass him to you straight away.
C: Hello, who am I speaking to?
A: Good morning (lawyer). It's Mr Serra here.
C: Good morning, Mr Serra, what can I do for you?

Call B:

A: Pronto, sono Giulio Tramonti. C'è Andrea per favore?
B: No, mi dispiace, è appena uscito.
A: Posso lasciare un messaggio?
B: Certo, *dimmi.*
A: Se possibile, Andrea dovrebbe richiamarmi stasera, dopo le 8. Devo *dirgli* una cosa importante.
B: Va bene. *Glielo* dirò certamente.
A: Grazie, arrivederci.
B: Prego, arrivederci.

A: Hello, it's Giulio Tramonti. Is Andrea there, please?
B: No, I'm sorry, he's just gone out.
A: Can I leave a message?
B: Certainly, tell me.
A: If possible, Andrea should call me back tonight, after 8 o'clock. I have to tell him something important.
B: OK. I'll certainly tell him.
A: Thanks, goodbye.
B: Not at all. Goodbye.

Appendix I
Spelling and pronunciation

Sounds and letters

It is often said that Italian is easy to learn, because it is spoken as it is written. This is not completely true, but certainly, compared with other languages such as English or French, Italian enjoys the advantage of an *almost* 'phonological' system of spelling, in which each letter of the alphabet almost always corresponds to one and only one 'sound' of the speech. Consequently it is usually easy to know how to pronounce an Italian word found in a written text, by simply following some straightforward general rules, to which there are no exceptions. The same is true when we need to write down words that we have heard in their spoken form.

However sounds and letters do *not* always correspond. There are some sounds ('phonemes') which are represented by two or three letters (e.g. [ʃ] = **sc-**), and some letters that can represent two different sounds (e.g. **c** can be either [k] or [tʃ] as in **ca** or **ce**).

Below, you will find a table of the relationship between the written letters of the alphabet and the sounds of the spoken language, represented both with the symbols of the International Phonetics Association (IPA) alphabet, and with some English words in which similar sounds can be found.

Following the table there are a few practical tips on some major difficulties of Italian pronunciation faced by native English speakers.

The alphabet

The Italian alphabet is composed of 21 letters. The letters *k j w x y* do not belong to the Italian alphabet, although they are often use to write words of foreign origin.

Letter	Phoneme		Examples
A	[a]		*a*more
B	[b]		*b*occa, ci*b*o
C	[k] c+cons.	*ca, co, cu, che, chi*	*c*rudo, *c*asa, *chi*esa
	[tʃ]	*cia, cio, ciu, ce, ci*	Lu*ci*ano, *c*era, ac*ci*uga
D	[d]		*d*ono, pie*d*e
E	[e]	see notes	*e*legant*e*, perch*é*

	[ɛ]	see notes	*ecco*, *vieni*
F	[f]		*facile*, *caffè*
G	[g] g+cons.	*ga, go, gu, ghe, ghi*	*grotta*, *gola*, *alghe*
	[dʒ]	*gia, gio, giu, ge, gi*	*rifugio*, *angelo*
H		no aspiration in Italian	
I	[i]		*idea*, *idiota*, *missile*
L	[l]		*lettera*, *collo*
M	[m]		*mela*, *ombrello*
N	[n]		*naso*, *anno*, *intelligente*
O	[o]	see notes	*voce, dito, ora*
	[ɔ]	see notes	*buono*, *ospite*, *Antonio*
P	[p]		*pelle*, *spalla*, *tappo*
Q(U)	[kw]		*acqua, questo, Pasqua*
R	[r]		*rosa*, *birra*, *pranzo*
S	[s]	see notes	*penso*, *solo*, *cassa*
	[z]		*rosa*, *socialismo*
T	[t]		*vita*, *petto*, *torre*
U	[u]		*uva*, *auguri*, *burro*
V	[v]		*volto*, *avventura*
Z	[dz]	see notes	*socializzare, zero*
	[ts]	see notes	*palazzo, zucchero*
	[ʃ]	sc- + e, i	*scena, pesci, piscina*
		sci- + a, o, u	*sciopero, usciamo, prosciutto*
	[ʎ]	gl- + i	*gli, figli, consigli*
		gli- + e, a, o, u	*foglie, bottiglia, aglio*
	[ɲ]	gn- + vowel	*agnello, gnomo, ogni*

Notes

The letter *h*

The letter **h** does not represent any sound in Italian; it is not pronounced. It is used to distinguish different consonant sounds as in the case of [k] or [g] before **e, i** vowels: **che chi ghe ghi**, as opposed to **ce ci** [tʃe] [tʃi] or **ge gi** [dʒe] [dʒi].

The consonants *s* and *z*

Each of the two letters **s** and **z** corresponds to two different sounds: voiced [z] [dz] and voiceless [s] [ts]. This distinction is not considered important by Italian speakers themselves. A few tips may however help in the pronunciation of the two different sounds of each letter:

S is voiceless [s]   at the beginning of a word, except before a

	voiced consonant (**spesa, scala, sale, sordo**)
	after a consonant (**falso, pensare, corso**)
	when double (**passo, assicurazione, messa**)
voiced [dz]	before a voiced consonant, even at beginning of a word (**asma, smetti**)
Z is voiceless [ts]	after **l** (**balzo, alzare, calze**)
	in **-ezza** (**bellezza, carezza, altezza**)
	before **-io -ia -ie** (**divorzio, zio, spazio, amicizia, pazienza**)
voiced [dz]	before a voiced consonant, even when at beginning of word
	in **-izzare, -izzazione**, etc. (**nazionalizzare, privatizzazione**)
	between vowels (**ozono, azalea**)

3 ## Open and closed vowels

There are two pairs of open and closed vowels: [ɛ] and [e], [ɔ] and [o]. The open vowels only occur in stressed syllables. When unstressed they are always closed. The two different vowels are represented in writing by the same letters **e** and **o**. The distinction between the two sounds is not very important in spoken Italian; Italians themselves may disagree on the 'correct' pronunciation of some words (especially when they speak different regional varieties of Italian).

Where necessary, the open and closed vowels can be distinguished by using the grave accent for the open sound **è ò** and acute accent for the closed **é ó**; many good dictionaries do this. However this is not done in normal written Italian, because of the fact that the distinction is simply not considered important.

Only in a few cases does the distinction become important in order to avoid confusion between two words. Then the written language indicates the open vowel sound with an accent, in this case obligatory, as in:

> **è** 'is' / **e** 'and'
> **tè** 'tea' / **te** 'you'
> **ho** 'I have' / **o** 'or'
> (here the **h** is used for historical reasons only)

4 ## Double consonants

'Double' or 'strong' consonants are a very common and frequent feature of the Italian language. Generally they are represented in writing by two letters (as in **palla**). In some cases however a consonant which is normally pronounced single is reinforced when speaking, due to its position in the utterance. This happens for instance in the case of consonants following some monosyllabic words (particularly in central and southern varieties of Italian), as in:

> **è vero** [ɛv'vɛro]   **a casa** [ak'kasa]   **sto bene** [stɔb'bɛne]

Likewise, the three consonants [ʃ], [ʎ], [ɲ] **sc, gl, gn** are always pronounced double when in the middle of a word, although this is not represented in writing (see 5).

Speakers of English mother tongue often find it difficult to reproduce exactly the sound of the Italian double consonants. Some practical help may come from knowing that a 'strong' consonant always follows a short vowel, while the corresponding single consonant always follows a long vowel, as in these examples:

pāla/pălla sēte/sĕtte   fāto/fătto cāro/cărro

5

The consonant groups *sc, gl, gn*

The consonants [ʃ] [ʎ] [ɲ] have no corresponding letters in the alphabet and are therefore represented by groups of two or three letters (see the table above). The pronunciation of these consonants is always strong when they are in the middle of a word.

Before the vowels **a o u**, [ʎ] [ʃ] are represented by the groups **gli** and **sci**. It should be noted that in these cases the letter **i** is only a written way of representing the consonants and is not to be pronounced as a separate sound. The same is true for the use of **i** in the groups **cia, cio, ciu** and **gia, gio, giu**.

6

Accent marks

In addition to the cases above, the accent mark is also used to distinguish between words with the *same vowel sounds*, but different meanings:

sé 'himself'/'herself'   **se** 'if'
lì là 'there'   **li** 'them', **la** 'her' (direct object pronouns)
né 'nor'   **ne** 'of it' (partitive)

Words with the stress on the last syllable are also written with an accent mark, as:

perché 'why'
città 'city'
caffè 'coffee'
università 'university'
libertà 'freedom'

Italians have tended to have a fairly flexible attitude to (and occasional disagreements over) the question of whether accents should be grave or acute. In recent years, there has been a tendency to use the acute accent on all the closed vowels including **a**, **i** and **u**. Serianni (*Grammatica Italiana*, UTET, 1989) recommends adopting the *grave* accent for **à, ì, ù** while keeping the option of *grave* and *acute* only in the case of *è/é* and *ò/ó* where it is needed to distinguish between open and closed vowels. This is the system adopted here.

Stress

Sometimes, particularly in dictionaries and textbooks, accent marks indicate on which syllable the stress falls, in words where there might be some doubt:

> **àncora/ancóra** 'anchor'/'still'
> **pàgano/pagàno** 'they pay'/'pagan'
> **chilogràmmo** 'kilogram'
> **chilòmetro** 'kilometre'

7

Spelling conventions

On the whole Italian spelling conventions follow English when it comes to capital letters. But note the following important differences:

Names of centuries:

> **il Duecento** 'the thirteenth century'
> **il Duemila** 'the year 2000'

Names of titles unless accompanied by proper names:

> **il Re** 'the King'
> **il Papa** 'the Pope'
> **il Conte** 'the Count'
>
> **re Vittorio Emanuele II**   King Vittorio Emanuele II

Appendix II
Irregular verbs

These two lists include all the common Italian irregular verbs. In the first list are included verbs with only two irregular tenses: simple perfect and/or past participle. In the second list are verbs with several irregular tenses. Verbs normally requiring **essere** in compound tenses are marked with a †. Tenses not appearing in the lists are regular.

 A   *List of verbs with two irregular tenses*

Infinitive	English	Simple Perfect	Past Participle
accendere	to light (up)	accesi	acceso
accludere	to enclose	acclusi	accluso
accorgersi	to realize	mi accorsi	accorto
affliggere	to afflict	afflissi	afflitto
aggiungere	to add	aggiunsi	aggiunto
alludere	to allude	allusi	alluso
ammettere	to admit	ammisi	ammesso
appendere	to hang	appesi	appeso
apprendere	to learn	appresi	appreso
aprire	to open	aprii (apersi)	aperto
assistere	to assist, witness		assistito
assolvere	to absolve	assolsi	assolto
assumere	to assume, employ	assunsi	assunto
attendere	to wait	attesi	atteso
avvolgere	to wrap	avvolsi	avvolto
chiedere	to ask	chiesi	chiesto
chiudere	to shut	chiusi	chiuso
comprendere	to understand	compresi	compreso
concedere	to concede	concessi	concesso
concludere	to conclude	conclusi	concluso
condurre	to conduct, lead	condussi	condotto
confondere	to confuse	confusi	confuso
conoscere	to know, meet	conobbi	
convincere	to convince	convinsi	convinto
coprire	to cover	coprii (copersi)	coperto
correggere	to correct	corressi	corretto
correre†	to run	corsi	corso

Infinitive	English	Simple Perfect	Past Participle
costringere	to force	costrinsi	costrettto
crescere[†]	to grow	crebbi	
cuocere	to cook	cossi	cotto
decidere	to decide	decisi	deciso
dedurre	to deduct, deduce	dedussi	dedotto
deludere	to delude	delusi	deluso
descrivere	to describe	descrissi	descritto
difendere	to defend	difesi	difeso
diffondere	to spread	diffusi	diffuso
dipendere[†]	to depend	dipesi	dipeso
dipingere	to paint, depict	dipinsi	dipinto
dirigere	to direct	diressi	diretto
discutere	to discuss	discussi	discusso
distendere	to distend	distesi	disteso
distinguere	to distinguish	distinsi	distinto
distruggere	to destroy	distrussi	distrutto
dividere	to divide	divisi	diviso
eleggere	to elect	elessi	eletto
emergere[†]	to emerge	emersi	emerso
erigere	to erect	eressi	eretto
escludere	to exclude	esclusi	escluso
esigere	to demand, require		esatto
esistere[†]	to exist		esistito
espellere	to expel	espulsi	espulso
esplodere	to explode	esplosi	esploso
esprimere	to express	espressi	espresso
estendere	to extend	estesi	esteso
estinguere	to extinguish	estinsi	estinto
fingere	to pretend	finsi	finto
fondere	to melt	fusi	fuso
friggere	to fry	frissi	fritto
fungere	to perform, act as	funsi	(funto)
giungere[†]	to reach	giunsi	giunto
illudere	to illude	illusi	illuso
immergere	to immerse	immersi	immerso
imprimere	to impress, stamp	impressi	impresso
incidere	to carve, record	incisi	inciso
indurre	to induce	indussi	indotto
infliggere	to inflict	inflissi	inflitto
infrangere	to infringe	infransi	infranto
insistere	to insist		insistito
intendere	to intend, understand	intesi	inteso
interrompere	to interrupt	interruppi	interrotto
introdurre	to introduce	introdussi	introdotto

Infinitive	English	Simple Perfect	Past Participle
invadere	to invade	invasi	invaso
iscrivere	to enrol	iscrissi	iscritto
leggere	to read	lessi	letto
mettere	to put	misi	messo
mordere	to bite	morsi	morso
muovere	to move	mossi	mosso
nascere[†]	to be born	nacqui	nato
nascondere	to hide	nascosi	nascosto
occorrere[†]	to be necessary	occorse	occorso
offendere	to offend	offesi	offeso
offrire	to offer	offrii (offersi)	offerto
perdere	to lose	persi (perdetti)	perso (perduto)
permettere	to allow	permisi	permesso
persuadere	to persuade	persuasi	persuaso
piangere	to weep	piansi	pianto
piovere[†]	to rain	piovve	
porgere	to hold out, offer	porsi	porto
prendere	to take	presi	preso
pretendere	to demand, expect	pretesi	preteso
produrre	to produce	produssi	prodotto
promettere	to promise	promisi	promesso
proteggere	to protect	protessi	protetto
pungere	to sting	punsi	punto
radere	to shave	rasi	raso
raggiungere	to reach	raggiunsi	raggiunto
redigere	to edit, draft	redassi	redatto
reggere	to support	ressi	retto
rendere	to return	resi	reso
resistere	to resist		resistito
respingere	to reject	respinsi	respinto
ridere	to laugh	risi	riso
ridurre	to reduce	ridussi	ridotto
riflettere	to reflect	riflessi (riflettei)	riflesso (riflettuto)
rincrescere	to regret	rincrebbe	
risolvere	to resolve	risolsi	risolto
rispondere	to reply	risposi	risposto
rivolgere	to turn, address	rivolsi	rivolto
rompere	to break	ruppi	rotto
scalfire	to scratch, undermine		scalfitto (scalfito)
scendere[†]	to descend	scesi	sceso
scommettere	to bet	scommisi	scommesso
sconfiggere	to defeat	sconfissi	sconfitto
scoprire	to discover	scoprii	scoperto

Infinitive	English	Simple Perfect	Past Participle
scorgere	to catch sight of	**scorsi**	**scorto**
scrivere	to write	**scrissi**	**scritto**
scuotere	to shake	**scossi**	**scosso**
seppellire	to bury		**sepolto** (**seppellito**)
smettere	to stop	**smisi**	**smesso**
soffrire	to suffer	**soffrii**	**sofferto**
sorgere†	to rise	**sorsi**	**sorto**
sorprendere	to surprise	**sorpresi**	**sorpreso**
sorridere	to smile	**sorrisi**	**sorriso**
sospendere	to suspend	**sospesi**	**sospeso**
spargere	to spread, scatter	**sparsi**	**sparso**
spegnere	to extinguish	**spensi**	**spento**
spendere	to spend	**spesi**	**speso**
spingere	to push	**spinsi**	**spinto**
stendere	to stretch, spread (out)	**stesi**	**steso**
stringere	to tighten, grip	**strinsi**	**stretto**
succedere†	to happen	**successe**	**successo**
svolgere	to develop, carry out	**svolsi**	**svolto**
tendere	to hold out, tend	**tesi**	**teso**
tingere	to dye	**tinsi**	**tinto**
tradurre	to translate	**tradussi**	**tradotto**
trascorrere	to pass	**trascorsi**	**trascorso**
uccidere	to kill	**uccisi**	**ucciso**
ungere	to oil, grease	**unsi**	**unto**
vincere	to win, defeat	**vinsi**	**vinto**
volgere	to turn	**volsi**	**volto**

B   *List of verbs with several irregular tenses*

accadere†	to happen
	as *cadere*
accogliere	to welcome
	as *cogliere*
andare†	to go

Pres. Indic. **vado, vai, va, andiamo, andate, vanno** *Future* **andrò**
Pres. Condit. **andrei**
Pres. Subjunc. **vada, vada, vada, andiamo, andiate, vadano**
Imperat. **va', andate**

apparire	to appear

Pres. Indic. **appaio, appari, appare, appariamo, apparite, appaiono**
Simp. Perf. **apparvi** (**apparii, apparsi**) ... *Past. Part.* **apparso**

appartenere	to belong
	as *tenere*
assalire	to assault
	as *salire*
avere	to have
	see Chapter 2
avvenire[†]	to happen
	as *venire*
bere	to drink
	Pres. Indic. **bev-o** ... *Simp. Perf.* **bevvi** ...
	Future **berrò** ...
	Pres. Condit. **berrei** ... *Pres. Subjunc.* **bev-a** ... *Past Part.* **bev-uto**
cadere[†]	to fall
	Pres. Indic. **cadrò** ... *Simp. Perf.* **caddi** ... *Pres. Condit.* **cadrei** ...
cogliere	to grasp, pick, take
	Pres. Indic. **colgo, cogli, coglie, cogliamo, cogliete, colgono** *Simp.*
	Perf. **colsi** ... *Past Part.* **colto**
comparire[†]	to appear
	Pres. Indic. **compaio, compari, compare, compariamo, comparite,**
	compaiono
	Simp. Perf. **comparvi (comparii, comparsi)** ... *Past Part.*
	comparso
dare	to give
	Pres. Indic. **do, dai, da, diamo, date, danno** *Simp. Perf.* **diedi,**
	desti, diede, demmo, deste, diedero (dettero) *Future* **darò, darai,**
	darà, daremo, darete, daranno *Pres. Condit.* **darei, daresti,**
	darebbe, daremmo, dareste, darebbero *Pres. Subjunc.* **dia, dia,**
	dia, diàmo, diàte, dìano *Imperf. Subjunc.* **dessi, dessi, desse,**
	dessimo, deste, dessero *Imper.* **da', date**
dire	to say
	Pres. Indic. **dico, dici, dice, diciamo, dite, dicono** *Simp. Perf.* **dissi,**
	dicesti, disse, dicemmo, diceste, dissero *Pres. Subjunc.* **dic-a** ...
	Imperf. Subjunc. **dic-essi** ... *Past Part.* **detto**
	Imperat. **di', dite**
disfare	to undo
	as *soddisfare*
dispiacere[†]	to displease
	as *piacere*
disporre	to arrange, place, put
	as *porre*
distrarre	to distract
	as *trarre*
dolere	to ache, hurt
	Pres. Indic. **mi dolgo, ti duoli, si duole, ci dogliamo, vi dolete, si**
	dolgono
	Simp. Perf. **mi dolsi, ti dolesti** ... *Future* **mi dorrò** ... *Pres.*
	Subjunc. **dolga, dolga, dolga, dogliamo, dogliate, dolgano**

dovere	to owe, to have to
	see Chapter 2
esporre	to expose, display, explain, set out
	as *porre*
essere†	to be
	see Chapter 2
estrarre	to extract
	as *trarre*
fare	to do, make

Pres. Indic. **faccio, fai, fa, facciamo, fate, fanno** *Simp. Perf.* **fecsi, facesti, fece, facemmo, faceste, fecero** *Future* **farò ...** *Pres. Condit.* **farei ...** *Pres. Subjunc.* **faccia, faccia, faccia, facciamo, facciate, facciano** *Imperf. Subjunc.* **facessi ...** *Past Part.* **fatto** *Imperat.* **fa', fate**

godere	to enjoy, benefit from

Future **godrò ...**

imporre	to impose, set, lay down
	as *porre*
morire†	to die

Pres. Indic. **muoio, muori, muore, moriamo, morite, muoiono** *Future* **morrò ... (morirò ...)** *Pres. Condit.* **morrei, morresti ... (morirei, moriresti ...)** *Pres. Subjunc.* **muoia, muoia, muoia, moriamo, moriate, muoiano** *Past Part.* **morto**

opporre	to oppose
	as *porre*
ottenere	to obtain
	as *tenere*
parere†	to appear, look, seem

Pres. Indic. **paio, pari, pare, paiamo, parete, paiono** *Simp. Perf.* **parvi, paresti ...** *Future* **parrò ...** *Pres. Condit.* **parrei ...** *Pres. Subjunc.* **paia, paia, paia, paiamo, paiate, paiano** *Past Part.* **parso**

porre	to place, put, lay down

Pres. Indic. **pongo, poni, pone, poniamo, ponete, pongono** *Simp. Perf.* **posi, ponesti, pose, ponemmo, poneste, posero** *Future* **porrò, porrai ...** *Pres. Condit.* **porrei, porresti ...** *Pres. Subjunc.* **ponga, ponga, ponga, poniamo, poniate, pongano** *Imperf. Subjunc.* **ponessi ...** *Past Part.* **posto**

potere	to be able to
	see Chapter 2
prevedere	to foresee, anticipate, forecast, plan
	as *vedere*
proporre	to propose, suggest, put forward
	as *porre*
raccogliere	to pick up, gather, collect
	as *cogliere*
rimanere†	to stay, remain, get, become

Pres. Indic. **rimango, rimani, rimane, rimaniamo, rimanete,**

	rimangono *Simp. Perf.* **rimasi, rimanesti** ... *Future* **rimarrò** ... *Pres. Condit.* **rimarrei** ... *Pres. Subjunc.* **rimanga, rimanga, rimanga, rimaniamo, rimaniate, rimangano** *Past Part.* **rimasto**
riuscire[†]	to succeed, manage to, prove to be as *uscire*
salire[†]	to go up, climb, rise *Pres. Indic.* **salgo, sali, sale, saliamo, salite, salgono** *Pres. Subjunc.* **salga, salga, salga, saliamo, saliate, salgano**
sapere	to know, learn; taste of, smell of *Pres. Indic.* **so, sai, sa, sappiamo, sapete, sanno** *Simp. Perf.* **seppi, sapesti, seppe, sapemmo, sapeste, seppero** *Future* **saprò** ... *Pres. Condit.* **saprei** ... *Pres. Subjunc.* **sappia, sappia, sappia, sappiamo, sappiate, sappiano** *Imperat.* **sappi, sappiate**
scegliere	to choose, select *Pres. Indic.* **scelgo, scegli, sceglie, scegliamo, scegliete, scelgono** *Simp. Perf.* **scelsi, scegliesti, scelse, scegliemmo, sceglieste, scelsero** *Pres. Subjunc.* **scelga** ... *Past Part.* **scelto**
sciogliere	to untie, loosen, melt, dissolve *Pres. Indic.* **sciolgo, sciogli, scioglie, sciogliamo, sciogliete, sciolgono** *Simp. Perf.* **sciolsi, sciogliesti, sciolse, sciogliemmo, scioglieste, sciolsero** *Pres. Subjunc.* **sciolga** ... *Past. Part.* **sciolto**
soddisfare	to satisfy *Pres. Indic.* **soddisfo, soddisfi, soddisfa, soddisfiamo, soddisfate, soddisfano** *Simp. Perf.* **soddisfeci, soddisfacesti** ... *Future* **soddisferò, soddisferai** ... *Pres. Subjunc.* **soddisfaccia** ... *Imperf. Subjunc.* **soddisfacessi** *Past Part.* **soddisfatto**
sostenere	to sustain, maintain, support, withstand as *tenere*
stare[†]	to stay, be, remain, be situated *Pres. Indic.* **sto, stai, sta, stiamo, state, stanno** *Simp. Perf.* **stetti, stesti, stette, stemmo, steste, stettero** *Future* **starò, starai** ... *Pres. Condit.* **starei, staresti** ... *Pres. Subjunc.* **stia, stia, stia, stiàmo, stiàte, stìano** *Imperf. Subjunc.* **stessi** ... *Imperat.* **sta', state**
supporre	to suppose as *porre*
svenire[†]	to faint as *venire*
tacere	to be silent, fall silent *Pres. Indic.* **taccio, taci, tace, taciamo, tacete, tacciono** *Simp. Perf.* **tacqui, tacesti, tacque, tacemmo, taceste, tacquero** *Pres. Subjunc.* **taccia, taccia, taccia, taciamo, taciate, tacciano**
tenere	to hold, keep *Pres. Indic.* **tengo, tieni, tiene, teniamo, tenete, tengono** *Simp. Perf.* **tenni, tenesti, tenne, tenemmo, teneste, tennero** *Future* **terrò, terrai** ... *Pres. Condit.* **terrei, terresti** ... *Pres. Subjunc.* **tenga, tenga, tenga, teniamo, teniate, tengano**
togliere	to remove, take away, take off

	Pres. Indic. **tolgo, togli, toglie, togliamo, togliete, tolgono** *Simp.* *Perf.* **tolsi, togliesti, tolse, togliemmo, toglieste, tolsero** *Pres.* *Subjunc.* **tolga** ... *Past Part.* **tolto**
trarre	to draw, pull, obtain, get
	Pres. Indic. **traggo, trai, trae, traiamo, traete, traggono** *Simp. Perf.* **trassi, traesti, trasse, traemmo, traeste, trassero** *Future* **trarrò, trarrai** ... *Pres. Condit.* **trarrei** ... *Pres. Subjunc.* **tragga** ... *Imperat.* **trai, traete** *Past Perf.* **tratto**
udire	to hear
	Pres. Indic. **odo, odi, ode, udiamo, udite, odono** *Future* **udrò** ... **(udirò)** *Pres. Subjunc.* **oda, oda, oda, udiamo, udiate, odano** *Imperat.* **odi, udite**
uscire[†]	to go out, come out
	Pres. Indic. **esco, esci, esce, usciamo, uscite, escono** *Pres. Subjunc.* **esca, esca, esca, usciamo, usciate, escano** *Imperat.* **esci, uscite**
valere	to be worth, to be valid
	Pres. Indic. **valgo, vali, vale, valiamo, valete, valgono** *Simp. Perf.* **valsi, valesti, valse, valemmo, valeste, valsero** *Future* **varrò, varrai** ... *Pres. Condit.* **varrei, varresti** ... *Pres. Subjunc.* **valga, valga, valga, valiamo, valiate, valgano** *Past Part.* **valso**
vedere	to see
	Simp. Past **vidi, vedesti, vide, vedemmo, vedeste, videro** *Future* **vedrò, vedrai** ... *Pres. Condit.* **vedrei, vedresti** ... *Past Part.* **visto (veduto)**
venire[†]	to come
	Pres. Indic. **vengo, vieni, viene, veniamo, venite, vengono** *Simp.* *Perf.* **venni, venisti, venne, venimmo, veniste, vennero** *Future* **verrò, verrai** ... *Pres. Condit.* **verrei, verresti** ... *Pres. Subjunc.* **venga, venga, venga, veniamo, veniate, vengano**
vivere[†]	to live
	Simp. Perf. **vissi, vivesti, visse, vivemmo, viveste, vissero** *Future* **vivrò, vivrai** ... *Pres. Condit.* **vivrei, vivresti** ... *Past Part.* **vissuto**
volere	to wish, want to see Chapter 2

Appendix III
Sequence of tenses

This is a simplified schematic outline of the 'sequence of tenses' between a main and a dependent clause. Here we indicate only the most frequent and important cases, with dependent verbs in the indicative, conditional and subjunctive moods. Other combinations are possible, as illustrated in Chapter 2 and in Chapters 30 and 31.

Main verb		Dependent verb	Example	
	Later	Indicative Future	**Pensa che tu**	**verrai**
		Indicative Present		**vieni**
		Conditional Present		**verresti**
		Subjunctive Present		**venga**
Present Tense	*Same time*	Indicative Present	**Pensa che tu**	**vieni**
		Conditional Present		**verresti**
		Subjunctive Present		**venga**
	Earlier	Indicative Compound Perfect	**Pensa che tu**	**sei venuto**
		Indicative Simple Perfect		**venisti**
		Indicative Imperfect		**venivi**
		Conditional Past		**saresti venuto**
		Subjunctive Past		**sia venuto**
		Subjunctive Imperfect		**venissi**
	Later	Indicative Imperfect	**Pensava che tu**	**venivi**
		Conditional Past		**saresti venuto**
Past Tense	*Same time*	Indicative Imperfect	**Pensava che tu**	**venivi**
		Subjunctive Imperfect		**venissi**
	Earlier	Indicative Pluperfect	**Pensava che tu**	**eri venuto**
		Subjunctive Pluperfect		**fossi venuto**

Main verb		Dependent verb	Example	
	Later	Indicative Future	**Penserà che tu**	**verrai**
		Conditional Present		**verresti**
		Subjunctive Present		**venga**
Future	*Same time*	Indicative Future	**Penserà che tu**	**verrai**
Tense		Indicative Present		**vieni**
	Earlier	Indicative	**Penserà che tu**	**sarai**
		Compound Future		**venuto**

Appendix IV
Word order

Italian is a language in which the word order is extremely flexible. You can see this illustrated throughout in both parts of the book. Here are just a few points to look out for:

Noun group

Noun + adjective
Unlike English where the *adjective + noun* order is rigidly fixed, in Italian the order is more flexible. We can say either:

> adjective + noun
> **un grande giardino**
> a big garden

or

> noun + adjective
> **un giardino grande**
> a big garden

The position of the adjective can make a difference in emphasis or even in meaning. This is fully illustrated in 1.4.5.

Sentence order

Subject – verb
English learners tend to translate sentences directly from English into Italian. In Italian too, the sentence can have the order *subject – verb*:

> *Subject*   *Verb*
> ***Gianni*   ha chiamato.**
> Gianni called.

> ***Il postino* è arrivato.**
> The postman's arrived.

But it is equally possible to reverse the order, to give *verb – subject*:

> *Verb   Subject*
> **Ha chiamato *Gianni.***
> Gianni called.
>
> **È arrivato *il postino.***
> The postman's arrived.

Often the 'normal' order is reversed or altered in order to emphasize who carried out the action:

> **Chi ha mangiato tutti i cioccolatini?**
> Who ate all the chocolates?
>
> *Verb   Subject*
> **Li ha mangiati *Sonia.***
> Sonia ate them.

But in the first examples above, no particular emphasis is given to the subject. It might just as well be the dustman who has called, or someone else who has telephoned.

In exclamative sentences, using **che** or **come**, the subject usually has to follow the verb:

> ***Com'è* bella *la tua casa*!**
> How lovely your house is!
>
> ***Che* begli occhi (che) ha *quel bambino*!**
> What lovely eyes that child has!

Similarly, in interrogative sentences, the subject often comes after the verb:

> **Finiranno mai questo libro *Franco e Anna*?**
> Will Franco and Anna ever finish this book?

And it *has* to come after the verb when the interrogative sentence is introduced by interrogative words such as **che cosa, come, quando, dove, quanto, quale, chi**:

> **Quando finiranno il progetto di ricerche *i nostri colleghi*?**
> When will our colleagues finish their research project?

Subject – verb – object

When there is a noun direct object, the normal sentence order is *subject – verb – object*:

> *Subject   Verb   Object*
> **Gianni   vedrà   la sua amica stasera.**
> Gianni   will see   his friend tonight.

Again, when we want to place emphasis on the *object* (in this case **la sua amica**), the normal order can be changed, so that the *object* is placed first in the sentence:

Object	Subject	Verb

La sua amica **Gianni** *la* **vedrà stasera.**
Gianni will see his friend tonight.
(*literally*: His friend, Gianni, will see her tonight.)

When we place the object first, we add a further direct object before the verb in the form of a direct object pronoun (**lo, la, li, le**). This is called *topicalization.*

It is equally possible to emphasize the object of the sentence by moving it to the *end*:

Lo **vedrò domani all'aeroporto** *mio padre.*
I will see my father tomorrow at the airport.
(*literally*: Him I will see tomorrow at the airport my father.)

Split sentence

In Italian – as in English – it is also possible to *split* the sentence, using a phrase with **essere**, to emphasize the person or object in question, while the rest of the sentence stays in the same position.

Emphasizing the *subject* of the action:

Sei tu **che mi chiami?**
Is it you who is calling me?

È Luca **che ci ha aiutato a fare il trasloco.**
It was Luca who helped us move.

(Compare the last example with the non-emphatic **Luca ci ha aiutato a fare trasloco.**)

Emphasizing the *object* of the action:

È lei **che ho visto con mio marito.**
It was she that I saw with my husband.

È Naomi **che sono andata a trovare a Genova.**
It was Naomi that I went to see in Genoa.

(Compare this with the non-emphatic **Sono andata a trovare Naomi a Genova.**)

Index

Note: the references are to sections, not to pages